Small Worlds

CHILDREN & ADOLESCENTS IN AMERICA, 1850–1950

Edited by Elliott West & Paula Petrik

UNIVERSITY PRESS OF KANSAS

Published by the University Press of Kansas (Lawrence, Kansas
66049), which was organized by the Kansas Board of Regents and is
operated and funded by Emporia State University, Fort Hays State
University, Kansas State University, Pittsburg State University,
the University of Kansas, and Wichita State University

Library of Congress Cataloging-in-Publication Data

Small worlds : children and adolescents in America, 1850–1950 / edited
by Elliott West and Paula Petrik.

p. cm.

Includes bibliographical references and index.

ISBN 0-7006-0510-x (hardcover : alk. paper) — ISBN 0-7006-0511-8 (paper : alk. paper)

1. Children—United States—History.   2. Teenagers—United States—History.

3. United States—Social life and customs. I. West, Elliott, 1945–   .

II. Petrik, Paula Evans.

HQ792.U5S575 1992

305.23'0973—dc20   91-40586

British Library Cataloguing in Publication Data is available.

Printed in the United States of America

10 9 8 7 6 5 4 3

The paper used in this publication meets the minimum requirements of the
American National Standard for Permanence of Paper for Printed
Library Materials z39.48-1984.

[P.P.]

For my stepchildren

Walter Noa Sylva III (1962–1983)

Kimberly Diane Sylva Carpenter

Kenneth Loren Sylva

Calvin Wayne Sylva

Cynthia Lalani Sylva (1967–1984)

and the grandchildren to come

and as always for my husband

Walter Noa Sylva, Jr.

[E.W.]

For my children

Elizabeth DuVal West

William Elliott West, Jr.

Richard Claiborne West

Garth Stoner Williams West

Anne Ellis West

The Mole waggled his toes from sheer happiness,
spread his chest with a sigh of full contentment,
and leaned back blissfully into the soft cushions.
"What a day I'm having!" he said.
"Let's start at once."
Kenneth Grahame, Wind in the Willows

Let the wild rumpus begin.
Maurice Sendak, Where the Wild Things Are

Contents

❖ ❖ ❖ ❖ ❖ ❖ ❖

Contents

Contents

Acknowledgments

The editors would like to acknowledge the early and critical support of Kate Torrey, formerly of the University Press of Kansas. She encouraged us to carry out this project and provided us with nudges when our enthusiasm waned or other projects threatened to distract us. Cindy Miller of the University Press of Kansas took up where Kate left off and furnished us with all necessary help, a critical eye, and the patience that authors and editors require in the home stretch. The essay, "The Youngest Fourth Estate: The Novelty Toy Printing Press and Adolescence, 1870–1886," owes a debt to two grants—a National Endowment for the Humanities Fellowship for College Teachers and a Kate B. and Hall James Peterson Fellowship awarded by the American Antiquarian Society—that subsidized the larger project from which the essay comes.

At this juncture we would normally name those foundations and agencies that supported our efforts to bring this book to publication. Unfortunately, there were not any. We would, however, like to note the signal contributions of Alexander Graham Bell and his legacy, the various Bell systems, the individual who invented the FAX machine, and the companies that brought us photocopy devices. It is a long way between Maine and Arkansas, and without these modern marvels this project would never have been completed. May the firms that manufacture these wonders grow and prosper. We are especially thankful also for the patient help in preparing the manuscript from Lindi Holmes, Dana Harris, and Mary Kirkpatrick.

Most of all, we would like to thank our contributors. Not only can they write interesting things; they are also professional writers of the first order. Their materials arrived on time (a wonder to behold), and they responded to criticisms with a practiced eye and an elegant pen. What more can editors desire? We think nothing.

(P. P. Finally I would like to thank my coeditor, Elliott West. From the point of view of a "sprinter," he is a "distance runner." He provided the ballast for this project. He consistently reminds me of why I became a historian in the first place and what fun the whole enterprise can be.)

(E. W. And thanks to Paula Petrik. The book was her idea at the outset, and her enthusiasm and unfailing good humor have buoyed us all. I cannot imagine a better or more congenial collaborator.)

Introduction

There is an irony in the study of children of past times. Today, adults seem nearly consumed with concern for their daughters and sons. In our contemporary "child-centered" society, parents devote enormous emotional and financial resources to rearing their young, and businesses draw on deep pools of capital to produce cereals, toys, gadgetry, and a vast array of other products aimed at children and adolescents. But those businesses are often disappointed, and many mothers and fathers feel neglected or at least unappreciated by their offspring. Ogden Nash summed up a common household lament: "Everyone needs something to ignore. / That's what God invented parents for." And yet when historians look backward toward previous generations, an odd reversal takes place: Adults receive virtually all the attention of those telling the stories of past societies while boys and girls, if mentioned at all, appear usually as passive and peripheral creatures, pliant parties to forces beyond their control or amusing figures playing at the edges of the main action. As parents, we lavish concern on children of the present; as researchers, we are typically guilty of child neglect.

The following essays are about children and adolescents. Not, that is, about how children have been treated or parents' and social commentators' ideas about youngsters and their upbringing or the place of children in our collective ideas about innocence and evil, anarchy and order. To be sure, all those topics appear, but they are secondary to the main theme—children and adolescents as influential actors in past societies.

We hope these essays will be of interest to specialists in American social history and the history of the family. Even more, however, this book, in content and style, is meant for general readers and beginning students in American history. The editors and contributors have tried to keep its scope broad and its paragraphs as free as possible of jargon. We hope that anyone who reads through these pages will find some insights into the

American story by looking backward from a slightly different perspective.

The proposition is simple: In telling that story, historians have virtually ignored a huge portion of its people. In 1850 roughly 42 percent of the population was under the age of fifteen; in 1950 that figure stood at 27 percent. Yet historians have rarely considered these persons as participants in the major events and developments of American society except in specialized ways. Although many previously neglected groups have recently been brought more onto the center stage of the national story— African Americans and immigrant groups, for instance—children have remained unseen and unheard even though in 1900 the number of people under fifteen was two and a half times that of all foreign-born persons and several times greater than the nation's African American population.

In a sense, however, the young have not been ignored. Children and adolescents have been a crucial part of the explosion of new works on family history published during the past twenty-five years. But the authors of those studies usually have considered the young as objects and motivators of adults' actions, part of the process summed up in the portmanteau term "socialization." Of the children's own motivations, goals, and acts—and, by extension, of their role as shapers of our past—very little has been written. In the essays that follow, the traditional historical point of view is moved closer to the ground (both literally and figuratively) as these writers consider children more in the active than in the passive voice.

The essays range in time from before the Civil War until the middle of this century. The topics, which only begin to suggest the range of possibilities, remind us of the diversity of children's lives. There are essays on native-born adolescents of the middle class and immigrant, working-class children, on slave youngsters and the sons and daughters of the western frontier, on teenage girls confined to reformatories and boys and girls amusing themselves with dolls, games, and printing presses. The essays in Part 1 focus on that diversity by considering some of the variables— cultural roots and geographical settings—that complicate and enrich the children's story. Part 2 concerns play, one of the most revealing and creative arenas in the lives of children and adolescents and the process by which they learn about their often bumptious selves and accommodate them to society. Part 4 is about the family, its emotional dynamics, and the complicated negotiations among young people, their parents, and institutions outside the home. Part 5 treats historical perspective and the ways adults reconstruct their own childhoods. Because one of the most ubiquitous records of childhood, both past and present, is photographs, a photographic essay (Part 3) stands at the center of the book. It serves to illustrate some of the book's themes and to make points of its own about the experience of growing up in America.

Not only will readers of these essays gain some insight into the diversity of children's lives, they can also expect to gain some sense of the difficulties of studying these subjects. One reason historians have paid so little attention to children and adolescents is obvious enough: Reconstructing their story is an extremely frustrating business. For one thing, researchers cannot rely on the usual kinds of sources in the customary ways. True, a surprising number of diaries and letters written by young people have survived, but these are still far less common than those by adults, and such documents are virtually all from the pens of school-age boys and girls of seven years and older. To enter the world of the young, particularly younger children, researchers must look even more carefully than usual at other evidence. Just as the observations of parents and other adults certainly are crucial, so are the documents of private and public institutions—census enumerations, school and church records, materials from benevolent and philanthropic societies and papers from government and law enforcement agencies.

The most common and revealing sort of evidence, the memoir or reminiscence, is also the most problematic. Such a document is an oxymoron, a "second-hand" primary source. On the one hand, the events in a reminiscence are described by the person who actually experienced them; on the other, that person has been separated from those experiences by time and deceived by the tricks that time plays on human memory. In a sense, the memoirist recounts what has been told by someone else, and the informant is the author as a child. The story becomes garbled as the words pass over the years. Writers sometimes admit these shortcomings. A man who had traveled to western Kansas at the age of four later recalled one day on the trip. "At noon we camped along the Solomon River beside a large stone mill," he wrote, "which I later had to agree was not there at the time." Besides outright misapprehensions, these authors shape their reminiscences typically in more subtle ways by what they choose to recall, by their arrangement of events and details, and by the emotional tone that they give to their recreated pasts. The writers' choices, of course, are themselves revealing. As Liahna Babener demonstrates in her essay, we can look for nuances, contradictions, and ambivalences that suggest the finer shadings of childhood experiences.

Historians of the young face an even more daunting difficulty. Children think differently from adults; they address the world around them in ways their elders find at least puzzling and sometimes impenetrable. This problem might seem quite similar to one that is common to all historians and readers of history. Telling or hearing a story from the past always requires imagining a way within someone whose mind works in ways quite unlike our own, since every past culture produced people with their own assumptions, values, and perspectives. *But historians of children are not dealing with people who have grown up with different cultural perspectives; they are dealing with people who have not grown up.* The difference between scholar and subject is not just cultural; it is also cognitive. A child is still developing intellectual schema—the ability to remember, to discriminate between detail and generality, to perceive cause and effect, and to draw conclusions from evidence—as well as moral processes—the ability to empathize with others, to discriminate between right and wrong. These are skills that most adults take for granted.

Curt Norton's diary entry for March 31, 1879, written on a Kansas homestead, illustrates both the puzzlements and the processes. "I hit Mary in the eye with a cowturd," he reported. "It was a dry one. At first she said she could not see. I was throwing at Charley but it hit Mary. She houled [*sic*] like a nailer." From an adult's perspective, the event appears commonplace enough. In a sibling donnybrook an older brother accidentally hits his younger sister instead of his younger brother with a cowflop. At the least, young Norton was guilty of discourtesy; at the most, he nearly inflicted a serious injury. Even so, there are interpretive problems. What, an adult reader might ask, is a "nailer" and what is the nature of its howl? Curt devoted about half his space to noting that the missile he hurled was dry, not fresh, and was tossed at his brother, not his sister. To him, these distinctions apparently were appreciable, but why? When he wrote about throwing at Charley, was he mitigating his guilt or criticizing his aim? And what of his not using wet ammunition? Did he consider his choice self-restraint or a missed opportunity? Without being too flip about the flop, we can say that Curt's words about that episode conceal a great

deal about a child's perceptual and moral perspective. The distance between his view and ours is not easily bridged. It may well be that adults
are further removed from the children at their own dinner tables than
from a milliner during the French Revolution, a Lakota mother, one of
Alexander's soldiers, or an ancient Sumerian farmer.

If we can apply our imagination to that formidable task (and happily
the essays herein illustrate its feasibility), there is a lot to be learned. At
the least, a youthful perspective on the past can provide a much better
understanding of changes in American material and economic life. The
years covered in these essays, from the mid-nineteenth century until the
1950s, were a time of extraordinary economic transformation. The part
that young people played in those changes varied considerably. Children
and adolescents of the urban middle class played less and less a part in
the nation's labors as workers and producers, but that trend was far from
universal. Among the cities' working classes, young people took on many
of the most essential tasks in industrial enterprises, ranging from employment in southern textile mills to work in shoe manufactories of New
England. In the countryside children moved out of the workforce more
slowly and at different paces in different regions. Southern children continued to play vital roles on their families' farms deep into the twentieth
century and, as Elliott West suggests in his essay, the economic contributions of children on the far western farming frontier were expanding, not
contracting.

Common to all classes and regions, furthermore, young people played
an increasingly influential role in American economic life as consumers. In
cities children found themselves with pocket money, time on the streets
away from parental supervision, and an expanding marketplace of new
products and services competing for their attention. Girls and boys became negotiators who insisted, by spending or withholding their nickels
and dimes, that some products be offered and others discarded. As David
Nasaw, Vicki Ruiz, and William Tuttle suggest in their essays, youthful
consumers were emerging as a force in shaping contemporary popular
culture and public tastes. Few readers scanning today's commercials and
advertisements could fail to appreciate just how powerful that force has
become.

Children's lives also can reveal much about the evolution of values in
American life. At first glance, that statement will surprise no one with the

slightest interest in social history. Arguably the most influential work in that field during the past half century is Phillipe Aries's *Centuries of Childhood*, which has compelled scholars to focus on the family, particularly on attitudes toward and treatment of children, both as a reflection of and an active force in society's broader changes. Yet most of this recent scholarship has explored parents' perceptions of their sons and daughters, their feelings toward the younger generation, and methods of childrearing. Most attention, in other words, has been given to adults' ideas about children and *to childhood*, not to the children themselves.

But common sense, not to mention experiences with our own offspring, should tell us that such an approach leaves out a lot. No child has ever been entirely "programmed," nor is socialization a one-way street. A boy or girl growing toward adulthood certainly feels the molding force of parents and society. Yet every child, moment to moment, is also evaluating and responding to what is received. Out of that mutual give-and-take come changes in attitudes and beliefs, both in individuals and societies, and an enormously complex evolution that continues as children mature and in turn try mightily to pass on values to a succeeding generation of children who, just as strenuously, work to make up their own minds.

If this observation seems overly obvious, we should ask some equally obvious, albeit deceptive, questions: Why have historians ignored almost totally the part children have played in this process? For all the attention given to how parents have perceived their sons and daughters, why have so few asked, as Robert Griswold does in his essay, how children have regarded their fathers and mothers? Much ink has been spilled on the psychological dynamics of slavery in antebellum America. Yet why has so little been done to address the questions, raised by Lester Alston, about the ways that slave children developed their own ideas of family, freedom, and authority? How can the process of acculturation be understood without examining, in the manner of Selma Berrol, Ruiz, and Griswold, accommodations made by the children of immigrants and resident minorities? Why, in short, has the calculus of change and continuity slighted essential parts of the equation?

Trying to answer questions like these inevitably will also shed light on the history of public institutions. During these years governments, semi-public organizations, and businesses assumed new relationships with children. The system of common schools expanded both in scope and purpose. The nation's legal apparatus adjusted to the changing views of childhood, now policing the activities of the young in new ways and providing them with special courts and protective laws. Overlapping these official institutions were others, ranging from the YMCA to the American Playground Association to groups promoting "Americanization" of immigrant youths, whose overarching goal aimed to mold the rising generations with an eye to larger social agendas. These changes, like the new styles of childrearing, have drawn much scholarly attention.

As with studies of childrearing, this work has been done almost wholly from the point of view of adults. Children, however, were no more passive in their relations with these institutions than they were with their own families. As Berrol shows, immigrant children absorbed some lessons in the classroom, modified others, and resisted some altogether, all the while trying to square public schooling with what they heard at home. The "wayward girls" studied by Ruth Alexander were challenging traditional sexual standards that courts and reformatories tried (imperfectly, as it turns out) to enforce. In so many ways, in fact, children and adolescents were actively engaging and thereby changing the very institutions designed to control and shape them. Such a process was more evident in children's play, an area of youngsters' lives apart from formal institutions. Children aggressively shaped "made, bought, and stolen" materials, converting toys and amusements to their own uses and purposes. Playing with dolls was a kind of politics, as Miriam Formanek-Brunell puts it, in which young girls tested prevailing values and developed their own distinctive fantasies. The "amateur" journalists of Paula Petrik's essay acted out the parts they soon would play as citizens. In so doing, they grappled with issues of class and race and framed their own variations of middle-class ideology.

The editors and contributors to *Small Worlds* hope their book will encourage students to pay more attention to the ways children and adolescents have made a difference in American history and to their perspective on our national experience. Beyond that, there is no unifying interpretation to these essays. Our approach has been eclectic. The topics are varied, the ideas diverse and occasionally in conflict. Our goal is to encourage a start. In "The Field," the poet Albert Goldbarth explored the idea of the guid man's croft, a fallow piece of land left open to possibility. He ended by finding his purpose in his poem's subject:

Introduction

Let this be my guid man's croft
That I will not finish or furnish or sign
with any name but my own true name.
I leave it: propitiary, begun, benign.

This book is such a field. We leave it: propitiary, begun, but hardly benign.

Part One

❖ ❖

Allee Allee Oxen Free

CULTURAL AND REGIONAL VARIATIONS

"Young man," laughed the farmer

"You're sort of a fool!

You'll never catch fish

In McElligot's Pool!"

"Hmmm . . ." answered Marco,

"It may be you're right.

I've been here three hours

Without one single bite.

There might *be no fish . . .*

But, again, well there might,

Cause you never can tell

What goes on down below!

This pool might *be bigger*

Than you or I know."

    – *Dr. Seuss*, McElligot's Pool

So then I chose another profession, and learned to pilot airplanes. I have flown a little over all parts of the world; and it is true that geography has been very useful to me. At a glance I can distinguish China from Arizona. If one gets lost in the night, such knowledge is valuable.

    – *Antoine de Saint-Exupery*, The Little Prince

How children act depends partly on what their surroundings are and what the children bring to them. That statement may sound obvious, but it has plenty of implications. Speaking about "typical" American children is as meaningless as talking about "the usual" American writers or clergy—or for that matter "typical" American houses or dogs. Consider a selective list of the backgrounds and settings among this country's children:

Anglo-American	Urban	New England
Native American	Suburban	Mid-Atlantic
African American	Small Town	Midwest
Hispanic	Rural	South
Irish		Plains
Italian		Mountain West
Polish		Southwest
Chinese		Pacific Coast

Now think of the possible combinations among these categories. Which of them (there are 256) do we use to generalize about growing up in the United States between the 1840s and 1950s? Suburban blacks in Ohio or the Irish of Butte, Montana? Anglo-American Alabama farmboys, San Francisco's Chinese, or Hispanics in Albuquerque?

As with the line from a game of tag used in our title for Part 1, in this first group of essays we "call home" four variations of American children's experiences. These barely begin to show the possibilities. They do, however, hint at how the variations of national life have made a difference as boys and girls have found their way from infancy to adulthood. The United States in these years was a bewildering cultural mosaic. Looking back on that jumble of patterns, a student can ask three questions about children and their families to help in understanding which aspects of their lives were among the most significant in their growing up.

First: How did they feed themselves? The economic environment and the family's means of support within it helped determine a child's responsibilities as well as the chances to explore his or her skills. On the lower east side of Manhattan and the high plains frontier, struggling parents depended on the labor of their children, and in both places the youngsters helped shape the economies emerging from profound and wrenching changes. But the particulars of the working worlds of Delancey Street and Norton County, Kansas, could hardly have been more different; girls and boys learned lessons specific to each place.

Second: Who was in the neighborhood? What was the population pattern, especially its ethnic composition, and what was its relation to its society's dominant institutions? The immigrant schoolchildren discussed by Selma Berrol were engaged in one of the most troublesome tasks possible in turn-of-the-century America—finding an accommodation between their adopted society's dominant values, as presented by their teachers, and the traditions they found at home. The adolescent Hispanic women studied by Vicki Ruiz also were grappling with the puzzles and pressures of "Americanization," but with a crucial difference. They were part of a numerically dominant ethnic population—a culture, geographically continuous with that of neighboring Mexico, that had been rooted in southwestern soil more than two centuries before the Anglo invasion.

And finally: What else did they see around them, and how was it changing? Within the United States, one of the most geographically diverse nations of its size on the planet, different regions were undergoing many sorts of changes that proceeded at varied rates. Northeastern and midwestern cities, homes to the children described by David Nasaw and Berrol, were growing at a pace rarely seen in modern times. The result was unprecedented congestion (parts of New York City were more crowded than any place in the history of the human race), a baffling array of problems, and a confusion of evolving authorities. The frontier children discussed by Elliott West were living through ecological and social transformations as rapid and sweeping as any the nation would ever see. The southwest of Ruiz's "star-struck" adolescents had been a region of great ranches, scattered villages, and a few larger cities. Now immigrants streamed into those cities to feed new industries. Roads and highways knit together the backcountry's isolated towns while radio, movies, and national periodicals ate away at the region's isolation.

In a sense, of course, we cannot separate these parts of a child's life. Like a pile of jackstraws, the whole structure changes when we try to pull out any piece. The economic setting, the pattern of population, and the changing landscape—each was influencing and supporting the others. In each case the unique combination of unique particulars helped make up a child's environment. And in every instance young people in turn were shaping what was shaping them.

Children grow up through a continual exchange among themselves, their families, and the societies outside their doors. The varieties of settings seen elsewhere in this book—from southern slave plantations to middle-class California suburbs to homefront households during World War II—raise challenging questions about how children have influenced and responded to the extraordinary diversity of our national life.

1

Children and Commercial Culture

Moving Pictures in the Early Twentieth Century

DAVID NASAW

❖ ❖ ❖ ❖ ❖ ❖ ❖ ❖ ❖ ❖ ❖ ❖ ❖ ❖

The history of children and commercial culture remains to be written, but primary documents from which to begin are abundant. In this essay we begin with the reports on children and moving pictures produced by reform groups in the early twentieth century. Like all historical sources, these reports were constructed from a particular perspective for particular purposes. Historians of childhood must not only collect and interrogate but also imaginatively wrestle with them to uncover their hidden stories.

The tale the adult reformers tried to tell was a simple one. The major characters were the children, the businessmen who preyed on their innocence, and the reformers who sought to rescue them from the snares of temptation. Poor, immigrant tenement dwellers, without proper parental supervision or adequate play space of their own, the children were drawn to the cheap theaters like moths to the light. Once inside, their impressionable young minds—clean slates waiting to be filled—were permanently marred by the pictures they saw on the screen. The young, it was charged, craved excitement and, though willing to sit through almost anything, gravitated to pictures about crime and criminals, "burglaries, hairbreadth escapes, accidents, thrilling adventures, flirtations, and every sort of practical joke."[1]

Working-class and immigrant children were, the reformers assumed, particularly susceptible to the tempting images exhibited in the "crime" pictures. They would learn from them a doubly pernicious lesson—that crime paid handsomely and required much less toil than labor in factory, mine, or mill. The Ohio Humane Society, which viewed 250 films in early 1910 and found 40 percent of them "unfit for children's eyes," identified stealing, murder, and house-breaking as the major categories of "objectionable matter." As a Cleveland teacher reported in a 1913 survey, "The effect of pictures is bad because . . . it teaches boys to become bandits, murderers, teaches arson. Shows how to get money without work." In 1909 one of the first actions of the newly established police censorship board in Chicago was to remove all scenes "of murder or robbing or abduction" from pictures approved for exhibition in that city. *The James Boys in Missouri* and *Night Riders* were refused licenses because, though lessons in history, they portrayed "exhibitions of crime" that "would necessarily be attended with evil effects upon youthful exhibitors."[2]

The danger to the children who attended the moving-picture theaters was ubiquitous, the adults reported. The Chicago Vice Commission charged in its 1911 report that the lack of adult supervision and the enveloping darkness encouraged boys to "slyly embrace the girls near them and offer certain indignities." In New York City, the Society for the Prevention of Cruelty to Children (SPCC), the most relentless critic of the cheap theaters, presented case after case of the "pernicious 'moving picture' abomination. . . . This new form of entertainment," the society claimed in its 1909 *Annual Report*, "has gone far to blast maidenhood. . . . Boys and girls are together in the room darkened while the pictures are on, and, . . . indecent assaults upon the girls follow, often with their acquiescence. Depraved adults with candies and pennies beguile children with the inevitable result. The Society has prosecuted many for leading girls astray through these picture shows, but GOD alone knows how many are leading dissolute lives begun at the 'moving pictures.' "[3] Because the children were incapable of resisting temptation, because their parents could not or would not protect them, because the movie exhibitors were driven only by profit, and because the state would not, without pressure, interpose itself between a business and its customers, no matter how young or innocent, the reformers were compelled (at least as they saw it) to cast themselves in the heroic role.

There was no consensus on what was to be done or indeed on how "bad" the new amusements really were. While some reformers such as

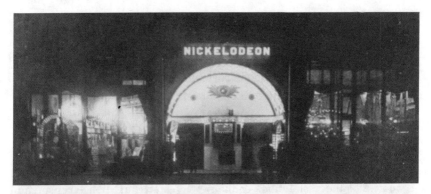

Nickelodeon audience in Homestead, Pennsylvania.
(Lewis Hine, photographer. From Margaret F. Byington,
Homestead: The Households of a Mill Town
[New York: Russell Sage Foundation, 1910], pp. 88ff.)

the SPCC in New York City called for mandatory state censorship and a ban on child attendance, others such as Jane Addams and her colleagues in Chicago believed it was possible to "reform" the pictures so that they could become a force for good. There was complete agreement, however, on two essential points: The children could not be given carte blanche to spend their nickels as they wished, and the movie producers and exhibitors could not be left alone to make and distribute pictures as they saw fit. The reformers appealed to the public to pressure legislators to write laws censoring the pictures and prohibiting or regulating the attendance of unaccompanied children. And they were successful. By the second decade of the twentieth century, only the rare municipality or state did not have such laws on the books.[4]

Regrettably, from the reformers' perspective, their laws had no noticeable effect on the numbers of children in the audience. By 1910 John Collier could report that "from 500,000 to 600,000 children attend picture shows in our country every day." A 1911 New York City study reported that 16 percent of the school children interviewed saw a nickel show daily. A 1913 Cleveland survey found that 67 percent of the almost six thousand school children canvassed "attended motion picture theaters almost daily." A 1914 Portland survey revealed that only 9.5 percent of the 2,647 children interviewed did not attend motion picture shows, and almost 30 percent attended them "twice a week or oftener."[5]

Whenever they could (and that was most of the time), the children simply disregarded the state laws and municipal ordinances that barred them from attending the shows without parent or guardian. The "underage" either sneaked into the theaters or found older children, neighborhood friends, or unacquainted adults to pose as their guardians. As a confidential investigator for the Jewish community organization, the Kehillah, reported of the Lower East Side movie houses in 1913, "Minors go in here with anyone who acts as their guardian and once they get inside they take care of themselves."[6] Although the reformers' continued complaints about the unaccompanied children were received and duly noted, action was seldom if ever taken. A letter from a National Board of Review official to the New York City Bureau of Licenses remarked that even though the SPCC had had special detectives assigned to it to procure "violations of moving pictures licenses as to the admission of [unaccompanied] children under sixteen," the ordinance "might just as well not be a law today for all that it is observed."[7]

More often than not, the police and the municipal agencies that licensed the moving-picture theaters looked the other way. The exhibitors paid the law no attention at all. The Mayor's Commissioner of Accounts reported in March 1911 that it had become "a common practice in most of the shows to admit children under sixteen years of age unaccompanied by a guardian or parents in spite of the provisions of section 484 of the Penal Code. Indeed, one important official of the Moving Picture Exhibitors Association stated in his testimony before us that 75 per cent of the moving pictures shows of this city would be driven out of business if this law were strictly enforced."[8] The problem was not confined to New York City. A 1913 survey in Cleveland found that more than half of the children attending the moving picture theaters were unaccompanied by adults. For the evening performances, the percentage exceeded two-thirds.[9]

The moving-picture theaters' low price and the increasing availability of money for children who worked on the streets made the nickel dumps as accessible as the vacant lot on the corner. Large numbers of working-class and immigrant children worked after school in the "street trades," hustling newspapers, blacking boots, peddling flowers, pencils, fruit, or candy, running errands, and delivering messages or telegrams. Every evening, the children handed over their earnings to their mothers. They got back enough money to buy the next day's papers, candy, or flowers from the wholesaler and, if they were lucky, an additional allowance to spend on themselves. Those who were not granted such allowances had to negotiate nightly for a bit of spare change or, as was often the case, hold back a bit of their earnings from the pocketful they delivered to their mothers. The children did not begrudge the family their nickels and dimes, but they regarded as inalienable their right to spend some portion of their earnings on themselves. Their parents were entitled to a portion of it, the largest portion, but not all. For the younger girls who worked at home after school, spending money was a bit more difficult to come by, but only a bit. They too had their means of teasing or "borrowing" it from their parents. "It is so easy for a girl, when sent to the corner grocery for 15 cents worth of coal oil, to get a dime's worth and save a nickel for the show," reported a social worker from Birmingham, Alabama, in 1911.[10]

The children of the city spent their money at the corner candy store; for clothes their parents would not buy them, especially hats—ostrich plumes for the girls, wide-brimmed caps for the boys; for weekend excursions to the amusement parks; and, most often, for a "show" at the penny arcades, the cheap vaudeville halls, and the moving-picture theaters. The rapid, uncontrolled expansion of storefront theaters and nickelodeons in the early years of the new century had placed cheap nickel and dime theaters within walking distance of the neighborhoods where the children lived or worked. And, as importantly, the picture show was, in its early years, never more than a half hour in length, making it extremely convenient for children who had to be home for dinner.

"Never before," wrote Jane Addams in 1909, "have such numbers of young boys earned money independently of the family life, and felt themselves free to spend it as they choose." When Ina Taylor interviewed over five hundred newsboys in St. Louis, she discovered that 87 percent regularly attended the cheap theaters. "In Chicago, William Hard, a journalist, claimed to have found a group of children who sold papers every afternoon for the sole purpose of raising money for movie tickets. They worked until they had their nickels for admission, quit to see the show, and then returned to work again until they [had] another nickel to be spent for the same purpose at another 'theatorium.'"[11]

With nickels in their pockets, the children were magically transformed into consumers worthy of respect. Adults who would otherwise have treated them with disdain opened their doors to welcome them inside. Although the boys had only spare change to spend, there were enough of them to interest the new show businessmen, who understood the calculus of mass commercial amusements. Hundreds of boys meant thousands of nickels every afternoon.

Some amusement entrepreneurs, such as the penny-arcade owners, went out of their way to attract the boys. Businessmen such as Herbert Mills, who promoted his arcades as "family entertainments," featured knife tosses, shooting galleries, strength-testers, and assorted games of chance that appealed primarily to young men seeking public proof of their masculinity. An investigator for the Chicago City Club who visited a Mills Amusement Company arcade at 177 West Madison Street in the heart of the Loop found dozens of boys "crowded around a knife board." For a nickel, the boys were given three rings, for a dime, seven, to throw at the knife handles protruding from the board. If they "rung" the knife, they got to keep it or trade it in for more chances and perhaps a better prize, like a watch. When the investigator informed the manager that such activity was "gambling" and thus outlawed, he was curtly warned to mind his own business. Later that afternoon, the investigator returned and found a police officer "watching the boys" throw rings at the board.

> "Isn't that chance, and aren't those boys learning mighty fast to gamble," I said to the police officer.
> "I suppose so," he said, "but it's allowed. I try to keep away small boys," and he turned and drove two little fellows away.

The police officer soon left the arcade; the investigator was thrown out by the manager.[12]

The knife tosses were not the only attractions designed for the boys. The Mutoscopes or peep-show machines in the back of the arcades displayed images—for a penny apiece—calculated to appeal to the boys: boxing matches, racing fire engines, speeding railroad trains, slapstick comedies, public hangings, and, under a prominently displayed "MEN ONLY" sign, girls "undressing" for bed or bath, pillow-fighting, or dancing the hootchi-kootchi. Though the pictures were labeled "for men only," the boys were seldom barred from looking through the peep hole. A New York City investigator claimed that the management in some of the arcades provided stools for the boys who were too small to reach the peep hole.[13]

In one arcade in Chicago, according to one investigator, the boys who paused before depositing their coins were encouraged by the attendant.

> "You mustn't miss this one," he says, "It's the hottest yet. She takes off everything from the top of her head to the soles of her feet." If the newcomer hesitates, he assures him that he takes him for no chicken, that unless his appearance belies him, he is a fellow who has seen the world and can stand anything. If our newcomer still hesitates before any of the machines, [the attendant] shows him the first picture without charge. A peep at this he tells the newcomer, "will send the shivers up his spinal column and make him feel like a man."[14]

Such was the come-on, punctuated by suggestive titles and lurid lithographs, most of them borrowed from the cheap melodrama houses.[15] The pictures themselves rarely if ever fulfilled the expectations raised by these displays. The arcade owners were well aware of the ordinances on the books that prohibited the sale or exhibition of immoral or obscene photographs or drawings. The police, had they wished, could have used these statutes to close down the moving-picture arcades. Instead of taking such risks, the owners promised their young male customers everything but delivered only what was legal. As a New York City investigator reported in 1906, "The signs on nine out of ten picture machines are deceptive—the effort in every instance being to make the customer believe that the exhibition within is most vulgar. It is a trick which serves the double purpose of catching extra pennies and impressing the casual observer [as well as the police and anti-vice crusaders] that there is nothing real bad about the place."[16]

In only two of the twenty arcades he visited did this investigator find "thoroughly indecent pictures," not enough, he reported, to interest Anthony Comstock in undertaking a more thorough investigation.[17] Elsewhere, in Boston, Buffalo, Philadelphia, Washington, D.C., Baltimore, Cleveland, Cincinnati, and Providence, reformers surveyed in 1906 and 1907 reported that the arcade owners were staying well within the spirit of the law, as defined by the cop on the beat. The pictures, as a Boston investigator reported in 1907, "come very near the line of obscenity, but, as a rule, are not such as can be reached by the law."[18]

The boys who patronized the penny arcades were no doubt captivated by the opportunity to do and see something "naughty," but they were also attracted by the clubhouse atmosphere. These establishments not only catered to the young but also left them alone to do almost as they pleased. The same freedom from adult surveillance and control—which the children adored and the reformers feared—characterized the neighborhood nickelodeons.

The nickel theaters were housed in tiny storefronts, filled with rented chairs, a makeshift screen in back, and a projector in front. They were usually staffed by the owner or a cashier, a projectionist, and sometimes a pianist to accompany the films and illustrated songs. There were as yet no laws on the books requiring the theaters to hire matrons to patrol the aisles. The children, as a result, were left to their own devices, especially during the afternoon, early evening, and weekend matinees when they were alone in the theaters.

The Bijous, Pictoriums, Theatoriums, Jewels, Electrics, and Dreamlands became the children's "general social center and club house." "Young people," Jane Addams reported from Chicago, "attend the five cent theaters in groups, with something of the 'gang' instinct, boasting of the films and stunts in 'our theater.'" When the lights

went down, they were free—as they were free nowhere else indoors—to behave like children: to shout, scream, howl, laugh aloud,
and jump up and down in their seats. "They were called silent pictures," Sam Levenson remembers. "Maybe the pictures were silent,
but the audience certainly wasn't." [19]

The children, with little privacy at home or in school, made the best possible use of their clubhouse/theaters. The younger ones played together
through the afternoon matinees, singing along with the illustrated songs,
eating candy and peanuts, throwing wrappers and shells at one another,
booing the villains, cheering the heroes, and generally making as much
noise as they could. In the larger theaters, many of them recently converted from vaudeville, the older children, if they chose, could retreat
to the balconies. Although the reformers had succeeded in most cities in
forcing the theater owners to turn up the lights, the balconies remained
in shadows. For couples looking for a place to be alone or to exchange
sexual favors, there was no better seat in the city. The SPCC worried about
"innocent" young boys and girls being led astray by depraved adults, but
those who ventured upstairs seldom went alone. All the children knew
what the balcony was for.

The children were at first so entranced by the magic of movement that
they paid their nickels to see whatever show the exhibitors arranged. If
the pictures were bad, they booed and hissed louder but still had fun.
Within a short time, however, they developed their own preferences and
began to patronize particular nickelodeons on the basis of the shows presented. The theater owners, for their part, quickly learned that to fill the
house they had to offer pictures of interest to the children.

When Jane Addams and her associates—under the impression that the
children would patronize any moving-picture show they offered—opened
a "clean" picture theater at Hull House, the first in what was supposed to
have been a "settlement-house circuit" of wholesome nickelodeons, they
were surprised to find only thirty-seven children in the audience. (The
experiment was soon terminated.) When questioned about the "clean"
show they had seen, the children responded that they had enjoyed watching *Cinderella* and travel scenes of Japan and Java but their tastes ran in
other directions. According to twelve-year-old Jimmy Flaherty (his words
recorded by adults who did all they could to make them sound cute and
tough), "Things has got ter have some hustle. I don't say it's right, but

people likes to see fights, 'n' fellows getting hurt, 'n' love makin', 'n' robbers, and all that stuff. I like to myself, even. This here show ain't even funny, unless those big lizards from Java was funny."

Had the choice been between *Cinderella* and nothing, the children would have paid their nickels to see *Cinderella*. But with dozens of local nickelodeons anxious to attract their nickels, the children could pick and choose what they wanted to see. Jane Addams's clean nickelodeon failed because it could not compete with the neighborhood nickelodeons ready to cater to the children's entertainment preferences rather than to their educational needs. The children, for their part, voted with their nickels to see *The Pirates*, *The Defrauding Banker*, *The Adventures of an American Cowboy*, *An Attack on the Agent*, and *The Car Man's Danger*, all playing within a few blocks of Hull House.[20]

When asked what kind of moving pictures they liked the best, the children occasionally answered "educational," no doubt to please the adults (often their teachers) asking the question. More often, however, they named comedy, westerns, and war pictures. The younger children, especially the boys, preferred the westerns with their gamblers, half-breeds, marauding Indians, heroic cowboys, and plenty of chases and battles. The comedies were popular with the girls as well as the boys. Louise de Koven Bowen reported from Chicago in 1911 that the comedy films were the "most popular" there. "They are silly, but harmless, and include among others the following: 'How Rastus Got the Turkey,' 'The Animated Armchair,' 'Bridget and the Eggs,' 'The Crazy Razors,' 'In Search of a Husband,' etc." The children also spent their nickels on special adaptations of classics such as *A Tale of Two Cities*, *Julius Caesar*, and *Ben Hur* and on dramas or melodramas, especially those "of a rather lurid type and sometimes showing criminal adventures."[21]

The censorship restrictions placed on (and accepted by) the producers had some effect on the story content and the images displayed on the moving-picture screens but not enough to cleanse the amusement of all the "bad" influences the reformers had found there. On their own initiative producers censored scenes dealing with white slavery, the seduction of women, prenatal and childbed scenes, drug habits, the "modus operandi of criminals," "gruesome and unduly distressing scenes," nudity, abortion, sacrilege, counterfeiting, adultery, incendiarism, drunkenness, gun play, vulgarities, "sensual kissing and love-making scenes," women smoking, venereal disease, and other forbidden subjects. But they still were left with a number of topics of interest to the children and myriad ways of disguising the banned ones.[22]

Even the crime pictures that had earlier been banned because of their supposed evil influence on the impressionable young were not kept out of the theaters for long. The producers and exhibitors soon found a way to reintroduce them without violating any censorship board restrictions. By 1910, according to John Collier, 20 percent of all the movies being produced dealt with dramatic themes in which characters were "tempted to commit crimes, and sometimes do commit crimes." As Collier proudly reported, however, none of these pictures portrayed crime "for its own sake" or allowed a criminal to go unpunished. In fact, crimes committed on the moving-picture screen were "invariably dealt with by a stern justice which is far more certain and terrible with its lightnings than is human justice in real life."[23]

The reformers struggled valiantly to convince the producers and the exhibitors to offer "educational" and "uplift" pictures for the young, but their powers of persuasion were never sufficient to supersede the logic of the marketplace. Because the young bought more tickets than the reformers, the pictures that the children wanted to see—and would spend their nickels on—were produced more often and exhibited more regularly than the educational fare.

Until the advent of television, when the reformers' focus would shift to the smaller screen, the adult discourse on children and the movies centered on the influence of the movies on the young.[24] And yet, ironically, when the full history of the subject is written, it may reveal that the children's effect on the industry was much greater than the moving pictures' effect on the children. Despite the reformers' considerable success in passing legislation that established censorship boards and regulated attendance, the children remained an important segment of the audience for the new commercial entertainments. The calculus of profit dictated that the show businessmen—with their cheap prices and abbreviated shows—fill and refill their houses dozens of times a day; they could not tolerate large periods with empty theaters. The children were an essential part of the weekly audience because they filled the theaters during the most fallow periods, in the late afternoons, the early evenings, and for the weekend matinees.

The producers and owners did whatever was necessary to keep their audience of children. They went out of their way to avoid controversy or conflict with the reformers, the police, or the public, and at the same time they did all they could to attract the children to their establishments. They accepted state censorship, kept the smallest boys out of the penny arcades, and turned on the lights in their theaters. Yet they ignored the laws barring underage, unaccompanied children and the pleas of the reformers that they substitute educational films for trashy crime melodramas and slapstick comedies. Through it all, they carefully and successfully walked the fine line between offending the reformers and boring the children.

"The nickelodeon," John Collier had written in 1908, "is almost the creation of the child."[25] Without the children's patronage after school and on the weekends, the early moving-picture industry would have been far less profitable. The children, for their part, no matter what the reformers may have believed, suffered little and gained much in the bargain. They not only saw the movies they wanted to see, but they also won for themselves a place to socialize and the right to consume amusements, a truncated right perhaps, yet, nonetheless a right that the adults were bound to respect.

2

Children on the Plains Frontier

ELLIOTT WEST

Frances Fulton found much to impress her when she moved to northern Nebraska early in the 1880s. She marveled at the rugged and beautiful valley of the Niobrara River, with its rich grasses and occasional splash of wild roses. Less pleasant, but still remarkable, was the brutal winter wind that moaned southward out of the Dakotas. The young woman sometimes found the people of the plains as unusual as her new homeland. They lived in holes in the ground called dugouts and faced an uncertain future with a dogged optimism. And they were forever behaving in ways she would never have expected in her native Pennsylvania: "It has been a novel sight to watch a little girl about ten years old herding sheep near town, handling her pony with a masterly hand, galloping around the herd if they begin to scatter out, and driving them into a corral."[1]

Like Fulton, many transplanted easterners noted that children seemed to live differently on the Great Plains. Just as she had, many observed that boys and girls also played prominent roles in meeting the daily needs of families on that part of the far-western frontier. Historians, however, have paid less attention to young people who came west to occupy the plains. That is a pity, for the children of the plains frontier have much to tell us about the pioneer experience and the history of American families.

Paying attention to children of the plains frontier can teach us three broad lessons. The first concerns the pioneer conquest during the second half of the nineteenth century. The invasion of the plains—a region larger than western Europe, from the Dakotas and Montana on the north

Children in Beaver County, Oklahoma, 1897.
(Berryman album no. 10, Kansas State Historical Society)

to the *llano estacado* of Texas on the south—involved a variety of forces and figures: soldiers, freighters, and merchants, land speculators, railroad promoters, and corporate kingpins. But most significant, both in numbers and in sheer impact upon the region, were the farming and ranching families who began arriving by the thousands on the eve of the Civil War.

This huge army of families began a radical transformation of vast stretches of the plains, destroying the economic base of Indian inhabitants and laying the foundation for long-term growth of population and political development. The efforts by families to begin making a living, then, was the key event in the Euro-American conquest of this region. And in that grabbing hold of the land the roles played by children were essential.

In describing the economic conquest of the plains, historians typically have concentrated on the tasks of "production." This rather misleading term focuses on those labors most celebrated in descriptions by journalists and travelers, in lithographs and chromos of the day. On the farming frontier, "production" meant breaking and plowing and planting the land, caring for the crops, and gathering the harvest. As with most frontier work, these accomplishments usually are attributed to those stalwart, barrel-chested pioneer males who, we are told, were most responsible for transforming the West.

Men did take part in all these tasks, of course, but they were not alone. In most aspects of farm production, women and children also had a hand, and boys and girls had some jobs all to themselves. The initial breaking of the sod, woven thick with the roots of grasses, was difficult work typically done by men. This first assault on the land, however, left a field full of large clods and matted soil that had to be broken up. In poorer families this work was done by hand. Everyone, young and old, took part. After Linneus Rauck broke up part of his Oklahoma homestead with a borrowed plow, he and his wife each took up an axe and his three children were handed butcher knives. Together they hacked their way through several acres to prepare the soil for a garden and their first seed bed of kaffir corn. Once a field was broken, children's help was more substantial. Accounts tell of girls and boys as young as eight plowing fields in the spring. R. D. Crawford of North Dakota, who plowed his first field at eleven, later claimed to have walked thirty thousand miles behind a plow during the next dozen years. His claim, although surely exaggerated, still emphasizes an important point. The revolution in agricultural technology during these years was allowing children to take over some jobs previously done only by men. Before moving to Kansas as a boy, Percy Ebbut had seen land plowed in his native England, a heavy labor performed by full-grown men using old-style plows. But on the plains, Ebbut wrote, a boy behind a new steel-tipped plow could handle the job easily: "I have plowed acre after acre from the time I was twelve years old."[2]

Fully capable of planting most crops, children were especially useful in the next stage—the care of the growing crops. Here, in fact, girls and boys probably played their most prominent part in pioneer production. During the long hot summer months, men often turned away from the fields to build and repair outbuildings, to fence gardens and fields, and to work in towns or at railroad construction for desperately needed cash. That left their children to protect the crops against a variety of threats. A Kansas farmwife filled her diary with similar entries, day after day, during June 1880: "The children was working in the corn field," and, "The children pull the weeds." Youngsters drove simple cultivators, or "go-devils," to throw a fresh layer of dirt against the plants and keep weeds on the defensive. They worked as living scarecrows, patrolling the fields for hours a day, disbursing the grazing cattle and horses and shooing away the whirling birds that threatened to devour the family's future. No tasks demanded a greater perseverance and outlay of time; none was more essential. For many families, the children's help was indispensable.[3]

At harvest time the entire family typically took to the fields, racing against the coming of fall hailstorms or an early frost that could wipe out the year's effort. Boys and girls cut and shucked corn; on the eastern fringe of the plains they picked cotton. Edna Matthews remembered blistering August days of her Texas girlhood, when the rows of cotton and corn stood "like a monster" before her. "Sometimes I would lay down on my sack and want to die," she wrote. "Sometimes they would pour water over my head to relieve me."[4] Children helped at harvesting by centuries-old techniques and by the newest mechanized methods. When wheat was cut by hand, children tossed the stalks into a wagon bed, then beat it with flails so the grain and chaff could be separated by tossing it on a winnowing sheet. When modern harvesting and threshing machines were used, children also played their parts. A boy would "turn bundles," handing sheaves of cut wheat to a man who built them into dome-shaped stacks. Next the thresher arrived. If it was horsedriven, a small girl might lead the animals around their circle, while one brother cut the bands of sheaves about to be threshed and another kept the machine cleared of straw to keep it from clogging. Haymaking was essential to the survival of herds on many ranches and stock farms. Here, too, young boys and girls were fully integrated into the tasks, both in the ancient forms of cutting and gathering by hand and in the new, mechanized methods used increasingly in the pastoral West.[5]

So in all the labors of farm production, from sodbusting to harvesting, whatever the techniques, with the simplest tools to the most sophisticated, plains children played essential roles in their families' efforts to transform the country and to make it pay.

But this was only the start of the youngsters' contributions. The work of production was possible only because of a wide range of other work, much of it highly productive in its own way. In this, the "subsistence" side of the family economy, the role of girls and boys was if anything even more important.

Most obviously they helped in preparing and caring for the gardens that provided much of the family's food after the first year. Even before the melons and squash had matured, however, children were putting food on the table, first by a job rarely mentioned in most histories of farm life—the gathering of wild plants. The meadows and watercourses offered a remarkable bounty for those who knew how to find it. Along the creeks were chokecherries, dewberries, elderberries, creek plums, fox and winter grapes, red and black haws. On higher ground were currants, wild onions, lamb's quarters, purslane and pigweed. At times this natural smorgasbord provided most of a family's food, and in any case it gave their diet a healthy diversity. Children grew up calling these plants "vegetables out of place," and they agreed with the O'Kieffe family's policy toward weeds: "If you can't beat 'em, eat 'em."[6]

Children put meat on the table as well. Common impressions to the contrary, grown men usually had little time for hunting. That job was left to sons and daughters, some as young as seven or eight, who stalked and killed antelopes, raccoons, ducks, geese, deer, prairie chickens, bison, wild hogs, and above all, rabbits. Young people came to love this work more than any other. Before she moved to western Kansas, the teenager Luna Warner apparently had done little of this work, but soon she was boasting to her diary of bringing down a variety of game. She accompanied friends and her father on a two-day bison hunt, and she took advantage of other situations not necessarily within the bounds of the hunter's code, once killing a steer mired in a nearby creekbed. "Hunting seemed to me the greatest sport in all creation," wrote Frank Waugh of his early years on the Kansas plains. "Compared with it, everything else was as dust in the cyclone."[7]

There is a nice irony here. As they brought the land under cultivation, farm families liked to think of themselves as redeeming this country from the native peoples who were retreating before the advancing fields. Yet even as they congratulated themselves, they were surviving by a kind of hunting-and-gathering economy quite like that of the Indians. During those first few years of settlement, when produce from the fields and gardens was least reliable, wild plants and animals were most abundant. By bringing them in, children in many cases were supplying most of their families' sustenance.

Children, in fact, generally labored at a wider variety of tasks than either mothers or fathers. They were in that sense the most accomplished and versatile workers of the farming frontier. These jobs inevitably brought a broad range of responsibilities as well. Together, the diversity of their physical chores and of their responsibilities demanded considerable adaptability—a willingness to wrestle with previously unconfronted problems and to call on unexplored individual resources.

The experience of one family suggests both the economic importance of children and the changes required of these and other girls and boys of the plains frontier. In 1877 Curt and Mary Norton left their Illinois farm to homestead near Fort Larned in western Kansas. With them came their eight children: Lottie (twenty), Willie (eighteen), John (fourteen), Curtie (twelve), Henry (nine), Charles (seven), Grace (five), and Mary (three). John's diary, which he began before departure and continued after arrival, shows clearly how rapidly and dramatically a pioneer youngster's world of work expanded. In Illinois he had drawn water and helped care for the stock. Once in Kansas, he helped build and grout the family dugout and plow and plant a large garden. Already he was herding and haying, and soon he was assisting in planting, harrowing, and helping his mother sweep and scrub the floors, wash clothes, and cook. He also brought in extra cash by killing and selling rabbits, and with Charles and Grace he went on long expeditions to gather bleached buffalo bones to sell in town. Remarkably soon John was also taking on considerable responsibilities in the family business. Within weeks of arrival he was negotiating arrangements with neighbors to care for the Norton cattle, and in less than a year he was negotiating egg and hay sales at Fort Larned and fussing over problems of storing barley seed. By then he was commenting critically on family economics—[Uncle's] "finances are in a very loose state"—and keeping meticulous tabs on the homestead's improvements.[8]

John's brothers and sisters, too, moved quickly into new roles. Henry gathered corn for a neighbor and helped his father plant, Charles herded and fetched items from the fort. Then in 1880 came a family crisis. As one of the period's worst droughts settled on the region, Curt, Sr., Willie, and John left to find work and income to prop up the Norton's sagging finances. Curtie and Henry suddenly were left with more responsibilities. While still herding, helping their mother with household chores, and tending the garden, they also had to maintain business arrangements in town and with neighbors.[9]

Throughout rural America, of course, young people helped in the labors and other duties of family farms. To some extent, the story of the plains frontier is merely a variation of a larger one that includes children of Alabama sharecroppers and of New York dairy farmers. Yet conditions in Kansas and the Dakotas after the Civil War were in some ways distinctive. Pioneer families were starting from scratch, building houses and outbuildings and fences, preparing soil for cultivation, and establishing their herds. They did these jobs in a demanding country that posed unfamiliar challenges, including an erratic, highly unpredictable climate. In the more settled regions to the east, networks of relatives and time-tested neighbors often were available to help families through the many labors of the annual agrarian cycle. On the frontier, however, these systems of support frequently had been left behind. All this meant that a typical plains family was thrown back more on its own resources to accomplish an extraordinary job of work. To meet such a challenge, children were probably even more important on the frontier than elsewhere in rural America.

The children's story offers a second lesson, besides broadening our understanding of westward expansion and young people's part in it. There is an "outer" and an "inner" history of the frontier. One concerns the process of conquest and transformation of the land; the other describes how people responded to that country and to what was happening there. The emotional dimension to the western settlement is just as important as the economic, and in understanding that inner history, the children's perspective is once again essential.

In particular, the responses of boys and girls suggest how the pioneer experience helped create a distinctive generation. In some ways, of course, the children of any time and place grow up with perspectives and attitudes different from those of their parents. But the peculiar nature of the frontier experience—and the distinctive angles of vision of adults and young people—deepened and widened those inevitable generational differences.

"The West" meant one thing to adults and something else to children. Adults had grown up someplace else—whether New York, Alabama, Ireland, or China. To them, the West was the "new" country. Typically they headed west in search of the better chance, but they knew they were leaving much behind: family, friends, the millions of details that made up the familiar world of their origins. This step was usually painful. Recent books about the great westward migration have emphasized the trauma of separation, a sense of loss and dislocation that was especially acute among pioneer women. The titles of these books often make the point: *A Scattered People* and *Far From Home*.[10]

In a sense the emotional base of these pioneers remained in the East. As their writings show, they were continually pulled between their hopes and their memories, now predicting a glorious future in the new country, now missing what they had put behind them. On the trip onto the plains, parents marveled at strange new sights, then longed for the spiritual solace of a familiar elm tree or an ivy-covered wall. Once settled in, mothers and fathers set out to change their new surroundings, not only for profit but also to make their world resemble the one they had left. Mothers strove to make their soddies and cabins "home like"; men lavished enormous energy on fragile maple and walnut saplings so these eastern trees might survive and flourish where nature obviously never meant them to be. These tasks were expressions of an emotional tug-of-war that parents never fully resolved. For the rest of their lives they remained psychologically disjointed.

But pioneer children, whatever other difficulties they faced, did not have to grapple with this irresolvable conflict. Growing up in the West, they felt no tug from another place. To understand the child's experience, we have to adopt a perspective different from virtually all books written about western settlement. Children did not see themselves as a "scattered people" since one must be scattered *from* someplace, and the West was the only place they had ever known first-hand. They were not "far from home"; they *were* home.

To say this may seem to belabor the obvious. Yet this distinction holds important implications for how young westerners grew to view the world in ways their elders could never approach. The process began with the earliest contact between children and their surroundings. During their first several years, infants and toddlers are establishing a sense of reality. They spend most waking hours exploring what is immediately at hand. From this they gradually learn something of what is to be expected of life—what brings pleasure and pain, what responses follow what actions, what is and is not permitted, what is hard and what is soft, whether snakes can be trusted. At the same time, children are engaged in another exploration. They are gradually coming to know themselves. They discover what they can and cannot accomplish and how they feel about this and that. They are forming their first opinions about what kind of people they are. In a more fundamental sense, they are for the first time becoming aware of themselves as individuals. They develop our most human trait; only people can step outside themselves and think about their own existence.[11]

Just what is happening during these momentous events is far from clear, but one point is well established: These two explorations, discovering the world and discovering one's self, continually affect one another. An infant girl cannot investigate her surroundings without learning something about herself, too; she can decide who she is and what she thinks only in terms of what she knows through experiences with what is around her. The psychological term for this interaction is "synesthesia" (or "co-enesthesia"), which refers to "a general awareness of your own existence through the sum of your bodily impressions." Behind the rather forbidding definition is a commonsensical notion. A child's emerging character and personality, her opinions of what is beautiful and ugly, her thoughts of the future, and her perceptions of herself—all these result in part from millions of impressions, sights and smells and sounds and feelings, that she has gathered from living in the particular place her parents have chosen to put her.

The poet and essayist Diane Ackerman calls synesthesia "a thick garment of perception."[12] Each person puts on his cloak of sensation gradually, taking on layer upon layer of impressions while moving through life, and because no two person's experiences are alike, each set of such "clothes" is unique. Just as obviously, there are degrees of difference. Adult pioneers carried and birthed their sons and daughters into an environment dramatically different from the ones they themselves had known as children. As these young western natives grew up, shaping and being shaped by their surroundings, their "garments of perception," those psychological outer layers through which they dealt with the world, were correspondingly very much their own. These children matured into individuals who, at the very least, often recognized that the gap between their generation and that of their parents yawned far wider than usual.

One hint of the importance of the dialogue between children and their environment is seen in the extraordinary energy and passion with which western boys and girls explored the world around them. "A happier set of children I think I never saw," wrote a mother soon after arrival on the Kansas plains; and she added about her two-year-old, "Johnny goes 'yout' to his heart's content." They were great collectors. They brought home beetles, snakeskins, fossils, pottery shards, bones, flowers, lizards, and an eclectic variety of animal dung. Some of these items they turned into playthings. A girl of the Flint Hills built an elaborate doll's house out of buffalo bones. Allie Wallace of Oklahoma made hats and other clothing out of cottonwood leaves. Some young Nebraskans took wild melon rinds, turned them inside out, strapped them on their feet, and skated around their cabin floor.[13]

Typically these were some of the most pleasant memories taken into adulthood, suggesting an identification between children and the natural setting. A Montana girl recalled that "from early March, when the snow was disappearing and the first flowers beginning to bloom, until October . . . , I with my brothers and sisters roamed the mountains and hills and explored the streams for miles in every direction."[14] The west Texan Ralla Banta wrote of her sheepherding days: "When we returned home in the evening, we enjoyed telling where we had been, to what creek, up what branch, and what we had seen." Charlie O'Kieffe referred to flora and fauna almost as people. He ascribed personalities to tumbleweeds and pocket gophers, bobolinks and sand cherries, and he remarked on the relative aesthetic virtues of cowchips and buffalo chips, comparing the latter to matzo and Swedish health bread. These richly sensual memories suggest a physical intimacy with the place. One girl would slip outside during winter to brush away the snow under a nearby tree; she filled her hands with the dirt she knew from summertime play, then smelled it and rubbed it against her cheeks.[15]

Not surprisingly, these young people acquired a remarkable knowledge of this country. Only four months after her arrival in western Kansas, Luna Warner had collected and cataloged 117 plants she had found around her family's homestead. Young settlers often seemed to know their surroundings far better than their elders. The Montanan Lillian Miller would write of the coloration patterns of curlews, finches, thrushes, and swallows. She also learned scores of wild-bird calls, although she specialized in domestic fowls, chickens in particular; she claimed to be able to crow in eight different keys. Ellison Orr described the flying and feeding habits of grouse, partridges, quail, pigeons, cowlinks, and shrikes.[16]

Children took pride in this knowledge, and often they made it clear that what they knew set them apart from their elders. Frank Waugh, who came to the Kansas plains at four, filled more than twenty pages of his memoir with descriptions and comments on plants and animals. He wrote not only of the differences between big and little bluestem but also on how compass plant could be told from rattle weed and where each stood in relation to buffalo pea, milk weed, flowering thistle, and wild aster. The adults he knew had been ignorant and uncaring about such things. His neighbor, a successful farmer, could identify only two plants: sunflowers and cockleburrs. To grown-ups, Waugh thought, "the stars above and weeds underfoot were equally nameless and therefore insignificant. Every wild plant was a weed. All wild plants, like all wild animals, had to be destroyed to make way for farms." [17]

This exploration continued from early infancy into and through adolescence. Children were finding and naming the many parts of their world; they were also discovering what they enjoyed and disliked and were testing their own abilities. The two processes were not only simultaneous; in a way, they were the same. In that, western boys and girls were making a special claim of possession. As children shaped who they would become, they did so in a world that was in a sense becoming more theirs than their parents'.

As children grew older, much of this exploration occurred as they played with friends and siblings and performed the multitude of jobs that were part of their annual regimen. The circumstances of this work and play, like the range and variety of labors, were in some ways distinctive to the frontier. Those circumstances in turn encouraged certain traits of personality in children. The same conditions that required children to work at many different tasks—a lack of outside help in establishing a farm from scratch—often left a child working largely on his own, frequently in the great yawning spaces of the plains. Wallace Woods's first job after moving to Kansas at seven was to carry food and supplies several miles every day over the unfamiliar plains to the place where his father was building a sod house. Agnes Morley and her brother, thirteen and eleven, once covered 130 miles of countryside in three days while helping their mother arrange a cattle sale. The needs of the day forced many parents to trust their youngsters' abilities. When Marvin Powe was nine, for instance, his father told him to find and return some runaway horses, assuming the animals were close by. In fact they had wandered miles from the ranch, and when Marvin could not find them, he just kept going, living off the land and camping for a while with some cowboys. It took him a week to locate the horses, yet his father was just starting out to look for Marvin when the boy showed up. Experiences like Marvin's suggest these sons and daughters developed a remarkable independence and self-reliance that surprised and sometimes shocked visitors from the East. In later years, at least, these children often attested to a confidence and self-respect. From traveling to supply the family's water and helping her father to build fence during her Oklahoma girlhood, Allie Wallace recalled, she first learned to know and trust her "established capability." [18]

Yet these same patterns of interaction may have had other, more troubling results. Frontier children seem often to have grown toward adulthood with contradictions inherent in their complicated relationships with their parents, with their peers, and with the country around them. So much of their work, for instance, brought children close to their families—not always physically, but in their perspectives and emerging identities. Girls and boys necessarily knew much about the state of family affairs and tribulations; they knew well their own worth and the part they played in family survival. Yet the particulars of their work and play took them away from the homestead, often to spend hours or even days by themselves. Nine-year-old Cliff Newland was hired to haul supplies every week to cowboys in line camps, a round-trip of seventy-five miles. Cliff knew that the pay—fifty cents a day—helped him and his widowed father pay for necessities on their small West Texas ranch. [19] The experience suggests that Cliff, like thousands of other plains youngsters, was being pulled, emotionally and psychologically, in different directions. His responsibilities and sense of worth bound him to his father; the particular actions with which he gained those feelings bred an isolation and an acceptance of separation from other people as the norm.

Many other lessons they learned seemed always to be bumping into each other. A lot of their work and play taught them to be independent, to rely on their own devices, and to move easily and confidently among adults. At the same time, their parents, especially their mothers, were trying to rear them by Victorian values, and these values told them that childhood was a precious time that should be prolonged as much as possible, that they should spend most of their time under their parents' close watch, that they should defer to their elders' opinions, and that they should step into adult roles only gradually. It must have been confusing.

Growing up western could be especially troubling for girls on their way toward womanhood. As children, they were expected to spend much of their time laboring at jobs typically assigned to men—plowing, planting, harvesting, hunting, herding. They often came to identify with this work. Even when they complained of its hardships, they usually enjoyed its freedom of movement, and they took pride in its highly visible accomplishments—the transformation of the land that was celebrated so lustily at the time.

Often they identified less with their mothers' labors, those essential, complex tasks of the household. Sometimes they resented it. Edna Clifton's mother used to tell her of her own girlhood in Tennessee, where she had spent much of her time sewing, cleaning, cooking, and tending the baby, chores impeccably feminine by the standards of the day. Edna, who spent her time herding, weeding, hunting, gathering fuel, and hauling water, was irate: "I thought my grandmother must have been the meanest woman in the world." The Oklahoman Susie Crocket, with her several brothers, supplied much of her family's income by trapping, then curing and selling the hides. Once, when she found a wolf in her trap, her brothers taunted her, saying she would have to ask for their help. "I won't," she said; then she beat the animal to death with a tent pole. She recalled all that with some affection, but she said, "I hated to see Ma come in with a big batch of sewing, for I knew it meant many long hours sitting by her side sewing seams." It was unfair, she wrote: "I could help the boys with the plowing or trapping, but they would never help me with the sewing." [20]

Then as they entered adolescence these girls received very different messages from their parents and elders. They had earned their confidence and their "established capability" by doing certain kinds of labor; they had gained a sense of themselves by confronting and learning from the country around their homes. Now they were told to put behind them the work and play they had known so long and to concentrate instead on jobs traditionally assigned to women: domestic tasks of rearing children and keeping the house and its immediate environs. They were told, quite literally, to come indoors. The result, naturally, was a dissonance between these women's pasts and futures. Some of these young women made this transition willingly; some did not.

Such contradictions—and other aspects of the inner history of frontier childhood—were not necessarily unique to the developing West. Certain tendencies among plains children, however, were accentuated by the special conditions of pioneer life: an identification with a new physical environment, the range of work and responsibilities, and the isolation in which much of that work took place. The resulting traits of personality may have contributed in turn to the formation of a distinctive regional character. During the late nineteenth and early twentieth centuries, as plains communities matured and political and social institutions took root, these boys and girls would mature to become many of the area's political and economic leaders, its farmers and ranchers, its housewives and schoolteachers, its drifters and crooks. Studying the emotional development of plains children can help us trace and define the emergence of the modern West.

The distinctive nature of plains childhood suggests the third lesson that these young people can teach us. This lesson concerns the history of American families generally and in particular the ways that history has often been oversimplified. Much has been written lately about the family, childrearing, and the relations between parents and their daughters and sons. Historians have given particular attention to the generations of the late nineteenth and early twentieth centuries, the same years in which much of the plains was being invaded by westering pioneers. Supposedly, American childhood was "reconstructed" during those decades, to use one scholar's word. Specifically, parents were encouraged to exert more control over the particulars of their children's lives. In the home, which was seen as a haven in a corrupted world, mothers especially were to use their superior virtue to nurture the nobler sensitivities of sons and daughters. Away from the hearth, public schools were to encourage those same higher values and to instill respect for dominant political and economic institutions.

Essential to this "reconstructed" childhood was an orderly, controlled introduction of young people into adult society, and vital to that was the withdrawal of children from America's workplaces. Only then could youngsters be shielded from adult vices and be tutored properly in personal and civic virtue. Besides, in an increasingly industrialized world of specialized, often highly technical occupations, a young boy or girl simply had less to offer. These changes were basic to the making of the contemporary ideal of the "child-centered" family, in which parents dedicate substantial time and resources to the careful, choreographed upbringing of the "economically useless child."[21]

This scenario is familiar to every student of American social history, and properly so. It is crucial in understanding the system of values and expectations in which both children and adults have come to live during this century. But this story of childhood's "reconstruction" is much less helpful in describing the ways most American families in fact have lived. In the first place, its focus is less on behavior than on goals—those of proper childrearing—as expressed mainly by social and educational reformers. On the question of how closely parents actually lived by these ideals, most examples have come from upper-middle-class families in towns and cities of the northeastern quadrant of the forty-eight contiguous states. In short, the story as now told essentially describes a rather small minority of Americans and the ideals to which they aspired.

Nothing close to a full picture of American children will be possible until we apply general notions—in this case that of a thoroughgoing re-making of childhood—to the many settings of national life. On the plains frontier many parents did seem to embrace such new ideals as a concern for youngsters' moral development, especially as directed by mothers and such public institutions as the common school. But these ideals were con-tinually colliding with the necessities of life on this fringe of an expanding national economy. Most pioneer families faced a dilemma: They would have to take on the increased burden of labor associated with starting farms from scratch, yet the move west often left them with fewer resources and less help to meet the demands of the day. Given this situation—and the fact that most of the essential work of pioneer farming was within the children's abilities—most parents relied heavily on their sons and daugh-ters in dealing with their load of labor. Far from being withdrawn from the workplace, children were, if anything, involved in a broader range of labor than their parents. Some of that work was done close to their parents, but much was not. That meant mothers and fathers were in no position to oversee closely how their girls and boys passed their days, to guide with much precision their steps into adulthood. Other frontier conditions—the high rate of mobility among its people, the newness of its shallow-rooted public institutions, its legendary vices often openly displayed—further complicated the task of implanting modern ideals of childrearing. As a result, plains children grew up shaped by a confusion of influences that reflected both emerging national values and the peculiarities of their place and time.

Surely the same general observation could be made of children else-where. Families of the rural South and in urban immigrant neighborhoods of the Northeast and Midwest also relied on their youngsters' wide-ranging labors, but other conditions set those places apart from pioneer settlements of Kansas and the Dakotas. Life in all these places, further-more, differed from that in Maine lumber towns, in Hispanic villages along the Rio Grande, and in well-to-do suburbs of Atlanta. Always a nation of dazzling diversity, the United States was experiencing some of the most profound changes of its history—great tidal movements of population, a prodigious industrial expansion that revolutionized national economic life, a splintering and reformation of class lines, and a blurring and refocusing of social distinctions. Seldom has so much in the lives of so many Americans changed so rapidly and in so many different ways.

The lesson for anyone trying to reconstruct the lives of children is clear: Be careful. Generalizing about the history of children, based mainly on the experiences of the boys and girls of one social class in one part of the country, tells us as much (or as little) as looking at the history of the United States entirely through the eyes of adults. The identities of plains children—their behavior and characters, who they were and who they became—all reflected in some ways the peculiar settings in which they found themselves. The same could be said of their cousins throughout the United States. Only when that diversity is recognized can we begin to bring children fully into the American story.

3

Immigrant Children at School, 1880–1940

A Child's Eye View

SELMA BERROL

There is no shortage of scholarship on the subject of immigrant children and the schools they attended. Most of the work, however, has focused on the reaction of the schools *to* the foreign children in their charge, not on the experience of the children themselves. Here I shall attempt to redress the imbalance.[1] The best way to do this is to listen to the voices of those youngsters who were born abroad or born in the United States but reared in households where English was not the family language and where the customs were those of the Old World. Some of the children will speak to us by way of memories recalled during interviews conducted by inquisitive scholars in recent years; others will be talking through their own memoirs.

Unfortunately, those sources are not evenly distributed. As a result, I shall describe only the views of children who attended urban public schools between 1880 and 1940. These youngsters, perhaps because they were more articulate than their rural peers or perhaps because the scholars interviewing them are themselves living in urban areas, are overrepresented in the sources and therefore in this essay. The picture that emerges is, as one would expect, multifaceted. The individual children were different from each other as well as from their native-born, English-speaking American peers. Under the umbrella term "immigrant child" were dul-

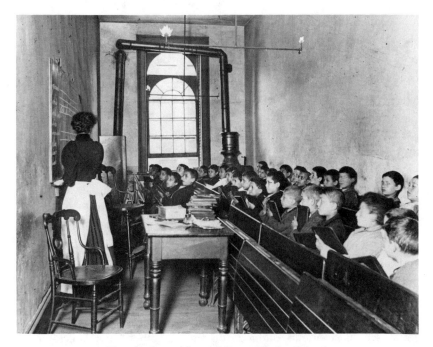

Class in the condemned Essex Market School.
(Photograph from the Jacob A. Riis Collection,
Museum of the City of New York)

lards and gifted students in every ethnic group. In addition, even a very young child might have learned something about school from parents or older siblings, and that knowledge, which would not be the same for all, would color his or her view of school even before entry.

Furthermore, despite the conventional view that portrayed all immigrant parents as avid for their children's education, recent studies have made it clear that no such unanimity existed. A number of the voices to be heard reinforce the revisionist position. Parents often placed greater stress on family goals than on individual success and thus encouraged their children to work and save for home ownership or entrepreneurship rather than to undertake careers through education. Sometimes children left school behind to help in the family's business. Placement in the family also made a difference; younger siblings, supported by older brothers and sisters, were more likely to stay in school longer. Gender made the greatest difference of all. Much to the unhappiness of many girls, daughters in immigrant families were usually discouraged from going to school for very long. Finally, some children simply disliked school. A Chicago survey in 1913 revealed that out of five hundred Slavic children, 82.4 percent declared that even if they were not forced to go to work by family need, they would prefer employment in a factory over continuing their education.[2]

To what extent can we generalize about immigrant children's school experience? As it turns out, quite a bit. Almost all children reported that they feared but usually respected their teachers. They were taught a common curriculum by similar methods and were distressed by the contrasts between school and home. Except for the last point, their view of school does not sound very different from what their native-born peers would have said, but in truth there were a number of differences.

At the start of the twentieth century, when immigration from southern and eastern Europe was at its peak, thousands of "little aliens" entered the public and parochial schools of large American cities, making them more congested than they had ever been before. Jam-packed classrooms and the resulting half-time schedules exemplified one way that the immigrant child's school experience differed from those of other American children. The neighborhoods in which they lived were old and their schools had been built for smaller populations. Thus, when the number of foreign-born children in the "ghettoes" increased, many schools were forced to go on half-day sessions or to seat two children at a desk made for one or sometimes to do both. Sadie R. recalled that on her first day of school she had to sit in a seat with another girl "and put an arm around her waist so I shouldn't fall off."[3]

The *Jewish Daily Forward*, speaking for many working-class Jews, reported that the poorest children on the Lower East Side of New York attended the worst schools. In one school on Henry Street eighty children were crammed into a room built for forty; another windowless classroom held seventy. In some schools, a teacher might face as many as one hundred children a day and, given the limitations on human strength, not convey much knowledge to any of them.[4]

Some immigrant children were turned away entirely because of overcrowding, postponing their entry into school and possibly shortening their entire school experience. This was also true for children who entered the United States at a later age than usual. Since most children finished their schooling by the age of twelve, the child who could not be admitted at the normal age of five or six and whose parents could not do without the income he or she could earn as a teenager might have little more than a primary school (grades one through three) education.[5]

School records in urban-immigrant districts showed great variations in the ages of students in any given grade, a circumstance not true of the schools that native-born children attended. A second-year class in a school that served an immigrant district resembled an ungraded one-room school found in rural areas; it might contain seven-year-olds, ten-year-olds, and occasionally a twelve-year-old. The disparity resulted from policy adopted by most school districts that received immigrants. A foreign-born child was placed at the level indicated by his or her ability to speak, read, or write English. Thus, a ten-year-old who knew little English would be assigned to a classroom with children three or four years younger.[6]

Most of the time a child who knew no English would be placed in a "sink-or-swim," total-immersion class when first entering school. After six months a student who did not "sink" would graduate to a class appropriate to his or her ability to cope with English. Bilingualism was not an option, and as a result many of the children schooled under this policy recall that their initial experiences were intensely traumatic. Isidor B., escorted by a neighbor to kindergarten in the Bronx, recalled his terror when she left and he realized that he could not understand what anyone around him, including the teacher, was saying. Edward Bok, a Dutch immigrant who later became the editor of the *Saturday Evening Post,* said that he did not know "a single word of English" when he entered school, an uncomfortable position he shared with Leonard Covello, who was to become a schoolmaster in "a great city" (New York City) when he grew up. Native-born children, of course, also did not know how to read and write English, but their ability to understand simple directions was one of the differences that set them apart from many immigrant children.[7]

Language difficulties for immigrants were a problem that could be alleviated only with the passage of time, but the intense crowding that marked the schools in immigrant districts could have been relieved immediately. Most large cities had a long-established tradition of neighborhood schools; when residential patterns shifted, some schools were underutilized. At the turn of the century there were usually empty seats in classrooms in parts of the city outside the immigrant districts. Busing, however, was unpopular with immigrant parents and often unacceptable to parents at the receiving schools, many of whom had left the poorer areas where most of the newcomers lived partly to avoid immigrants.[8]

Outdoor School for Tubercular Children (organized charity).
(Photograph from the Jacob A. Riis Collection,
Museum of the City of New York)

Wherever immigrant children appeared, teachers and administrators did all they could to get them into school and to keep them there until they were old enough to leave school legally. In some places that meant completion of the sixth grade, in others the eighth year. Success was difficult to achieve. Primarily for economic reasons, parents of every ethnic background were often forced to send a child to work at the earliest possible age. Sometimes the work was part-time but very demanding. Several former students, for example, described selling newspapers from 4 A.M. to 7:45 A.M. and then again at 4 P.M. Vicenzo M., in Syracuse, New York, had such a schedule but was able to cope. Harry Roskolenko, however, who followed a similar schedule on New York City's Lower East Side, slept selectively in class, staying "partially awake during history and English lessons" but not during civics, arithmetic or "most of everything else."[9]

Sometimes the work done by foreign-born children was full-time, possibly at home doing piecework or, in the case of girls, attending to the household so the mother could earn some much-needed money. It was not difficult for a child to find work; small jobs could be obtained at the docks and errand boys were always in demand. The absence of birth certificates, a common situation for children born abroad, made it easier to fool the truant officer or another authority figure, especially if the child was tall for his or her age.[10]

Although most immigrant children did not want to avoid school, the acute discomfort some experienced in the classroom led them to evade the compulsory-education laws as much as possible. As Eva Morawska said in her book on the east central European immigrants in Johnstown, Pennsylvania, children from foreign homes who attended the public schools in that community between 1890 and 1940 recalled "recurrent feelings of embarrassment and inferiority to the American children caused by [their] difficulty with the English language . . . foreign dress . . . and unpronounceable names."[11]

For many reasons, boys and girls of the immigrant generation and many of their children did not attend school for very long. In many cases it was the schools themselves, and especially the teachers in them, that were to blame. Then as now, the teacher was central to the entire school experience, and then as now, many were not equal to their task.

During these years, most immigrant children faced an unmarried woman, usually although not always a WASP or an Irish Catholic, who had completed a teacher-training program at a normal school.[12] In addition to differences in background, age, and training, these teachers, like most human beings, differed in personality and ability. If the perceptions of most of their former students are to be trusted, however, they were alike in one very important way: They were antagonistic to their students. One after another, the men and women who were once immigrant children discussed the hostility that they felt emanating from the front desk. Some youngsters felt this early in their school careers. Samuel C. described his first-grade teacher as "cold and forbidding," an image reinforced by her habit of calling on her six-year-old charges by their surnames and requiring an instant response to her commands. Alfred Kazin wrote that his teachers "grimly, wearily, often with ill-concealed distaste, watched against their students relapsing into savage Brownsville boys."[13]

Other students had other complaints but all revealed unfavorable memories of those who had instructed them. Mike T., whose given name was distinctly Serbian, recalled that "at school I went as Tomas . . . because the teacher would not pronounce or spell my own." A student of

Slovenian background in a Pittsburgh public school, Stanley N., echoed this, recalling that his teachers, despite his corrections, continued to mispronounce his unfamiliar surname, which made him angry and contributed to his decision to drop out of school at twelve. Rosemary P., also from Pittsburgh, was told that she "talked funny" by her first high-school teacher and, to avoid further embarrassment, she spent a precious twenty-five cents on a self-improvement pamphlet and locked herself in the bathroom to "practice English" in secret until she could "pronounce properly the difficult 'th' sound."[14]

Rightly or wrongly, former students recalled some painful experiences. Tanya N., for example, got into trouble on her first day of school:

> My mother gave me a bagel and an apple which I brought to school with me. My teacher was talking and I didn't understand a word she said. I got bored so I bit into my bagel. The teacher's face looked a little angry, so I thought something was wrong, but I didn't know what was wrong. I just kept eating the bagel and after a few minutes the teacher went over to me, took me by the hand, walked me to a corner of the room [and] sat me up on a very high teacher's chair. I took my bagel with me. She put a dunce cap on my head and the children began to laugh. I didn't know that it was a dunce cap. I learned later.[15]

Food was often a problem. During Passover, Jewish children substituted matzo for their usual bread sandwiches. As anyone who has ever tried to manage a matzo sandwich would expect, a terrific mess resulted and led to harsh criticism from the teachers assigned to patrol the lunchroom. In general, lunch, brown-bagged from home, caused particular difficulty. Italian mothers made Italian-style lunches, but WASP teachers said that American foods were healthier. One interviewee told Leonard Covello that he threw his lunch away "rather than ruin his reputation" with his non-Italian peers and his teachers.[16]

Some teachers did not hesitate to use humiliation in order to teach. Sadie R. recalled such an incident when she was learning English at a Lower East Side school:

> On one occasion in the lower grades . . . I raised my hand and the teacher said, "What is it, Sadie?" "Can I leave the room?" I say. She

said, "Yes, you can leave the room." So I picked myself up and I go and she said, "Where are you going?" And I said, "I asked you and you said I could leave the room." And she said, "I said you *can* leave the room, but you didn't ask me whether you *may* leave the room!" I was so embarrassed with the whole thing, I never forgot the difference between can and may.[17]

Alfred Kazin, as well as others, remembered his teachers as always being angry; often their anger resulted in physical punishment. Felix B., in a Chicago school in 1915, said that he "wanted to stay out of school because every time my work was wrong, the teacher hit me." His classmate, Edward R., had a slightly different experience: When he could not do the assigned work, his teacher used "proxy punishment" and encouraged his fellow students to hit him. Edward Bok recalled being "hit hard" as a pupil in the Philadelphia public schools; Sol L. said his New York City first-grade teacher struck him "with a pointer if he talked at the wrong time" because "talking was illegal and hitting was common." In his next grade, the treatment got worse. A Miss Bower broke a ruler on him for reading under the desk.[18]

Harry Roskolenko recalls being hit by his teachers and the school principal, possibly because he fell asleep in class, something Leonard Covello reported was not unusual. Jerre Mangione and Sam R. agreed that they feared their teachers because, as Sam said, "they would send you up to the principal and the principal would beat the hell out of you." Paul W. said that the nuns who taught him "seldom used the ruler to measure anything except the distance between a long overhead swing and the [offending] student's hand." Parents did not complain because usually they did not know. Most of the memoir writers never told their fathers or mothers, fearing that another beating would result; parents typically believed that for good or ill authority had to be respected.[19]

Many immigrant children, especially girls, were well behaved and suffered no punishments. As a result, they had good memories of their teachers. Mary Antin was an example; at twelve, recently arrived from Russia, she entered the Chelsea, Massachusetts, public schools to find that her teachers "were patient, persevering, sweet and ready to help her at any time." She had special praise for a Miss Dillingham, who gave her private tutoring in the pronunciation of *v* and *w*. Other children, especially girls, had similar memories. Sadie R. recalled a loving first-grade teacher who "put me on her lap after school and [would] teach me English words."[20]

Rose J. loved her fifth-grade teacher, Miss Bliss, partly because she had never known a real person with that surname but had seen the word only in books. She cared even more for her sixth-grade teacher, who was "beautiful and young" and encouraged her interest in music. Hannah T. remembered a teacher who "would help me, hug me and nurture me. My mother was not a nurturer." Rose J. agreed: "I loved my teachers . . . I always sought a surrogate mother because my own was not demonstratively an affectionate person."[21]

On the other side of the United States, Jade Snow Wong, later to become an author and ceramicist, also found her American teachers to be very kind. Her third-grade teacher appreciated her ability and allowed her to skip a grade, and her next teacher was "loving." Harry Roskolenko recalled one teacher: "a grand lady . . . a beautiful woman [who] smelled of heaven . . . , had small hands and seemed much concerned with him." He adored her and paid her the highest tribute in his power to bestow— he did his homework that year.[22]

Different children liked their teachers for different reasons, but Dora W., speaking of her teacher in grade five, said it all: "I had such a dedicated teacher. She was an absolutely beautiful person. She changed the course of my life. She gave me everything she had and more. Because of her I was introduced to everything that was good in the United States."[23]

Dora's reaction was to be expected. Teachers of immigrant children were "representatives of a different, ineluctably more attractive way of life" to the young girls they taught. Apparently to everyone's satisfaction, immigrant children learned WASP etiquette along with WASP speech and dress from their teachers, who also brought culture into their lives. Rose J. cited her attraction to music and "things cultural," which she would not have had without the teachers who set her an example to follow. She learned to love music in appreciation classes. "I had a fabulous memory," she reported and thus recognized all the songs and operatic excerpts that were played. As a result, "I won all the prizes."[24]

More down-to-earth training was also part of her education. Girls in the upper grades of elementary school attended home-economics classes, later favorably recalled. Mary F. told her interviewer: "I didn't know what the [table] utensils were for. We'd set the table and Miss Themig [said]

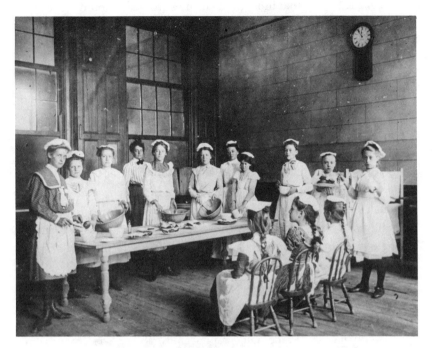

Domestic science class in public school.
(Photograph from the Jacob A. Riis Collection,
Museum of the City of New York)

to me 'You don't have a butter knife there,' so I took a knife and put it down. She then said . . . [no], 'that is an ordinary knife.' " Mary did not mind the correction because she learned that there was a special knife for butter.[25]

These girls discovered, however, that their mothers did not always respond happily to such lessons. One mother, told by her ten-year-old daughter that her cooking was not American enough and that she should use a cook book, asserted her supremacy in the kitchen in no uncertain terms; others welcomed the new knowledge as a window to the outer world. That, of course, was the reason for introducing home economics into the curriculum and also why it caused trouble for many girls. The recipes used in these classes, for example, involved mixing dairy and meat products and using pork. This created difficulty for both Orthodox Jewish girl students and for those from less observant but nonetheless traditional Jewish homes. No concessions to religious law were made, however. On the theory that immigrant cuisines would not produce healthy new Americans, young girls were taught to prepare and value American foods, including bacon and ham.

While their female peers were involved in the demonstration kitchen, boys were attending workshops. The reasoning behind workshops for boys differed somewhat from that behind home economics. Although most immigrant children were not expected to remain in school long after the legal school-leaving age, boys in particular were expected to leave quite early. Thus knowing a trade would have great value. Some of the memoirs indicate that the children liked workshop classes and took great pride in "bringing home a project from carpentry class," but others felt that such lessons had little long-term value. As with so many issues in immigrant history, reactions varied with ethnicity. Some Jewish parents, for example, considered learning manual skills a waste of time better spent in preparing for a profession, but others, notably Italians and Slavs, welcomed the opportunity for their children to learn skills that might enable them to enter a higher echelon of manual work.[26]

In all areas of the curriculum, a good memory was much prized. Leonard Covello memorized the states, capital cities, poetry, wise sayings, and "memory gems," which by themselves were intended to create a better memory. Good handwriting was another highly rated skill. Edward Bok recalled his inability to learn a Spencerian style of writing, which led to the principal's hitting his hand with a rattan rod hard enough to cause swelling. Bok does not specify the kind of paper he was told to use, but other sources indicate that at the start of the first grade, wide-lined paper was used. The lines soon grew narrower; a sample of Thomas S.'s writing as a student in the second half of first grade (1B) was done on paper with normal line spacing.[27]

Handwriting was not considered an individual trait. Many respondents recall the horizontal chart that adorned their primary-school classrooms showing the only correct way to write the letters of the alphabet in upper and lower case. Students also did exercises to improve muscle control and thus produce the clearest possible writing. From an inspection of one valuable source, materials collected by the recently created Board of Education of the City of New York and presented at the Paris Exposition in 1900, this practice paid off. Many second graders and even more third graders wrote with a clarity that many adults would envy.

But what were they saying in this eminently legible handwriting? Some wrote poetry and many wrote short essays. Hyman G., age nine, in the second grade at P.S. 75, Manhattan, gave us a sample of the former:

> Dear Rain, without your help, I know
> The trees and flowers could not grow
> My roses all would fade and die
> If you stayed up behind the sky

His classmate, Max A., provided a mini-mini-essay reflecting weather changes: "The birds are going South. It is too cold here."[28]

Max's topic reflected another subject many former students recalled, most with great pleasure. Nature study was introduced into urban schools on the theory that city children, especially if they grew up in the "congested districts," would barely know what a tree looked like. In some schools such study took the form of gardening. Isidore B. remembered the elaborate ceremonies surrounding Arbor Day at his Bronx school, and Mary F., from a third-grade class in Brownsville, Brooklyn, described her experience on a nature trip: "We traipsed over to New Lots Avenue and there was this huge wilderness under the El [elevated trains] and [the teacher] gave us all kinds of implements but our job was to weed. And we weeded and we got burrs in us and we planted." Mary may have been more enthusiastic than most. She also planted seeds on her own and "used to pick up manure [for fertilizer] in the street."[29] Most children liked physical education, but few schools in immigrant neighborhoods were equipped to hold such classes. As a substitute, Sophie Ruskay said, teachers held an exercise period when, with the window partially open, the children were ordered to "breathe in; breathe out" and to do simple exercises.

Gardening, cooking, carpentry, and physical education were not taught in every school because they were often seen as unnecessary frills. Everyone agreed, however, on the basics; arithmetic, grammar, spelling, and speech were thoroughly taught.

In retrospect, given the crowding and the problems of poverty, poor health, and adjustment presented by immigrant children to the schools, it is amazing to see how much was attempted on the elementary level. How well the schools succeeded is another matter, but judging from what the children said about the teaching methods, there was certainly no lack of trying. Charlie M. explained how he learned to read: "We had a book, story books, a progressive reader. We didn't have a formalized reading method. We had a primer. In the primer were stories: 'the sky was falling down.' We children actually repeated that story with the teacher, so we learned it by repeating it. We would match the words we had learned with the words in the book, and this way we acquired a vocabulary." [30]

Leonard Covello, although in a different school, learned by a similar method: memorizing assigned word lists. Children at P.S. 188 on New York City's East Side learned the English words for the parts of their body by physically locating them. This led one small newcomer to say "Dis ist a piece of mine head" when the teacher patted her hair and asked what part of her body was being touched. [31]

Phonetic methods, later used to teach reading, do not appear in the recollections of those interviewed, but recitation certainly does. Over and over, the children tell us that they were required to recite, often standing at attention. Henry Klein, who graduated from P.S. 4 on the Lower East Side, liked this approach and said that he was always ready with answers in arithmetic, history, geography, and grammar. If he also enjoyed the regular Friday tests, however, he was unusual; most children dreaded them. Tests of various kinds were an integral part of schooling. Teachers would dictate words, which children were expected to write well and to spell correctly. There were also daily oral drills and frequent spelling bees. Mistakes in spelling, wherever they occurred, might lead to a special assignment—writing each misspelled word ten times or more. [32]

Americanization was at the top of the public-school agenda. Although immigrants had been coming to America since the colonial era, the years from 1880 to 1920 saw extraordinarily heavy immigration from areas of Europe previously underrepresented in the American population. The volume and "foreignness" of the new immigrants gave rise to much concern among those whose ancestors had come earlier. "Balkanization" was much feared; ethnic separatism was much deplored. The public school was seen as the agency best equipped to provide the remedy: assimilation. As a result, the central purpose of schools in immigrant neighborhoods became Americanization. Through reading and writing the national language and learning the national heritage and value system, the "little aliens" were expected to become socialized in American ways.

This goal was complicated because in most urban neighborhood schools children of the same ethnic background could speak to their peers in their own first language. Recognizing this, Julia Richman, the district superintendent of the Lower East Side schools from 1903 to 1912, forbade the use of Yiddish anywhere in her domain and enforced the rule by directing teachers to wash out offending mouths with kosher soap.[33]

Unable to change the ethnic configuration of their classes, teachers took the advice of one expert and attempted to "wrest" the immigrant children in their care from their foreign backgrounds by a host of different methods, both negative and positive. They began with names. In Morreville, Pennsylvania, Slavic names were "adapted" for the teacher's convenience; in Boston, Philadelphia, and New York, first names might fall prey to the Americanizing teacher. Sadie would become Sylvia, Becky, Rebecca, and so on. Some of the newly named youngsters seemed to like the change, but others were confused because at home they continued to be called by their original names. One memoirist said that when her school friends called at her home and asked for her under her American name, her parents told them no one by that name lived there.[34]

Methods of Americanization, although they varied with individual teachers, were insensitive. Several of the Russian Jewish students who were interviewed years later remembered the inspections they were subjected to by school nurses and teachers who assumed that because they were poor they were also dirty. The nurse's inspection visits were purposely irregular; when she entered the classroom "the insides of the little immigrant daughters would begin to slide—slide" because the examination was done in groups of five in front of the class, and the public humiliation if one was found offensive was almost unbearable.[35]

Dozens of times each day, teachers sought to "Americanize" their immigrant children into "little citizens." As the children learned the three Rs, for example, their primers, textbooks, and assignments were used to inculcate love and pride in their adopted land. History, especially American history, occupied a central place in the curriculum, with civics and geography in only a slightly lower spot. Harry L. remembered that "American holidays and Puritan roots were emphasized: We had a textbook about Puritans, pictures of Puritans with big hats and Thanksgiving and so on, and then about Betsy Ross and George Washington, and those things we learned." Other memoir writers agreed that they were taught a history that left them with "strong positive feelings about the United States."[36]

Given their mission, the public schools ignored and often derogated the first culture of the students they were teaching. With the exception of an occasional settlement-house resident, "immigrant gifts" were not much prized. Parents did not protest. Most accepted the Protestant exercises that began the public-school day as well as the highly nationalistic American history taught in the classroom. Although most parents certainly wanted to preserve at least some aspects of their home culture and language, they seemed to agree that the public school was not obligated to do this for them. Instead they relied on the home or on an additional ethnic or religious school, for which they paid tuition, to teach the language and culture of their ethnic group.

Authors Jade Snow Wong and Maxine Hong Kingston followed this path, attending and enjoying Chinese school after public-school classes were over. Both described the long hours that they spent in the afternoon and evening classes as strengthening their feelings of self-worth, which had been somewhat damaged by classmates, and to a lesser extent, by teachers, in public school. Kingston also recalled the differences in children's behavior in the two schools. Children who were withdrawn and passive in their American classes became raucous and wild in Chinese school; depression and silence gave way to gaiety and chatter in an atmosphere where they felt at home.[37]

Exhausting as attending two schools might be, ethnic schools did lessen the painful feelings of marginality frequently expressed in the memoirs and interviews of those recalling immigrant childhoods. Which model were they to follow? Their parents' behavior and ideas or the teachers'? Harriet Pawlowska's father, for example, left Poland, as most immigrants did, to earn a better living. He remained proud of his native land, however, and wanted his children to feel the same way. As a result, Harriet expected to see a large nation called Poland on the map when she first studied geography and was extremely puzzled when she could not find it. Papa had never told her that as a physical entity, his beloved land had ceased to exist at the end of the eighteenth century. Whom was she to believe? Patriotic Papa or the map? Where did the child belong? Was he or she an American or something else? Or, as Jere Mangione's father said, was the answer "half and half"?[38]

Immigrant children became aware of this duality from their first day of school because many of them were meeting Americans for the first time. One such child, Samuel O., likened going from his own street to school to a trip to another planet. For some, it was a hostile planet; for others, the problems came from home; for still others, there were no differences. Rosemary P.'s reminiscence exemplifies what Samuel meant. As with so many other children of her time, the 1930s, she learned to read from the

Dick and Jane series, and, as for so many other immigrant youngsters, the contrasts between the idealized life portrayed in the primer and her own thoroughly Slovenian family created conflict:

> I became ashamed that my parents spoke "funny"; that we laughed too loud; that we drank homemade wine; that our walls were papered in flower patterns; that we grew our own vegetables; that my father raised chickens in our garage; . . . that he repaired all our shoes in the basement; that my mother never sat down to dinner with us (she cooked, served and ate when everyone was finished); that our clothes and our curtains and towels were homemade, some of them out of feed bags from the local granary; that stockings and worn clothing were never thrown away but given to my uncle who transformed them into rag rugs.[39]

Classroom procedures helped create feelings like Rosemary's. Two Jewish girls remembered a handkerchief problem. "I had a cold," recalled Mary F., "and I had a rag with which to blow my nose, but no handkerchief." Her teacher was "really disgusted" and made it clear that a rag was no substitute for a handkerchief. Rose K. reported that her teacher "came to school with stacks of clean handkerchiefs" and would call students up to her desk to blow their noses. On hygienic grounds the teachers could not be faulted, but at the same time their attitudes increased the problem of marginality for their students by making them doubt the customs of their homes.[40]

Such doubts led to fear of exposure and feelings of inferiority such as those recalled by the Slavic interviewees in Morreville, Pennsylvania, who discussed the past with Ewa Morowska years later. Italian children interviewed by Leonard Covello echoed this, describing their shame at being Italian, their embarrassment at dressing "Italian style," and their envy of those "boys and girls fortunate in not having Italian parents." In view of such feelings it was not surprising to learn that many youngsters changed their first names and said that they came from Rome instead of Sicily. Covello himself said that he was nervous from 9 A.M. to 3 P.M. while he attended an integrated school and was much relieved when he and his family moved and he changed to a de facto segregated school in Italian East Harlem.[41] There he no longer felt that he lived "in a different world," feelings also expressed by other immigrant children who were uncomfortable in schools where they were a minority but who bloomed when they attended a school where differences in speech, dress, food preferences, and other activities did not matter. As we have seen, this was also true for the children in the after-school Chinese classes described by Jade Snow Wong and Maxine Kingston.

Harriet Pawlowska described her own experience when she attended a Detroit high school where many teachers and students came from Polish backgrounds, the Polish language was taught, and electives in Polish history were offered. Here, in contrast to the more integrated school she had previously attended, her name was pronounced properly and no one joked, "It looks like Pavlova, but you don't." [42]

Clearly, segregation brought the security that the newly arrived child needed. In a class where almost everyone came from a similar background, childish bigotry, evidenced by name-calling and physical assault, was less likely. There was also less embarrassment if one's dress and school supplies indicated that one's family could not afford better, because in a "ghetto" school everybody's parents were poor. Several memoir writers, usually women, who attended integrated schools recalled that their inability to match the wardrobes of their Americanized peers caused them to leave school at the earliest possible age. [43]

Richard Gambino, on the other hand, was unhappy in a school where Italians were in the majority because as a child who did well, he was "tormented" by his peers. He laid the blame for this on the conflicting messages Italian children were getting from school (do well) and at home (school is not important, don't bother). Certainly it was difficult for a child to be a high achiever in the face of hostility from his parents and his peers, and if he tried to be one, his feelings of marginality could only increase. [44]

Several of the interviewees, however, recalled that their parents' attitudes helped them to endure these feelings. Some mothers and fathers told their children to overlook the school's efforts to change their culture and cuisine and to concentrate on what was to be gained by "going along." As Isidore B.'s father asked rhetorically, "Do you want to be an expressman [truckman] when you grow up? No? Then don't pay attention to anything else, just study!" Sam S.'s father gave another reason for his son to "go along." When Sam showed his dislike of school by being fresh to his teachers, his father was forced to come to school, thus losing a much-needed half-day's pay. [45]

Some parents went further. Max W., born in Chicago in 1908, told his interviewer that his mother and father valued education so much that "the fact that [their] child was . . . celebrating the birth of Jesus and making Christmas decorations" was acceptable because it was "part of [his] education." When President William McKinley was assassinated, Jewish children sang "Nearer My God to Thee" along with their Christian classmates, and there is no evidence that anyone protested. William D'Antonio's parents took a middle course. Although they were Catholics, they sent their son to a public school where the Protestant version of the Lord's Prayer was recited every day but told him not to say the words. Jewish youngsters, without instructions from home, did something more inventive. They substituted their own, sometimes hostile words for the original verses in hymns and Christmas carols.[46]

A few of the immigrants interviewed did not recall any difficulties. Thomas N., for example, says that he got the same messages at school as at home—work hard, respect your elders, learn as much as you can; as a result, he did not feel any marginality. Only the physical setting was different; the values were the same, and thus what he learned in school reinforced what he had already learned at home. Shirley K. also felt no conflict, but for quite a different reason. Her father urged total Americanization on his wife and children. Play baseball, the American game, he told his sons; join the Girl Scouts of America, he told his daughters. In his heart he may have wanted the Russian-Jewish food of his childhood, but he insisted that his wife prepare the broiled meats and bacon and eggs that Americans ate. Although he was more comfortable in Yiddish, he forbade its use in his home. With such a model, his daughter asked, who could resent Americanization at school?[47]

There were other immigrant children who also welcomed Americanization, even against their parents' wishes; yet many more did not. Viewed from an adult's perspective, American public education might seem a homogenizing experience; certainly, this was the intent. Teachers and administrators were charged with tutoring their students in many of the same broad, general lessons and with instilling in them similar ideals and behavior. But from the child's eye view, education was diverse and disparate. Schooling meant one thing to immigrant children, quite another to native-born students. The experiences *among* those young immigrants differed as well, depending on a multitude of factors—not only their own personalities and inner resources but also their backgrounds, the teachers they faced, and the views they heard when they returned home each evening.

Thus the public school, the one institution that most of the children had in common, stands as a convincing reminder that we shall begin to understand the history of American childhood only when we accept the complexity and diversity of the children themselves and of their lives.

4

"Star Struck"

Acculturation, Adolescence, and

Mexican American Women, 1920–1950

VICKI L. RUIZ

SIGA LAS ESTRELLAS
[Follow the stars]
Max Factor Cosmetic Ad,
La Opinion, June 5, 1927

Ethnic identity, americanization, and generational tension first captured the historical imagination during the 1950s with the publication of Oscar Handlin's *The Uprooted* and Alfred Kazin's *A Walker in the City*.[1] These issues continue to provoke discussion among humanists and social scientists. Within the last decade, feminist scholars have expanded and enriched our knowledge of acculturation through the study of immigrant daughters. Cross-class analysis of adolescent culture provides another window into the world of ethnic youth.[2] This vibrant discourse on generation, gender, and U.S. popular culture has a decidedly East Coast orientation. Are patterns typical of working-class immigrants in New York City applicable to those in Los Angeles?

Mexican American woman, ca. 1941.
(Collection of the author)

Here I shall address the forces of americanization and the extent to which they influenced a generation of Mexican American women who came of age during the 1920s and 1930s. The adoption of new cultural forms, however, did not take place in a vacuum. The political and economic environment surrounding Mexican immigrants and their children would color their responses to mainstream U.S. society. The Spanish-speaking population in the United States soared between 1910 and 1930

as over one million Mexicanos* migrated northward. Pushed by the economic and political chaos generated by the Mexican Revolution and lured
by jobs in U.S. agribusiness and industry, they settled into the existing
barrios and forged new communities in both the Southwest and the Midwest, in small towns and cities. For example, in 1900 only 3,000 to 5,000
Mexicans lived in Los Angeles, but by 1930 approximately 150,000 persons
of Mexican birth or heritage had settled into the city's expanding barrios.
On a national level, by 1930 Mexicans, outnumbered only by Anglos and
blacks, formed the "third largest 'racial' group."[3]

Pioneering social scientists, particularly Manuel Gamio, Paul Taylor,
and Emory Bogardus, examined the lives of these Mexican immigrants,
but their materials on women appear sprinkled here and there, at times
hidden in unpublished field notes. Among Chicano historians and writers
there appears a fascination with second-generation Mexican American
men, especially as *pachucos*.[4] The lifestyles and attitudes of their female
counterparts have gone largely unnoticed, even though women may have
experienced deeper generational tensions.[5] "Walking in two worlds,"[6]
they blended elements of americanization with Mexican expectations and
values. To set the context, I shall look at education, employment, and
media as agents of americanization and assess the ways in which Mexican
American women incorporated their messages. Drawing on social science
fieldwork and oral interviews, I shall discuss also the sources of conflict
between adolescent women and their parents as well as the contradictions
between the promise of the American dream and the reality of restricted
mobility and ethnic prejudice.

This study relies extensively on oral history. The memories of thirteen
women serve as the basis for my reconstruction of adolescent aspirations

*"Mexicano(-a)" designates someone of Mexican birth residing in the United States.
Mexican American denotes a person born in the United States with at least second-
generation status. Mexican is an umbrella term for both groups. I use the term
"Chicano(-a)" only for the contemporary period as most of the older women whose
oral interviews contributed to this study did not identify as Chicanas. "Latino(-a)"
indicates someone of Latin American birth or heritage. I refer to "americanization"
within the context of immigration history, that is, as an idealized set of assumptions
pushed by state agencies and religious groups to "transform" or "anglicize" newcomers. Bureaucrats and missionaries narrowly defined "America" as signifying
only the United States.

and experiences (or dreams and routines). Of the thirteen full-blown life histories, ten are housed in university archives, eight as part of the Rosie the Riveter collection at California State University, Long Beach. I became familiar with most of these interviews during the course of my research for *Cannery Women, Cannery Lives,* and two surfaced as student oral-history projects. I personally interviewed three of the informants.

The women themselves are fairly homogeneous by birth, class, residence, and family structure. With one exception, all are U.S. citizens by birth and attended southwestern schools. Ten of the interviewees were born between 1913 and 1929.[7] Although two came from families once considered middle class in Mexico, all can be considered working class in the United States. Their fathers' typical occupations included farm work, day labor, and busing tables. Two women had fathers with skilled blue-collar jobs (a butcher and a surveyor), and two were the daughters of small family farmers. The informants usually characterized their mothers as homemakers although several remembered that their mothers took seasonal jobs in area factories and fields. The mother of the youngest interviewee (Rosa Guerrero) supported her family through domestic labor and fortune-telling. Eleven grew up in urban barrios, ten in Los Angeles. Most families were nuclear rather than extended, although kin usually (but not always) resided nearby. Rich in detail, these interviews reveal the complex negotiations across generation and across culture.

Education and employment were the most significant agents of americanization. Educators generally relied on an immersion method in teaching the English language to their Mexican pupils. In other words, Spanish-speaking children had to sink or swim in an English-only environment. Even on the playground, students were enjoined from conversing in their native Spanish. Admonishments, such as "Don't speak that ugly language, you are an American now," not only reflected a strong belief in Anglo conformity but also denigrated the self-esteem of Mexican American children and dampened their enthusiasm for education.[8] Ruby Estrada remembered that corporal punishment was a popular method for teaching English. "The teacher was mean and the kids got mean."[9] At times children internalized these lessons, as Mary Luna reflected: "It was rough because I didn't know English. The teacher wouldn't let us talk Spanish. How can you talk to anybody? If you can't talk Spanish and you can't talk English, what are you going to do? . . . It wasn't until maybe the fourth or fifth grade that I started catching up. And all along that time I just felt I was stupid." [10]

Students also became familiar with U.S. history and holidays (e.g., Thanksgiving). In recounting her childhood, Rosa Guerrero elaborated on how in her own mind she reconciled the history lessons at school with her own heritage. "The school system would teach everything about American history, the colonists and all of that," she explained, "then I would do a comparison in my mind of where my grandparents came from, what they did, and wonder how I was to be evolved and educated." [11]

Schools, in some instances, raised expectations. Imbued with the American dream, young women (and men) believed that hard work would bring material rewards and social acceptance. In fact, a California grower disdained education for Mexicans because it would give them "tastes for things they can't acquire." [12] Some teenage women aspired to college; others planned careers as secretaries. "I want to study science or be a stenographer," one Colorado adolescent informed Paul Taylor. "I thinned beets this spring, but I believe it is the last time. The girls who don't go to school will continue to top beets the rest of their lives." [13]

Courses in typing and shorthand were popular among Mexican American women even though few southwestern businesses hired Spanish-surnamed office workers. In 1930 only 2.6 percent of all Mexican women wage earners held clerical jobs. Anthropologist Ruth Tuck noted the contradiction between training and placement. When she asked one teacher why Mexican women were being trained for clerical positions largely closed to them, the educator replied, "To teach them respect for the white collar job." Skin color also played a role in obtaining office work. As one typing teacher pointed out to young Julia Luna, "Who's going to hire you? You're so dark." [14]

Many young Mexican women never attended high school but took industrial or service-sector jobs directly after the completion of the eighth grade. As with the eastern European and French Canadian workers studied by John Bodnar and Tamara Hareven, their family needs took priority over their individual goals. Family obligations and economic necessity propelled Mexican women into the labor force. One governmental study appearing in a 1932 issue of *Monthly Labor Review* revealed that in Los Angeles over 35 percent of the Mexican families surveyed had wage-earning children. [15] By 1930 approximately one-quarter of Mexicana and

Mexican American female wage earners in the Southwest obtained employment as industrial workers. In California, they labored principally in canneries and garment firms.[16] Like many female factory workers in the United States, most Mexican operatives were young, unmarried daughters whose wage labor was essential to the economic survival of their families. As members of a "family wage economy," they relinquished all or part of their wages to their elders. According to a 1933 University of California study, of the Mexican families surveyed with working children, the children's monetary contributions constituted 35 percent of the total household income.[17]

At times working for wages gave women a feeling of independence. Historian Douglas Monroy asserted that outside employment "facilitated greater freedom of activity and more assertiveness in the family for Mexicanas." Some young women went a step farther and used their earnings to leave the family home. Facing family disapproval, even ostracism, they defied parental authority by sharing an apartment with female friends.[18] Conversely, kin networks, particularly in canneries and packing houses, reinforced a sense of family. Working alongside female kin, adolescents found employment less than liberating. Yet the work environment afforded women the opportunity to develop friendships with other Spanish-surnamed operatives and occasionally with their ethnic immigrant peers. They began to discuss with one another their problems and concerns, finding common ground both as factory workers and as second-generation ethnic women. Teenagers chatted about fads, fashions, and celebrities.[19]

Along with outside employment, the media also influenced the acculturation of Mexican women. Movie and romance magazines enabled adolescents (and older women as well) to experience vicariously the middle-class and affluent lifestyles heralded in these publications, thus nurturing a desire for consumer goods. Radios, motion pictures, and Madison Avenue advertising had a profound impact on America's cultural landscape. According to historians John D'Emilio and Estelle Freedman, "Corporate leaders needed consumers . . . who were ready to spend their earnings to purchase a growing array of goods designed for personal use. . . . Americans did not automatically respond to factory output by multiplying their desire for material goods; an ethic of consumption had to be sold."[20] The Mexican community was not immune to this orchestration of desire, and a propensity for consumerism appeared among second-generation women. In his 1928 study of Mexican women in Los Angeles industry, Paul Taylor contended that second to economic need, the prevalent motive for employment among single women was a desire to buy the "extras"—a radio, a phonograph, jazz records, fashionable clothes. As Carmen Escobar revealed, "After I started working, I liked the money. I love clothes—I used to buy myself beautiful clothes."[21] As members of a "consumer wage economy," daughters also worked in order to purchase items for their families' comfort, such as furniture, draperies, and area rugs.[22] Other teenagers had more modest goals. After giving most of her wages to her mother, Rosa Guerrero reserved a portion to buy peanut butter and shampoo. "Shampoo to me was a luxury. I had to buy shampoo so I wouldn't have to wash my hair with the dirty old Oxydol. I used to wash my hair with the soap for the clothes."[23]

The American cinema also made an impression. Although times were lean, many southern California women had dreams of fame and fortune, nurtured in part by the proximity to Hollywood. Movies, both Mexican and American, provided a popular form of entertainment for barrio residents. It was common on Saturday mornings to see children and young adults combing the streets for bottles so that they could afford the price of admission—ten cents for the afternoon matinee. Preteens would frequently come home and act out what they had seen on the screen. "I was going to be Clara Bow," remembered Adele Hernández Milligan. Another woman recounted that she had definitely been "star struck" as a youngster and attempted to fulfill her fantasy in junior high by "acting in plays galore." The handful of Latina actresses appearing in Hollywood films, such as Dolores Del Rio and Lupe Velez, also whetted these aspirations. Older star-struck adolescents enjoyed afternoon outings to Hollywood, filled with the hope of being discovered as they strolled along Hollywood and Vine with their friends.[24]

The influential Spanish-language newspaper *La Opinion* encouraged these fantasies by publishing gossipy stories about movie stars like Charlie Chaplin and Norma Shearer as well as up-to-the-minute reports on the private lives and careers of Latino celebrities. It also carried reviews of Spanish-language films, concerts, and plays.[25] Although promoting pride in Latino cultural events, the society pages reflected the public fascination with Hollywood. One week after its first issue, *La Opinion* featured a Spanish translation of Louella Parsons's nationally syndicated gossip column. Furthermore, the Los Angeles-based newspaper directly capitalized on the dreams of youth by sponsoring a contest with Metro-Goldwyn-Mayer. "Day by day we see how a young man or woman, winner of some contest, becomes famous overnight," reminded *La Opinion* as it publicized its efforts to offer its readers a similar chance. Touted as "the unique opportunity for all young men and women who aspire to movie stardom," this promotion held out the promise of a screen test to one lucky contestant.[26]

For many, show business had obvious appeal; it was perceived as a glamorous avenue for mobility. One could overcome poverty and prejudice as a successful entertainer. As an article on Lupe Velez optimistically claimed, "Art has neither nationalities nor borders."[27]

Americanization seemed to seep into the barrios from all directions—from schools, factories, and even from their ethnic press. Parental responses to the americanization of their children can be classified into two distinct categories—accommodation and resistance. These responses seem more rooted in class than in gender. Based on the sample of thirteen interviews and on my survey of early ethnographies, I can find no indication that intergenerational tension occurred more frequently between fathers and daughters than between mothers and daughters. Although parents cannot be viewed as a monolithic group, certainly both took an active interest in the socialization of their children. Resistance was the norm, but some parents encouraged attempts at acculturation, and at times entire families partook of adult-education programs in a concerted effort to become "good Americans." Paul Taylor argues that middle-class Mexicans desiring to dissociate themselves from their working-class neighbors had the most fervent aspirations for assimilation. Once in the United States, middle-class Mexicanos found themselves subject to ethnic prejudice that did not discriminate by class. Because of restrictive real estate covenants and segregated schools, these immigrants had lived in the barrios with people whom they considered as their inferiors.[28] By passing as "Spanish," they cherished hopes of melting into the American social landscape. Sometimes mobility-minded parents sought to regulate their children's choice of friends and later their marriage partners. "My folks never allowed us to go around with Mexicans," remembered Alicia Mendeola Shelit. "We went sneaking around, but my Dad wouldn't allow it. We'd always be with white." Interestingly, Shelit married twice, both times to Anglos. As anthropologist Margarita Melville has concluded in her contemporary study of Mexican women immigrants, "aspirations for upward mobility" emerged as the most distinguishing factor in the process of acculturation.[29] Of course, it would be unfair to characterize all middle-class Mexican immigrants as repudiating their mestizo identity. Or as one young woman cleverly remarked, "Listen, I may be a Mexican in a fur coat, but I'm still a Mexican."[30]

Although enjoying the creature comforts afforded by life in the United States, Mexican immigrants retained their cultural traditions, and parents developed strategies to counteract the alarming acculturation of their young. Required to speak only English at school, Mexican youngsters were then instructed to speak only Spanish at home. Even in families that permitted the use of English, parents took steps to ensure the retention of Spanish among their children. Rosa Guerrero fondly remembered sitting with her father and conjugating verbs in Spanish "just for the love of it."[31] Proximity to Mexico also played an important role in maintaining cultural ties. Growing up in El Paso, Texas, Guerrero crossed the border into Ciudad Juárez every weekend with her family in order to partake of traditional recreational events, such as the bull fights. Her family, moreover, made yearly treks to visit relatives in central Mexico. For those who lived substantial distances from the border, resistance to assimilation involved the building of ethnic pride through nostalgic stories of life in Mexico.[32] As one San Jose woman related:

> My mother never . . . tired of telling us stories of her native village in Guanajuato; she never let us children forget the things that her village was noted for, its handicrafts and arts, its songs and its stories. . . . She made it all sound so beautiful with her descriptions of the mountains and the lakes, the old traditions, the happy people, and the dances and weddings and fiestas. From the time I was a small child I always wanted to go back to Mexico and see the village where my mother was born.[33]

Though many youngsters relished the folk and family lore told by their parents or grandparents, others failed to appreciate their elders' efforts. "Grandmother Perez's stories about the witches and ghosts of Los Conejos get scant audience, in competition with Dick Tracy and Buck Rogers."[34]

In bolstering cultural consciousness, parents found help through youth-oriented community organizations. Church, service, and political clubs reinforced ethnic awareness. Examples included the "Logia 'Juventud Latina' " of the Alianza Hispano Americana, the Mexican American Movement initially sponsored by the YMCA, and the youth division of El Congreso De Pueblos Que Hablan Español. Bert Corona, a leading California civil rights advocate for over four decades, began his career of activism as a leader in both the Mexican American Movement and the youth auxiliary of the Spanish-speaking Peoples Congress.[35]

Interestingly, only two of the thirteen women mentioned Catholicism as an important early influence. The Catholic church played more of a social role; it organized youth clubs and dances and was the place for baptisms, marriages, and funerals.[36] For others, Protestant churches offered a similar sense of community. Establishing small niches in Mexican barrios, Protestant missionaries envisioned themselves as the harbingers of salvation and americanization. Yet some converts saw their churches as reaffirming traditional Mexican values. "I was beginning to think that the Baptist church was a little too Mexican. Too much restriction," remembered Rose Escheverria Mulligan. Indeed, this woman longed to join her Catholic peers who regularly attended church-sponsored dances: "I noticed they were having a good time."[37] Whether gathering for a Baptist picnic or a Catholic dance, teenagers seemed more attracted to the social rather than to the spiritual side of their religion. Certainly more research is needed to assess the impact of Protestant social workers and missionaries on the attitudes of adolescent women. Mary Luna, for example, credited her love of reading to an Anglo educator who converted a small house in the barrio into a makeshift community center and library. Thus the dual thrust of americanization: Education and consumerism can be discerned in this excerpt from Luna's oral history. "To this day I just love going to libraries. . . . There are two places that I can go in and get a real warm, happy feeling; that is, the library and Bullock's in the perfume and make-up department."[38]

Blending new behavior with traditional ideals, young women also had to balance family expectations with their own need for individual expression. Within families, young women, perhaps more than their brothers, were expected to uphold certain standards. Indeed, Chicano social scientists have generally portrayed women as "the 'glue' that keeps the Chicano family together" as well as the guardians of "traditional culture."[39] Parents therefore often assumed what they perceived as their unquestionable prerogative—the right to regulate the actions and attitudes of their adolescent daughters. Teenagers, on the other hand, did not always acquiesce in the boundaries set down for them by their elders. Intergenerational tension flared along several fronts.

Generally, the first area of disagreement between a teenager and her family would be over her personal appearance. During the 1920s a woman's decision "to bob or not bob" her hair assumed classic proportions within Mexican families. After considerable pleading, Belen Martínez Mason was permitted to cut her hair, though she soon regretted her decision. "Oh, I cried for a month."[40] Differing opinions over fashions often caused ill feelings. One Mexican American woman recalled that as a young girl, her mother dressed her "like a nun," and she could wear "no make-up, no cream, no nothing" on her face. Swimwear, bloomers, and short skirts also became sources of controversy. Some teenagers left home in one outfit and changed into another at school. Once María Fierro arrived home in her bloomers. Her father asked, "Where have you been dressed like that, like a clown?" "I told him the truth," Fierro explained. "He whipped me anyway. . . . So from then on whenever I went to the track meet, I used to change my bloomers so that he wouldn't see that I had gone again."[41] The impact of flapper styles on the Mexican community was clearly expressed in the following verse taken from a *corrido* (ballad) appropriately entitled "Las Pelonas [The Bobbed-Haired Girls]":

> Red Bandannas
> I detest,
> And now the flappers
> Use them for their dress.
> The girls of San Antonio
> Are lazy at the *metate*.
> They want to walk out bobbed-haired,
> With straw hats on.
> The harvesting is finished,
> So is the cotton;
> The flappers stroll out now
> For a good time.[42]

With similar sarcasm, another popular ballad chastised Mexican women for applying make-up heavily enough to resemble a piñata.[43]

Once again bearing the banner of glamour and consumption, *La Opinion* featured sketches of the latest flapper fashions as well as cosmetic ads from both Latino and Anglo manufacturers. The most elaborate layouts were those of Max Factor. Using celebrity testimonials, one advertisement encouraged women to "Follow the Stars" and purchase "Max Factor's Society Make-up." Factor, through an exclusive arrangement with *La Opinion*, went even further in courting the Mexican market by answering beauty questions from readers in a special column—"Secretos de Belleza [Beauty Secrets]."[44]

The use of cosmetics, however, cannot be blamed entirely on Madison Avenue ad campaigns. The innumerable barrio beauty pageants, sponsored by mutualistas, patriotic societies, churches, the Mexican Chamber of Commerce, newspapers, and even progressive labor unions encouraged young women to accentuate their physical attributes. Carefully chaperoned, many teenagers did participate in community contests from La Reina de Cinco de Mayo to Orange Queen. They modeled evening gowns, rode on parade floats, and sold raffle tickets.[45] Carmen Bernal Escobar remembered one incident when, as a contestant, she had to sell raffle tickets. Every ticket she sold counted as a vote for her in the pageant. Naturally the winner would be the woman who had accumulated the most votes. When her brother offered to buy twenty-five dollars worth of votes (her mother would not think of letting her peddle the tickets at work or in the neighborhood), Escobar, on a pragmatic note, asked him to give her the money so that she could buy a coat she had spotted while window-shopping.[46]

The commercialization of personal grooming made additional inroads into the Mexican community with the appearance of barrio beauty parlors. Working as a beautician conferred a certain degree of status, "a nice, clean job," in comparison with factory or domestic work. As one woman related:

> I always wanted to be a beauty operator. I loved makeup; I loved to dress up and fix up. I used to set my sisters' hair. So I had that in the back of my mind for a long time, and my mom pushed the fact that she wanted me to have a profession—seeing that I wasn't thinking of getting married.[47]

Although further research is needed, one can speculate that neighborhood beauty shops reinforced women's networks and became places where they could relax, exchange *chisme*, and enjoy the company of other women.[48]

Conforming to popular fashions and fads cannot be construed as lacking ethnic or political consciousness. In 1937 Carey McWilliams spoke before an assembly of 1,500 walnut workers in Los Angeles and was "profoundly stirred" by this display of grass-roots labor militancy by eastern European and Mexican women. Describing the meeting he wrote, "And such extraordinary faces—particularly the old women. Some of the girls had been too frequently to the beauty shop, and were too gotten up— rather amusingly dressy."[49] I would argue that dressing up for a union meeting could be interpreted as an affirmation of individual integrity. Although they worked under horrendous conditions (actually cracking walnuts with their fists), they did not surrender their self-esteem as evidenced by their collective action and personal appearance.

The most serious point of contention between an adolescent daughter and her parents, however, centered on her behavior toward young men. In both cities and rural towns, close chaperonage by a family member was the prerequisite for attending a movie, dance, even church-related events. Recalling the supervisory role played by her "old-maid" aunt, María Fierro laughingly explained, "She'd check on us all the time. I used to get so mad at her." Ruby Estrada recalled that in a small, southern Arizona community, "all the mothers" escorted their daughters to the local dances. Even talking to male peers in broad daylight could be grounds for discipline.[50] Adele Hernández Milligan, a resident of Los Angeles for over fifty years, reported, "I remember the first time that I walked home with a boy from school. Anyway, my mother saw me and she was mad. I must have been sixteen or seventeen. She slapped my face because I was walking home with a boy."[51] Describing this familial protectiveness, one social scientist aptly remarked that the "supervision of the Mexican parent is so strict as to be obnoxious."[52]

Faced with this type of situation, young women had three options: They could accept the rules set down for them, they could rebel, or they could find ways to compromise or circumvent traditional standards. "I was *never* allowed to go out by myself in the evening; it just was not done." In rural communities where restrictions were perhaps even more stringent, "nice" teenagers could not even swim with their male peers. "We were ladies and wouldn't go swimming out there with a bunch of boys." Yet many seemed to accept these limits with equanimity. "It wasn't devastating at all," reflected Ruby Estrada. "We took it in stride. We never thought of it as cruel or mean. . . . It was taken for granted that that's the way it was."[53] In Sonora, Arizona, as in other small towns, relatives and neighbors kept close watch over adolescent women and quickly reported any suspected indiscretions. "They were always spying on you," Estrada remarked. Women in cities had a distinct advantage over their rural peers in that they could venture miles from their neighborhood into the anonymity of dance halls, amusement parks, and other places of commercialized leisure. With carnival rides and the Cinderella Ballroom, the Nu-Pike Amusement Park of Long Beach proved a popular hangout for Mexican youth in Los Angeles.[54] It was more difficult to abide by traditional norms when excitement beckoned just on the other side of the streetcar line.

Some women openly rebelled. They moved out of their family homes and into apartments. Considering themselves free-wheeling single women, they could go out with men unsupervised as was the practice among their Anglo peers. "This terrible freedom in the United States," one Mexicana lamented, "I do not have to worry because I have no daughters, but the poor *señoras* with many girls, they worry."[55] Those Mexican American adolescents who did not wish to defy their parents openly would "sneak out" of the house in order to meet their dates or to attend dances with female friends. A more subtle form of rebellion was early marriage. By marrying at fifteen or sixteen, these women sought to escape parental supervision; yet it could be argued that many of these child brides exchanged one form of supervision for another in addition to the responsibilities of childrearing.[56]

The third alternative sometimes involved quite a bit of creativity as these young women sought to circumvent traditional chaperonage. Alicia Mendeola Shelit recalled that one of her older brothers would always accompany her to dances, ostensibly as a chaperone. "But then my oldest brother would always have a blind date for me." Carmen Bernal Escobar was permitted to entertain her boyfriends at home but only under the supervision of her brother or mother. The practice of "going out with the girls," though not accepted until the 1940s, was fairly common. Several Mexican American women, often related, would escort one another to an event (such as a dance), socialize with the men in attendance, and then walk home together. In the sample of thirteen interviews, daughters negotiated their activities with their parents. Older siblings and extended kin appeared in the background either as chaperones or as accomplices. Although unwed teenage mothers were not unknown in the Los Angeles barrios, families expected adolescent women to conform to strict standards of behavior.[57] As one might expect, many teenage women knew little about sex other than what they picked up from friends, romance magazines, and the local theater. As Mary Luna remembered, "I thought that if somebody kissed you you could get pregnant." In *Singing for My Echo*, New Mexico native Gregorita Rodriguez confided that on her wedding night, she knelt down and said her rosary until her husband gently asked, "Gregorita, *mi esposa*, are you afraid of me?" At times this naiveté persisted beyond the wedding. "It took four days for my husband to touch me," one woman revealed. "I slept with dress and all. We were both greenhorns, I guess."[58]

Of course, some young women did lead more adventurous lives. A male interviewer employed by Mexican anthropologist Manuel Gamio recalled his "relations" with a woman he met in a Los Angeles dance hall. Though born in Hermosillo, Elisa "Elsie" Morales considered herself Spanish. She helped support her family by dancing with strangers. Although she lived at home and her mother and brother attempted to monitor her actions, she managed to meet the interviewer at a "hot-pillow" hotel. To prevent pregnancy, she relied on contraceptive douches provided by "an American doctor." Although Morales realized her mother would not approve of her behavior, she noted that "she [her mother] is from Mexico. . . . I am from there also but I was brought up in the United States, we think about things differently." Just as Morales rationalized her actions as "American," the interviewer perceived her within a similar though certainly a less favorable definition of americanization. "She seemed very coarse to me. That is she dealt with one in the American way."[59] In his field notes, Paul Taylor recorded an incident in which a young woman had moved in with her Anglo boyfriend after he had convinced her that such living arrangements were common among Americans. Popular *corridos*, such as "El Enganchado" and "Las Pelonas," also touched on the theme of the corrupting influence of the United States on Mexican women.[60]

Interestingly, both Anglo and Mexican communities held almost identical preconceptions of each other's young female population. While Mexicanos viewed Anglo women as morally loose, Latina actresses in Hollywood found themselves typecast as hot-blooded women of low repute. For example, Lupe Velez starred in such films as *Hot Pepper*, *Strictly Dynamite*, and *The Mexican Spitfire*.[61] The image of loose sexual mores as distinctly American probably reinforced parental fears as they watched their daughters apply cosmetics and adopt the apparel advertised in fashion magazines. In other words, "If she dresses like a flapper, will she then act like one?" Seeds of suspicion reaffirmed the penchant for traditional supervision.

Tension between parents and daughters, however, did not always revolve around adolescent behavior. At times teenagers questioned the lifestyles of their parents. "I used to tell my mother she was a regular maid," Alicia Shelit recalled. "They [the women] never had a voice. They had to have the house clean, the food ready for the men . . . and everything just so."[62] As anthropologist Tuck observed, "Romantic literature, still more romantic movies, and the attitudes of American teachers and social workers have confirmed the Perez children in a belief that their parents do not 'love' each other; that, in particular, Lola Perez is a drudge and a slave for her husband."[63]

I would argue that the impact of americanization was most keenly felt at the level of personal aspiration. "We felt if we worked hard, proved ourselves, we could become professional people," asserted Rose Escheverria Mulligan.[64] Braced with such idealism, Mexican Americans faced prejudice, segregation, and economic segmentation. Though they considered themselves Americans, others perceived them as less than desirable foreigners. During the late 1920s the *Saturday Evening Post*, exemplifying the nativist spirit of the times, featured inflammatory characterizations of Mexicans in the United States. For instance, one article portrayed Mexicano immigrants as an "illiterate, diseased, pauperized" people who bear children "with the reckless prodigality of rabbits."[65] Racism was not limited to rhetoric; between 1931 and 1934 an estimated one-third of the Mexican population in the United States (over five hundred thousand people) were either deported or repatriated to Mexico even though many were native U.S. citizens. Mexicans were the only immigrants targeted for removal. Proximity to the Mexican border, the physical distinctiveness of mestizos, and easily identifiable barrios influenced immigration and social-welfare officials to focus their efforts solely on the Mexican people, people whom they viewed as both foreign usurpers of American jobs and as unworthy burdens on relief rolls. From Los Angeles, California, to Gary, Indiana, Mexicans were either summarily deported by immigration agencies or persuaded to depart voluntarily by duplicitous social workers who greatly exaggerated the opportunities awaiting them south of the border.[66] According to historian George Sanchez:

> As many as seventy-five thousand Mexicans from southern California returned to Mexico by 1932. . . . The enormity of these figures, given the fact that California's Mexican population was in 1930 slightly over three hundred and sixty thousand . . . , indicates that almost every Mexican family in southern California confronted in one way or another the decision of returning or staying.[67]

By 1935 the deportation and repatriation campaigns had diminished, but prejudice and segregation remained. Historian Albert Camarillo has demonstrated that in Los Angeles restrictive real estate covenants and segregated schools increased dramatically between 1920 and 1950. The proportion of municipalities in the Los Angeles area with covenants prohibiting Mexicans and other minorities from purchasing residences in certain neighborhoods climbed from 20 percent in 1920 to 80 percent in 1946. Many restaurants, theaters, and public swimming pools discriminated against their Spanish-surnamed clientele. In southern California, for example, Mexicans could swim at the public plunges only one day out of the week (just before they drained the pool).[68] Small-town merchants frequently refused to admit Spanish-speaking people into their places of business. "White Trade Only" signs served as bitter reminders of their second-class citizenship.[69]

In 1933 a University of California study noted that Mexicans in southern California were among the most impoverished groups in the United States. Regardless of their birthplace, they were often dismissed as cheap, temporary labor and were paid "from 20 to 50 percent less per day for . . . performing the same jobs as other workers."[70] This economic segmentation did not diminish with passing generations. Writing about San Bernardino in the 1940s, Ruth Tuck illustrated the situation:

> There is a street . . . on which three families live side by side. The head of one family is a naturalized citizen, who arrived here eighteen years ago; the head of the second is an alien who came . . . in 1905; the head of the third is the descendant of people who came . . . in 1843. All of them, with their families, live in poor housing; earn approximately $150 a month as unskilled laborers; send their children

to "Mexican" schools; and encounter the same sort of discriminatory practices.[71]

Until World War II, Mexicans experienced restricted occupational mobility as few rose above the ranks of blue-collar labor. Scholars Mario García and Gilbert González have convincingly argued that the curriculum in Mexican schools helped to perpetuate this trend. Emphasis on vocational education served to funnel Mexican youth into the factories and building trades.[72] In the abstract, education raised expectations, but in practice, particularly for men, it trained them for low-status, low-paying jobs. Employment choices were even more limited in rural areas. As miners or farm workers, Mexicans usually resided in company settlements where almost every aspect of their lives was regulated, from work schedules to wage rates to credit with local merchants. In 1925 a newspaper editor in Greeley, Colorado, bluntly advocated "a caste system," explaining that "it will be worse upon us, the aristocracy, than upon the Mexicans in their serfdom."[73] In both urban and rural areas, ethnicity became not only a matter of personal choice and heritage but also an ascribed status imposed by external sources.[74]

Considering these circumstances, it is not surprising that many teenagers developed a shining idealism as a type of psychological ballast. These adolescents, like the members of the Mexican American Movement, believed that education was the key to mobility; others placed their faith in the application of Max Factor's bleaching cream.[75] Whether they struggled to further their education or tried to lighten their skin color, Mexican Americans sought to protect themselves from the damaging effects of prejudice.

Despite economic and social stratification, many Mexicanas believed that life in the United States offered hope and opportunity. "Here woman has come to have place like a human being," reflected Señora ——.[76] More common perhaps was the impact of material assimilation, the purchase of an automobile, a sewing machine, and other accoutrements of the United States consumer society. The accumulation of these goods signaled the realization of (or the potential for realizing) the American dream. As Margaret Clark commented:

In Sal si Puedes [a San Jose barrio] where so many people are struggling to escape poverty and want, a "luxury item" like a shiny new refrigerator may be the source of hope and encouragement—it may symbolize the first step toward the achievement of a better way of life.

One of Clark's informants aired the more direct statement, "Nobody likes to be poor."[77]

The era of World War II ushered in a set of new options for Mexican women. In southern California some joined unions in food-processing plants and negotiated higher wages and benefits. Still others obtained more lucrative employment in defense plants. As "Rosie the Riveters," they gained self-confidence and the requisite earning power to improve their standard of living. A single parent, Alicia Mendeola Shelit, purchased her first home as the result of her employment with Douglas Aircraft.[78] The expansion of clerical jobs also provided Mexican American women with additional opportunities. By 1950 23.9 percent of Mexican women workers in the Southwest held lower white-collar positions as secretaries or sales clerks.[79] They could finally apply the office skills they had acquired in high school or at storefront business colleges. Although beyond the scope of this study, intermarriage with Anglos may have been perceived as a potential avenue for mobility.[80]

Most of the thirteen interviewees continued in the labor force, combining wage work with household responsibilities. Only the oldest (Ruby Estrada of Arizona) and the youngest (Rosa Guerrero of Texas) achieved a solid, middle-class standard of living. Though one cannot make facile correlations, both women are the only informants who attained a college education. Six of the eleven California women took their places on the shop floor in the aerospace, electronics, apparel, and food-processing industries. Two became secretaries and one a sales clerk at K-Mart. The remaining two were full-time homemakers. Seven of these eleven informants married Anglo or Jewish men, yet their economic status did not differ substantially from those who chose Mexican spouses.[81] With varying degrees of financial security, the California women are now working-class retirees. Their lives exemplify upward movement within the working class rather than rags-to-riches mobility. Though painfully aware of prejudice and discrimination, people of their generation placed faith in themselves and faith in the system. In 1959 Margaret Clark asserted that the second-generation residents of Sal si Puedes "dream and work toward the day when Mexican Americans will become fully integrated into American society at large."[82] The desire to prove oneself appears as a running theme in twentieth-century Mexican American history. I should hasten to add that in the process, most people refused to shed their cultural heritage. "Fusion is what we want—the best of both ways."[83]

In this essay I have attempted to reconstruct the world of adolescent women, taking into account the broader cultural, political, and economic environment. I have given a sense of the contradictions in their lives—the lure of Hollywood and the threat of deportation, and in so doing, an intriguing question has arisen. Can one equate the desire for material goods with the abandonment of Mexican values? I would argue that the ideological impact of material acculturation has been overrated. For example, a young Mexican woman may have looked like a flapper as she boarded a streetcar on her way to work at a cannery; yet she went to work (at least, in part) to help support her family, as one of her obligations as a daughter. The adoption of new cultural forms certainly frightened parents but did not of itself undermine Mexican identity. The experiences of Mexican American women coming of age between 1920 and 1950 reveal the blending of the old and the new; fashioning new expectations, making choices, and learning to live with those choices.

Part Two

❖ ❖ ❖ ❖ ❖ ❖ ❖ ❖ ❖ ❖ ❖ ❖ ❖ ❖ ❖ ❖

Eenie Meanie, Minie Moe

CHILDREN, PLAY, AND SOCIETY

So they went off together. But wherever they go, and whatever happens to them on the way, in that enchanted place on the top of the Forest, a little boy and his Bear will always be playing.

   – A. A. Milne, The House at Pooh Corner

The right clothes of the Match-Man faded and his straw hat turned into his old ragged cap again. Mary Poppins turned and looked at him, and she knew at once what had happened. Standing on the pavement she gazed at him for a long minute, and her glance explored the wood behind him for the Waiter. But the Waiter was nowhere to be seen. There was nobody in the picture. Nothing moved there. Even the Merry-go Round had disappeared. Only the trees and the grass and the unmoving little patch of sea remained.

But Mary Poppins and the Match-Man smiled at one another. They knew, you see, what lay behind the trees.

   – P. L. Travers, Mary Poppins

The rhyme referred to in the title of Part 2 reminds us that children are often choosing, despite the efforts of adults to control the younger generations. And in no part of their lives do children enjoy greater freedom of choice than in their play. In playground games "team captains" might "choose up sides" with a series of alternating selections, an activity involving strategy, diplomacy, and shrewd evaluation of personality and physical prowess. Or players might divide their ranks through the "eenie meanie" scheme, a crudely democratic process of distributing talent. Just as important is the rhyme's second line, usually "Catch a —— by the toe," with the missing word varying by region, ethnicity, and even nation. Filling in the blank involves a kind of moral choice of an "out group" of unfortunates doomed to "holler" after being caught by the toe. These methods of choosing are a perfectly acceptable part of childhood and adolescence; but in many other ways, adults try to direct their children. They do so partly by encouraging certain activities and by selecting the material possessions, the "things" for their youngsters' amusement.

Such things, as much as ideas, appear at different historical moments for different reasons. Architectural historians, for example, have argued that nineteenth-century housing designs and cooperative neighborhood plans were material manifestations of ideology, whether bourgeois or socialist. Styles of furniture appeared and disappeared because different people needed to define their social status or lifestyle more clearly. The hall stand, a massive combination of coatrack, mirror, seating, and umbrella holder, provided a suitable object for the entry to the nineteenth-century middle-class home and for a time became a sign of middle-class gentility. Children's furniture and clothing designs also corresponded to different ideas about status, health, and the place of the child within the family.

The same can be said about play and toys. Although both have always been part of American culture, the advent of mass-produced toys coincided with the formation of the American middle class and that group's emphasis on mother-centered childrearing. Just as the new middle class built its houses as stages on which to display its aspirations and achievements and to exhibit its values, so it required different props. Toys became part of the paraphernalia of the new middle-class childhood and a means for introducing young men and women to values useful for achieving white-collar success or domestic gentility. But young people themselves, beginning in the early part of the nineteenth century, created their own subculture based on play that embodied different activities with toys and different values.

To ferret out the relationship among children, play, and toys presents certain conceptual difficulties. Historians can know a great deal about parents' expectations regarding play and toys; they can know somewhat less about what toy businesses had to offer and how successful they were with their options; but researchers will be challenged to know how children played, what playthings or amusements appealed to them, and what they thought of the experience. Anyone who has watched children play understands how toys may be put to entirely different uses. Imagine a tea party—the dolls and teddies drawn up around a miniature table set with small crockery and cutlery. Suddenly the imitation of life alters. The teddy wears a tea cup as a chapeau, and a doll has pins stuck in her head to simulate a crown. The saucers fly like frisbees as the teddy and doll oppose each other in a tea war. Barbie dolls, too, may be transformed from fashion models to commandos to better negotiate an obstacle course in which one Barbie perishes in a rope trap. Toy trucks leave a dwarf construction project to become animals with the box and body of the truck transformed into snapping jaws. What sense can adults make of this, if any at all?

These difficulties aside, a good deal of contemporary debate revolves around the notion of the effect of play, toys, and amusements. Each holiday season, magazines and television programs debate the questions of "good" and "bad" toys. Do toy guns promote aggressive behavior among children? Do dolls socialize girls into traditional female roles? Does a Nintendo outfit isolate children socially and render them less able to understand ambiguity? Hardly a discussion among educators occurs without the group's bemoaning the effect of television on children's and adolescents' academic performance, and librarians fuss over the place of series books and the debilitating effect of comic books. Implicit in all these discussions is a historical interpretation. Somewhere in the nation's early history was a "golden age" of play. In this period, so the scenario goes, children played with a few sturdy toys. If they did not have toys, either their parents or preferably the children themselves made them, and these homemade toys were the more valuable and instructive because of their noncommercial origins. Such a regimen resulted in a wholesome, innocent childhood in which children learned a healthy, useful ethic. After World War II, however, plastic war toys, unusual for their military realism, and dolls with unbelievable anatomies and wardrobes appeared on store shelves along with other toys, bringing with them a host of pernicious values: jingoism, materialism, sexism, to name a few. Children moreover possessed or desired rooms full of these too often breakable delights. The result: too many socially toxic toys rendered childhood a contentious, dangerous time in which boys and girls might acquire pernicious values.

Although it is often useful for public policymakers and toy manufacturers to posit a golden age, historians find the popular history of play and toys entirely too short and shortsighted. Historical inquiry regarding play and toys is a broad area, but it can be summarized in several major questions. How and with what did children play in times past? How has the nature of play and amusement changed over time? What was the effect of play and toys on children? And what did children think of their play and playthings? The essays in Part 2 set out to answer these questions. Bernard Mergen furnishes an overview of play and provides some tentative answers to the first two questions. Miriam Formanek-Brunell tackles one of the most popular toy categories—dolls—and explores both adult views and expectations regarding doll play as well as children's responses to their dolls. With the exception of the Handy Andy Toy Printing Press, printing presses as toys are not as familiar as dolls. Yet as Paula Petrik points out, they were an enormously popular toy for nineteenth-century adolescents and provide a means to uncover adolescent thinking on two important issues: race and gender. William Tuttle rounds out this group of essays by considering more generally popular amusements during World War II and their messages for youngsters.

5

Made, Bought, and Stolen

Toys and the Culture of Childhood

BERNARD MERGEN

"During my youthful days I found the penknife a source of great amusement and even of recreation. Many a long winter evening, many a dull, drizzly day . . . have I spent in great ecstasy, making candlerods, or some other simple article of household goods, for my mother, or in perfecting toys for myself and my young friends."
—Samuel Goodrich (1793–1860)

"My prized possession was a white leather two-gun holster, studded with fake stones."
—Caryl Rivers (b.1937)

A century and a half separate the childhoods of the authors of these two quotations.[1] It would be difficult to find better summations of the meanings of toys at the beginning of the nineteenth century and the middle of the twentieth. When Goodrich, a popular children's writer, recalled the prized possession of his Connecticut boyhood, it was in the context of making things of wood. When Rivers remembered her favorite toy in suburban Washington, D.C., it was a set of pistols manufactured in imitation of movie and comic-book heroes.

Toys are the material culture of play. Like other forms of material culture—artifacts such as tools, weapons, or clothing—they have different meanings in different contexts. Their significance may be generally recognized or intensely personal. From the child's point of view, a toy is some-

December 27, 1909.
(Photo by Underwood & Underwood, Library of Congress,
Prints and Photographs)

thing to be used for personal amusement. Pleasure is a private emotion even when it arises in a group experience. A toy that pleases a child one minute may be discarded the next. One child's favorite toy may be another's junk. Historically, toys have been relatively unimportant to children compared to games and play that do not require objects. The evidence offered in this essay comes from autobiographies that present childhood as a time of exploration and education through work and play.

The authors who grew up before the Civil War fondly recall their toys, both manufactured and homemade, but only in the context of certain kinds of play. Objects were transformed by the child's imagination rather than having fixed meanings. Although this remains true to the present, two new attitudes toward toys emerge in the 1870s. One emphasizes the accumulation of toys for their own sake, material possessions indicating the status of the owner. A second attitude, reflected in the quotation from Caryl Rivers's *Aphrodite at Mid-Century: Growing-Up Catholic and Female in Post-War America*, is that certain toys have special significance; they define the identity of the child. Children, the autobiographers suggest, attempt to create through play their own alternative to the adult world, even though it is clearly modeled on that world. This culture of childhood uses toys—objects made, bought, and stolen—to define itself in space and time. In the twentieth century the toy industry has attempted to sell its own definitions of that culture based on children's toy preferences. Yet although manufactured toys have overwhelmed the culture of childhood physically, children continue to maintain their identities by selecting, modifying, and rejecting the baubles televised each week.

The history of childhood is not simply the extinction of a once-vibrant children's culture and the replacement of handcrafted toys by metal and plastic. On the contrary, American children continue to show an ability to use what is available to them in unintended and unexpected ways. The very meaning of the word "toy" is still contested by children and adults. "The word 'toy,'" writes Dorothy Mills Howard, a folklorist who reconstructed her own childhood in *Dorothy's World*,

> was not in the vocabulary of the Mills children. They had "playthings" and "play pritties." A "plaything"—a stick, for example—was not a stick but (metaphorically) a horse to ride, a thermometer for playing doctor, a writing or drawing tool for marking on the ground, a log for building log cabins, a boat to float down a rivulet from a spring shower, play candy, a shotgun for hunting, or another person. A "plaything" could be and was anything the mind willed—for a moment, an hour, for months or years. The definition, unarticulated, was communicated by action in a context common to and understood by all the players.[2]

Tools that provide amusement, possessions that are prized, sticks that can be transformed by the imagination, all enter into a child's definition of toys and playthings. As with all words, the meaning changes according to context. When is a "G.I. Joe" an "action figure?" When is it a toy soldier? When is it a doll? Why is Barbie a doll and not an action figure, when she is so clearly looking for action? The answer depends on whether a little boy has learned that dolls are only for girls. It depends too on whether judges on the United States Court of International Trade apply a strict, dictionary definition of doll—"a representation of a human being used as a child's plaything"—for the purpose of imposing the tariff on G.I. Joes made in Hong Kong.[3] It depends on whether G.I. Joe's owner of the moment is playing by himself, with boys, with girls, or with a group that brings to the occasion a cast of figures representing R2D2, She-Ra, Transformers, and Teenage Mutant Ninja Turtles. It depends a bit on whether G.I. Joe is 11 ½ inches tall, 8 ½ inches, or just 3 ½ inches.[4]

Children quickly learn what kinds of things adults call toys and learn to demand them. Almost as quickly, adults learn to label all other possessions of the child as junk and to ask, "Why don't you play with your toys?" Brian Sutton-Smith has explored many of the paradoxes of toys in his book *Toys as Culture*, and he demonstrates that toys are as important as they are difficult to define. Toys are gifts meant to form bonds between adults and children, especially at family-centered rituals such as Christmas and birthdays. Yet the child is told, either explicitly or implicitly, to take the toy and play by himself. He is also told that the toy is not "real" but that he should learn something by playing with it. Moreover, *he* learns that as a boy he can expect more toys than a girl.[5] Caryl Rivers was not stereotyped by the kind of toys she had as much as by the number. Nor is this a phenomenon of the recent past. Karin Calvert's study of portraits of children painted between 1830 and 1870 shows that while 66 percent of the boys were depicted with some sort of plaything, only 20 percent of the girls were shown with toys, and these were limited to dolls and domestic objects.[6] Toys are used to define gender, age, social class, even race, but the definitions are not usually those of the children themselves. There is good evidence that children simply place less importance on toys than adults do. Learning to value toys is part of growing up.[7] Here I shall attempt to recreate the meanings of toys to American children from the early nineteenth century to the mid-twentieth century using autobiographies, writings on toys by adults, and artifacts that have survived and been collected.[8]

Edward Everett Hale was born in Boston in 1822 and grew up in a family both prosperous and prominent. He became a popular writer of moralistic fiction, including "The Man without a Country." In 1892 he published his description of childlife, *A New England Boyhood*, one of about a dozen autobiographies that provide a glimpse of the meanings of toys in pre–Civil War America. Young Hale made boats from hemlock bark three or four feet long and fitted them with sails made of wrapping paper and sheets from writing books. "Then," he writes, "you could sail them from wharf to wharf, on voyages much more satisfactory than the shorter voyages of the Frog Pond." The inspiration for this activity, Hale makes clear, came from his reading of *Robinson Crusoe* and other adventure books, but the context was his defiance of his father's order to stay away from the docks and to come directly home from school. This, plus the thrill of stealing the wood, which was imported as kindling for coal-burning stoves, is clearly what makes Hale recall his boats and to comment,

> Whether what we did were right or wrong in the view of magistrates I do not know. I do know that it was morally and eternally right, because we thought it was. That is one of the queer things about a boy's conscience. I do not remember that, till the time when I dictate these words, for nearly sixty years, it has once occurred to me to ask whose was the property we used on these occasions, or what the owners would have said to our use of it.[9]

Hale's commentary on the distinct moral life of children, though self-serving, is insightful. As the psychiatrist Robert Coles and others have observed, children fashion moral codes from the experiences of everyday life, balancing gratification and altruism within the contexts of family and friends.[10] Hale mentions many other playthings—whalebone, spiral springs, pulleys, catgut, a magnifying glass, building blocks, broomsticks—used in making locomotives and large boats he calls "floats." Floats consisted of planks a foot wide, four feet long, and an inch thick, which were placed on rollers made of broomsticks. A child seated on the plank propelled himself across the attic or barn floor with paddles made of shingles. "If you have a companion on another float in the same room," Hale writes, "you can have naval battles, or you can go to the assistance of shipwrecked crews." Hale's juxtaposition of childhood games of war and peace is an indication of the suppleness of a boy's make-believe play. The most elaborate fantasy involving a plaything that Hale recalls was carrying the daily mail. Boys made small newspapers by clipping the ones their parents discarded and then "delivered" them by rolling their hoops around the Common and hiding the papers in trees and buried boxes designated "post-offices." Each hoop, an imaginary steed, was named. Hale's was "Whitefoot," formerly part of a sea-going cask. The detail with which Hale reconstructs this memory and his clear preference for this kind of play over checkers, chess, lotto, battledore and shuttlecock, indicate that objects, whether called playthings or toys, become identities "around which a child organizes his or her actions and concepts of the world." [11]

Lucy Larcom, whose *A New England Girlhood*, published in 1889, inspired Hale to write his memoir, played with objects in similar ways. Her girlhood in Beverly, Massachusetts, was in a more rural setting than Hale's, but she too made imaginary voyages in boats and "traveled" to distant towns in a sleigh overgrown with summer weeds. She made rag dolls rather than locomotives, but doll play was secondary to her memories of outdoor play with her brother and friends. And although she was an unusual woman for her time because she became a successful writer and editor, she does not recall her playthings or her games as specifically masculine or feminine. The sexes played tricks on each other, stole sweets, and decorated themselves with wild flowers with utter disregard for gender roles. [12]

In addition to dolls, pre–Civil War girls had playhouses furnished with broken pottery from home, rubber balls, jump ropes, rings, and bracelets. Laura Howe, the daughter of Julia Ward and Samuel Gridley Howe, describes the playthings of her 1850s childhood in rich detail. Her older sister invented a "school-loan" system, renting treasures from her desk to younger children for so many pins an hour. "Then there was a glass eye-cup without a foot; that cost ten pins, and was a great favorite with us. You stuck it in your eye, and tried to hold it there while you winked with the other." [13] Howe's rough treatment of her paper dolls and her younger sister's successful attempt to remove the eyes from her expensive doll so she could pretend to have a blind friend are vivid reminders that children's ideas about destructiveness differ considerably from their parents'.

In city and country, boys were given more freedom to roam than their sisters, although not all chose to do so. Samuel Clagett Busey, who was born on a Maryland farm just outside of Washington, D.C., in 1828, played with marbles, hoops, tops, kites, balls, and pocket knives with his younger brother and two young slaves. John Albee, born in 1833 in

Children playing on a wagon, 1890.
(Robert Redfield, photographer. The Library Company of Philadelphia)

Bellingham, Massachusetts, used his mother's clothespins as soldiers, and another New Englander, Thomas Bailey Aldrich, set up a theater in a barn. William Dean Howells, whose *Boy's Town* is one of the most detailed accounts of childhood, also created plays, minstrel shows, and circuses in imitation of those he saw in Hamilton, Ohio, in the 1840s. Gene Schermerhorn moved into a house on Twenty-third Street just west of Sixth Avenue in New York City in 1848, across the street from George Christy. Soon he and his playmates were blackening their faces and putting on minstrel shows of their own. Recalling his boyhood in Dansville, New York, in the 1850s and 1860s, H. W. DeLong describes a panorama he helped to build in a cigar box and several other shows and circuses he and friends performed for a neighborhood audience.[14]

As the abolition movement grew in strength, children became aware of the impending war and their play incorporated it. James Langdon Hill was impressed by a performance of *Uncle Tom's Cabin*, collected Union Army gear, and emulated his hero, Robert Gould Shaw, in play. In all these activities, homemade playthings were props in a larger drama. In the years immediately after the war, "boughten" toys were more available but were considered inferior to homemade items, even sleds. Yet by the 1870s children clearly were becoming more dependent on toys in their play and new definitions of childhood were emerging.[15]

Walter Brooks, born in 1856 in Boston, grew up in this transitional period and recorded his memories and later his feelings about the changes in playthings. "The rag doll and the monkey on the stick were . . . emblems [of a simpler time]—not yet replaced by the dressy little princess from the Parisian atelier or the mechanical toy from a German workshop." Yet his inventory of toys included a boy doll dressed in a red shirt with gilded buttons and black velvet trousers, a toy house made of "sanded cardboard" with isinglass snow on the roof and a Santa in a sleigh, and an elaborate Noah's ark with brightly painted animals. Brooks recalls that the paint came off when wet and that he broke the brim off Japhet's hat and the legs off various animals before he finally tired of playing with them. Brooks describes the destructiveness of children's play better than most writers. He remembers building a fort of newspapers and bombarding it with firecrackers to impress his "puppy love." One of his favorite indoor games involved turning over chairs and making believe that they were horses and coaches, an activity mentioned by several autobiographers, including Lincoln Steffens and Meta Stern Lilienthal a generation later.[16]

The Civil War inspired the play of Margaret Campbell (Deland), who spent her childhood in the 1860s near Pittsburgh, and Hamlin Garland, whose earliest memory at age four is of his father's returning to their Wisconsin home in his army uniform. Deland remembers being inspired by the word "compassion," used by her grandmother in relation to slaves and wounded soldiers, to build her own hospital in the lattice-work summerhouse. Here she made "medicines" from crushed brick and scraps of lilac leaves, which she labeled "Bricktiva" and "Leafiticus." She also made beds and coffins, but the only patients she was able to treat were two woolly caterpillars who escaped. Garland played soldier with broomsticks and drummed on dishpans. Like Brooks, he had a monkey on a stick. Another Christmas present was a red and blue tin horse. His sled was made by a local blacksmith. A lasting legacy of the war was baseball, which few writers born before 1860 recall playing but which is mentioned frequently by both men and women born later.[17]

Playthings and toys before the growth of the toy industry, the expansion of a national railroad system, and mail-order catalogs were generally limited to a handful of simple items, supplemented by household furnishings and the indispensable pocket knife. The memories of the autobiographers are confirmed by paintings and lithographs—Henry Inman's *Mumble the Peg* (1842) shows two boys playing a game of skill with a pocket knife. George Comegys's *Little Plunderers* (1845) shows children costuming themselves from a trunk full of clothes, and Lilly Martin Spencer's *War Spirit at Home* (1866), with its armed and marching children, documents the effect of the war on children of both sexes and all ages. Currier and Ives's *Burning Glass* (c. 1860), based on a painting by John George Brown, shows a boy holding a little girl's hand while he waits for the sun's rays to pass through the glass and burn her.[18] If Edward Hale did not recall using his magnifying glass for this purpose, one of his playmates probably did.

Catalogs and articles in children's magazines in the 1870s suggest that adults were beginning to take a new interest in children. The result was an increase in toy manufacturing and the concomitant increase in presents from adults to children as well as a redefinition of the word "toy" to include equipment used in baseball and other games. This led to an emphasis on the similarities between child and adult play and to a more serious treatment of both. A writer for *St. Nicholas Magazine* in 1879 reviewed the history of toys, compared the toys of various nations, and concluded that

> our own toy shops have all the wonders of European make, but the kinds we invent ourselves are mostly mechanical toys,—creeping dolls, bears that perform, horsemen that drive furiously, boatmen that row, steam cars that go; and we have a monopoly of baseballs and bats, for no other people use them. None but English-speaking people indulge in plays so violent as to be dangerous to life and limb, as is our base ball, and the cricket of our English cousins.
>
> When we begin to talk of these games we reach the amusements of the grown-ups, which perhaps they wouldn't like to have called "playthings", though—between you and me—they are just as much toys as are dolls and tops.

The message conveyed to young readers was clear. A kind of nursery-story Darwinism explained how the finest mechanical toys had evolved from simple rattles and terra-cotta dolls and how our national game helped the fittest survive. The subtext for parents was the importance of toys for their children's development and happiness; the children themselves learned that "the real 'Paradise of Babies' is Japan—as has been said many times—for not only do the children have every imaginable toy, but many persons get their living by amusing them." [19] To demand more toys was an act of patriotism.

The generations of children who grew up in the 1840s, 1850s, and 1860s became the adults of the 1870s, 1880s, and 1890s who extolled the simple playthings of their childhoods in their autobiographies while supporting the nacent toy industry with purchases for their children and grandchildren. Yet the irony was lost, chiefly because the majority of children in the late nineteenth century could only dream of the toys they saw in shops and mail-order catalogs. One child of the 1870s later noted the changes that took place. William Allen White, the widely admired editor of the Emporia, Kansas, *Gazette*, commented in his autobiography that the arrival of the railroad "in the boy's world, . . . meant that homemade sleds and little homemade wagons would pass; that the bows and arrows which boys made by seasoning the hickory behind the stove and scraping and polishing them with glass would as an art disappear forever out of the life of American boys." But he did not lament the things he accumulated by selling subscriptions to *Youth's Companion*—a scroll saw, musical instruments, skates, balls and bats, masks, books of games and magic, dumbbells, and boxing gloves. Nor did the increasing availability of manufactured toys prevent him from making hickory whistles, stick horses, or "little railroads with whittled ties." He was an only child, but White's memories of play and playthings are unusual only in their detail. Like other boys and girls he found "secret" places to play; fought, stole, and discovered sex; and escaped into play when school and work were over. "The home, the barn, the river, and the school made this Willie White. The school only taught him superficial things—to read, write, and figure, and to take care of himself on the playground. But those ancient institutions of learning taught him wisdom, the rules of life and the skills which had survival value in the world of boyhood." [20]

More than a thousand miles away on a plantation in North Carolina, Mary Alves Long played with her dolls, one a wax doll that could open her eyes and say "Mama" when squeezed, the other a boy doll her mother had knitted. The dolls were married and lived in a house built by Mary's brother and rode in a carriage basket woven by her mother. Yet Mary, like Willie, played "Round Town," the local version of baseball, rode saplings, and built dams in a stream. In Pennsylvania, Katherine Stauffer went sledding on both homemade and factory-made models. In Wisconsin, the future novelist Zona Gale buried snow so that she could eat it in the summertime. Both Katherine and Zona had their doll play disrupted by boys playing vandals, who destroyed their villages and dolls' houses. Only Zona, however, turned her anger into a grievance she harbored for forty years. "They [boys] were always producing something from their pockets and examining it, with their heads together, or manufacturing something or burying something, or disputing about something unguessed and alluring. Their whole world was filled with doing, doing, doing, whereas ours was made wholly of watching things get done."[21]

Under the pressure of parents, schools, and supervised playgrounds the small world of girls grew smaller in the period from 1880 to 1920, although differences of race, region, social class, and parental supervision allowed wide variations. Eleanor Abbott of Boston played with toy soldiers, Una Clarke of Cincinnati built stagecoaches of cardboard, and Estilline Bennett of Deadwood, South Dakota, went sledding with the few black and Chinese children in her frontier community. Girls often knew better than boys the bondage of gender-typed toys, as Zona Gale did when she threw her dolls away as an act of defiance against what she felt were limits imposed on her identity.[22]

Increasingly in the 1880s and 1890s, the growth of cities, immigration, the toy industry, and adult supervision of children shaped play. Henry Mencken, a child of Baltimore's German community, replayed Sebastopol, not Gettysburg, with his toy soldiers. He also recalls being heldup by three boys with cap pistols who took his "pocket knife, a couple of seashells, three or four nails, two cigarette pictures, a dozen chewing-tobacco tags, a cork, a slate pencil, an almost fossil handkerchief, and three cents in cash." The bad boys returned the three cents so they could not be accused of stealing and "hooked" the rest. An hour and a half north by rail, Philip Goodman played in a Jewish neighborhood in Philadelphia, where he called an Irish policeman a "son of a bitch" when he was arrested for riding his bike on the sidewalk. Philip had more to fear from the gangs of boys who controlled nearby sections of the city of brotherly love. The anthropologist Stewart Culin described his youth and the initiation rituals all boys in these gangs had to endure:

Hide the Straw.—Bounds are agreed upon, and the new boy is made "it." All close their eyes while he hides the straw, and afterwards they searched for it, apparently with much diligence. At last they go to the boy and say: "I believe you have concealed it about you. Let us search him." Then they ask him to open his mouth, and when he complies they stuff coal and dirt and other objects into it.[23]

Although *Youth's Companion, St. Nicholas,* and other magazines offered children ideas for playthings for almost fifty years, a new kind of adult influence emerged in the 1880s, the book-length compendium of activities thought suitable for boys and girls. Daniel Beard's *The American Boys Handy Book: What to Do and How to Do It*, published in 1882, was one of the first and most successful of these. His sisters brought out *American Girls Handy Book: How to Amuse Yourself and Others* six years later. In 1890 John D. Champlin and Arthur E. Bostwick published the first edition of *The Young Folks' Cyclopaedia of Games and Sports.* Although few toys are mentioned among its more than four thousand entries, there are some interesting selections. A bandilore (*sic*), not yet called a yo-yo, is described, but forty years would pass before it became popular with children. Tops, on the other hand, had for centuries been one of the most esteemed toys, especially for boys, and Champlin and Bostwick devote seven pages to several varieties, including a rubber-band-powered airplane they call a "fly-fly." This kind of information and the success of the kite-flying Wright brothers opened the skies to children's playthings. Both Beard and Champlin provide elaborate instructions on how to build snowforts and have snowball fights, which seems gratuitous until we read that frozen snowballs soaked in water are forbidden and that no blows by hand or foot are allowed. Children did not need to be taught to play, only to play gently.[24]

There is evidence that boys' play was becoming rougher as the twentieth century began. The reasons are many. Town and urban concentrations of children permitted more frequent confrontations and made them more visible to others. Enforced attendance at school and the segregation of the sexes created a male subculture dominated by older, larger boys. Increased awareness of violence in society may also have resulted in a willingness to write about it. Whatever the causes, a number of autobiographers, recalling their childhoods in the 1890s and in the first decades of the twentieth century, emphasize fights, play fights, gun play, and play guns.

"Those who believe little boys are turned toward crime by playing with toys pistols would certainly have picked me for an outlaw in the making," writes Harvey Fergusson in his *Home in the West: An Inquiry into My Origins*. Born in New Mexico territory in 1890, Fergusson recounts his love of guns and his boyhood fights in detail before revealing that he became a newspaper editor in Washington, D.C. Marquis James remembers being whipped by a teacher in Oklahoma and responding by organizing a "Kid Nation" that was temporarily independent of state and parental authority. Samuel N. Behrman, the playwright, remembers throwing a cat on its head and hearing its skull crack, and Taylor Gordon, one of the few blacks in White Sulphur Springs, Montana, recalled a chase and tag game so violent that it destroyed a cart and resulted in injuries that put an end to the game for months. On the streets of New York, immigrant boys Mike Gold and Jimmy Savo fought for their territories with rocks and sticks. Gold writes of his defense of a vacant lot on Delancey Street: "Some of our boys stole tops of washboilers at home, and used them as shields. Others had tin swords, sticks, blackjacks. The two armies slaughtered each other in the street. Bottles were thrown, heads were cut open." Savo's earliest memory is of a rock fight at Ninety-seventh Street and Third Avenue.[25]

None of this can equal the violent childhood described by Richard Wright in *Black Boy*, which includes killing a kitten, being robbed by a gang, being beaten by his grandmother, and rock fighting with whites, unless it is the Oklahoma oil-field memories of Woody Guthrie, which involve insanity, arson, and rock fights that imitated World War I, with barrels as tanks and hot rocks thrown by slingshot. Flannery Lewis, focusing on a few months in 1918 when he was just five, remembered a store selling "soldier suits and . . . machine guns that fired wooden bullets, a dozen bullets to a belt." In the 1920s Robert Paul Smith treasured his BB gun, probably a Daisy air rifle, which came with a copy of "A Boy's Bill of Rights." Guthrie's fellow Sooner, John O'Dell, knew how to make a half-dozen different kinds of rubber guns, from the basic single-shot pistol to repeating rifles. A few hundred miles west in Lea County, New Mexico, Bill Tate pretended to be Buck Jones the movie cowboy at the same time that older boys were shooting holes in the skating rink to scare the patrons. A generation later the news of Pearl Harbor caused young Fielding Dawson of Kirkwood, Missouri, to play with guns and to collect Dinky Toy warplanes.[26]

Selecting references to guns and fighting and assembling them out of context obviously distorts their meaning in the lives of children. Nonetheless, the frequency with which guns are mentioned in the autobiographies

Clifford Shorts's children playing, Aliquippa, Pennsylvania, July 1938.
(Arthur Rothstein, photographer. Library of Congress [LC-USF34-26597-D])

of the period 1890–1945 illustrates some of the problems in understanding the child's view of play. Adult descriptions of children seldom mention fighting except to condemn it.

Five surveys of children's play between 1896 and 1959 provide data against which the memories of the autobiographers can be checked. Because these surveys were conducted by teachers and social workers they use the words *play* and *toy* differently from children, although the children obviously recognize the meanings the adults employ. All but one of the surveys asked children to rank their activities, to choose one game over another as if specific contexts were not important. Yet for all the artificiality of the exercise, it forced children to think about the significance of their play and toys. The meaning of their answers may be obscured by the phrasing of the questions, but they remain answers, all the more valuable because they are so rare.

The earliest and still the best survey was done in Worcester, Massachusetts, with two thousand children between the ages of six and eighteen. Children were asked by their teachers to write a list of their favorite play, games, toys, and playthings for each season of the year, for indoors and outdoors, alone and with others. The 2,000 children listed over 700 different kinds of amusement, indicating the personal nature of play. In raw numbers, ball was mentioned by 679 boys and football by 455. Marbles were named by 603 boys. Sleds, skates, tag, relievo (a chase-and-capture game), hockey (shinney), checkers, hide and seek, and express wagons followed at the top of the list. Wooden guns were mentioned by 17 boys as something they played with alone, but 64 listed guns, hunting, and rifles as pastimes. Girls mentioned dolls 621 times, followed by sleds, jump ropes, tag, hide and seek, skates, balls, playhouses, jackstones, and play-school. A smaller study in nearby Westfield asked children ages seven to sixteen about their toys. The overall favorites for boys were tops, balls, marbles, express wagons, and footballs, although railroad trains ranked fourth with nine-year-olds and guns fifth among eleven-year-olds. Girls chose dolls (including paper dolls), tea sets, doll carriages, books, and tops, with the popularity of tea sets declining after age nine. By age thirteen, balls were the fourth most popular toy, moving ahead of books and tops. Dolls also declined in popularity after age twelve.[27]

In 1898 a survey of more than four thousand South Carolina children was conducted by teachers in May and again in December. The overwhelming favorites—baseball, football, swimming, marbles, fox and geese for the boys and dolls, jump ropes, croquet, clap in-clap out, and drop the handkerchief for the girls—are both more specific and include more team play than the Massachusetts sample, suggesting either regional differences or adult influence. Nevertheless, there are some other intriguing choices. Three hundred forty-nine boys and 36 girls played Buffalo Bill and 278 boys and 40 girls played policeman. In both states, boys mentioned more kinds of toys. Comments by children in Worcester reveal that children soon understand both the joy and the disappointment of toys. "The toys I like best," wrote a boy of eleven, "are Brownies, printing press, electric motor, scroll saw, Welch's steam engine, type writer, tool chest, small shot gun and a rifle. The reason I like to play with these toys, because these are toys for bigger children and the others are for babies and other small children. Also for another reason, you can use some of these toys and gain money from them." A girl of eight who was exploring her place in the world wrote, "I like to play with my dolls because I make believe they are alive. I like to play with my cart because I make believe I am a horse and have somebody for a master." One thirteen-year-old girl rejected fantasy: "The playthings I like best to play with are my kittens, my dog. I like these best of all because they are alive and can move; dolls cannot move nor walk, so I do not like to play with them." Another clung to childhood by replacing one favorite plaything with another: "I like to play with my dolls when we are many to play, but now I don't care much for dolls. We often make party and eat in little toy dishes. I like to eat in small dishes because I think the food tastes better." [28]

A one-day survey of June 23, 1913, by social workers in Cleveland, Ohio, revealed that more than half of the 14,683 children observed were in the streets and that the majority of them were "doing nothing" or "just fooling." Baseball, kites, playing in sand piles, tag, and jacks topped the list of approved activities, but far too many were seen fighting, teasing, pitching pennies, shooting craps, stealing apples, breaking windows, building fires, writing in chalk on walls, shooting air guns, and picking up junk. The solution offered by the superintendent of physical recreation was more school and playground activities. Play was defined as organized games; anything else was "idling." [29]

A 1921 survey of 474 children in San Francisco by the psychologist Lewis Terman shows the continued popularity of baseball, kites, and tag among boys, as well as the new importance of the bicycle. More dramatic changes are recorded in girls' choices. Dolls drop to eighth place on the list of favorite play, which is dominated by tag, sewing, bicycling, baseball, hide and seek, and basketball. A survey by Brian Sutton-Smith and B. G. Rosenberg in northwestern Ohio in 1959 confirms some of the trends that seem to emerge in the 1930s, 1940s, and 1950s. In their list the five top boys' activities are football, throwing snowballs, bicycling, hide and seek, and basketball. Girls in Ohio ranked jump rope first, followed by hide and seek, tag, bike riding, and hopscotch. Because these surveys were conducted in different ways it is difficult to draw firm conclusions. Sutton-Smith points to the sixty-year decline in singing and dialogue games and a rise in games that encourage strategy and imagination. He thinks that girls are less limited now than they were, while the range of play deemed appropriate for boys has narrowed. [30]

Clearly, smaller families, attendance in nursery and preschool for longer periods of time, movies, and television have had an enormous impact on children and their play. Some evidence in the autobiographies supports the conclusion that young women during the years 1920 to 1950 also enjoyed new opportunities for play as a result of the toy industry's efforts to expand its markets. In general the surveys, whether by questionnaires or by observation, confirm the autobiographers' memories concerning toys. Toys and playthings were part of the games and play of children in the 1890s as well as in the 1950s, but in neither generation were they the most preferred play except in the choice of dolls by girls in the 1890s. By 1917 at least one little girl had put away her dolls in favor of a Meccano set.

Eda Lord, like Flannery Lewis, recalled the impact of World War I on her play with an older brother:

> Our most pressing concern was what we were going to make with the Meccano sets. With the sheets of metal and the girders we could build almost anything but we wanted to make something which needed some of our pulleys. We were limited by not having traction wheels. No matter what shape our construction took, it turned out to be a lifting crane. It would lift objects large in comparison to its size but never so large that we couldn't lift them ourselves with one hand. Finally we left it as a dock crane to supply the fleet with food and ammunition. For a short time we changed over from a war footing to a merchant fleet but the continuous loading and unloading was dull. We tried freighters-attacked-by-pirates but the booty and excitement went to whoever was pirate, and that wasn't fun.[31]

Lord was living in the Midwest in 1917, but she moved frequently, forcing her to discard unwanted toys yet making them all the more important because she often played by herself.

Businessmen were quick to adjust to changes in American life brought about by the war and the breakdown of traditional family organization. An editorial in the January 1920 *Playthings*, the leading journal of the toy industry, called attention to an exhibit of toys designed by children and cited a number of toys that had been copied by manufacturers from homemade playthings. Recognizing the importance of the child-created plaything in children's culture, the manufacturers also knew that some of that culture was disappearing under the impact of migration, smaller families, and the willingness of prosperous parents to indulge their children with store-bought toys. The editor also published Professor Patty Smith Hill's view that the industry should produce fewer toys and improve their quality because her opinion lent the authority of Columbia

University Teacher's College to the idea that toys are important in the education of children. Later in the same year, *Playthings* published an article on the Americanization of immigrant children through supervised toy-making in settlement houses. Men and women in the toy industry did not try to change children's toy play; rather, they exploited what they saw as fundamental to a child's life. A 1940 article, however, listing hundreds of items appropriate for each season of the year, from indoor board games for winter to traditional marbles, kites, and hoops for spring to beach and camp equipment for summer and educational toys for the fall, shows how rapidly the toy industry permeated every moment of childhood. The influence of the automobile on children's play and the industry's ability to incorporate it are seen in a separate line of "travel toys (to encourage quiet play)." [32]

Estha Briscoe, who grew up in Oklahoma between the time of Woody Guthrie and John O'Dell, had many of the same playthings they had. "We played with everyone who was big enough to run, ride a stickhorse or chase a ball," she writes. "Outdoor toys were scarce with this group. There were no bicycles or tricycles. A few children had balls, and old shovel handles made good bats. Most of the time we improvised with whatever became available. We used empty tomato or corn cans along with pieces of bailing wire to make tin-can walkers. With a foot on each can and each hand holding a wire loop, we could 'walk tall' and cut little round circles in the hard dirt." In an interesting reversal of perspective, O'Dell remembered that if you were barefoot "the raised rim on the cans [which he calls "Tom Walkers"] would leave red indentations on the soles of the feet that wouldn't go away for hours." Briscoe also treasured her roller skates and a boy doll in overalls that she chose over a ruffled girl doll. [33]

Further evidence of the place of treasured toys in a child's life comes from a unique collection of the playthings of three generations of a Philadelphia family. Recently donated to the Please Touch Museum, Philadelphia, Pennsylvania, the collection of over seven hundred objects contains material from 1888 to the 1950s, the toys and games of Katharine Parker Taylor, her parents, her husband, Daniel Chappell Frysinger, and the four Frysinger children, who were born between 1944 and 1953. It is not necessary to analyze the scratches, stains, and dents on old toys as closely as a taphonomist examines the marks on prehistoric bones to see the patterns of wear and use. The toys in the Frysinger collection clearly reveal such patterns. Some are in excellent condition, even their original boxes are preserved, but others have been played with until they are worn almost beyond recognition.[34]

A miniature electric iron belonging to Katharine was either used carefully or seldom. A similar iron cost ninety-seven cents according to a 1930 Montgomery Ward catalog. Further research may reveal whether its present condition is the result of some special memory associated with it, relative disinterest in ironing by Mrs. Frysinger or her daughter, or some other factor. A twelve-inch wooden sail boat with a metal keel, purchased for one of Mrs. Frysinger's children in the 1950s, has been remodeled in several ways. The original rudder was replaced by a tin can lid bent over the wire extending from the tiller. Neither the sails nor the rigging is original. The replacement sails are tattered and stained with what seems to be bird droppings, suggesting that the boat may have been left outdoors for some period of time. The broken mast was not replaced. Interviews might determine the process by which the boat was wrecked and salvaged and wrecked again and possibly how long the process took, but the evidence is clear that this was a treasured toy on which considerable time and interest were spent. Multiply these two examples by 350, and one quickly sees the dimensions of the historical reconstruction of childhood through toys.

One of the oldest toys in the collection is a badly worn, stuffed dog about ten inches long and six inches high on wheels. It is identified as belonging to Mrs. Frysinger's husband, who was born in 1915, but it may be older. A similar toy was advertised in the 1889 Montgomery Ward catalog, suggesting that it may have been handed down from Mr. Frysinger's father. Its association with the toys donated to the Please Touch Museum implies that it was played with by his children, who themselves had a similar toy—a tin, clock-work cat holding a ball, made by the Marx Company. It too shows signs of long, hard play. Its rubber ears are gone; its wind-up springs jammed. Like the other toy animals in the collection—a stuffed gingham dog and a stuffed oilcloth rabbit with a painted face—the wheeled dog and the mechanical cat were obviously played with often. The rabbit's left ear is badly chewed and hanging by a thread. It is not difficult to imagine the child who loved it carrying it by its ear and dragging it around kitchen and yard until it acquired a fine patina of stains from food and tears and dirt. The blue dog is stained and missing an eye on its left side, its tail is almost off, but its ears are in good condition, perhaps replaced or repaired. It is faded on its right side, as if left in the sun too long. Possibly it decorated a window after its owner grew too old to play with it.

Although there are few handmade toys in the collection, there is evidence that the Frysinger children did make and modify some toys. The orange paint on a three-inch metal airplane appears to have been carefully scraped to make it two-toned, and a wooden model Piper Cub was constructed but never painted. Its tail is missing and its wing struts broken, suggesting that it was played with before it was finished, the builder more anxious to fly it than to patiently paint it and apply the decals. Sixteen cardboard turtles cut out and decorated by the children are reported to be part of a game created by Margaret Brown Frysinger in the 1950s. Several Kix cereal boxes with cut-outs of rodeo riders and an Indian village were saved but never constructed.

The people who played with these toys can probably no longer recall what it meant to receive, play with, and collect them. There is a risk in overinterpreting the remains of their toys and certainly nothing is unusual in the collection. All the familiar types—dolls, cars, soldiers, cap pistols, games, whistles, blocks, boats (including a Marx Company speed boat, "Miss America '55," made in Japan)—are represented. We can safely assume that these and other toys amused their respective owners during appropriate periods of their childhoods. Most of these toys are the kind that encourage the development of imagination and are a part of fantasy play. Some required skill in building; others, the physical development necessary for roller-skating or bicycling. The fairly large numbers of whistles, jumping insects, and rubber worms should remind us that the sounds of shrieks and laughter are also part of play.

In the same years that the younger Frysinger children were playing with their cap pistols and building their model airplanes, Caryl Rivers was holstering her six-shooters and Susan Allen was trying to build Ferris wheels with her Tinker-toys. Annie Dillard was throwing snowballs with her neighborhood gang in Pittsburgh.[35] These young women seem to have escaped gender stereotyping to some degree. The advent of television and the birth of Barbie brought a return of sexual segregation.

"Barbie wasn't just a toy, but a way of living that moved up suddenly from tea parties to dates with Ken at the soda shoppe," Joyce Maynard writes.[36] Mattel's success in exploiting children's storytelling abilities during play with its packaged narratives of Barbie's life has led to the marketing of other dolls and action figures, chiefly through television programs. Care Bears, My Little Pony, G.I. Joe, Rambo, He-man, She-ra, and most recently, Teenage Mutant Ninja Turtles sell a whole universe of characters and plots with each doll. A recent study of the content of television programs for children argues that these programs promote two kinds of fantasy play with toys, one involving role playing, such as pretending to be Barbie's sister, the other involving identification with an imaginary character, such as pretending to be G.I. Joe. In both cases the play depends not on knowing the rules to a game but on knowing the rules of the narrative, providing story and dialogue appropriate to the character of the doll or action figure. Character toys are stereotyped by gender, too, with boys' toys limited to fantasy galaxies filled with violence and girls' dolls dwelling in worlds where they require nurturing, evidence that once again the range of adult-approved play for little girls has narrowed.[37]

Television, however, is not the only source of adult-sanctioned children's fantasies, nor are girls as passive in the acceptance of TV commercials as many parents fear. Toys marketed with books have long been popular. Winnie-the-Poohs, Paddingtons, and plain old Teddy bears are still a staple of most children's imaginary play, joined now by Snoopys and Garfields, Muppets and dinosaurs. Some of these toys come with scripted stories, but bears and dogs and cats and prehistoric monsters are generic. They are able to escape the momentary confines of commercialization. The evidence presented in autobiographies, in the Frysinger collection, and in photographs of children at play shows that toys have meaning only when children play with them. The objects they choose in play—made, bought, or stolen—may be defined as toys or dismissed as junk by adults, but if they are meaningful to the child they will be reused and remembered. What adults call toys may be accepted as such by children and may even achieve the status of prized possession when small and large worlds coincide.

6

Sugar and Spite

The Politics of Doll Play in Nineteenth-Century America

MIRIAM FORMANEK-BRUNELL

"It seems to me," wrote a contributor to *Babyhood* magazine, "there is no occupation of childhood so devoid of outlook and uplift, so stupefying to the natural activity and curiosity of childhood, as doll playing."[1] This turn-of-the-century critic articulated what feminists, historians, and other scholars have been arguing since—that dolls are symbols of patriarchal oppression and even worse, its agent. In this social history of girls' doll play I challenge the dominant interpretation that dolls limited the development of girls to domestic and maternal concerns in late-nineteenth-century America.

What follows is about nineteenth-century dolls, the purposes they served as adults saw them, and the uses to which girls put them. We begin in antebellum America, where the political ideology, class values, and cultural and economic forces of the young nation shaped new attitudes about doll play. Mothers, informed by the literature of the new domestic advisers, instructed their daughters to be "useful" within the matrix of the family. Daughters of the evolving middle class made cloth dolls in an attempt to facilitate sewing skills that integrated leisure with training in domestic economy. Dolls, of which there were few, served as training in everything *but* emotional development and expression. Outdoor play, education, and a schedule of daily, weekly, and seasonal responsi-

Girls with dolls, ca. 1900.
(Kansas State Historical Society)

bilities (punctuated by the Sabbath) limited the role that dolls played in girlhood. These utilitarian purposes of dolls, however, became obsolete in the Gilded Age as simplicity yielded to splendor. Children's magazines, books, poems, songs, and stereographs revealed that girls were encouraged by adults to imbue their numerous dolls with affect, to indulge in fantasy, and to display their elaborately dressed dolls at ritual occasions such as tea parties and while visiting. To adults such as the nineteenth-century poet Robert Southey, girls were "sugar and spice and all things nice."

It is my thesis that although adults, especially parents, perceived dolls as useful vehicles in feminine socialization, their daughters—with a different agenda—appropriated dolls and used them for purposes other than training in the emotional and practical skills of mothering. Girls' funereal doll play, for example, revealed far more evidence of resistance than of accommodation to both prescriptions and proscriptions. Memoirs, autobiographies, biographies, and oral histories suggest that through their doll play, an unquantifiable number of girls challenged parental authority, restrictive social customs, and gender roles. These girls, in late nineteenth-century America, engaged their parents in a political struggle to define, decide, and determine the meaning of dolls in their own lives and as representations of their own culture.

Dolls and their clothing, argued Catharine Beecher and Harriet Beecher Stowe in *The American Woman's Home*, will provide girls with "another resource . . . to the exercise of mechanical skills." Children should be "trained to be healthful and industrious."[2] Earlier in the nineteenth century, advice books, ladies' magazines, and other printed sources similarly urged mothers to apply Christian principles to the regulation of the bourgeois family, their recent domain, and to direct their children's play toward useful ends.[3] Printed material that offered practical advice and philosophical explanations to middle-class mothers standardized methods of antebellum childrearing.[4] In the prescriptive literature published after the early 1800s, middle-class girls and their mothers were kept informed of genteel decorum, bourgeois values, and domestic training.

Girls were urged toward usefulness as natural training in the republican values they would need as future wives of citizens. New attitudes about girls' play were shaped in part by the political ideology of the young nation. According to the Beechers and other "experts," mothers were to use "gentle nurture" to teach their children to be self-governing and to exercise "self control" while at play.[5] Miss Eliza Leslie, author of the *Girls' Book*, suggested, as did other prescriptive writers, that making dolls rather than indulging a love of dress and finery would prevent degeneration into godless anarchy.[6] In her moral tracts, Mary Sewell exhorted mothers to inculcate "habitual restraint" in children by structuring play periods with "habitual regularity."[7]

"In this land of precarious fortunes, every girl should know how to be 'useful,'" wrote Mrs. Lydia Maria Child, one of the best-known writers of the period. A girl's vocation, to which dolls contributed, was to be a domestic one, surprisingly untouched by sentimentality and shaped in response to the world beyond the proverbial Victorian hearth. A canon of domesticity contrasted the safety of the home, where women presided, to the restlessness, competition, selfishness, and alienation of the masculine world beyond. Girls' play was viewed as training in genuine adult usefulness, especially in the wake of an unstable market economy dependent upon international trade and finance. Although the reality of slipping down the ladder was obscured by the mythology of the self-made man whose life of hard work, moderation, and temperance promised untold rewards, young ladies were nevertheless forewarned to make themselves useful should misfortune strike.[8]

Mothers' Monthly Journal, one of the leading maternal-association periodicals with a broad readership, advised that dressing dolls provided "a semblance of the sober activities of business."[9] Making dolls, family nurture, and household duties constituted a girl's informal apprenticeship in preparation for being a wife and mother.[10] According to experts such as Maria Edgeworth, who "firmly believed in the utility of toys," sewing dolls and their clothing stressed a pragmatism useful in the domestic economy of the antebellum household.[11] Popular ladies' magazines often included directions for making pen wiper dolls (to clean nibs), sewing dolls (whose pockets held thimbles and other tools for sewing), and pincushion dolls.

It was from their mothers, endowed with both the ability and the social responsibility to determine the fate of their children, that girls were to learn their lessons, both practical and moral.[12] Although the widespread availability of cloth was dramatically altering the ways in which women spent their days, family comfort still depended on skillful use of the needle. Catharine Beecher, who felt "blessed with the example of a most ingenious and industrious mother," suggested that

> when a little girl begins to sew, her mother can promise her a small bed and pillow, as soon as she has sewed a patch quilt for them; and then a bedstead, as soon as she has sewed the sheets and cases for pillows; and then a large doll to dress, as soon as she has made the undergarments; and thus go on till the whole contents of the babyhouse are earned by the needle and skill of its little owner. Thus, the task of learning to sew will become a pleasure; and every new toy will be earned by useful exertion.

In her treatise on household management, the nineteenth-century architect of domesticity boasted that she "had not only learned before the age of twelve to make dolls, of various sorts and sizes, but to cut and fit and sew every article that belongs to a doll's wardrobe."[13] In the absence of mothers, other female kin such as Lucy Larcom's "adopted aunt" provided instruction in how to knot thread and how to sew clothing for rag dolls.[14] A doll in one children's story recalled that "there were hours and hours when she [her owner] had to sit quietly beside grandmother, and sew her stint."[15]

In addition to adults, older sisters often helped younger ones create homemade dolls. "I once knew a little girl who had twelve dolls," wrote Lydia Maria Child, "some of them were given her; but the greater part she herself made from rags, and her elder sister painted their lips and eyes."[16] One of Lucy Larcom's older sisters outlined faces on her dolls with pen and ink.[17]

Despite the practical suggestions provided to girls by antebellum experts, the hours during which toys were expected to absorb their attention were limited by genuine household responsibilities.[18] Few matched the ideal as represented in the numerous extant canvases of girls leisurely holding dolls, painted by itinerants for socially conscious, middle-class parents. Though the texture of girls' lives was changing, childhood was still neither as precisely demarcated nor as prolonged in early nineteenth-century America as it would be by the end of the century. Instead, a mother of a large and rural family was likely to be assisted by the eldest of her children, especially her daughters, whose participation began as soon as possible despite decreasing household productivity and the increasing availability of goods. Thus for a girl the number of hours spent in play would have been circumscribed by immediate familial obligations. Though minding younger siblings combined amusement with training, it also bore the weight of sober responsibility.

Time spent in doll play was also limited by school attendance, which required more girls to spend a portion of their day in decidedly unleisured activities. In a children's story from the 1850s, retribution was delivered upon two girls who skipped school in order to play with their dolls.[19] Similarly, on Sundays, which were "not like any other day," girls were expected to pray, not play. Cutting across the economic stratifications within the middle class, all Christian children were expected to observe the Sabbath as did the adults, even those who were not very religious. "We did not play games nor read the same books," and church services and Sunday school seemed to last forever.[20]

Consequently, girls were less likely to devote much of their time to doll play. Though the number of toys had increased since the colonial period, there were still few dolls around, a fact of doll demography that would change dramatically only after the Civil War. "Life for children was simple in the extreme [as] there were no array[s] of costly toys," recalled one New England girl in her autobiography. [My sister and I] "had the regulation rag doll with long curls and club feet, very ugly but dear to our hearts," and no others.[21]

Because of the scarcity and sheer market value of dolls, parents and relatives tended to treasure those purchased far more than did their daughters, grandchildren, and nieces. One father in Petersburg, Virginia, included the two large dolls he had bought for his daughter in his will.[22] With little regard for a doll's economic value, however, girls like Lucy Larcom rejected the "London doll that lay in waxen state in an upper drawer at home." To her, this "fine lady did not wish to be played with but only to be looked at and admired." Larcom, instead, preferred the "absurd creatures of her own invention."[23] Antebellum expert Eliza Leslie similarly observed that cloth dolls "remain longer in favor with their young owners, and continue to give them more real satisfaction, than the handsomest wax doll that can be purchased."[24]

Yet many girls who lived in rural areas preferred to spend their time outdoors. Lucy Larcom played on farms and in fields, rivers, quarries, and cemeteries in addition to schoolrooms and local stores.[25] Emily Wilson and her sister preferred skating, sledding, and running to playing with dolls as did Frances Willard in her youth.[26] Nor were such activities unusual. Whether writing about a New England boyhood or girlhood, the authors' play activities were remarkably similar.[27] According to Anne Scott MacLeod, little girls lived "as unfettered and vigorous an outdoor life as their brothers."[28]

In both the city and the country, middle-class girls born in the years after the Civil War amassed quantities of dolls unknown to Willard's generation. In contrast to the four decades preceding the Civil War, during the remaining years of the century dolls sold widely. Revolutions in European doll production enabled jobbers, manufacturers' agents, importers, and distributors to funnel European toys to retail stores, where mothers and fathers purchased greater quantities of dolls, ones made of china or bisque, ones with open mouths and little teeth, or ones with closed lips.[29] Some of the most expensive French lady dolls in the 1870s and 1880s arrived with fully packed trunks, a factor that often tripled the original price of the doll. French and German dolls—"ladies" with hourglass figures and French *bébés,* idealized and romanticized representations of children—flooded American markets at a time when most Americans enjoyed increasing affluence.

The standard of living was climbing, and a rising personal income meant that most middle-class Americans could become consumers of articles formerly available only to the rich, whom they emulated. Nevertheless, buying imported dolls still required a solid bank account. In 1890, when the annual income of an industrial worker was $486, French jointed, kid dolls with composition heads cost between $3 and $30.00. As a result, the majority of dolls remained prohibitively expensive for working-class families.[30] In one doll story, a poor seamstress is unable to purchase a wax doll because she "could not afford to spend her money that way." "Does she cost a great deal, mamma?" asks a little girl. "It would be a great deal for us—she costs $10, Lucy," replies her mother.[31]

Shopping at home using mail-order catalogs gave those living far from urban centers but with financial resources opportunities to share in the consumer-goods market for dolls. Seven years after Richard Sears began advertising watches to the rural market, Sears and Roebuck broadened their wares to include dolls.[32] Wholesale suppliers such as Butler Brothers and Marshall Field provided the small merchant of the rural Midwest with dolls and other items.[33]

Beginning in 1865 department stores such as Macy's, Jordan Marsh, and Marshall Field dazzled shoppers as spectacular "palaces of consumption."[34] Macy's was the first to establish a toy department, and others soon followed their lead.[35] "Most of us adults can recall the time when the toy shop exhibited but a slim stock," commented one observer. But in the years after the Civil War, toy shops, some of which would issue illustrated catalogs, increased in number and size. "Enter one of our big toy shops now and there is really an *embarrass de richesses.*"[36] In fact, "the first impression of the visitor to the big toy shop [now] is . . . apt to be one of bewilderment."[37]

Toy stores catered to a clientele of middle-class women, most of whom did not work outside the home and for whom shopping for self, friends, and family was becoming a central activity.[38] According to an 1881 *Harper's Bazaar,* dolls and other toys were "chosen by mothers with a view to giving their girls correct ideas of symmetry and beauty."[39] In stories, nurturing women traders patiently assisted female customers.[40] In "A Doll's

Story," a jointed bisque doll recalled seeing from inside her glass display case "mostly mothers and young children—sometimes nurses with small children."[41]

Women were the largest group of consumers, but fathers also purchased dolls—some of which said "Papa"—for their daughters at each birthday or homecoming.[42] Giving gifts to one's children instead of to adult employees as in the Victorian Christmas was a bourgeois father's ritual that had been gaining in popularity since about mid-century even though most dolls were too expensive for working-class parents to afford. One middle-class daughter of German immigrants recalled that she received gifts only on Christmas and for her birthday but then typically in an abundance suitable for several children.[43]

Generous gift giving, whether on Christmas or during other times of the year, had been a recent consequence of a number of factors, including the increasing distance between parents and children. Busy parents with fewer children provided their daughters with the companionship of dolls, thereby lengthening childhood and prolonging their "dollhood."[44] Middle-class women had become not only increasingly isolated from production but also from their children. Fashion and etiquette, shopping and visiting dominated the life of the matron. Fashion magazines, as one indicator, far outnumbered mothers' magazines. Mothers' contact with their children became circumscribed shortly after their births. By the late 1890s, leading pediatrician Luther Emmett Holt observed that "at least three children out of every four born into the homes of the well-to-do-classes" were not fed at the breast.[45] Many children probably saw more of "nanny" in their own sphere than of their mothers and fathers in theirs.

In doll stories "papas with weary heads" committed to a business ethos were frequently too preoccupied to notice a sick or a sad daughter.[46] Fathers were typically separated from the family during the day, especially those who commuted from the sprouting suburbs. Sons might have been more acutely affected by their diminished opportunities to assist fathers, but the relationship of fathers to their daughters was influenced as well. Gift giving could solace an alienated father and reinforce his belief that he was fulfilling his role as provider.[47] As a result, "most fathers," observed a writer for the *Doll's Dressmaker*, "are inclined to overindulge their daughters."[48] Pearl's father, for example, "bought me a beautiful bedstead," narrated a doll in one story, "round which were hung some elegant blue silk curtains." [49] In *A Doll's Journey*, a story written by Louisa May Alcott, one sister reassured another that "papa will give you a new doll." [50]

Daughters living in urban and newly created suburban homes were given far less productive work, fewer responsibilities and siblings to look after, and far more toys, books, magazines, clothing, and furniture made especially for them.[51] Most middle-class mothers had successfully limited the number of births, spaced them farther apart, and ceased childbearing earlier than had previous generations.[52] Though this process freed women from a lifelong process of childbearing and elevated the status of the child, it made a daughter's life potentially more solitary than social. There were fewer brothers and sisters to watch, which increased the amount of time for play but decreased the number of friends and kin with whom to share it. As a single child of well-to-do parents, Margaret adored the numerous dolls she received—now the foundation of the Margaret Woodbury Strong Museum in Rochester, New York.[53]

Doll play in antebellum America emphasized learning and developing skills, but such was not the case in the decades that followed the Civil War. Gradually, dolls began to serve a more modern or symbolic function than a utilitarian one. Doll play in the postwar era emphasized the display of fashion. In one story from the period, Pearl adored the doll she saw in Mrs. Lieb's toy shop though she hesitated to purchase it because it was undressed. "You know, dear mother," she said in a whisper, "how badly I sew." [54] Although teaching girls to make doll dresses had been an essential function earlier in the century, the emphasis on sewing for dolls had become obsolete. Instead, organized doll play developed rules that became nearly as formalized as those recently devised for baseball. During the Gilded Age, Americans became participants and spectators of baseball and football as specific forms of leisure and amusement. Pastimes that had made previous generations of well-to-do Protestants uneasy now became acceptable. As with production and consumption, amusement in general became a more organized activity.

The middle-class nursery became an arena where, as with organized sports, values, attitudes, and standards of behavior were imparted. Changes in the family, childhood, and the needs of married adults had given rise to the middle-class nursery by the second half of the nineteenth century, differentiating households as well as the space between family members. The nursery, a place to keep the large numbers of dolls, their accoutrements, and other toys, became an indispensable feature of the middle-class home in the last quarter of the nineteenth century. Although Victorian houses were spacious they were also cluttered with possessions too precious to risk the consequences of uncontrolled child's play. In the autonomous space of the nursery described by J. M. Barrie in *Peter Pan,* children lived a life apart from parents and the rest of the household.[55] Miniature-sized furniture altered the landscape of the children's nursery and became a standard feature of the spacious upper-middle-class Victorian home. Some chairs were stenciled with affectionate names such as "My Pet," and miniature tea tables painted to represent marble imitated adult lavishness.[56]

Adults expected girls to imitate the new social rituals of high society with their dolls in their nurseries.[57] For instance, elaborately dressed dolls were thought useful in the instruction of social conventions such as housewarmings.[58] Far more common, however, were dolls' tea parties, another social ritual frequently depicted as a heterosocial activity in stereographs, tradecards, and books such as *The Dolls' Tea Party.*[59] Dolls' tea parties were staged with great regularity whether in the Midwest or the Northeast. As a girl growing up in Wisconsin in the 1870s, Zona Gale dressed her eleven dolls for outdoor tea parties. According to one study of school-aged girls in Worcester, Massachusetts, 73 out of 242 considered tea parties their favorite activity.[60] Adults proudly noted that "the children's doll parties of to-day are counterparts of grown-up people's receptions."[61]

In addition to tea parties, girls were urged to imitate another adult social ritual of polite society in the Gilded Age, that of visiting. Dolls could be purchased wearing "a stylish visiting dress, and also accompanied by a trunkful of clothes ready for all the demands of fashionable occasions."[62] Miniature calling cards, which represented self, family, and possessions to neighbors and friends, served as a *carte de visite* for girls who paid formal visits with their dolls.[63] Now instead of singing, "Here we go round the mulberry bush," girls were encouraged to sing, "This is the way we carry them . . . when we go visiting."[64] Popular magazines such as the *Delineator* advertised instructions for making visiting dresses and even "a stately toilette for Miss Dolly to wear on the promenade."[65] "With their companions or dolls you will hear them imitating the discussion [on fashion] . . . that they daily hear in the parlor or nursery from their mother . . . ," observed Mrs. H. W. Beecher in 1873.[66]

Of all the newly constructed middle-class rituals girls were urged to imitate, doll funerals, not weddings, were by far the most common. Adults encouraged rather than discouraged doll death rituals. For example, mourning clothes were packed in the trunks of French lady dolls in the 1870s and 1880s. Fathers constructed doll-sized coffins for their daughters' dolls instead of the more usual dollhouses.[67] To middle-class parents in the second half of the nineteenth century, devising imaginary and miniaturized funerals was not seen as evidence of a child's morbid preoccupation with death. According to Harvey Green, "Visiting ill or dying relatives and friends was an expected and socially required part of women's sphere, part of the broad set of nurturing responsibilities with which she was charged."[68]

The process of learning about the meanings of grief began early in life, as the etiquette of mourning became an integral part of a girl's upbringing. Young students in private schools learning the decorative arts created countless embroidered mourning pieces filled with new iconographic symbols such as willow trees and morning glories.[69] Even Rebecca of Sunnybrook Farm routinely staged deaths and funerals with her friends.[70] As the ritualization of mourning increased over the century, all maintained within the feminine sphere, it is no wonder that parents encouraged funereal ceremonies meant to properly sanctify the "bodies" and protect the "souls" of those poor, deceased dolls.[71]

Short stories of dying dolls were included in the popular fiction aimed at an audience of children and provided them with a source of new ideas about how they should play with dolls. Earlier in the century so few stories about dolls had been written that one disappointed doll in a story from the 1840s remarked, "I never heard any stories about dolls, and what they thought, or what happened to them!"[72] In the years after the Civil War, however, a conspicuous doll culture unfolded in widely available children's books and popular magazines. Beginning in the late 1860s, colorfully illustrated and miniature-sized books were printed for girls and their dolls. Nursery shelves were lined with books about dolls, books for them, such as *The Dolls' Own Book*, which went through numerous editions, and even books by dolls.[73] Stories such as "Dolly's Experience, [as] Told by Herself" or dolly memoirs were ostensibly written by doll authors.[74]

Unlike the antebellum literature, which stressed the development of skills and morals, doll fiction of the Gilded Age emphasized the exploration of self, interpersonal relationships, and fantasy. Despite the innumerable images of girls washing their dolls and their clothing, grooming had not yet become a primary justification for doll play because most dolls had little chance of surviving a good dunking. Instead, it was through her relationship to her female dolls, also portrayed as passive, pretty, enigmatic, domestic, dainty, mute, vain, and delicate, that the doll player learned about the essence of "true love" and how to distinguish it from more superficial feelings. One bisque sophisticate observed, "Oh, it's nice to be grand and all that, I suppose / But of late I'm beginning to reap / The Knowledge that happiness isn't fine clothes / And that beauty is only skin deep."[75] Although hopelessly unfashionable, even rag dolls had keen insight.

> Lillian Grace is a fine city girl
> I'm but a queer "country cousin,"
> I have one dress of coarse cotton stuff,
> She has silk gowns by the dozen.
>
> She is so pretty, and dainty and gay,
> I am so homely and funny;
> I cost a trifle, I'm but a rag doll,
> She costs a whole heap of money.
>
> She came from France in a big handsome box,
> I, from a country bazaar,
> Things are more precious I've often been told
> That travel so long and so far.
>
> Yet it is strange, but Oh! it is true
> We belong to the same little mother
> And though she loves Lillian Grace very much
> It is queer, but somehow or other,
>
> I have a spot in her dear loving heart
> That Lillian Grace cannot enter;
> She has a hold in the outermost rim,
> But I have a place in the center.
>
> And all the silk dresses and other fine things,
> Though they do look so fair to the eye,
> Are not worth a thought since they cannot win love.
> O a happy rag dollie am I![76]

The portrayal of love between a doll and a girl, which often straddled the boundaries between mother love and romantic love, was reciprocal, communicative, and passionate.[77] Beginning in the early 1890s, the growing emphasis placed on the importance of mothering and child study had influenced popular ideas about doll play for girls. The *Doll's Dressmaker* (a monthly magazine first appearing in New York City in 1891) reprinted images of girls with their bevies of dolls, which conveyed maternal fecundity out of step with demographic changes (families were becoming smaller) but in step with newer ideas about mothering. Thereafter, in numerous images girls cradled *bébés* with maternal sentimentality while contemporaries rhetorically asked, "Is it not the harmless, childish joy that develops and educates the young girl's maternal instinct, and in so doing helps to elevate her to the pinnacle of true womanhood?"[78]

Elsewhere, fictional characters encouraged the achievement of feminine submission to masculine dominance. In fact, girls' dolls were often portrayed as hapless victims of mischievous boys who taunted girls and tortured dolls. The incorrigible boy was a familiar one in popular fiction, art, cartoons, advertisements, and stereographs of the period.[79] One doll in a story recalled that her "little mistress" had a book entitled *Mischievous Tommy*, "about a troublesome, rude boy" who had disgusting manners.[80] As Mary Lynn Stevens Heininger and others have noted, the boys in *Tom Sawyer* and *Peck's Bad Boy* practiced masculine behavior through mischief and manipulation.[81] Such was the case in another popular story in which Gladys was portrayed as defenseless against her scheming, scissors-wielding brother who "cut a great patch of hair out of the poor doll's head."[82]

In addition to bad boys, other threats restricted the boundaries of safety for girls' dolls and hence for their owners.[83] In numerous stories, birds, cows, and monkeys like "Naughty Jacko" stole, pecked, gnawed, and kicked defenseless dolls unable and unwilling to resist.[84] In *The Dolls' Surprise Party*, a roving mother pig and her piglets attack a bevy of dolls enjoying their picnic.[85] Although most stories departed from realism long enough to attribute powerful emotional responses to dolls and thus to girls, fictionalized dolls and girls often sat by helplessly with "wooden legs" while dogs hounded them.

Home provided little safety for two dolls in a Beatrix Potter tale in which "two bad mice" destroy domestic security and fantasy. In this 1904 children's story, two working-class mice, a foul-tempered husband and his thieving wife, ransack the house of two wooden dolls absent from the nursery. Returning from their stroll in the perambulator, the dolls are shocked into victimized passivity. One doll merely "sat upon the upset kitchen stove and stared," while the other "leant against the kitchen dresser and smiled—but neither of them made any remark."[86] Instead, nurse and policeman dolls (brought into play by the girl whose dollhouse has been burglarized) set mousetraps. To make a short story even shorter, the repentant mouse husband pays for everything he broke and "very early every morning—before anybody is awake—Hunca Munca [his wife] comes with her dust pan and her broom to sweep the Dollies house!"[87]

In the last decades of the century stereographs and other images revealed a middle-class ideal of girls, overflowing with metaphors of abundance, yet we know far more about adult expectations than we do about childhood reality. How did girls feel about the dolls they heard about in nightly bedtime stories? What did they think of the dolls they cradled in studio portraits? Did they actually prefer dolls to other toys and activities? How did boys play with dolls? Were girls who played with dolls more gentle and nurturing than were boys?

There is no disputing that girls in late nineteenth-century America liked their dolls—but not just any doll. According to one study, girls preferred dolls made of wax, paper, rag, and china over those made of rubber, china and kid, wood, tin, or celluloid. Among the favorite dolls were those often made of cloth.[88] Emily Kimbrough disliked the fashionable doll her grandmother gave her but adored her Topsy-turvey rag doll.[89] Adults were often at a loss to understand why their daughters preferred ragged and "countrified" dolls to brightly colored and elaborately dressed ones.

Among rag dolls, black ones were a favorite among white children, observed one contemporary shopper.[90] Both Mary Hunt and her friend favored black dolls over white ones.[91] "My little girl has two such [rag] dolls," commented a mother, "one white and the other black, but her affections are centered on the colored woman . . . never going to bed without Dinah in her arms, and crying for "di" if the nurse had forgotten to put it in her crib."[92] Increasingly, African American women played a significant role in the rearing of middle-class children.[93] Suggesting a relationship born of affection, one four-year-old girl fed everything that tasted good to her black rag doll.[94]

Despite their uniform portrayal as fictional adversaries, boys were also among doll lovers. The examples of boys who were especially fond of their dolls are numerous. G. Stanley Hall found that 76 percent of the boys he studied played with dolls to age twelve.[95] According to the records of the Wenham Museum, a boy doll (c. 1875) named "Theodore" became a "chum" to a little boy for eight years.[96] The only man who participated in the Doll Oral History Project conducted at the Margaret Woodbury Strong Museum in 1987 recognized a painted cloth boy doll similar to his childhood toy.[97] One contributor to a mother's magazine reported that her son treated the doll he loved with "the greatest care and tenderness."[98]

In their play, boys and girls sang to and rocked the dolls, which they endowed with emotional, intellectual, physiological, moral, political (e.g., a "democrat"), and religious qualities. They fed dolls milk, bread, buttons, or pickles when they were "hungry," occasionally breaking tiny teeth and heads in order to do so. Children succored dolls sick with measles or brainfever with remedies such as tapioca and paper pills or dissolved candy. According to one ten-year-old girl, "My doll Liz had a headache, so I put on her micado and read her some of Longfellow's *Hiawatha*, as she wanted me to."

Girls and boys often played with their dolls in socially prescribed ways. While girls pretended to be little mothers to their dolls, boys often assumed authoritative roles such as doctor, preacher, and undertaker to sickened, dying, and dead dolls. One eight-year-old doll dentist used toothpicks as dental tools. Another boy shot his doll full of holes with a bow and arrow so that he could dress its wounds.[99] Boys' play with dolls also included crucifixions and executions.[100] Unlike the girl characters in doll stories, however, girls did not always mind.[101] "When my brother proved my doll had no brains by slicing off her head, I felt I had been deluded; I watched him with stoicism and took no more interest in dolls."[102]

The examples of girls such as this one—who preferred all other activities to doll play—are also numerous. Less than one quarter of the girls in T. R. Croswell's study of two thousand children in Massachusetts considered dolls to be their favorite toy.[103] School-aged girls preferred sledding, jumping rope, tag, hide and seek, tagging games, or any other game to playing with dolls.[104] Eleanor Hallowell (granddaughter of Jacob Abbott, author of the *Rollo* series) preferred paper dolls, toy soldiers, or fighting with her brother to dolls.[105] "In my own immediate family," recalled an aunt, "a canvass through three generations of women shows only two doll-lovers out of fifteen little girls, the rest decidedly preferring rough and tumble, active play in the open air." "Wouldn't you rather play with dolls?" someone asked a girl playing horse and driver with her friend. "We'd rather run," replied the pair.

Although historian Karin Calvert found few dolls mentioned in the late nineteenth-century girls' diaries she read, dolls nevertheless played a prominent role in the lives of many. Surprisingly, however, their play behavior was neither submissive nor instinctively maternal; evidence reveals that doll players pushed at the margins of acceptable feminine and genteel behavior in late nineteenth-century America. A wide variety of sources suggests that in their doll play, numerous "hoydenish little girls" expressed anger and aggression nearly as frequently as love and affection.[106] "Of doll-haters, I have known a few," wrote a contributor to *Babyhood* magazine in 1905.[107] George Eliot's fictional heroine, nine-year-old Maggie Tulliver, expresses her rage by hammering nails into her wooden doll's head, beating it against a wall, and grinding it against a rough brick. (In numerous stereographic images, girls used more typical domestic tools, cutting their dolls with scissors or forcing them through clotheswringers.) Punishments often could be particularly brutal. One thirteen-year-old girl broke her doll by knocking it against a window as punishment for crying.[108] A four-year-old girl disciplined her doll by forcing it to eat dirt, stones, and coal.[109] (Swatting and slapping dolls was interpreted by adults as evidence of being spoiled, uncaring, and generally worrisome in stories and poems.)[110]

Although parents perceived doll funerals as an acceptable accommodation to femininity, such was not always the case. In the numerous doll funerals that appear with startling consistency in doll stories, memoirs, and questionnaires, it was not the passive grieving that provided doll players with pleasure.[111] Instead, for some, it was the expression of aggressive feelings and hostile fantasies. According to an article in the *Pittsburgh Post* (and reprinted in *Doll's Dressmaker*), a five-year-old girl purposely broke her doll, then declared with satisfaction, "It was dead."[112] Girls like this one changed the emphasis from cathartic funerals to ritualized executions. Using available kitchen utensils she dug a grave in the backyard and then invited other little girls to do the same. "I have vivid memories of harrowing games with Mary Gordon," wrote Ethel Spencer in her turn-of-the-century memoir, "during which our children [dolls] became desperately ill and died."[113] Though this gruesome scenario bordered on the unacceptable by the end of the nineteenth century, the fascination and determination of the children were not at all unusual. "Funerals were especially popular, with Becky [doll] ever the willing victim," confided one doll player. "No day was too short for a funeral, just so they [my friends] all got home for supper."[114]

Many dolls were buried, but more were both intentionally and unintentionally dismembered. George Eliot remembers that she "only broke those [dolls] . . . that could not stand the test of being undressed, or that proclaimed their unfleshy substance by falling and breaking their noses."[115] Meta Lilienthal's elegant doll could join the rest of her doll family only after becoming soiled.[116]

For some, a doll's worth was determined by its ability to subvert convention and to undermine restrictions. For example, doll parties, considered entirely too sedate for some, were transformed into invigorating activities unlikely to win the approval of adults. Some girls preferred exhilarating "indoor coastings"—sliding down the stairs while sitting on a tea tray—to dull tea parties.[117] Zona Gale and her friend wreaked havoc on their tea party by smashing their unsuspecting dolls to bits.[118] Gale, who became a writer and a feminist, had been consciously determined to live life unencumbered by sex roles. Nor was it the social ritual that appealed to at least one doll player. "I like to eat in small dishes," explained one girl, "because I think the food tastes better."[119]

Through their doll play, girls also enjoyed challenging established authority. One autobiographer recalled deliberately sewing clothes for her doll on Sundays, "quite as on other days," until finally sobered by the warning that "every stitch she sewed on Sunday, she would have to rip out with her teeth when she got to Purgatory." Still, not intending to give up this activity, she decided to learn how to rip out the stitches with her teeth before she got there. The task, however, proved to be so difficult that she gave up sewing on Sundays until her mother purchased a Wilcox and Gibbs chain-stitch sewing machine. Thereafter, she did all her sewing on Sundays after having triumphantly yanked out sample seams with her teeth. "After that, I did all my Sunday sewing on the sewing machine, feeling it would only be an additional pleasure to rip it out in Purgatory, and with a deep satisfaction at having gotten the best of the Devil."[120]

Girls who played with dolls in late nineteenth-century America could develop a sense of self that was anything but submissive. Late nineteenth-century autobiographies reveal that, contrary to the adult version, girls whose dolls fell victim to taunting or teasing boys defended themselves and their dolls instead of seeking male protection. One young girl "burst out" and "flew at" her friend, Harry (who bullied and teased), after he bit a hole in her favorite doll. She "grabbed him by the shoulders, . . . ready to fight to the death for [her] rights, [when] he burst into cries for help. . . . I shall never forget my surprise and triumph as I realized that I conquered—conquered in spite of being small, with a strength I could always command. I only had to set Una Mary free, to let her come, outside, and she could do anything." [121]

By the turn of the century, dolls with their own wardrobes, literature, and ideology had altered the nature of doll play from that of the early years of the nineteenth century. Girls born and raised in middle-class, antebellum households had few dolls, and those were mostly of their own making as prescribed and instructed by a literature directed at mothers and daughters. Making dolls and playing with them had fostered skills useful to character development, self-government, and a more simple domestic economy. In the years after the Civil War, however, dolls proliferated, became more splendid, and their importance in the lives of little girls changed as it increased. Doll stories provided companionship and the development of fantasies, which brought girls beyond the confines of the material world. Girls were encouraged to display the store-bought dolls they received on holidays and from indulgent relatives. The productive and "useful" activities of their mother's generation had left the doll house as it had the American household, gradually replaced by new values and skills in regard to status and kin. Previous generations had learned skills useful to a domestic economy, but girls in the Gilded Age were encouraged to play with their china and bisque dolls in ways that increasingly exhibited the conspicuous display of consumer goods and social status. Nevertheless, girls rejected elaborate dolls for coarse ones, favored black dolls over white ones, resisted play rituals, and preferred physical culture to doll culture. At times, boys challenged sex-role stereotyping and at other times reinforced it. Those girls who resisted patriarchal prescriptions in their play with dolls developed conviction and confidence.

7

The Youngest Fourth Estate

The Novelty Toy Printing Press and Adolescence,

1870–1886

PAULA PETRIK

One of the consequences of the formation of the new white middle class in the Northeast in antebellum America was the lengthening of childhood. Children's longer dependency within the family helped create and support institutions, namely, private and public schools, which provided skills and knowledge for the new white-collar occupations. But the rising sons of the middle class could not spend all their time at study, and hours apart from school became playtime, increasing the need for suitable recreation for adolescents. Besides participating in typical boyish pranks, organized sports, and junior political and reform activities, boys between twelve and eighteen published their own newspapers in which "the youngsters practiced for adulthood in a world all their own."[1] Not only do these amateur journals demonstrate the pervasive influence of contemporary children's authors, but they also reveal a new set of values regarding money, athletic ability, and gender and suggest how both young men and women recast middle-class standards to shape the ideology of their own generation, especially ideas regarding race and gender.

Juvenile newspapers sprang up all over the Northeast during the 1840s

COMPOSITOR AT WORK.

THE PRINTER.

"Now Papa," said Alfred Benson, on the evening of the day on which he had visited the paper-mill; "can you spare a little time to tell me about printing?"

Mr. B. But suppose you were to tell me what you know about it. You have been more than once to the printing office at A—.

Alfred. You know the printing office at A—, is a very small one, and they have only a common press. There were only two men at work, when I was there last.

Illustration of printer at work.

(*From* Trades Described: A Book for the Young *[London: The Religious Tract Society, 1845], Department of Special Collections, Kenneth Spencer Research Library, University of Kansas)* and 1850s as their youthful editors scavenged used type and cast-off composing sticks and put their mothers' abandoned cheese presses back into service. Some teenage pressmen depended on their mechanical skill and copied their machines from engravings of Benjamin Franklin's press.[2] However they were able to gather the tools of their trade, the young editors became part of a vast amateur journalistic pastime; on March 16, 1846, the editor of the Boston *Germ* noted that the city boasted eight juvenile papers and Worcester an equal number.[3] Amateur newspapers continued to be a feature of boys' teen years (and, to a lesser extent, of girls') until 1867, when the invention of the Novelty Press and its imitators brought publishing within financial reach of an even larger number of children. Selling for between fifteen and fifty dollars, depending on the style, the Novelty Press guaranteed professional albeit slow results. For those young people who had the economic wherewithal, the Novelty Press provided the means to test their literary and journalistic talents and organizational abilities.

The advent of the small toy presses, moreover, ushered in the golden age of amateur publishing during the 1870s. Because subscription lists were large and because exchanging papers was an important element in amateur journalism, the hobby spread from the Northeast across the nation, creating a mass culture for teenagers who shared the experience of reading the same stories and debating the same issues.[4] Many of the papers of the 1840s and 1850s generally imitated their adult counterparts by reprinting selections from other periodicals, but the juvenile papers of the 1870s were firmly committed to original work. Bereft of stylistic sophistication—metaphor, symbol, character development, and sometimes plot—the amateur papers and miniature novels provided a forum for young people's thinking as they used a toy to mark the longer time between childhood and adulthood. Because they were novice writers, the authors often copied or, more precisely, plagiarized plots and characters created by their favorite authors: Captain Mayne Reid, Horatio Alger, and especially Oliver Optic.

Of the mid-nineteenth-century authors who wrote for young people Optic (William Taylor Adams) was one of the most popular and prolific. Beginning in 1856 with the publication of the *Boat Club* and through his editing of *Student and Schoolmate* and later in the pages of his own enormously successful *Our Boys and Girls, Oliver Optic's Magazine*, Optic beguiled teenagers with his tales of adventure. Unlike the purely moralistic stories of earlier decades, Optic's stories stood between the didactic tales of Jacob Abbott, which did more to instruct than to entertain, and the violent adventures of the dime novels, which aimed at the cheap entertainment of titillation and sensation. The theme of Optic's books normally involved a solitary boy of between sixteen and eighteen years old who, whether through choice or circumstance, was without parents. In the course of the narrative the boy confronted dangers and people that he bested through "impudence and self-possession." To be sure, Optic did not neglect the moral side of his characters or plot, but his affirmations of honesty and generosity and his condemnations of tobacco, alcohol, and gambling were secondary to the action of the story, in which the boy hero flummoxed his opposition with quick wits and sheer Yankee bluffing. Optic's emphasis on action and on the "smart" aspects of his protagonists later set him at odds with Louisa May Alcott, the *St. Nicholas* establishment, and professional librarians, who criticized his work as sensational, unrealistic, and detrimental to young minds.[5] Optic's work disappeared from library shelves but not from the hearts of his readers; each year he sold thousands of books. For whatever reason, Optic's novels enchanted boys and girls alike, and his fans kept on buying and reading.

For some boys Oliver Optic's influence went beyond casual reading; many who aspired to literary recognition began a conscious program of association and imitation. Almost as soon as Optic's magazine appeared, many of the young writers under their pen names "Alert," "Wide Awake," "Hautboy," "Gold Pen," and "Downsey" began to write to the popular author and submit puzzles, charades, rebuses, and so forth for Optic's "Headwork" department.[6] For many of these puzzlers and for other young amateur authors, Oliver Optic was a patron saint. For his part, Optic encouraged them in their literary and publishing efforts and recognized their achievements.[7] Years later, "Sancho Panza," an early puzzle contributor who had become a deputy postmaster in a western town, indicated some measure of Optic's influence over young men when he recalled

I wrote to you every week in 1868 and 1869, with the usual batch of headwork; and the magazine—you don't know how I prized it! I vowed over and over again always to work for it; and take it as long as I lived. I meant it then; but I didn't know of the busy world ahead that would soon claim me; but though I haven't taken the magazine, I can assure you I have frequently thought of Oliver Optic and those so happy days. I should so love to live them over again! I look back to them as among the happiest of my life. I often think of Tempest, Hautboy, Alert, Quiz, Yorick, Ned Sketchly, and the host of others that rallied around the "Letter Bag" in those halcyon days.[8]

And when "Alert" (Edwin Farlane, Jr.), one of amateur journalism's favorite members, died at the age of twenty in 1870, Optic fondly dedicated his book *Desk and Debit* to the young man.[9] Naturally enough then, these novice writers, as with most writers, adopted another's style and subject until they found their own literary voices.[10] Such was the case with William H. Downes, the "Downsey" of Optic's early puzzlers, who recast Oliver Optic's best-selling *Soldier Boy, or A Tale of the Great Rebellion* (1864) in his own serial story, "Roger Dale" (1871).

Born March 1, 1854, Downes was seventeen·years old when he wrote "Roger Dale," his chronicle of the Civil War. That he should choose *A Soldier Boy* for his model was not simply a matter of caprice; Gettysburg loomed large in Downes's experience just as the Battle of Fredericksburg and the low ebb of Union fortunes had absorbed Optic in *Soldier Boy*. In a "later" biographical essay, written when he was eighteen, Downes noted that his first memories were of northern troops leaving for war and that his first interests involved "the daily history of the campaign" and Gettysburg. "In 1865," he wrote, "my grandfather took me to Getysburg to see the great battlefield. It was the longest journey I had ever taken, and I enjoyed it to the utmost."[11] Born thirty years apart, Optic and Downes shared many of the same attitudes and values. Patriotism ranked high for both, and both attached some weight to principle, although Downes gave it even shorter shrift than Optic. Similarly, both approved of boys' using their wits and their fists to solve problems and attributed their heros' successes to their actions rather than to their moral attributes. Optic's protagonist, Tom Somers, received his military promotions as a consequence of his deeds, but his kind and obliging nature made his premature preferment acceptable to his company. Despite these basic similarities, there are some significant differences in Downes's story, variations that appeared in works by his fellow adolescent publishers and writers that allow a glimpse of the new boy hero, one who possessed a different perspective on the world and who held different values.[12]

First, the most obvious contrast is in Downes's emphasis on economic status. All of Downes's characters are wealthy except for one who is in partnership with his father and merely well-to-do; Optic's Tom Somers comes from modest and endangered means. Optic's rich boy, moreover, drifts into obscurity by the end of *Soldier Boy*, but the millionaire's son in "Roger Dale" becomes a romantic figure in death and remains a well-loved friend. Similarly, in Richard "Humpty Dumpty" Gerner's *The Lord of Monteith, or the Secret of the Red Chamber*, money is a central element. In an odd deathbed scene, Gerner's protagonist listens to his father's last words: "I leave you to a merciless and cold world and naught to brave it but your wealth, keep far from vice and virtue will protect you, shun evil companions, they are like vipers and will rob you of every cent under friendly pretenses."[13] In another of Gerner's miniature novels, *"?", a Tale of Baden-Baden*, the hero styles himself as an "American planter," whose plantation looked on the "fairest landscape of the South."[14] Unlike Optic and his more famous contemporary, Horatio Alger, whose characters rose from rags to respectability, Downes and his peers preferred characters drawn from the elite. When they used the ubiquitous orphan, bootblack, or newsboy, they translated these characters into misplaced merchant princes who had fallen from riches to rags and risen again to riches.[15]

Second and more subtly, an element of athleticism appears in Downes's story that is wholly absent from Optic's writing. Downes's character, even though he is wounded, clears a fence "with a touch of one hand, as he had been accustomed to leap boxes in Chambers Street" and runs, "using the long slouching trot, so breath-saving when a long distance is to be traveled rapidly."[16] In Will H. Dennis's *Dick Marlowe*, the heroes run a virtual marathon in their pursuit of boarding-school burglars. "And he ran off like a deer through the shadows," wrote Dennis, "with Harry close behind. For *twenty minutes* [italics mine] nothing was to be heard but their footfalls as they ran and an occasional word which passed between them."[17] In contrast, Optic's hero slogs through northern Virginia on his way to battle or rides when he can.

Predictably, in both Downes's and Optic's tales no African Americans appear. Although Optic wrote his book just after the announcement of the Emancipation Proclamation in 1863 and although the aftermath of slavery occupied the minds of the reading public, no black appeared in Optic's *Soldier Boy* or in his later works. Similarly, Downes includes no person of color. The same was largely true of other amateur and professional writers. Despite their absence from fiction, African Americans were part of amateur journalism, and their presence among the elected officials of the hobby group occasioned a widespread discussion, revealing a range of adolescent views on race.

In 1878 the amateur journalists grappled with the issue of race as the election of sixteen-year-old Herbert A. Clarke, an African American youth, to the third vice-presidency of the National Amateur Press Association (NAPA) provided the occasion for a long discussion, later known as the Civil Rights Controversy. Thomas Harrison (*Welcome Visitor*, Indianapolis, Indiana), in a somewhat patronizing fashion, remembered his meeting with Clarke at the Chicago convention:

> While in the club room, on the first day of the NAPA convention, a friend of mine came to me and said that there was a "colored fellow, outside who said he was an amateur." "Why doesn't he come in?" I asked, and my friend replied that he had requested him to enter, but that "the poor fellow, with tears in his eye," had said he did not like to, because he was afraid the boys would not like it, on account of his color. I mentioned this to several near me, and we went out and hunted the boy up, greeted him warmly, and brought him in with us, and introduced him right and left. This was the first introduction of Herbert A. Clarke, then editor of the *Boys' Argus* of Mt. Vernon, Indiana, since made famous by a combination of circumstances, to the amateur fraternity. He was cordially greeted by us, and made to feel that an amateur was respected as an amateur, whatever his color.[18]

The circumstances of Clarke's election revolved around the byzantine requirements of the NAPA constitution. Proxy voting was part of the constitution, but at most amateur gatherings these votes almost invariably were disallowed on technicalities or charges of corruption. Although George M. Carr (*North Carolina Amateur*, Rose Hill, North Carolina) and Louis Schliep had been nominated, neither had attended the gathering. Clarke had. In a surprising decision, the assembled body of forty boys elected Clarke, and the response from the rest of amateurdom divided along sectional lines and filled the columns of their editorials for the next two years with debate over civil rights.

Most of the southern boys rehearsed racist and white-supremacist arguments in one form or another. For the southern partisans, the chief obstacles to Clarke's membership and office holding were not political rights but social equality. Edward Oldham, "Odd Trump," reminded the association that "we of the South know more concerning the creatures who were once in slavery, than do our brothers of the North, and it is our advice and request that something be done against their admittance into our national association at least." Oldham further advised that integrating NAPA would divide the organization irrevocably. The editor of *Our Free Blade* argued against the social equality of blacks and saw the event as an insult to the other candidates. George M. Carr, the losing candidate, frankly propounded the ideology of racial inferiority and proposed a "separate but equal" amateur press association for black amateurs. He ended his piece with a frank call to secession: "From this day onward we declare ourselves seceded from the National Amateur Press Association (?) and do earnestly hope that all who coincide with us will lend their assistance to establish a white boys' Amateur Press Association and let the negroes and their equals have the one which they have already taken possession of." [19]

Clarke's northern supporters countered somewhat naively with arguments of simple justice, honor, equality of opportunity, and personal knowledge of Clarke's character. Styling themselves "Jeffersonian Democrats," they viewed the southerners simply as bigots who laid claim to outmoded notions of chivalry, honor, and Confederate politics to defend their position. The lessons of the Civil War were uppermost in the memories of some. "The Southern fire-eating rebels," one wrote, "whom the North condescended to whip several years ago and of whom the brilliant youths of North Carolina are fair samples, have not yet lost their ideas of 'chivalry,' and probably with all the persistency of bigots and with all the characteristics of the fool will adhere to them."

But it was Herbert Clarke himself in his own paper (*Le Bijou*, Cincinnati, Ohio) who advanced the most articulate arguments and countered his detractors with forceful rejoinders, demonstrating breadth of knowledge and intellectual sophistication. Initially, however, he pled his case on the basis of individual achievement by pointing out that he had come up through the amateur ranks the hard way by submitting puzzles to the commercial juvenile magazines and then by successfully sending material to the amateur papers themselves. Clarke asserted that he came from a distinguished free black family who had fought for American principles since the Revolutionary War. Still, Clarke maintained, had he come from a slave background, "nonetheless would [he] demand the right to stand in the dom upon an equality with any." [20] When the anti-Clarke contingent, not above using the most vicious of stereotypes, charged that Clarke and his fellow blacks were "not morally trustworthy," especially with a neighbor's wife, Clarke shot back that his critics were on delicate ground in this regard and reminded his readers of the miscegenation that accompanied slavery. His critics were, according to Clarke, "expounders of that southern morality, which has never been wedded to any decent principle."[21] And Clarke was not above twitting his southern opponents with sexual innuendo: "Ed Oldham favored us with a tintype of himself lately. We've placed it in our album opposite our Black gal's photo. Sh—Sh—Ed don't run—She won't hurt you."[22]

Shortly, however, Clarke moved away from a purely individual claim for equality and began to argue for equality for African Americans as a class. In answering Harry Legler, who had asserted that "the negro race [was] the most detestable one in existence," Clarke pointed out that the "detestable race" had formed the capital and labor of the South and that environment affected a people's progress. "The disposition and character of a race," he wrote, "depend greatly upon the surroundings and, however detestable the negro race may be, its condition is the handiwork of the South." Moreover, slavery had affected African Americans' progress by denying them education, and for Clarke, education was the linchpin of African American progress. He used statistics in his editorial to demonstrate that levels of educational funding and attendance were much lower in the South and had a great impact on the region's black residents who formed the bulk of the population. Clarke also saw that his race bore some responsibility for this state of affairs. "So long as the negro suffers himself to be oppressed," Clarke claimed, "he deserves the title of 'pretty good nigger,' but perchance obtaining a little knowledge and daring to assert his . . . dormant manhood he will earn the title detestable because of his assertiveness."[23]

In 1879 seventeen-year-old Benjamin Pelham, editor of the *Venture* (Detroit, Michigan), joined NAPA and the civil rights discussion, supporting Clarke's position.[24] More personal in his opposition, Pelham hammered away at the southern editors' claims, exposing their hypocrisy. In response to an editorial declaring that the South was the backbone of the nation, Pelham wrote, "You have only to think of Hamburg Butler, of the numerous Ku Klux bands, of the White Leaguers to see how far he is justified in making that statement."[25] At another time Pelham took on James O'Connell and by extension Irish Americans when he mounted an attack on O'Connell's anti–African American stance. Essentially, Pelham argued that O'Connell's alliance with the southern faction stemmed from a personal animosity involving some rejected poems and not from a political belief.[26]

By 1880 the controversy still lingered, and the northern boys had refined their arguments, in short, retreating from their former liberal positions. *The Egyptian Star* (Cairo, Illinois) and its editor encapsulated this view under the unfortunate headline, "Damn the Nigger." He addressed his audience:

> [You] speak of "the admittance of negroes" as if it were a general and continual occurrence. They don't seem to remember that Mr. Clarke is perhaps the only colored boy engaged in journalism. They don't seem to consider that in admitting him into fellowship they are simply recognizing his abilities and encouraging his endeavors. . . . The admittance of negroes to our organization will not be general, never fear. . . . His color is but a shade darker than a white person. . . . The negroes will not take possession of our association, but mark you so long as Mr. Clarke—who entered it at the solicitation of its members—so long as he commands respect just so long will he receive it at the hands of those who compose our representative association.[27]

Early on, the *Egyptian Star*'s editor along with other like-minded northern editors articulated the familiar ideology of tokenism and its rationales, accordingly premising their argument on the exceptional black.

Although others were less frank than the *Egyptian Star* about their position on civil rights, some wished that Clarke and his supporters were less inflammatory and insistent. Clarke clearly knew what was at stake and tolerated no liberal, genteel posturing. When the female editor of the *Pen* suggested that the subject of civil rights be handled "delicately," Clarke praised her fearless denunciation of wrong on other subjects but took to task her caution on the matter of race. "Reluctantly we think her one of that class of Americans who would restrict the American negro to a little corner in life by himself. . . . The time is now past when in defining the future of the American negro, it is to be narrowed down to the sphere of his own race."[28]

Pelham's paper also noted the tensions between white women's aspirations and African American progress in its sometimes strident opposition to female participation in NAPA and women's rights in general. In 1882 the *Venture* published "The Female Phalanx," an antiequal-suffrage editorial characterized by distinct claims to divinely ordained and scientifically proven male superiority. The editorial writer, relying heavily on contemporary scientific research into the relationship of brain physiology and gender, filled his essay with such passages as

> if woman were allowed to appropriate to herself the faintest glimmering of scientific research, she must know that it shows a lack of taste, not to mention the absence of other qualifications to jostle her "intellectual superior" into the mud. But as she marches a "century behind" him in these matters, does it not behoove that lofty, masculine superiority to be lenient toward her natural, and thereby unavoidable trespasses?" [29]

On a more personal level, the *Venture* made cruel sport of the young female editors when Libbie Adams ("Nettie Sparkle"), editor of the *Youthful Enterprise* (Elmira, New York), nominated Eva Britton, editor of the *Hurricane* (Charleston, South Carolina), for a NAPA office. "By the way, Nettie," wrote Pelham, "are you, too, trying to convulse amateurdom? The nomination of Miss Eva E. Britton is enough to draw a smile from, from—well from almost anything." [30]

If African Americans were absent from Downes's "Roger Dale" and Optic's *Soldier Boy*, the same was not true for women. Women assume a larger, far different role in Downes's tale and those of his scribbling young brethren from the women in Optic's fiction. For Downes and his contemporaries, although their heroines tend to appear at odd moments and circumstances, women are exciting, autonomous, physical characters who add important action to the story. Downes's heroine, Agnes Chaloner, is an independent young woman who forsakes her skulking family to take work as a nurse in a Union field hospital behind Confederate lines. In Richard Gerner's story, *A Tale of Baden-Baden*, the young author seems deliberately to subvert the nineteenth-century female role embodied in the "cult of true womanhood." He introduces Beatrice, the object of the hero's infatuation, in the process of breaking a casino bank. "And here she sat gold-thirsty, and unwomanly; passionate, excited and heated," Gerner wrote. "She behaved madly flashing with wit and brilliancy." [31] Beatrice is hardly the typical "true woman" of the nineteenth century, but the hero falls in love with her and fights a duel to avenge an insult to her honor, although Beatrice seems perfectly capable of handling herself in any situation. In *Edith, the Girl Detective*, Dave and Dolph, the twin teenage detectives, find much to admire in Edith, who disguises herself as a boy clerk, engages in a brawl, and slips into a Chicago gambling den to trap her larcenous cousin.[32] The boys' literary delight in independent women sometimes took a frankly sexual turn; the *Boy's Journal* invited "gay boys" to send fifteen cents for "those nude and festive photographs" or a quarter for the "Lola Montez gay book."[33]

To be sure not all the boys agreed with the *Yankee Land*'s position that "the world has changed, and the time has fallen into the dead past when woman is to be chained at home and made the slave of a man, who, as is often the case, is not worthy of her."[34] In J. A. Fynes's *Love's Discovery*, Lily White, an astronomer and the object of the hero's affection, trades her discovery of the eighth moon of Jupiter and a handsome astronomy prize for the hero's love. "God bless my cousin," muses the hero, "her woman's wit was ever fertile, even inventive; for her sake, for her love I allowed it to be said that I had discovered the eighth satellite of grandiose Jupiter." Lily replies that she has made the sacrifice for Hal and that his love, his "whole confiding passionate love," will repay her. Despite the story's emphasis on female self-sacrifice, Fynes portrays Lily as an accomplished scientist.[35] For Optic, unlike his intellectual young followers, women existed as photographs or appeared in brief, uncomfortable meetings where they were notable for their "silvery screams."

Having once created their bold new heroines, the young editors encountered flesh and blood counterparts of their fictional creations. Though far fewer in number, women entered the ranks of amateur journalism almost as soon as they acquired presses. Because girls were rare among the youthful press corps, they garnered a disproportionate share of attention and served as the focus for boys' thoughts and opinions about gender. Eventually, fact proved more difficult than fiction. Even as the boys delighted in their new fictional women, they were unwilling entirely to dispense with traditional gender roles. Reacting to girls' greater participation in the amateur scene, the boys increasingly resorted to conventional nineteenth-century definitions of manhood and womanhood in the editorial columns of their papers.

During the early 1870s, the years when young men like William H. Downes described new perceptions of women, the boy editors seemed more willing to include women in their group on an equal footing. When the Lukens girls, publishers of *Little Things* (Brinton, Pennsylvania), attended the National Amateur Press Association meeting in 1873, the boys, pleased with their attendance, enrolled them as members in the organization immediately. In the editorial columns of their sheet, the Lukens sisters affirmed the general egalitarian themes that appeared in boys' fiction. "We think," they wrote, "most people are beginning to give girls the credit which is due them of being pretty nearly as smart as boys." The Lukens were, however, quick to point out that in addition to their publishing they were responsible for all the housework.[36] One young editor, Virginia J. Stephens of the *Pen* (Springfield, Massachusetts), sounded a frank women's-rights note when in one issue she advocated equal pay for equal work and in the next stressed the need for both classical and practical female education.[37] And when a boy editor invited Belle Mantates and Franny Pringle of the *Dreamer* (Jackson, Michigan) to defend pull-back dresses, they replied that they did not think a defense necessary. The dress, for the girls, possessed distinct advantages. "No boy can successfully disguise himself in a pull-back dress," they wrote playfully. "Our wardrobes will be safer on this account, and the dangers of amateur editors *escaping* will be less."[38]

By the late 1870s the early generation of young men and women had given up their adolescent journalism and passed into adulthood to be replaced by the next group of eager editors. Though the national organization had been generally receptive to girls in the early 1870s, matters were very different when NAPA revised its constitution in 1876. Young male editors enthusiastically supported the recruitment of women into the amateur ranks as writers and puzzlers but were far less comfortable with girls as editors or critics and were frankly opposed to their participation in the politics of the national organization. As long as girls acted in a subsidiary role, the boys were content; when they did not, the boys attempted to "put them in their places"—and not always kindly. Usually, the boys emerged from these contests the worse for their efforts. In 1882, for example, a boy editor dismissed Eva Britton as a "small bit of female vanity." Eva replied, "Haven't we the right to be vain? We are under the impression this characteristic belongs to ladies as much as bravery to the opposite sex. One thing, though, my friend, we are not vain enough to have our picture taken in a cabinet with twenty others and offer the entire number for forty-one cents. Tra, la, la."[39] Later, when a Virginia paper erroneously reported that Britton had been arrested in New Orleans for obtaining money under false pretenses as she enrolled additional sub-scribers for the *Hurricane*, the *North Carolina Amateur* (Lenoir, North Caro-lina) commented: "We never had a very exalted opinion of Miss Britton and her paper, and we are glad for the sake of our cause, that she did not claim allegiance to it."[40] Britton responded with a triumphal tour through the country, gathering subscriptions as she went.

Various superficial resentments against female editors crystallized in the early 1880s when more girls entered amateur journalism in the wake of an enthusiastic article published in *St. Nicholas*. The newcomers im-mediately understood that they were disenfranchised from the major business of youthful journalism because they could not participate in the electioneering, political reporting, and editorializing attached to NAPA's annual meeting.[41] Originating with Zelda Arlington of the *Violet* (Cin-cinnati, Ohio), the organizing drive to create the Ladies Amateur Press Association (LAPA) for girls involved in writing, editing, and publish-ing began in 1884 with a call to band together in mutually beneficial and sustaining sisterhood.[42]

Concomitant with her organizing effort solely on women's behalf, Ar-lington pressed the national organization for the admission of women, and in 1885 at the group's meeting in San Francisco the male member-ship obliged, after a fashion. In an amendment to the constitution, the association voted to admit girls without the payment of initiation fees or annual dues. Arlington and other female editors correctly perceived that the boys' action guaranteed them no equality of membership. Arlington and her supporters wanted the right to membership, not membership on sufferance. She wrote:

> Let us feel that we have a right to every privilege that is given to the young men of the association. . . . Can we as ladies accept such gallantry and compliments and maintain our pride and dignity? Is it right to place us under obligations to the association and members, when we wish to be accepted as any other person? Is it right to make us feel that we are not equal, active, working members, who assist in supporting the cause?

Borrowing from the rhetoric of the American Revolution, Edith May Dowe summarized the girls' position in the LAPA column: "We desire no taxa-tion without representation and no representation without taxation. Let us have equality,—and none of this false stuff yclept 'gallantry.' "[43] Without the payment of dues, the girls understood that they would always be second-class citizens in NAPA.

Zelda Arlington's advocacy of women's equality went beyond the issues involved in the membership fracas; her personal life also highlighted the young editors' struggle with ideas about masculinity and femininity. As the very young wife of Edwin B. Swift, a young dentist who also had an interest in presswork, Zelda elected to retain her maiden name on the masthead of the *Violet*. As a result, she received several "spoony" letters from her fellow editors. When she revealed that she was married, her amorous correspondents in an effort to cover their faux pas denounced Arlington.[44] Zebbie Hunt of the *Mirror* (San Francisco, California), among others, quickly came to Arlington's aid, defending her right to privacy and condemning the boys' immaturity. Hunt wrote, "What if she is married? That is HER business not YOURS, and if she chose to play a harmless joke on a lot of boys, they should have kept still and not have told it on themselves. Boys we say, because a boy with any manliness about him would have had more respect for himself than to do such a thing."[45] In the end the girls' efforts prevailed, and in 1886 they convinced NAPA to admit them as full, dues-paying members. But by that point, the character of NAPA was changing; less of an independent organization for adolescents, it had become more of a hobby group for university-age men and women and older adults. In any event, admission of young women to NAPA marked an important political victory, albeit a minor one.

In editorials and in the discussions surrounding women's admittance to NAPA, young women editors confronted subtle and not-so-subtle discrimination. As the teenage girls sorted out their arguments, they took increasingly strong positions and mounted critiques, in some cases far more penetrating than the rank and file of their older counterparts in the national women's-rights movement. The boys argued against these determined girls and for the most part supported aspects of traditional womanhood even as they articulated the idea of an independent, sensuous woman. In short, when both boys and girls explored their ideas about manliness and womanliness, they discovered that both sexes were more than willing to dispense with traditional ideologies regarding gender roles, but they were not quite so willing to give up their expectations of ladylike and gentlemanly conduct. For twentieth-century readers, the debate over the civilities of equality among the amateur journalists should come as no surprise. That it occurred so early, prompted such a wide-ranging discussion, and resulted in the girls' triumph may indeed partially explain the renewed participation of women in the woman-suffrage movement at the turn of the century.

Most historians who have discussed children or adolescents in the nineteenth century have imputed little influence to either group's control over their own futures. Most practitioners have confined their discussions to socialization and measured its success by the extent to which youngsters conformed or not to parental wishes and plans. Others have noted structural changes and argued that the absence of land, economic transformation, or demographic alterations have constrained one generation's strategies. But the amateur newspapers produced by the owners of Novelty Toy Printing Presses show that nineteenth-century adolescence was much more complex than explanations of socialization involving structural shifts or parental exertions. The issues taken up by the young journalists capture young men and women in the mutually educative process of interpreting for themselves the complicated array of relationships in their society and reveal them in the act of exploring the possibilities of their own perceptions.

The Novelty Toy Printing Press and other similar presses literally put the power of the press into youngsters' hands and allowed them to debate difficult issues before a wide audience of their contemporaries. Although Clarke, Pelham, and their peers reflected society's diverse views on race, the amateur press allowed the editors to grapple with the problem of racial equality in post–Reconstruction America in terms of a personal and an intellectual dilemma. In doing so, the boys not only marshaled their own politics—for better or for worse—but also articulated and anticipated attitudes and policies that would govern black and white relations until the mid-twentieth century. Similarly, the discussion of women's rights allowed adolescents to explore the complexities involved in achieving gender equality, and they too anticipated cultural paradoxes that would travel into the next century. Thus, the debates among amateur journalists over civil rights and later over women's rights demonstrate the continuity and discontinuity involved in adolescent socialization and suggest how a toy might assist youngsters in assembling the raw material of their experience in constructing a personal system of belief and practice.

The connections between amateur journalism and domestic policy might seem strained, yet they are not so tenuous as might be imagined.

The post-Reconstruction years saw the persistence of the Ku Klux Klan in the South, despite its prohibition, and the enactment of Jim Crow legislation; the history of amateur journalism mirrored this development. Shortly after Clarke's election, several friends of the defeated southern candidate formed a secret association—the Amateur Anti-Negro Admission Association (AAAA), aimed at preventing the admission of African Americans to amateur press organizations. The AAAA was ultimately credited with inserting the word "white" in the constitution of the Columbian Amateur Journalism Association and in an ironic twist was also responsible for revealing yet again the racism of those northern amateurs who espoused the admission of blacks.[46]

During the same period, however, African American political groups, self-improvement societies, and educational associations became a significant part of African American life, and the careers of the African American amateur journalists, too, reflected this evolution. Herbert A. Clarke, who had taught summers in Mississippi schools during his career as an amateur journalist, maintained both his interest in journalism and his vocation as a teacher. He founded the *Daily Searchlight* (Muskogee, Oklahoma), the first African American paper in Indian Territory, and ended his career as principal of Frederick Douglass School in Columbia, Missouri.[47] Benjamin Pelham, too, kept faith with his politics. In 1883 Pelham, his brother, and two friends founded the weekly *Plaindealer* (Detroit, Michigan) as a successor to the *Venture*. An adult, professional paper, the *Plaindealer* became a well-known voice for black affairs and politics in the Midwest and provided the impetus for a Colored Men's State Convention in 1884 and later for a national convention. Pelham also led a successful campaign for the election of an African American to the Republican National Convention held later in 1884. After the demise of the *Plaindealer* in 1893 in the midst of national financial stringencies, Pelham joined Wayne County government, becoming in 1906 the county accountant, the highest nonelective local office.[48]

Although William "Downsey" Downes and his peers did not reject their parents' views in toto, they experimented with different relationships with women—relationships that included female autonomy and sexuality—and described a boundless confidence in their bodies and minds, bodies that could seemingly run forever without tiring and minds that could sustain a dramatic financial reversal and contrive a miraculous recovery of status and wealth. In their amateur stories, the boys neither defined success synonymously with moral virtue nor relied solely on virtue to solve problems or to defeat their opponents. Success equaled commercial prosperity; problem solving became the combination of cunning and force. The girls, too, attempted different relationships with men and tested their intellectual capacity. Just as the African American editors did, the early proponents of women's rights kept faith with their adolescent politics. Downes, the creator of Agnes Chaloner, Union nurse, in the final number of his paper, the *Boy's Advertiser*, reported that his studies and other responsibilities precluded his carrying on the paper. In the same message he also observed that he had been elected secretary of the local woman-suffrage association.[49]

Numerous folk sayings, various proverbs, and several poetic couplets related to childrearing point out that "as the twig is bent, so grows the tree." Implicit is the idea that twigs and children inevitably respond to external stimuli and mature accordingly. Boys and girls, unlike twigs, are not passive. Certainly the literary tyros of the 1870s showed themselves to be active participants in their own socialization as they confronted the issues of their time. Historians have overlooked the most obvious of clues: Children and adolescents have had more command over their lives in times past than their elders or their researchers have suspected.

8

The Homefront Children's Popular Culture

Radio, Movies, Comics—Adventure, Patriotism, and

Sex-Typing

WILLIAM M. TUTTLE, JR.

"Mom, what was on the radio before the war started?" one of the home-front girls asked. Hers was not an isolated question; children's radio adventure programs during World War II were integral to their homefront experiences and had a memorable cultural impact on these boys and girls. "I tried to never miss 'Captain Midnight,'" wrote a homefront boy. "He was constantly chasing down Nazi spies." Captain Midnight had taken an oath, to which many of his listeners also subscribed, "to save my country from the dire peril it faces or perish in the attempt." Other radio adventure shows were "The Shadow," "The Green Hornet," "Gangbusters," "Jack Armstrong—the All American Boy," "Hop Harrigan," "Dick Tracy," "Don Winslow of the Navy," "The Lone Ranger," "Tom Mix," "Sky King," "Terry and the Pirates," and "Superman." Many of the radio heroes were young—really, not much older than their audience—such as Jack Armstrong, a high-school student, and Hop Harrigan, "America's ace of the airways," an eighteen-year-old aviator who fought the enemy and constantly escaped capture while dodging bullets. Moreover, the radio villains were vicious and truly despicable. Jack Armstrong battled the Vul-

*Photograph of mother and children sent to father
overseas during World War II, ca. 1943.
(Collection of the author)*

ture and the Silencer, and Captain Midnight's "arch rival" was Ivan Shark, who was first "a Russian mastermind" in 1940 but during the war became part of "the oriental peril." Shark repeatedly escaped, and as late as 1949 Captain Midnight was still in pursuit. While some heroes operated abroad, others, such as Superman and the Green Hornet, fought the war at home, tracking down spies and saboteurs and functioning essentially as urban vigilantes.[1]

Whatever their mission, most of the radio "superheroes and super-sleuths" shared one characteristic: They were male. There were far fewer women adventure heroes; women usually starred not in these shows but in daytime serials such as "Stella Dallas," "Portia Faces Life," "Our Gal Sunday," and "Ma Perkins." One of the few crime-drama heroines was Little Orphan Annie, and although some of the male heroes such as Jack Armstrong and Captain Midnight had girls for sidekicks, their roles were subordinate, much as was the Lone Ranger's faithful Native American or the Green Hornet's loyal Filipino valet. Interestingly, it was two soap operas, "Our Gal Sunday" and "The Romance of Helen Trent," with an audience largely of women, which had positive black characters, one a serviceman who spoke movingly—and frequently—of his loyalty to the United States, the other a doctor who saved Helen Trent's life.[2]

America's radio adventure shows had a moral tone similar in its righteousness to the war games that the homefront children played. Good confronted evil, and justice prevailed. In this spirit, the radio shows focused on the heinous Germans and Japanese and the need to defeat them, and they exhorted the children to collect scrap materials, to buy War Bonds, and to plant victory gardens. In 1943, for example, listeners to "Dick Tracy" took the five-point pledge to combat waste, vowing "to save water, gas and electricity, to save fuel oil and coal, to save my clothes, to save Mom's furniture, to save my playthings." These girls and boys had the satisfaction of having their names placed on the Victory Honor Roll, which, the show's announcer guaranteed, would be read by General Dwight D. Eisenhower at his headquarters. Also in 1943 more than a million children joined the Jack Armstrong Write-a-Fighter Corps, pledging to write once a month to a service person as well as to collect scrap and to tend victory gardens. But most of all, the shows' messages reaffirmed the nation's homefront patriotism. Every week during the war, the western hero Tom Mix fought spies and saboteurs on his show, so he was a credible spokesperson on V-E Day, May 8, 1945, when he told his listeners,

"We've shown Hitler and his gang that we know how to lick bullies and racketeers, but we've still got a big job to do . . . fighting the Japs."[3]

To appreciate the impact of radio during wartime, it is important to remember that as in other cognitive areas the impact varied depending upon the child's age. According to a study of radio in education, between the ages of four and seven a child began "to take an active, continuous interest in radio entertainment," including requesting particular programs and listening intently. By age six the child had become "an habitual listener," who not only could identify the characters but also could imitate them and who, according to one study, "could enter freely into fantasy and whimsy" and use radio as "an exciting realm for imaginative wanderings." At age nine or ten, however, interest in fairy tales flagged before the escapades of the homefront radio heroes. As this study concluded, these children's desire for "more realism or pseudorealism" took precedence, and they demanded "greater verisimilitude in situation and character."[4]

Homefront children, who listened to radio an average of fourteen hours a week, had their special times to tune in. On weekday afternoons, the standard children's fare was "blood-and-thunder melodrama." Between about 4:30 and 6:00, they listened to "Jack Armstrong," "Captain Midnight," and other shows, expressing their gratitude by eating "Wheaties, the Breakfast of Champions," drinking Ovaltine, the drink for "young, red-blooded Americans," and consuming the products of the other advertisers. They also bought the premiums offered by the shows, such as Captain Midnight's "Code-o-graph," with which children decoded messages from the Secret Squadron. "You are the keen-eyed fliers of tomorrow," stated one of the messages, "the skippers of . . . atomic powered ships that will girdle the world. . . . America needs you—healthy, alert, and well trained to guard her future. . . ." Of all the radio heroes, Superman was probably the most popular—and perhaps the most imitated by children—partly because the show had "considerable physical action and fighting in exciting, fast-moving episodes." An overnight sensation when he was introduced in 1938, Superman vigorously fought the enemy, whether mobsters or the Germans and Japanese. Larger than life, Superman provided assurance of righteousness. Parental objections to this hero rested on other grounds. "Parents find it noisy," an article in *Child Study* reported, but this was another "factor which children seem to enjoy." Superman's extraordinary gifts included long-distance hearing, X-ray vision, and supersonic speed; and he battled against such societal evils as racial intolerance and juvenile delinquency. Children had other favorite listening times as well. On weekdays, for example, from 10:00 A.M. to mid-afternoon were the soap operas, which, like the other shows, "went to war." Children feigned sickness and stayed home to listen to the serials. A popular listening time for boys was Friday evening when the boxing matches were followed by "The Bill Stern Sports Show." Both genders enjoyed the Saturday morning shows "Grand Central Station" and "Let's Pretend," which told fairy tales about kings and queens and about princes rescuing "beauteous maidens" from "witches, dragons, gnomes, dwarfs, and other mythical fauna." There were plenty of popular family shows too, and everyone gathered around to listen to singers such as Bing Crosby and Kate Smith and to such comedians as Fred Allen, Jack Benny, Bob Hope, and Edgar Bergen, whose shows topped the "Hooper's ratings." Other favorites with all members of the family included musical programs and mystery shows as well as a new genre, exemplified by "The Aldrich Family" and "Meet Corliss Archer," that probed teenagers' problems with love, school, and their parents.[5]

During the war, radio entered the children's lives significantly in another way; it conveyed the war news. Indeed, as one of the homefront girls queried her mother, "What did the news have to talk about when a war was not going on?" Or as another girl asked, "Has there always been war? Has there ever been other news besides war news?" A survey conducted in November 1942 estimated that three-fourths of the people used the radio as their major source of information about hostilities. Rural and urban children alike vividly remembered listening to the war news, but everywhere the decorum expected of the children was the same: Be quiet. "When the news was on," one of the girls wrote, "we did not make a sound." And children recalled the seriousness of their parents as they bent forward to listen; sometimes the room was dark except for the glow of the radio. Among the popular newscasters were Gabriel Heater, H. V. Kaltenborn, and Walter Winchell. Some of the broadcasts, such as those by Edward R. Murrow from London, were live transmissions, and after listening to the news, families updated their war maps by moving the pins showing the locations of battles. Children in Cincinnati had their own news program, with the station supplying world maps and tiny flags on pins to the boys and girls; each afternoon, the "announcer would read the war news and tell us where to insert the proper flag pin." Georgia Brazil's father operated a restaurant in Beatrice, Nebraska. "Everything at the restaurant came to a halt at news time," she recalled, "so Daddy could listen" and then update the map hanging on the wall. Georgia also remembered wondering "what could possibly fill up the allotted time for news when the war was over?"[6]

Radio provided material for the children's fantasies. And even though television, which saw its first transmission in 1927, was not commercially broadcast during the war, some people were already worrying about the effects of "blind broadcasting" on children. Would children stop using their imaginations? As Rudolph Arnheim, the psychologist, warned before the war, "The words of the story-teller . . . , the voices of dialogue, the complex sounds of music conjure up worlds of experience and thought that are easily disturbed by the undue addition of visual things." Arnheim's apprehension was not groundless; postwar research showed that radio stimulated the child's imagination "significantly more" than television did.[7]

As for the imagination, wartime parents, teachers, police officials, and child-guidance experts worried that, if anything, radio overstimulated children's fantasies, encouraging them to commit antisocial acts. This was not a new fear; public apprehension about radio violence had first risen in the 1930s. During the war critics pointed out that the "radio crime dramas" featured violence in the form of murder, not to mention sabotage, robbery, arson, assault, and drug peddling. Sound effects amplified these crimes, "with nothing left to the imagination," complained one critic. "One hears the thud of the lead pipe against the head of the victim as well as the resulting crashing of the skull and his blood-curdling shrieks for help and mercy." Another critic argued that these homefront children suffered from "addiction" so acute that at night "they dream about killings and have fears of kidnapings." The critics' chief concern was radio's impact on boys; the debate only marginally addressed girls' fantasy lives and the possibility of radio's destructive impact on their behavior. An article entitled "*His* Ear to the Radio," for example, voiced foreboding about the future of the boy who, after listening to his radio shows, "may sit brooding over the terrors, refuse to eat his meal, fight against going to bed; and when he does get to sleep, toss restlessly until morning."[8]

Still, the girls as well as the boys listened to the radio adventure and crime shows; in fact, the girls' programming preferences were similar to the boys'. Although there is a paucity of studies on the gender differences in children's listening habits during the war, one such study—of children in the fifth through the seventh grades in New Rochelle, New York—concluded "that, on the whole, girls were almost as interested in crime and mystery shows as boys." But the study also observed that even though the boys and the girls both "liked stories of the lives of successful men and women," the boys "had a tendency to look upon the detective or the 'superman' as a hero while the girls preferred stories presenting the 'good mother' or the 'nurse' or the 'faithful wife' as a heroine." It seems likely, then, that the girls and boys listened to the same programs but heard different things. There are no definitive findings, however; sadly, the handful of other studies of the homefront children's favorite shows examined age as a variable, but none considered gender even tangentially.[9]

Yet gender differences were evident in all areas of "the people's" culture. During the war, for example, two of the loudest boosters of American patriotism, not to mention two fundamental shapers of sex-role images, were advertising and popular music. On the homefront, advertising both reinforced patriotism and exploited it. Many ads urged Americans to do their part. "Who gets hurt if you buy gas in the black market?" asked one ad. "Will you give a pint of life insurance?" asked another in an appeal for blood donors. Most of the wartime ads, however, sold not the war effort and service to country but the products of the marketplace—everything from breakfast cereals, eyeglasses, and liquor to cigarettes, electric ranges, and vitamin pills. "What was offensive in peace time," wrote Raymond Rubicam, himself a leading advertising executive, "was ten times more so in war." In selling products, the ad agencies presented an idealized, sex-typed American society.[10]

Regardless of the product, the wartime ads presented the viewer with drawings and photos intended to appeal to "the reader's patriotic interest in the war effort": pictures of tanks, airplanes, and other war equipment as well as of civilian trucks and tractors "in the service of the country"; pictures of busy factories and farms as well as of air, land, and sea battles; and "scenes portraying the desirability of . . . the American way of life." Likewise, carefully selected patriotic symbols adorned the ads, such as Uncle Sam or his hat, the eagle, a minuteman, the "V" sign, red, white, and blue colors, and, of course, the flag. Targeted mainly at women, the ads' jingles and slogans were predictably patriotic. "In times like these serve hearty breakfasts," stated an ad for a pancake mix. "Uncle Sam's workers must be well fed. Do your part for national defense right in your own kitchen." An ad for hats urged women to wear "Victory colors—let your hat be brave, bright, a banner of your courage." A store advertising its "lower prices" announced: "Thrift is no longer a private virtue. It is a patriotic duty." And lest they forget, a cosmetics ad told America's women: "Your first duty is your beauty—America's inspiration—morale on the home front is the woman's job."[11]

As for the music of wartime, it too was patriotic. The homefront children sang all the service songs, and they thrilled to hear Kate Smith sing "God Bless America." They played 78 rpm records and listened to music on the radio. One boy in Brooklyn delighted in cranking up his grandmother's RCA Victrola "and moving the metal arm . . . on to the record to play 'Remember Pearl Harbor' and 'We're Gonna Kill the Dirty Little Jap.' . . . I marched around the Victrola for hours." If the songs were not rousingly patriotic or jingoistic, they were sentimental ballads reflecting not only the mood of sadness and loneliness of couples being separated by the war but also the sex-typed scenario of women waiting while their men fought abroad. "Don't sit under the apple tree with anyone else but me," enjoined an exceedingly popular number, "'til I come marching home." Children knew the words to this song and to "I'll Never Smile Again," "I'll Walk Alone," "Sentimental Journey," "When Johnny Comes Marching Home," and "The White Cliffs of Dover." Sometimes these sentiments became unbearable to mothers whose husbands were overseas. One girl recalled that every time her mother heard "I'll Be Home for Christmas," it "totally reduced" her to tears. "It got so I was forbidden to play the radio when she was within earshot." Another girl's mother loathed hearing "White Christmas" on the radio. Besides patriotic songs and sentimental ballads, there were novelty songs, most of them silly and some of them incomprehensible, such as "Mairzy Doats" or with lyrics like "Send up in smokio the city of Tokyo, / Show the Nipponese that Uncle Sam does not jokio!"[12]

Whether broadcasting music or adventure shows, the radio was a vital link to the homefront for children. And because numerous homefront girls and boys have expressed pride in being the last pretelevision children, it is difficult not to speculate about the different effects on childhood of homefront radio and postwar television. Homefront children generally listened in silence to the radio while the parents discussed the news among themselves. Sometimes the parents answered the children's questions, painting visual images that the children took away with them from the broadcasts. Thus, the homefront children tended to be in a passive position compared to their elders. But with television, the parents ceased to be the major interpreters of events, the main filterers of the news. As the anthropologist Margaret Mead observed, "For the first time the young are seeing history made *before* it is censored by their elders." Yet there was a downside for the television generations born after the war. Joshua Meyrowitz, the psychologist, has contended that the television years "have seen a remarkable change in the image and roles of children. Childhood as a protected and sheltered period of life has all but disappeared. . . . In the shared environment of television, children and adults know a great deal about one another's behavior and social knowledge—too much, in fact, for them to play out the traditional complementary roles of innocence versus omniscience." [13]

Even without television, however, American childhood during the war was anything but innocent, for the homefront children did have access—direct and immediate—to powerful visual images, including sources of "uncensored" news in which no adult stood between image and child. One example was the pages of *Life* magazine, another the newsreels that the children saw at their local movie theaters. *Life*'s impact could be shattering, compelling the girls and boys not only to reorder their sense of what was right and wrong but also to recalculate the outside limits of what human horrors were possible. "*Life* did more than anything else," wrote Ed Morris, a boy in Aaron's Fork, West Virginia, "to give me an adult's perspective of the war." At the outbreak of war, Ed's family did not have a radio or a newspaper subscription, but its copy of *Life* arrived weekly in the mail. Decades after the war, the images of *Life*'s photographs—those "fiercely gruesome photos," one homefront girl called them—are still vivid and still evoke deep emotion. For one girl, it was a photograph "that showed a very young boy standing on his stumps . . . that brought home to me the horrors of war." For another, it was a picture "of a Japanese officer beheading a blindfolded American flyer. I see it in my mind very clearly," she wrote forty-seven years later. "I remember particularly one shot of frozen bodies in Russia, stacked like cord wood," wrote Ann Parker, a girl who lived in Philadelphia. Ann's family did not subscribe to *Life*, but she read it at her school. Those images were still vivid years later when she visited the Holocaust Museum in Jerusalem and saw them again, dead bodies in piles, in the pictures of "the Nazi extermination camps." [14]

Not surprisingly, *Life*'s photographs of the Holocaust have stayed with the homefront children. "Most of my life," wrote a homefront girl, "I have been haunted by a photograph from *Life* magazine" that showed a young woman "standing in a Betty Grable-like pose, looking over her shoulder. Her skirt was raised, rather like a 'pin-up girl,' but, instead, she was displaying horribly disfigured legs, the result of medical experimentation." For another girl, the Holocaust photographs "exceeded anything we could have imagined—even in our wildest nightmares."[15]

So too it was with other uncensored visual images such as the newsreels, which one reporter called "a sort of *Life* magazine made animate." The newsreels were "our only view of the war," recalled a homefront girl. Not only did they bring "The Eyes and Ears of the World" to the audience, but as a homefront girl wrote, it was through them that "the war became very real." In black and white, the children saw scenes from air, land, and sea battles. During the war, about three-fourths of the newsreels showed either the hostilities or war-related governmental activities, with much of the combat footage shot by professionals trained by *The March of Time*, *Fox Movietone*, and Hearst's *News of the Day*. Early in the war, there was strict governmental censorship of both the newsreels and the combat photographs in *Life*; not for a year, for example, did the government release footage of the attack on Pearl Harbor. Fearing that civilian morale was flagging, however, the government later cleared pictures of atrocities and vicious battle scenes that would shock sensibilities in an effort to redouble people's commitment to the war effort.[16]

"The most terrifying thing I can remember," wrote a homefront girl, "was our weekly walk to the movie theater." Shown in between the double feature, she recalled, were the newsreels, which gave her "terrible nightmares. It was apparent, even to a child, that this was not part of a movie but reality." When a newsreel came on the screen, she remembered, some people began to cry, others shouted at the images of Hitler and the Japanese, and "some were terrified," she wrote, "—as I was." It was through the newsreels too that other children learned about the Holocaust. These films were "very upsetting," remembered a homefront girl. "There were scenes of rooms full of eye glasses. . . . Pictures of gas chambers . . . [of] skeletal people." Some theater managers edited out the Holocaust footage; the manager of Radio City Music Hall said that he did not want to risk "sickening my squeamish persons in the audience which is usually family trade, mostly women and children." But Frances Degen, a girl in New York City, saw the unabridged black-and-white newsreels at her local theater. Years later, in 1973, she was in Israel when the Yom Kippur War erupted. She thought to herself that this was not at all like war because it was in color, not in black and white. It was "really a lovely day," she reflected, with blue skies and bright sunshine.[17]

Of course, the homefront children paid their dime or twelve cents to see not only the newsreels but also two full-length features, a serial, the previews, and several cartoons. In addition to the war movies, children saw westerns and musicals. In fact, in 1943 Hollywood, perceiving that the public was tiring of war movies, began concentrating on "escapist" films—musicals and comedies.[18] At some theaters the children viewed classic films funded by the government, notably the documentaries in Frank Capra's *Why We Fight* series as well as John Ford's *The Battle of Midway* (1942), John Huston's *Report from the Aleutians* (1943) and *The Battle of San Pietro* (1944), and William Wyler's *Memphis Belle* (1944). They also saw government-sponsored public-service films and cartoons, the most famous being Walt Disney's *Der Fuhrer's Face* (1942), starring Donald Duck, which gave the nation a hit song based on the unlikely topic of flatulence: "We heil [Bronx cheer], heil [Bronx cheer], right in der Fuhrer's face." Less heroic, but no less a hero, was Minnie Mouse. Her cartoon *Out of the Frying Pan and into the Firing Line* exemplified Disney's sex-typing, which was fully consonant with the gender-role assignment evident in all forms of popular culture. This sex-typing was probably not the result of a conscious effort or of maliciousness, but it was done so consistently as to heighten its power in forming or confirming images of gender roles. Thus, Minnie's task was not to confront Hitler but to show "why it was important for housewives to save fat." [19]

Movie attendance skyrocketed during World War II. Some people wanted escape; others wanted to see the war through newsreels and war-related features. And, with burgeoning employment, they could afford to go to the movies several times a week. In response, Hollywood studios released fifteen hundred films during the war, one-fourth of which were combat pictures. Weekly attendance in 1942 was an estimated 100 million—at a time when the national population stood at 135 million; the previous high had been 90 million tickets sold per week, reached in 1930. Moviegoers often attended more than once a week, for in numerous theaters the films usually ran from Thursday through Saturday and changed on Sunday, with the new films continuing through Wednesday. Double features were widespread. People of all ages responded to these offerings, and box office receipts soared, doubling from $735 million in 1940 to $1.45 billion in 1945.[20]

The homefront children said they were going to "the show," and the most popular was the Saturday afternoon matinee. For many children, going to the movies was an experience in independence. They went to the theater with their siblings or playmates or were dropped off by a parent or a grandparent, to be picked up later. In either case, the children enjoyed being at "the show" without adult supervision. Most ushers were only teenagers, and reports were frequent of unruly boys and girls. Children screamed in their seats, ran up and down the aisles making war sounds, whistling and screaming, and pretended they were bombs falling. The theater could be a rough place. Willie Morris, the writer, described the Saturday matinee in his Mississippi hometown as always "crowded, noisy, filthy, full of flying objects; one of the Coleman boys from Eden had his eye put out when somebody threw a BB." A theater manager in El Paso, Texas, complained that "from the beginning, the boys and some of the girls . . . decided they were going to run things as they pleased." Sometimes, he said, "when told not to roam the aisles, to quit talking, . . . they would sneer or spit in your face." But there was a more serious threat in Philadelphia, where a gang of children, led by a six-year-old boy, "crawled under seats, opened purses in the dark, and pocketed the contents."[21]

"Comics—Radio—Movies," proclaimed an article in *Better Homes and Gardens*. "What are they doing to our children? And what should parents do about them?" Despite its effort to be inclusive, the article failed to discuss another favorite entertainment of the homefront children: movie serials. Children thrilled to these serials, featuring such anti-Axis heroes as Captain Marvel, the Spider, Batman, Spy Smasher, and Special Agent X–9. These heroes were all variations on the Superman theme, and girls and boys flocked to see the serials; children's wartime obsession with spies also boosted the demand. In *Captain Marvel*, the first fifteen adventures of which were released in 1941, the boy Billy Batson became "the World's Mightiest Mortal" simply by shouting the magic word "Shazam." *Spy Smasher*, who in reality was Jack Armstrong's twin brother Alan, started in 1942. *The Black Commando* also debuted that year; he trapped the leader of the alien spies in America by offering to provide the secret formula for synthetic rubber. The next year, with the release of another new fifteen-chapter serial, Batman began to pursue the nation's enemies, including "Dr. Daka," the "Japanese superspy" who was conspiring to seize control of the United States. "You're as yellow as your skin!" Batman railed at him. Also in 1943, the Masked Marvel took to the screen in pursuit of "Sakima," a Japanese spy intent on sabotaging America's defense industries. And in 1944, Captain America donned his red-white-and-blue tights and did battle with Nazi spies.[22]

As with radio, parents and educators worried about the psychological effects of the movies. Yet based on the relative coverage given the issue in popular and professional magazines, there was far less concern about the injurious effects of films than there was about radio. For one thing, parents could monitor the movies more closely than they could the radio, which could be listened to almost surreptitiously by children lying in their darkened bedrooms at night. The film production code, adopted by the Motion Picture Producers and Distributors in 1930, seemed to reassure American parents; and some states and communities had their own censorship codes and boards that licensed films and removed scenes and dialogue considered objectionable. But the production code, in effect until 1968, was a curious document. On the one hand, it allowed the presentation of arson, dynamiting of trains and buildings, and the use of firearms as well as of murder so long as "the technique of murder" was not "presented in a way that will inspire imitation." On the other hand, nudity was "never permitted," including "nudity in fact or in silhouette, or any licentious notice thereof by other characters in the picture." As for sexuality, "excessive and lustful kissing, lustful embraces, suggestive postures and gestures, are not to be shown." Finally, "*miscegenation* (sex relationship between the white and black races) is forbidden."[23]

Perhaps there should have been greater concern about the movies' effects on children, particularly the psychological results of the violence portrayed on the screen. Certainly many of these films were gruesome, a fact recognized by Bosley Crowther of the *New York Times*, who wrote in 1943: "It is one of the ironies of warfare that such dubious films . . . manifestations which, in peace time, would be regarded as outside the pale— can be palmed off as righteous inducements to a true war consciousness." These violent and horrifying films agitated most children and frightened the rest. More than radio or the comics, concluded a survey of "psychiatric opinion," it was the "visual experience—the movies—[that] are likely to have the greatest and most lasting impact." The writer Scott Momaday remembered that the children in his New Mexico town "would not let go of the movies, but we lived in them for days afterwards." After seeing a swashbuckling adventure film, "there were sword fights in the streets, and we battered each other mercilessly." Many children, girls and boys alike, took movie-inspired warfare with them after they left the theater and headed for playgrounds and vacant lots. Others, however, were terrified and took those emotions home. According to one wartime study, this was especially true for girls; for them the films were too vivid. "I felt I was actually *there*," remembered a homefront girl, "and I would be terrified for days afterwards." Another girl recalled a "totally horrifying film" in which a Japanese pilot fired bullets through the windshield of an American airplane, and "the starburst in the windshield is repeated in the starburst of the [American] pilot's goggles and the trickle of blood that ran down his face is indelibly imprinted in my memory." And Susan Yarin, a girl who lived in Springfield, Massachusetts, remembered going with her mother to see *The North Star*, a 1943 film in which Nazi doctors inflicted medical atrocities on children. "My mother put her hand over my face during the bad parts. I still saw. In later years," Susan wrote, "it was on television. I [still] couldn't watch it."[24]

Radio and movies were relatively recent entertainments in children's lives; readers and literature allowed a more traditional interaction. Given the nation's multifaceted war enthusiasms, publishers released surprisingly few war titles for children. At that time too librarians' published recommendations of children's books were relatively devoid of war-inspired stories. There was a canon in children's literature, and its self-appointed guardians were active in its exposure to a new generation of readers, war or no war. Among the magazines that published the librarians' lists were the *Nation, Horn Book, Newsweek, Journal of the National Educational Association,* and the *Atlantic*; they also appeared in publications of the Children's Bureau and other child-welfare agencies and associations. Frequently throughout the war the *Library Journal* and *Publishers Weekly* recommended selected children's books for all reading levels, from "Picture Book Age" to the "Middle-Age Child." These magazines boosted the adventures of Mary Poppins, Homer Price, Lassie, and other fictional characters of the day and such classics as *The Adventures of Huckleberry Finn, Little Women,* and *Treasure Island*. They recommended animal stories, fairy tales, and biographies of George Washington, Davy Crockett, Abraham

Lincoln, Julia Ward Howe, George Washington Carver, and other great Americans as well as books about children in other war zones, such as Mollie Panter-Downes's *Watling Green*, which told of a girl in England.[25]

Added to this genre was the war-related story, evident in such titles as *PT Boat*, *Bombadier*, and *Navy Gun Crew* and in books about antifascist adventures, such as *Shadow in the Pines*, about a boy in New Jersey who foils a Nazi plot. Lining the shelves of both the bookstores and the libraries were children's war stories, especially for those over age eight or nine. Most of these books, unlike the movies, did not spotlight warfare's blood and gore; they tended to be more on the order of Theresa Kalab's *Watching for Winkie*, a book for grades three to five, which tells of a carrier pigeon that saved the lives of four Royal Air Force aviators.[26] Much of the credit for the ongoing innocence of children's books was due to individuals such as Edward Stratemeyer and John R. Tunis. In 1910 Stratemeyer founded a syndicate specializing in children's books, which over the next sixty-five years originated over one hundred series, featuring Honey Bunch, the Bobbsey Twins, the Hardy Boys, Nancy Drew, and Tom Swift, and published more than twelve hundred titles. According to the novelist Bobbie Ann Mason, a fan of Stratemeyer, he was "keenly attuned to what turned children on, and he gave them the action-jammed adventures of ideal, wholesome, all-American characters who lived in ideal places. His own favorite," she noted, "was the Rover Boys, a series he wrote personally, with love." Many girl readers, however, preferred Nancy Drew, "the first official girl sleuth."[27]

No scholar who was a homefront child and a member of the reading public at the time could fail to pay tribute to John R. Tunis, the author of a series of sports novels published during the war. Tunis's baseball players—guys like Roy Tucker, the Duke, Highpockets, Sourpuss, Rats, and Fat Stuff—were a diverse group racially, religiously, and ethnically; this was precisely the point. He told exciting sports stories, avoiding the predictable. His stories dealt with the hot hitter who "whangs the old apple" and "thumps the old tomato" and with grown men who affectionately call each other "lads" or "chaps." But his novels were bold for the 1940s. "What made Tunis' novels particularly fine," journalist Toby Smith has written, "was that they were less about sports than about social concerns," notably, the need to confront racism and anti-Semitism. One of the heroes of Tunis's football story, *All-American* (1942), is Ned LeRoy, a black wide-receiver subjected to bigotry at his school. In this novel as in the others, tolerance triumphs. In *Keystone Kids* (1943), for example, a Jewish catcher, Jocko Klein, joins the Dodgers only to be taunted as "Buglenose" by the fans and opposing players. Jocko is an excellent player, but he becomes discouraged. "He won't last," says a team veteran. "The bench jockeys will get him. You'll see. They'll ride that baby to death. Besides, these Jewish boys can't take it. Haven't any guts." In time, the fans jeer at Klein; "Yer yeller kike, look out there or he'll pare your beak offa ya." But Spike, the manager, takes Jocko aside, telling him that the club "can win if you play like you can. . . . Once they see you're a scrapper, they'll be for you, all the way." And naturally Spike is correct. At last, the bigots confront their intolerance, unite to overcome it, and witness "the re-birth of their team." The new spirit is evident in the postgame nods in Klein's direction. "Nice catching, Jocko," "You sure handled those pitchers, Jocko." During the war, Alice Dalgliesh, a children's book editor, praised Tunis's "craftsmanship and his ability to make the reader *feel* and like characters before he hits—and hits hard—at intolerance." Children, especially boys, eagerly read Tunis's other wartime books, *World Series* (1941) and *Rookie of the Year* (1944), and they went to the library shelves for such prewar publications as *The Kid from Tomkinsville* (1940). Toby Smith spoke for readers of several decades when he paid tribute to Tunis: "He made a world—where winning and losing and bad bounces all have a place—come alive . . . for an 11-year-old."[28]

Some children's wartime heroes owed their existence not to writers of fiction but to cartoonists and animators. Whether cartoon heroes or comic-book heroes—and there was a great deal of overlap—these illustrated images were integral to the homefront children's experiences. Donald Duck and Minnie Mouse starred in both the cartoons and the comics as did Bugs Bunny, Mighty Mouse, and others. The plots varied little from one medium to the other, and the messages were invariably the same. Death to the enemy, or at least a severe maiming, was usually the goal. In *Bugs Bunny Nips the Nips*, the rabbit hero is on a Pacific island where he sells Japanese soldiers "Good Rumor" ice cream bars that have grenades hidden inside. "Here y'are, Slant Eyes," says Bugs as he hands out the treats.[29]

Many of the comic books, however, demanded a level of sophistication uncalled for in Bugs Bunny or Donald Duck cartoons. This was the golden age of comic books; as with numerous heroes in the cartoons and on the radio, several leading comic-book stars were born just prior to

World War II. In June 1938 Superman made his debut on the cover of the first issue of Action Comics. *Batman* comics arrived the next year. Many of these heroes could fly, and after the Pearl Harbor attack still others began to pilot airplanes. As exemplified in the comic books *Hawkman* and *Blackhawk* and by other comic-book aviator heroes, World War II was "a time when the evil and the airborne were both simplified in the comics' pages." During the war there were 150 different comics books selling 20 million copies each month. "Here come the comics!" wrote the experts, who identified the years from age five up to eleven as the period of children's fixation on comic books. At age twelve their fascination peaked; but of the homefront children between the ages of six and eleven, 95 percent of boys and 91 percent of girls "read comic books regularly." Children's comprehension of the comics mounted with both age and enthusiasm, as they progressed from simple description to the interpretation of events. Just as there was no discernible gender difference in this mass readership, so, concluded a researcher for the Child Study Association, "the comics appear to have an almost universal appeal to children . . . regardless of I.Q. or cultural background." The "Captain Marvel Club" had 575,000 members, and in 2,500 classrooms during the war school children learned to read from "Superman workbooks." To offset the perceived evil influence of comic books, in 1942 the publishers of *Parents' Magazine* brought out the first issue of True Comics, "designed deliberately to look like other comic magazines . . . [but] free of vulgarity and slang [and] the trashy horror fiction." With monthly sales of comic books so high, however, these sanitized comics were unlikely to cut substantially into the sales of the others.[30]

Although most of the superheroes of the comics were men and boys, there was a notable exception—and for numerous homefront girls, she was a magnificent hero: Wonder Woman. A homefront girl in Toledo, Ohio, Gloria Steinem was seven when Wonder Woman made her debut in 1941. Before that time, her heroes had performed "superhuman feats," but all were men. In watching these heroes, she wrote, "the female child is left to believe that, even when her body is as grown-up as her spirit, she will still be in the childlike role of helping with minor tasks, appreciating men's accomplishments, and being so incompetent and passive that she can only hope some man can come to her rescue. . . . 'Oh, Superman! I'll always be grateful to you.'" But then Wonder Woman came to the rescue. She was "as wise as Athena and as lovely as Aphrodite, she had the speed of Mercury and the strenght of Hercules." She also was an Amazon and had honed her superhuman skills in training with her sisters on Paradise Island, their home. Like the male heroes, Wonder Woman had marvelous gadgets. She had a golden magic lasso that she threw with unerring accuracy, and she reacted with incredible quickness to stop speeding projectiles with her bullet-proof bracelets. She flew on her missions in an invisible airplane, which was also a time machine. Since this was wartime, Wonder Woman was a patriot who fought Axis spies in her red-white-and-blue costume. Like her male compatriots, she could be jingoistic and racist. Yet clearly there was a difference: Wonder Woman's message was feminist. She says in one episode that she could never love "a dominant man"; it is a woman villain who proclaims that "girls want superior men to boss them around." In another episode, Wonder Woman rescues Prudence, who in the process discovers her self-worth and agency: "I've learned my lesson. From now on, I'll rely on myself, not a man." Although written during the war by a man, William Marston, Wonder Woman's plots revolved around "evil men who treat women as inferior beings." This, Steinem wrote, was exhilarating because "in the end, all are brought to their knees and made to recognize women's strength." Recalling Wonder Woman years later during the rebirth of feminism, Steinem observed that the Amazon's was "still a passable version of the truisms that women are rediscovering today." [31]

In an era when women were breaking stereotypes on the labor front and in the armed services, Wonder Woman did not originate in a vacuum, but she was a rare exception in wartime popular culture. In the preponderance of children's radio adventure and crime shows, in their comics books and animated cartoons, and in their movies and serials, men invariably were the heroes, the action figures, the ones who took risks. Women's role, on the other hand, was usually that of supportive-nurturant, as evidenced by the title of one radio serial, "Mary Noble—Backstage Wife." Women also were sidekicks, "his girl Friday." And so it was with the sex-typing in children's war games, demonstrated by the gender roles that prevailed on the battlefields and in the foxholes in side lots, woods, and vacant fields. Again, the prevalent sex-typing assigned the girls to the role of nurse if not to the roles of enemy and prisoner of war and the boys to soldiering and warfare.

Admittedly, there were exceptions to this sex-typing. By their example, working mothers and other working women, dressed in slacks and making their own decisions, clearly undermined gender roles in the minds of many children. So too did the 350,000 women who joined the armed forces. Nevertheless, sex-typing was a powerful force in wartime America, and prescribed gender roles were not only strong but also long-lasting, perpetuated in the popular culture. The wartime films exemplified both the depth and the persistence of gender identification in popular culture. One paradigm showing sex-typing was the romance film, which the homefront girls vividly recalled. While the war raged abroad in these films, a homefront girl recalled, the "wives and sweethearts [were] at home waiting for the men to return, fearing that they would not." One of the most memorable of these films was *Since You Went Away* (1944) in which the husband, and father of two daughters, is missing in action and presumed dead. It is Christmas, and Claudette Colbert, the wife, unwraps the present that her husband has left her, a music box that plays "Together." Sitting there alone, she listens to the song. Suddenly, the telephone rings. It is her husband; he is alive. As one girl remembered, "there was not a dry eye in the theater."[32]

For the girls the films were also lessons in "subtle sexuality" or how to "trap" a man. Personified by Betty Grable and Rita Hayworth, "these movies," according to a study of women in popular culture, "portrayed images . . . which were at great variance with the working girl image popular with audiences of real working women." Produced with the serviceman in mind, these movies often had a chorus girl as the female star. "Into the wartime musical melee," this book explained, "danced the sweet little sex kitten who, underneath the chorus-girl figure, was all mother love." Herein lay major future conceptual problems for both the girls and the boys. Interestingly, too, several significant 1940s films about independent women were released not during the war but before or after it, such as *Woman of the Year* (1941) and *Adam's Rib* (1949), both starring Katharine Hepburn. Another study, M. Joyce Baker's *Images of Women in Films*, concurs that during the war the films strengthened rather than weakened Americans' attachment to traditional roles for women. America's women participated in the national defense, but in popular culture the institutions that they defended were their traditional domains: romance and marriage, the family and the home. As for working women, in the film version they joined the labor force entirely for patriotism and to work only for the war's duration.[33]

The messages of these films and much of the wartime popular culture were simplistic. In reply to questions about what the United States was fighting for, the answer in several movies was "pumpkin pie!" Or as an aviator in *Thirty Seconds over Tokyo* (1944) put it, "When it's all over . . . just think . . . being able to settle down . . . and never be in doubt about anything." Just as the films indulged in sex-typing, so too they spun myths about American society. "One big family—that is America," stated one film character. "We all see eye to eye," asserted another. "This has been a happy home," was a third expression of this American myth.[34]

Because it engaged in mythmaking and the presentation of "ideal types" of both genders, the wartime popular culture functioned to mislead the American people, including the children, about the past, present, and evolving future of their country. For one thing, as was evident during the race riots that swept the country in 1943, the United States was not "one big family." But the myriad myths derived from the popular culture were as persistent as they were powerful, and they continued to influence Americans' notions of men, women, and gender for the next two decades. Indeed, as one of the homefront boys wrote, "a lot of the perspective of the war was taught to the children . . . after the fact through the movies made *after* the war." These films also romanticized war, diminished the realities of separation, absence, and death, and deepened society's already exaggerated notions about gender roles. Indeed, the war's legacy for the homefront children was a system of virtually unchallenged representations in mass culture about what properly constituted the male sphere and the female sphere. This ideology, which exercised its hegemony in subtle but overpowering ways, helped to govern the homefront girls' and boys' behavior in the years after the war. These images of men's bravery and women's self-sacrifice were the same ones that America's Baby Boomers, born after the war, absorbed, from the 1940s well into the 1960s, when the reborn feminist movement issued its challenge to sex-typing.[35]

Although scholars can debate whether films and other forms of popular culture are "social artifacts" from which one may extrapolate "what's afoot in the society at large," there is no denying either the power or the persistence of these images in the minds and lives of Americans. Jean Bethke Elshtain, a homefront girl, later wrote a book entitled *Women and War*. Her story, she said, is "not-a-soldier's story; it is, instead, a tale of how war, rumors of war, and images of violence, individual and collective, permeated the thoughts of a girl growing up . . . in the 1950s." "Born in 1941," she wrote, "I knew the war only at second hand." Her encounter "as a child and citizen-to-be with the larger, adult world of war and collective violence" was, to a significant extent, "filtered down to me through movies." Through them, she and countless others, boys as well as girls, learned lessons—and myths—and developed idealized, sex-typed notions, some of which in fact had been around for ages in epic tales of good versus evil. And in the absence of new story lines, Elshtain recalled, the film images of World War II told of "the Just Warrior and the Beautiful Soul."[36]

Multiple cultures, some of them oppositional, existed in wartime America. Even while patriotism and shared national goals animated popular culture, homefront unity often papered over deep racial, ethnic, religious, and class tensions. Nevertheless, on key ideological issues, the war's imprint was deep from the 1940s to the 1960s. With few dissenters, Americans trumpeted the glories of their country, boasting that it was the greatest nation in the world—and getting better all the time. Having won World War II and persevered in the Cold War, the United States, the British journalist Godfrey Hodgson has written, "entered the 1960s in an Augustan mood: united, confident, conscious of a historical mission, and mobilized for the great task of carrying it out." As they had since World War II, Americans "felt the maturity of their power" and "accepted the legitimacy of their institutions. They believed not in the perfection, but in the perfectibility of their society," which they saw as "essentially just and benevolent." Indeed, as one reflects on the American consensus that emerged during World War II—and on the patriotism and the shared beliefs and values that prevailed afterward—what is remarkable is not that it finally collapsed but that it enjoyed the hegemony it did and that it endured for as long as it did.[37]

Part Three

❖ ❖ ❖ ❖ ❖ ❖ ❖ ❖ ❖ ❖ ❖ ❖ ❖ ❖ ❖

Seen but Not Heard

CHILDREN IN AMERICAN PHOTOGRAPHS

N. Ray Hiner

The Hatter opened his eyes very wide on hearing this; but all he said was "Why is a raven like a writing desk?"

"Come, we shall have some fun now!" thought Alice. "I'm glad they've begun asking riddles—I believe I can guess that," she added aloud.

"Do you mean that you think you can find out the answer to it?" said the March Hare.

"Exactly so," said Alice.

"Then you should say what you mean," the March Hare went on.

"I do," Alice hastily replied; "at least—at least I mean what I say—that's the same thing, you know."

"Not the same thing a bit!" said the Hatter. "You might just as well say that 'I see what I eat' is the same thing as 'I eat what I see'!"

– Lewis Carroll, Alice's Adventures in Wonderland

The history of American children and the history of photography are inextricably linked. As the writers in this book show, children had considerable influence on their societies, but they did not exercise power in the ways historians usually have defined the term. As a consequence, they left behind few of the documents typically used to describe how the movers and shakers of American life changed their world. Children initiated no legislation, though they were certainly the objects of many laws passed by adults; they executed no wills, though countless wills were executed on their behalf; they delivered no major political speeches, preached no influential sermons, and published no essays on the pressing public issues of their day, though they were often the subjects of these activities; and they created no large public or private institutions, though many institutions were created for them. Some children kept diaries and wrote letters, but not nearly as often as adults. Because boys and girls left little behind in the places historians have looked for evidence, they have often been shunted to the shadowy margins of history, barely visible to those who write or study our past.[1]

This historiographical invisibility of children is understandable but unwarranted. Children played a much more important role in our history than has been commonly assumed. For one thing, children were far too numerous, too ubiquitous to be ignored. Throughout much of our history, children under the age of sixteen constituted between one-third and one-half of the population.[2] Adults had to devote an enormous amount of time, energy, and resources to their care and supervision. Children were everywhere—in fields, in factories, in families, schools, churches, prisons, and custodial institutions; they were on ships, on the streets, and even on battlefields. They were, many of them, producers as well as consumers, wanted and unwanted, pampered and abused, cherished and exploited.

Some of the clearest evidence of the omnipresence and pervasive influence of children can be found in the millions of photographic images created by Americans from the early 1840s, when the daguerreotype was introduced to the United States from Europe, until the present, when pictures of children are all around us, in advertisements, on milk cartoons, in movies, on television, in newspapers, and in our wallets and family albums. Anyone who reviews a representative sample of these images past or present can hardly escape the conclusion that children are important to adults, that children profoundly affect the lives of their elders,

Frank and Helen Chapman, 1925.
(Museum of New Mexico, neg. no. 28174)

both individually and collectively, and that the historical experience of children has been as diverse and often as complex as that of adults.

Photographs are among the most efficacious sources for the study of children in the past because children are among the most inarticulate of historical subjects. Photographs permit children to be seen who would not normally be heard. Through photographs, we can look into the eyes of children who never kept a diary or wrote a letter. We can see them at play, at work, in school, at home, at their mother's breast, at their father's knee; we can see what kind of clothes they wore; we can to some extent see what they and their world looked like. By seeing in this way we can gain an understanding of children and their lives that would otherwise be closed to us.

Young children make especially interesting photographic subjects for the historian. As Susan Kismaric has noted, they "face the camera innocent of all but the present moment, and often with a startling purity of motive."[3] Unlike adults, who have learned how to put on masks for the camera, children are often oblivious of the photographer's social function or the symbolic purpose of the event or moment to be photographed. Children are often simply uninterested in or unable to participate consciously with adults in creating the photograph as social artifice. This is not to argue that adults do not control and manipulate children when they are photographed. They obviously do, but the spontaneity and honesty of children occasionally break through the conventional forms of photographs to reveal something about themselves or those around them that goes beyond the intended purpose of the photograph. For example, in the photograph reproduced on page 168, did the photographer intend to capture the uncertain, equivocal, perhaps deferential but ultimately ambiguous expressions on the faces of Helen and Frank Chapman, or was the intent simply to photograph two very cute kids all dressed up on a sunny winter morning? Without more information about this photograph, we shall never know, but these children have in their own way made a visual statement about their lives, even if it is a highly ambiguous one.[4] Like most photographs, this image raises more questions than it answers. It invites us to speculate, to ponder its meaning on several different levels, from the feelings of the individuals involved to the social and cultural functions of the photograph itself. If they do nothing else, photographs generate questions, which are at least as important to the intellectual vitality of a field as the answers they produce.

Photographs not only provoke questions; they can also provide powerful, vivid illustrations that enhance and deepen what we have already learned from other sources about the history of children. It is one thing to read congressional reports about child labor but quite another to see a Lewis Hine photograph of a young girl in a southern textile factory or one by Jacob Riis of a young boy in a New York sweatshop. As Alan Trachtenberg has said, "The past is always immeasurably more complex than any written narrative can suggest."[5] Photographs give us an additional understanding of this complexity.

The value of photographs as illustrations of what we know about the historical experience of children is greatly strengthened by the sheer number of images that have survived and by the extraordinary extent to which photography rapidly became available to ordinary people. Although daguerreotypes of the 1840s and 1850s were produced by a rather cumbersome process (exposures required twenty to forty seconds on the average), intense competition soon made them affordable to the middle class and even to relatively poor families.[6] For example, Beaumont Newhall has stated that more than four hundred thousand daguerreotypes were produced in Massachusetts alone during the year ending June 1, 1855.[7] And when the box camera and roll film were developed, culminating in the introduction of the Kodak camera by George Eastman in 1888, photography became accessible to almost everyone. Kodak advertisements pro-claimed, "You Press the Button, We Do the Rest."[8] The rest, as they say, is history.

Photography has become so much a part of American life that today virtually everyone is photographed. According to Susan Sontag, "Not to take pictures of one's children, particularly when they are small, is a sign of parental indifference."[9] This national obsession with photography has produced a vast repository of photographic images available for schol-ars to study. The Library of Congress alone has at least fifteen million photographic images in its collection, and the National Archives houses at least five million.[10] Additional millions of images are preserved in other libraries, archives, and homes throughout the country.

It should be obvious that the brief photographic essay that follows can hardly be seen as representative of the huge mass of photographs of chil-dren that exists today. The images reproduced here can illustrate only a very small portion of what we know about children in the past and suggest just a few of the questions that these images can generate. The photographs have been arranged in rough chronological order from the 1840s to the 1960s to demonstrate both the evolution of photography as a social phenomenon and to identify some of the major forces, events, and processes that have affected American children over time. Many of the photographs are paired by placing two photographs on the same page to encourage the viewer to consider their possible relationships to each other as well as to the photographs that precede and follow them in the essay. The reader is also invited to review the photographs reproduced at the beginning of each essay in this book.

Charles Shaw and Mary Louise Leonard, Providence, Rhode Island, ca. 1847.
(Kansas State Historical Society, Museum of History)

Left: *Rowena Charles and daughter Aristene. Daguerreotype, ca. 1840.*
(Kansas State Historical Society)
Right: *Jennie Terry. Daguerreotype, ca. 1859.*
(Kansas State Historical Society)

Above: *Woodsawyer's Nooning. Daguerreotype by George N. Barnard,
Oswego, New York, 1853. (George Eastman House, Rochester, New York)*
Below: *Jeremiah (1838–1912), Edwin (1845–1908), and Sara Remington
(1836–1903). Daguerreotype, ca. 1858. (Kansas State Historical Society)*

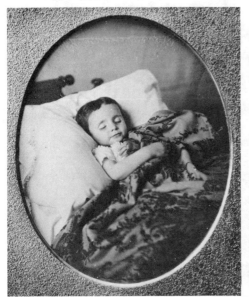

Left: *Dead child. Photographer unknown, ca. 1845. Sixth-plate daguerreotype.*
(Collection of Richard Rudisill, Santa Fe, N. Mex.)
Right: *William Black, who was wounded in the Civil War.*
(Mathew Brady Collection, National Archives.
Records of the Chief Signal Officer [111-B-2368])

Left: *Beeler baby, New Mexico, ca. 1885–1892.*
(J. C. Burge, photographer. Museum of New Mexico, neg. no. 76607)
Right: *Louise, Caroline, and Margaret Walbridge opening*
Christmas presents, ca. 1900.
(Kansas Collection, University of Kansas Libraries)

Above: *The halt. A journey through Navajo country, ca. 1890.*
(Ben Wittick, photographer. Museum of New Mexico, neg. no. 3083)
Below: *Victorian interior. William Culver family, Topeka, Kansas, ca. 1890.*
(Kansas Collection, University of Kansas Libraries)

Higdon family, Junction City, Kansas, 1898.
(Joseph Pennell Collection, Kansas Collection, University of Kansas Libraries)

❖ 177 ❖

Birney Public School, Washington, D.C., 1899.
(F. B. Johnston, photographer. Library of Congress [LC-USZ62-4553])

Above: *Gilbert Emick and friends at Smoky Hill River,*
Junction City, Kansas, 1902.
(Joseph Pennell Collection, Kansas Collection, University of Kansas Libraries)
Below: *Boys playing pool in St. Louis, Missouri, 1910.*
(Lewis Hine, photographer. Library of Congress)

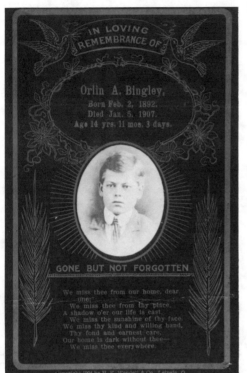

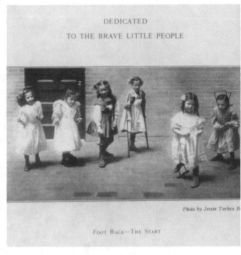

Left: *Orlin A. Bingley (1892–1907) memorial card.*
(Courtesy of Marietta Davis)
Right: *Frontispiece from a book on crippled children, 1914.*
(Jessie Tarbox Beales, photographer. In Edith Reeves, Care
and Education of Crippled Children in the United States
[New York: Russell Sage Foundation, 1914])

Left: *Self-portrait with children, ca. 1914.*
(Lewis Hine, photographer. Spencer Museum of Art,
University of Kansas. Museum purchase)
Right: *Child labor poster, ca. 1915.*
(Lewis Hine photographer. Spencer Museum of Art, University of Kansas.
Museum purchase: Peter T. Bohan Fund)

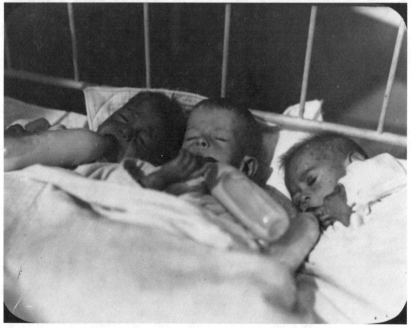

Above: *Street scene, ca. 1910. (Lewis Hine Lantern Slide Collection.*
Spencer Museum of Art, University of Kansas)
Below: *Three tenement children, ca. 1910. Lewis Hine Lantern Slide Collection.*
Spencer Museum of Art, University of Kansas)

Above: *Newsgirls, ca. 1910. (Lewis Hine Lantern Slide Collection.*
Spencer Museum of Art, University of Kansas)
Below: *Boy Scouts starting camp fire, New Mexico, ca. 1920.*
(Museum of New Mexico, neg. no. 8351)

Above: *Snapshot of Aspray children and friends, Blytheville, Arkansas, 1910.*
(Courtesy of Joseph Robert Wilson)
Below: *Family portrait, 1924. Paul David Wilson, Joseph Robert Wilson, and*
Azzie Lee (Aspray) Wilson.
(Courtesy of Joseph Robert Wilson)

Above: *Unidentified wedding group, Santa Fe, New Mexico, 1912.*
(Jesse L. Nusbaum, photographer. Museum of New Mexico, neg. no. 61817)
Below: *Farm family in Arkansas, June 1914.*
(R. C. Hughey, photographer. National Archives,
Records of the Forest Service, 95-G-18909A)

Above: *Family in Hood River country, Oregon,*
listening to early radio, July 20, 1915.
(Unknown photographer, National Archives.
Records of Federal Extension Service [33-SC-4849])
Below: *Ransom family picnic in Franklin County, Kansas, ca. 1920.*
(Kansas Collection, University of Kansas Libraries)

Left: *Page from Lawrence, Kansas, Memorial High School Yearbook, 1926.*
(Collection of the author)
Right: *High school graduation portrait of salutatorian Azzie Lee Aspray*
(Wilson) and her sister, valedictorian Ivey May Aspray (Segerson), Senath,
Missouri, May 4, 1917.
(Courtesy of Joseph Robert Wilson)

Teck family celebrating Passover Seder, Brooklyn, 1928.
(Courtesy, Myrna Teck)

Left: *Teofolo Ortega with unidentified child and dog,*
Tesuque Pueblo, New Mexico, 1920.
(T. Harmon Parkhurst, photographer. Museum of New Mexico, neg. no. 47271)
Right: *Joseph Robert Wilson meeting Grandma (Sara Angeline Aspray) at Frisco*
Station, Cape Girardeau, Missouri, summer 1928.
(Courtesy of Joseph Robert Wilson)

Baby Rose Marie, 1930.
(Orval Hixon, photographer. Spencer Museum of Art,
University of Kansas. Gift of the artist)

❖ 190 ❖

Above: *School for African American children in Arkansas church, 1938.*
Below: *One-room school in Alabama, 1939.*
(Both photos by Arthur Rothstein, photographer. Library of Congress.
From The Depression Years as Photographed by Arthur Rothstein
[New York: Dover Publications, 1978])

Left: *Elementary school children, Greenbelt, Maryland, 1938.*
(Arthur Rothstein, photographer. Library of Congress. From The Depression
Years as Photographed by Arthur Rothstein
[New York: Dover Publications, 1978])
Right: *Children reading Sunday comics, St. Charles County,*
Missouri farm family, 1939.
(Arthur Rothstein, photographer. Library of Congress [LC-USF34-25121].
From The Depression Years as Photographed by Arthur Rothstein
[New York: Dover Publications, 1978])

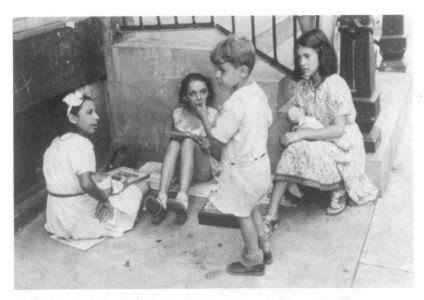

Above: *Children Playing on East Sixty-first Street, New York City,*
August 23, 1938.
(Walker Evans, photographer. Library of Congress [LC-USF3301-6722-M2])
Below: *Children on streets of planned suburban development*
in Greendale, Wisconsin, 1939.
(John Vachon, photographer. Library of Congress [LC-USF33-1433-M2])

Georgia farm children, 1941.
(Jack Delano, photographer. Library of Congress [LC-US534-439970-D])

Left: *Boy watching July 4th parade in Vale, Oregon, 1941.*
(Russell Lee, photographer. Library of Congress [LC-USF3301-13103-M5])
Right: *Japanese-American boy awaiting relocation in Salinas, California, 1943.*
(Russell Lee, photographer. Library of Congress [LC-USF34T01-72499-0])

Left: *Four generations of the Mary Machado family,*
Gloucester, Massachusetts, 1943.
(Gordon Parks, photographer. Library of Congress [LC-USW3-31668-C])
Right: *Children of Cochran family washing dishes, Cincinnati, ca. 1943.*
(Esther Bubley, photographer. Library of Congress [LC-USW3T01-37545-E])

*To the Colored Waiting Room, Florida, 1946–1949.
(Marion Palfi, photographer. Spencer Museum of Art,
University of Kansas. Gift of the artist)*

Phyllis (Hansard) Gilmore using a walking bar constructed by her father to help her recover from polio, late 1940s, St. Louis, Missouri.
(Courtesy of Phyllis Gilmore)

Frank Archuleta and sons Donald (left) and David (right),
Taos Pueblo, ca. 1950.
(Tyler Dingee, photographer, Museum of New Mexico, neg. no. 120214)

American family watching presidential debates, September 26, 1960.
(United Press International. The Bettman Archive)

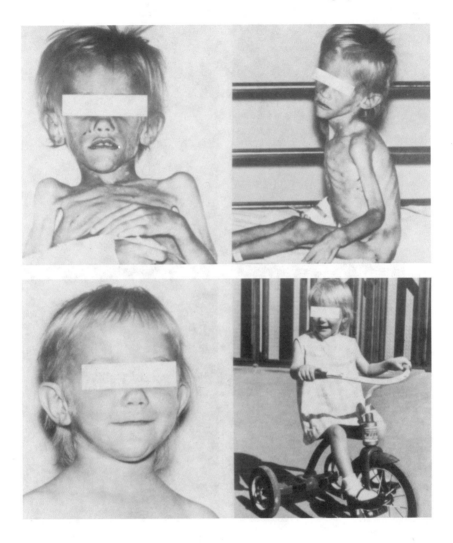

*Abused children before and after admission to the University of
Colorado Medical Center.
(From Ray E. Hefler and C. Henry Kempe,* The Battered Child
[Chicago: University of Chicago Press, 1968])

Children on Castillo Street, Santa Fe, New Mexico, 1960.
(Museum of New Mexico, neg. no. 10589)

Part Four

❖ ❖ ❖ ❖ ❖ ❖ ❖ ❖ ❖ ❖ ❖ ❖ ❖ ❖ ❖

One, Two, Buckle My Shoe /

Three, Four, Shut the Door

CHILDREN AND THE FAMILY

It was the best place to be, thought Wilbur, this warm delicious cellar, with the garrulous geese, the changing seasons, the heat of the sun, the passage of swallows, the nearness of rats, the sameness of sheep, the love of spiders, the smell of manure, the glory of everything.

   – E. B. White, Charlotte's Web

As [the woodcutter] was tossing and turning in bed in the evening because of his worries, his wife said to him: "Listen husband, tomorrow morning take both the children, give each one a little piece of bread, then take them out into the forest . . . and then go away and leave them there, for we cannot feed them any longer."

   – the Brothers Grimm, "Hansel and Gretel"

"The silver shoes," said the Good Witch, "have wonderful powers. And one of the most curious things about them is that they can carry you to any place in the world in three steps, and each step will be made in the wink of an eye. All you have to do is knock the heels together three times and command the shoes to carry you wherever you wish to go."

Dorothy now took Toto solemnly in her arms, and having said one last good-bye, she clapped the heels of her shoes together three times, saying,

"Take me home to Aunt Em."

   – L. Frank Baum, The Wonderful Wizard of Oz

"There's no place like home, there's no place like home."

   – Florence Ryerson, Noel Langley, and Edgar Allen Woolf, screenplay, The Wizard of Oz

The old counting rhyme referred to in the title to Part 4 is intended to aid children in numeracy and obedience, but metaphorically it can just as easily apply to childhood. Early on, children learn the basics —the buckling-the-shoe part—later on, they come to understand—the shutting-the-door part—that a door closes or opens as they reach certain important times in their lives or make critical decisions. Nursery rhymes and children's jingles are the stuff of childhood, and children are the heart of the family. However brief that association might have been or however profound or superficial the relationship, children have defined and continue to define a family. Even the phrases "to have a family," "to be in the family way," and a host of others imply the presence or expectation of children. A childless husband and wife or any other kind of affective or legal association was (and is) not always considered a family, despite social scientists' best efforts to expand the definition. Children, in short, are critical to our idea of family.

Important as the family has been, with few exceptions historians paid little attention to the development of the family in history. Since the 1960s, however, the history of the family has increasingly become a topic of historians' interest and attention, and their steadily growing body of information has revised previous notions of family life. (Policymakers and social commentators have largely ignored historians' beaver-like activity. The federal government, for example, bases its family welfare policy on a household of four persons in which the husband and father is the major breadwinner and the mother the homemaker, even though less than 25 percent of American families conform to this happy paradigm.) To be sure, historical families tended to group themselves in nuclear units composed of parents and children but with significant variations.

Colonial families, for example, lived in nuclear units. Besides having a greater number of children, however, they often had another person or two—servant, apprentice, or relative—living with them in a very small physical space. For a variety of reasons, colonial families lived remarkably public lives. Persons outside the family moved in and out of the family's business with little regard for household privacy. The family's business was community business and vice versa. By the mid-nineteenth century, family life had become remarkably varied. Middle-class white families had become significantly smaller; immigrant families occupied whole urban neighborhoods and rural enclaves; slave families were King Cotton's chattel with all the pressures that role placed on African Americans. The Native American families of the Northeast, for the most part, were no more, and American Indians of the West had begun to feel the pressure of white settlement. Certainly the trend toward smaller families had been a long time developing, and by the nineteenth century this phenomenon was pronounced and noticeable among the white gentry. But it was hardly universal. Different ethnic groups, economic strata, and social classes adopted different reproductive strategies. For a variety of reasons the middle class of the mid-nineteenth century determined that limiting its offspring had economic and social advantages. In the absence of birth control, white-collar families and couples who aspired to the middling ranks disciplined themselves to limit the number of their offspring to almost twentieth-century birth rates. At the same time, immigrant families and agricultural families saw no similar blessings in restricting their number of children, for a larger family meant a greater number of workers and a larger family wage. Against impossible odds, slave families labored to maintain family relationships and identity. Whatever its social or economic class, the nineteenth-century family of whatever background sheltered people from outside its circle. Among white middle-class families, a servant or two remained a prominent feature, although the servants occupied a separate space in the house itself. Working-class families squeezed a boarder (a relative or a work mate) into the household. And the slave family accommodated another person, whether at the behest of the owner or at the contrivance of the slave family itself. Increasingly, however, among certain classes, families became more private, holding the community at arm's length or at commuting distance.

Except for a few brief discussions, historians of the family have mentioned children only insofar as they have played vague or undifferentiated walk-on parts in these larger, adult dramas: biological reproduction, demographic birthrates, women's childrearing responsibilities, or acculturation. Of their own thinking about their parents, their siblings, their peer group, or society as a whole and the transformations around them, the record is largely mute.

The contributors to Part 4, although they do not include a discussion of the relationships between children and certain important family members—brothers and sisters, children and mothers, or specifically (except by inference) between extrafamilial groups and the family—begin to think about family relationships from a youngster's perspective. Admittedly speculative and based in psychohistorical methodology, Lester Alston examines slave children's response to their condition and its effects on their lives. Victoria Brown moves the discussion forward in time and westward in space as she talks about middle-class girls in the Land of the Lotus Eaters and their accommodation to gender prescriptions in a locale that allowed girls wide range in their early years and mandated compromise later on. Robert Griswold tightens the focus on familial relationships by looking at the particular relationship between fathers and children in the early decades of the twentieth century. As a student once remarked in another context, "not a pretty picture." What fathers expected from relationships with their children was far from what they received. In the last essay in Part 4 Ruth Alexander studies the young women who "crossed the line" that demarcated the "good" working-class girl from the "bad" one. By examining the extreme cases, she opens the aperture on the thinking of those girls who did not cross the boundary between "good" and "bad" and so clarifies and by extension outlines the influence of peers on adolescent behavior.

9

Children as Chattel

LESTER ALSTON

When emancipation released some four million black slaves in 1865 the one million of them who were minor children were simply the last of many millions of children whose experiences of childhood were framed by the conditions of chattel slavery in the United States. These children were born into slave communities that were as distinct from the African communities of their forebears as they were from the social communities of their white owners. Their experiences of childhood were shaped by an African American slave subculture that by the time of the Civil War was four to six generations old and was peopled by parents and elders who themselves had been born on these shores into slave families and slave communities.[1] Fashioned by the imperatives of slavery and shaped by the social, familial, and moral fabric of the slave subculture, the childhoods of antebellum slave children might find some analogies but no counterparts in the childhoods of other groups. They shared with other nineteenth-century American children—for instance, rural, immigrant, frontier, and urban poor—childhoods that were short, impoverished, exploited, without schooling, and with limited opportunity for self-determination. Unique to slave children's experience was the impact of the peculiarities and requirements of chattel slavery on virtually all of their psychosocial experiences and the roles played by everyone the children encountered in fitting them for a lifetime of bondage.

Attempts to sketch the slave child's development must be speculative, since most accounts of slave childhoods, whether through narratives, tes-

African American family in South Carolina, ca. 1864.
(Library of Congress)

timonies, autobiographies, or diaries, understandably focus on the treatment accorded children or the children's activities rather than on the course of their personal and psychological development. Unfortunately, interest in the history of childhood came well after the effort that produced the greatest amount of information about slave childhoods—the 1936–1938 Federal Writers' Project that compiled the slave narrative collection. The narratives provide fascinating details on how children lived during slavery but because of limitations in the interview questions only scattered glimpses of how slave children *as children* wrestled with the experience of slavery. However, systematic research into the narratives and (to some extent) the autobiographies using psychohistorical inquiry and content analysis and focusing specifically on developmental and formative events might well yield deeper understanding of how children experienced slavery.

As one reads the slave literature a number of persistent themes or questions emerge that from a contemporary perspective compel attention and analysis. These were the tensions and contradictions produced in slaves by the nature of the institution itself that appear to have permeated the slaves' lives and experience: the conflicts between loyalties to parents, to the slave community, and to the owner that were expressed in divided allegiances in some slaves throughout their lives; the ways slaves handled the irony that increases in their competencies and skills aided owners and the purposes of slavery as much as and often more than these increases benefited the slaves themselves; the kind of future slaves projected when so little of that future was under their control; and the toll on the slaves' emotional state by the constant threat of separation and loss. The psychological mechanisms by which slaves adjusted, resolved, or quieted these tensions haunt the study of slavery; any account of how children developed under slavery has to address the ways these tensions were incorporated into their early lives.

❖ ❖ ❖

INFANCY AND ATTACHMENT

Studying the accounts of family life in slavery, one is struck by the limited amount of time slave infants and toddlers spent with their biological mothers. According to Blassingame, the "routine of the plantation prevented the lavishing of care upon the infant."[2] A slave mother, having worked in the fields until shortly before her baby was born, was given a lying-in period of just a few days to a few weeks to spend with the newborn before being returned to her regular sun-up-to-sun-down schedule of labor. In the largest slaveholdings, nursing infants and babies not yet walking were cared for during the day in separate cabins called "chillun's houses" or "nurse houses" that contained rows of cradles and some space for eating and playing. Many of the nursing and weaning functions were performed by wet nurses.[3] Once the slave children became toddlers, many in holdings of various sizes spent most of the day under the care of a nurse—an older slave woman who no longer had the strength or health to be a productive laborer in the fields.[4] In all too many instances, however, even infants were simply placed in the care of siblings just older than themselves. The readings suggest that slave infants early on experienced a practice of communal child care and multiple surrogate caretakers that was to persist throughout early childhood. While time spent with the natural mothers was limited, it is likely that in most cases it was sufficient to establish initial parent-infant bonding and that for virtually all slave infants the natural mother became an attachment figure.[5]

The concept of communal childrearing was continued by the system of having slave children eight to twelve years old tend to and in effect "raise" their younger siblings while the latter's parents were out in the fields. This nursing practice was probably most prevalent on the larger plantations, but throughout slavery many children were often raised and cared for by slightly older children and where the numbers were large enough were raised in cohorts of (roughly) same-age companions.

❖ ❖ ❖

SATELLIZATION

Although bonding and attachment within the slave child's natural family could have proceeded normally, the issue of whether the slave child could have satellized normally on his or her family is clouded. A reciprocal process, satellization permits children to develop sources of status and self-esteem around two years of age, once the "inflated sense of self-worth" and the omnipotence of infancy are ended. At that point, a derived status from the parents, a taking-on of their power, competence, skills, and omniscience substitutes for the previous loss and becomes the basis for a new self-esteem. In return, the child identifies with or introjects the parents' values, mores, attitudes, and behavioral patterns—thus gradually becoming over the next few years a "satellite" of the parents.[6]

For a number of reasons satellization on the slave parents would have been difficult. First, toddlers learned easily that the focal point of authority, privileges, and control was the owner and the owner's family, and this sense may have been firmly established long before the term "slave" could mean anything to the child. The most impressive rewards and privileges came from the owners, who were able to bestow small gifts, toys, and candies on young slave children; parents generally could not. Owners were able to display attitudes of indulgence, ease, and gentleness around slave children; slave parents, in the short time they had with their children, often had to be harried caretakers and restrictive disciplinarians. As children grew they perceived that the owners viewed a slave child's parents as his or her temporary custodians or guardians—again a realization that may have come before children were aware they themselves were slaves. The parents as guardians had some vested interests and affective and emotional ties to their children, which were recognized by others in the slave quarter, but these ties were denied or not recognized by the owner.

The perception that the parents' authority and responsibility was clearly secondary to the authority of the slave owner undoubtedly created ambivalence or conflict within children at some points, but satellization on the owner would have been accelerated precisely by the children's needs to resolve this conflict. The path of authority was clear as recalled by Sarah Fitzpatrick: "When de young fo'ks wanted to go an'wah' dey didn't have to ax deir mama an' pappa, dey axed de white folks an' ef de white fo'ks sed yes it wuz all right wid dem. See we b'long to de white fo'ks, not to our mamas and pappas."[7]

Some owners, affecting a paternalistic style of slave ownership, deliberately drove a wedge between slave parents and their children that made it virtually impossible for children to satellize on their parents. For instance, "good masters" seldom scolded or punished slave children; when they felt some reprimand or correction was necessary, they would have the child's parents do it. Owners emerged as the ultimate protectors of the child, sometimes protecting children from their own parents by admonishing the parent to go easy in whipping a child or even by permitting a young child to flee to them for safety to avoid parental punishment. As was true with adult slaves, the owners sought whenever possible to have someone intercede between them and the child on matters of coercion, discipline, and unpleasantness but made sure that the young chattel had access to them in issues of protection and benevolence. Susan Hamlin, in a defensive but deliberate assertion that her former master deserved the affection of his slaves, experienced such a wedge in a childhood incident:

> Dey [slave parents] couldn't send you out in the cold barefoot neither. I 'member one day my mama want to send me wid some milk for her sister-in-law what live 'round de corner. I fuss cause it cold and say 'how you going to send me out wid no shoe, and it cold?' Mausa hear how I talkin' and he turn he back and laugh, den he call to my ma to gone in de house and find shoe to put on my feet and don't let him see me barefoot again in cold weather.[8]

The slave parent's power and authority would have been eroded further by the child's growing awareness that he or she had a worth to the owner independent of the parent. As children learned how slaves were valued from talk in the quarter, from gossip about sales, and through speculation among peers and as they saw their worth grow, relative to that of their parents, satellization on the owners who determined and controlled worth would have been strengthened.

Satellization was also reinforced by the owner's concern and attention to slaves when they were ill. This attention came at times when the slaves were most vulnerable and when their own medicines and healing efforts had been unsuccessful (or had been judged so by the owner). At such times, whether he ministered to the slaves himself or, as was more rarely done, sent for doctors, an owner could be seen as a healer or a "lifegiver." For impressionable young children the owner's presence and attention during illness must have been seen as highly comforting and caring. Years later former slaves would remember such instances vividly and cite them as proof of their importance to the owner and as justification for their identification with and affection for the owner.

A final factor that influenced satellization patterns—especially in the larger holdings—was the practice of raising children in cohorts. This practice may have blunted a given child's sense of being a satellite of a particular family, since the time spent away from parents in these group arrangements was structured by the owner and spent in activities and chores that furthered the owner's interests. Within the cohorts children had time to reinforce each other's consciousness of the power of the owner and to develop a sense of their being shared satellites of the owner. And the satellization may well have been supported and encouraged by the old nurse or the elders in the quarter who monitored and disciplined young slaves' behavior on the owner's behalf.

Children learned to look to their owners for confirmation of their worth rather than to their parents, and for much of their childhoods, possibly until they approached the teen years, the most important part of their derived status may have been that conferred by association with the owner and the owner's family. If the owner was prosperous and powerful and had esteem among owners, the children sensed that these qualities reflected on them. If the owner was petty, ungenerous, and lacked wealth and esteem among owners, the children felt that also. In the so-called "good master paradox," slaves, both as children and later as adults, may have wanted to see their masters and mistresses as powerful, kindly, and indulgent. They chose to view them as protectors of their welfare, arbiters of their best interests, and even fair in doling out punishment—often despite behavior and evidence to the contrary—because of their own needs for derived status. The strength of this need is shown in the statements of strong affection, intense loyalty, and even compassion made by former slaves for their owners, years after slavery.

❖ ❖ ❖

AUTONOMY

We do not know how slave parents or caretakers handled or viewed the emergence of autonomy in young children at its earliest points around ages two to three. The readings indicate that the power-assertive and restrictive control practices that marked subsequent parental behavior would have been operative here. Yet since many slaveholders monitored and took active interest in the welfare of infants and young toddlers and wanted to see healthy, contented babies, slave parents or caretakers might have adopted more lenient practices with infant and toddler children, accepting spontaneous, even willful behavior from them. The slave child could have developed and expressed an early autonomy, but the picture is likely to have changed markedly as the child gained greater command of language, could begin to express and delineate individual or personal autonomy, and could discern and interpret patterns of authority and control within the slaveholding or the quarter. Possibly well before the age of six strong efforts would have been made to train the child to suppress any public expressions of individual autonomy or willfulness and to begin to cede to the owner (or to the owner's children) rights to override or to disregard the child's urges for autonomy. This was probably accomplished principally by direct teachings and warnings or by the suppression of autonomy commanded by parents and surrogates in their handling of the child. Observing the behavior and overhearing the talk of adult slaves would also have provided many lessons. Transmitted largely through maternal anxiety and sensed in the fearfulness and obedience of adult slaves, the suppression was achieved before the child could understand its purpose or imagine the consequences of resisting. Once autonomy was suppressed, however, a major milestone in the young child's acculturation to slavery would have been passed.

❖ ❖ ❖

SOCIALIZATION

The forces that socialized the slave child were concentrated and clear; they did not extend beyond the parents, the quarter elders, and the master's family. The feudal-like structure of slaveholdings assured each owner virtually absolute control of the slaves and control over many of the influences that might affect them—particularly the children. Except for those living in cities, slave children seldom encountered any other slave children whose acculturation was much different from theirs, even on those occasions when (with the owner's permission) they could visit or mix with children from other holdings. The most notable variation may have been observed in slave children who were favorites of the owner, but even here owners are not likely to have practiced favoritism in ways that encouraged problems in the socialization of the other slave children. White children of nonslaveholding families are not likely to have been much of an influence since the association of slave children and the children of nonslaveholding whites tended to be discouraged by both slave parents and owners.

Masters left it to parents to shape the character of young slaves, and their socialization to proper behavior in the quarters and to slavery was achieved through a consensus of teachings and expectations shared by the parents and the older slaves.[9] Children were of course socialized to the pattern of behaviors that bound the slave community. These included a strong emotional bonding to one's family, an extension of kinship ties to a network of relations in the quarter, a respect for elders, the obligation that each child (and person) would contribute to the family's welfare, the basic Christian teachings, and rather strict moral teachings regarding the behavior toward others in the quarter.

But the most important lesson that had to be learned by every black child during this period was how to conform to the social forms, manners, and etiquette demanded of black people; to some extent it superseded and informed all other aims of socialization. A major portion of the limited time slave parents could spend with their young was probably devoted to the teaching and reinforcement of this racial etiquette. Learning this etiquette was an imperative of the social system; it permeated the slave community, and the child was presumably assisted in acquiring it by all the adults in the community. The child had to learn to conform to the slave codes, to affect submissive and subservient manners, to respond to and obey whites as symbols of power, and to become indoctrinated in the "rightness" of slavery. Parents were no doubt intense and uncompromising in accomplishing this; in fact, many may have seen it as their principal objective in rearing their children and thus judged their competence and success as parents accordingly. Given the relatively short childhood of slave children and the relative danger and ineffectiveness of training the child through other methods of control, parents adopted strict and physical methods of discipline to instill this etiquette. Children would have sensed the parents' urgency to mold their behavior and felt some compulsion to adapt quickly.

Parents also taught children how to survive and occasionally triumph despite their slave status. They taught their children how to sabotage, how to play dumb, how to use sarcasm and humor and laughter to thwart their oppressors, how to communicate by code with each other through song, gestures, and voice inflection—in short, how to make their subservient status work for them so far as the political and social system of slavery would permit. In fact, slave children learned that both slaves and masters shared equally in the practiced, institutionalized deceit of the other that was so integral to the social fabric of slave society. Slavery was enforced by law and fear and ultimately by the gun, but it operated through a set of social conventions, caste behaviors, and mutual "deceptions [that] fed upon each other and were compounded, becoming an inextricable part of daily life."[10] Former slave Edward Jones recollected the reciprocal nature of this deceit some years later:

> The white folks' house must have been tall off the ground, 'cause we would get under it to hear what the white folks was talking about. The white folks would come to our house to eavesdrop, too. It was a habit for us to talk about "white horses" when we meant white folks, so if they heard us they wouldn't know we was talking about them. That's the reason you can't 'pend on nothing colored folks tells you, to this good day—they learned to be so deceiving, when they was young.[11]

❖ ❖ ❖

COMPETENCE AND SELF-ESTEEM

It is difficult to know how slave parents encouraged or viewed competencies in their growing children or the benchmarks in development they looked for. When parents expressed satisfaction in their children's progress, what were the behaviors, skills, or signs of maturity they singled out? We know that obedience and even submission were instilled by parents in the children; while parents may not have admired these traits in their children—or would have done so only with pained ambivalence— they were probably comforted (and may have prided themselves) on seeing them there. Apart from these qualities, others, such as being dutiful and respectful and loving, would have gratified the parent (and the quarter community) even as they served the interests of the owner. Since the child's future work was largely controlled by the slaveowner, parents could do little to prepare the child with the character traits that might bring success in specific roles other than that of field hand.

Slave children would have prided themselves on and gained a sense of their abilities through games and children's play, however. They would have learned early that the competencies and skills to be pursued most avidly were those that brought recognition and increased their standing in the quarters and in their peer group and not necessarily those that would increase their value and productivity to the owner. Among these skills were hunting, fishing, trapping, or gardening, to increase the diet, quickness in identifying the herbs and roots used in cookery and medicine, and the sewing and carpentry that would enable one to use found scraps to fashion furniture, to make repairs to the cabin, or to patch together wearables to supplement or embellish a meager clothing allotment. Children also would have received recognition for the emergence and mastery of skills that increased the slaves' amusements—the playing of instruments, the memorization of chants and toasts and songs that signaled the development of a storyteller or a preacher, the verbal quickness and the wit that helped one excel at the social repartee of the quarters (and the guile needed to fast-talk the master or overseer), the speed, strength, and agility to win at wrestling or dance competitions, cornhuskings, logrollings, and quilting bees that were the entertainments for older children and young adults.

Recognition and esteem would have been accorded to those slave children assigned to learn the crafts and skills of older slaves despite the clear benefit to the owner because of the pleasure adults in any culture take in seeing children learn the skills they themselves employ. To some extent, status in the quarter was based on one's labors within the plantation-work hierarchy, and children apprenticed to learn skills or to become house servants or personal retainers would have received more recognition.[12] Finally, consistent with the many ironic and perverse sets of values engendered by slavery, the adults of the quarter and the children themselves were aware that skilled slaves were more valuable. Willis Cofer, describing slave sales, said, "Cyarpenters and bricklayers and blacksmiths brung fancy prices, from three thousand to five thousand dollars, sometimes. A nigger what warn't no more'n jes' a good field hand brung 'bout two hundred dollars."[13] Possession of a skill may even have provided some sense of security for children since they could have believed that a more skilled slave was less likely to be sold.

Yet even young children might have realized that increasing their competencies and skills in ways valuable to the master could only rarely be parlayed into the most important asset in the slave quarter—freedom from the mistreatment, deprivations, and abuse slaves suffered. Slaves were forced to function in a system in which the master wanted productivity, and slaves wanted above all the security of kind treatment, humane protection, and generous food and clothing allotments. Children could look around and see from the behavior of adults in the quarter that while "production affected the master's humour, . . . the slave had good reason to believe that pleasing the master, ingratiating oneself to him, was a more direct route to better treatment than harder and more efficient work." [14] Many may have expended as much effort learning the arts of ingratiation as they did learning the skills needed by the owner.

❖ ❖ ❖

AWARENESS OF FAMILY AND COMMUNITY

Slave children lived in families quite unique by standards of that period or of today, and their families both mirrored and created the tensions under which the children developed. The composition and structure of these families have been the subject of a century-long debate. [15] Since the establishment of households and families was under the control of the owners and since any number of arrangements could suit the owner's needs, varied patterns of ownership and dispersal characterized the slave family. All may have appeared quite natural to a young slave growing up in the milieu of a slave quarter. In one of the larger holdings a child could have witnessed a variety of families or households: families headed by mothers and fathers with all their children sharing the same quarters; families with only younger children living with the household head(s), the older siblings having been systematically sold or hired away to neighboring holdings; families headed by women with their natural children from several husbands, the result of their being sold along with their children several times and forced to cohabit with men in each new holding; families of informally adopted children of parents who had died, been sold away, or hired out; families with siblings owned by different members of the slave owner's family; families whose children included half-siblings who were the offspring of the owner; households of adult males who were part of one holding but who periodically visited their wives and families residing in a neighboring holding; couples who had once headed families but whose children had—individually or as a group—been sold away; and families with children or a parent who lived in structures near or attached to the owner's house because of their assignment to "bighouse" work or as personal retainers. Slave children also saw families headed by men and women who begged and risked whippings to see each other and cohabit; these children saw that mutual affection and compatibility were deemed irrelevant by owners who denied them permission to marry. Conversely, they would have been aware of families and households that came about through coercion by an owner or the collusion of several owners. For the slave child, families were flexible social units that extended and re-formed themselves in whatever ways were necessary to accommodate new members, changed circumstances, or an owner's directives.

It is possible, however, that for the slave child the phenomenological experience of "family," or what we would call the *primary* family, ex-tended beyond the natural family to encompass the owner or members of the owner's family. Given the authority that the owner represented, the owner's psychological presence and importance in the life of the slave child's natural family, and particularly the owner family's position as the source of privileges, rewards, and punishments, the young child during the satellization process may have invested some members of this family with affective bonds, loyalties, attachments, and identifications of familial intensity and quality. In this case, what constituted family for the child may have been a bifurcated concept with two distinct lines of authority and networks of affiliation bonds developing and existing simultaneously, although not necessarily of equal strength. Alternatively, the child may have developed a hierarchically organized, extended, pyramidal concept of family with a single line of authority descending from the slaveholder through widening strata that would have included at the higher levels the older and then the younger children of the holder and at subsequent levels the child's parents and fictive kin who acted as parents.[16] Under certain conditions, the strength, persistence, and resistance to separation that characterized natural family ties would be extended—often throughout a lifetime, as the former slave accounts show—to the owner's family.

The extension of bonds to the owner's family did not necessarily mean weaker or compromised emotional bonds between the slave children and their families. It is likely that slave children, especially the younger ones, simply established bonds of varying strengths with those who rewarded them, had power, and accorded privileges to them or to members of their natural families. Bonds within the slave child's natural family would have developed out of the early attachment to the mother; this subsequent con-tinued attachment would have been a function of patterns of handling by the parent. Similarly, the strength of ties to the owner or to the owner's family would have been a function of factors such as kindness and the ab-sence of cruelty that characterized the owners' relationships as the child perceived them. In either case, we would expect that in some cases attachments held and even intensified for some children even in the face of maltreatment—as is often the case with young children.[17]

Ample evidence indicates a *consciousness* of the natural family as distinct from the slaveholder's family and that the natural family members worked hard—possibly self-consciously so—to encourage and nurture familial affections. Child care and discipline were viewed and judged by the owners and the slaves as a family responsibility. Children were exhorted to remember to love, protect, assist, and to stay close to each other and particularly the mother (a frequent recollection of former male slaves). When the families were divided, family members went to great lengths to have the family reunited, sometimes requesting owners to arrange sales to achieve this or, braving and accepting the punishment if caught, running away or traveling without permission to visit separated kin. Most freed slaves set about immediately—where it was possible—to purchase the freedom of family members still in bondage or to live as close to them as possible. Despite the extensions of familial-like feelings, the slave child was aware of the natural family.

Some sense of this extension of ties across natural and slaveholding families and the slaves' consciousness of the natural family can be seen in the narrative of former slave John Crawford, who was born into owner "Grandpappy" Jake Crawford's holding of some nine hundred slaves on a Mississippi plantation. "I come up in his backyard and I served him past eighteen years," Crawford recounts. "My pappy was named Henry Crawford for Grandpappy Jake Crawford's pappy. My pappy and Grandpappy Jake used to say we is all Crawfords and we got to stick together, and they is always been fools 'bout each other." And later: "When the Civil War come, my real grandpappy was one that went with Grandpappy Jake and measured three-quarters of a mile from the house to bury the gold and silver . . . [to prevent it from falling into Union hands]."[18]

The slave family functioned in unique ways among nineteenth-century American families; one would have to go to feudal societies to find parallels. First, fundamental decisions about the family could not be made by family members themselves. Even under the most lenient master, children could see that their family's destiny was not in the control of the family. Families were provided for but parents were not the providers. The slave parent could shape the child's welfare, character, or life's work only marginally and only as their efforts were compatible with survival under slavery and the owner's needs. The children looked to their owners and not to their parents for their future. Second, the child saw that the family's intactness and structure were established by the owner and were dependent on the economic circumstances and the continuity of the owner's family. Changes in either were feared since the latent threats of sale or separation often became realities at such times. Third, children learned early that products of a family's labor did not benefit the family as a unit, and, with the principal exception of the small plots of land some owners allotted to an individual or a family to cultivate garden crops, that the child's slave family could do little to better itself or to amass food, material goods, or wealth. Finally, children learned to accept markedly contradictory roles in their parents. A parent with a defined set of personality and character traits was present in the cabins and slave quarters, while a different parent, one showing the docility, shuffling demeanor, impassiveness, or simple-mindedness of the slave group persona, emerged in the fields and in the presence of whites. Young children would have been confused and pained by this, but as they grew they learned that the group persona was play-acting quite unconnected to the real personality of the parent and in fact was an acting ability that they themselves had to master and to manipulate to avoid pain and harassment. Children then began to develop this "other self"—a duality of personality[19]—that allowed them to negotiate both the world of the fields and the world of the quarters. As they moved toward puberty they probably measured and assessed each other—possibly even competed—in how smoothly or convincingly they could mimic this group persona.[20]

❖ ❖ ❖

IDENTIFICATIONS

Like children everywhere, slave children developed a consciousness of self and fashioned personal identities in early childhood based on the "true" personalities and traits of their parents or the surrogates who predominated in their early care. And as they grew older, the circumscribed caste status of slaves and the distinct subculture of the quarter assured that their group identities—the sense of placement of their group within the stratification system of the society—were clearly formed early in their lives.[21] Clear group identities encompassing the slave-caste status would have been established even by those slaves who reported the first realizations that they were slaves in late childhood or in early puberty (most likely when events or demands first challenged their acceptance of bondage).

However, the shaping of identity for slave children involved some unique twists. The slave child's identity emerged in a world where that identity was tied to ownership—was in fact inseparable from ownership. Even in the quarters, the child saw that slaves were identified by a given name quickly followed by the name of the person's owner; they learned that the genealogy of slaves consisted of mention of the parent, of where they were born, and of who had owned them and sold them. A group of slave children, challenged by patrollers while foraging for brush, might be required to state only who owned them or what plantation they were from, as if this manifest of ownership was the only certification of their existence and position in the world.

The development of slave children's identities had to be disturbed by repeatedly seeing the principal adult identification figures in their world humiliated or destroyed. Many had the shattering experience of seeing their own parents flogged in the highly ritualized whippings that occurred in slavery. In addition to the sense of rage, fear, and impotence such an experience must have engendered, the child saw the parents treated as children in ways that they themselves were treated and for much the same reasons. If the parent's behavior displeased or irritated the owner—whether it was failing to make one's daily quota for carding cotton or picking sweet potatoes, being late to the fields, forgetting to perform a chore, or persisting in a request to the owner—the subsequent impatience, scolding, cuffing, or whipping was precisely what the child realized he or she received for similar acts. Older children may have managed an understanding of this that permitted continued respect for the parent's position; but for all slave children there was probably an earlier time when such infantilizing treatment of the parent allowed them to see little or no difference in circumstance between them and their parents, only a puzzling difference in size and age. The treatment of slave parents as children was structured into the slave child's everyday life. Mingo White recalls his involvement in it:

[My mother's] task was too hard for any one person. She had to serve as maid to Mr. White's daughter, cook for all of de hands, spin and card four cuts of thread a day, and den wash. Dere was one hundred and forty-four threads to de cut. If she didn't get all of dis done she got fifty lashes dat night. Many de night me and her would spin and card so she could get her task de next day.[22]

To what extent this disrupted the common wish of children to be like their parents we cannot know. It is conceivable that for many a major humiliation or the flogging of a parent may have been a transition point in the child's satellization on the owner or the owner's family.

The children were likely to see the most impressive figures in the quarter—the strongest field hands, the quarter's most esteemed leaders, the best musicians and songsters, the most quick-witted youths—verbally scolded, broken by the lash, maimed, or sold, especially when such persons exhibited behavior that appeared defiant or rebellious or in any way encouraged other slaves to be less docile. To the young preteen children, such experiences could have altered radically the identification process (shifted from models who were racially like them to models who were racially unlike them), the nature of their play (to incorporate not only the triumphs of their heroes but also their heroes' destruction), and their self-concepts (to be confident and assertive was to increase the risk of humiliation, pain, or separation). Once children entered their teens they may have been able to come to grips with such experiences, being capable at that point of isolating the figure's humiliation or debasement while retaining admiration for the person's distinguishing qualities or skills. For younger children, however, the disruption in identification would have been severe.

The identifications of slave children and much of their socialization were also reinforced through play. Of course, most of their play activity differed little from that of children in any culture. Accounts tell of slave children through many areas of the South playing rhythm or unison games, hide and seek, marbles, horseshoes, variations of baseball or stickball using sewn bags stuffed with beans for balls, dramatic play using dolls in simple domestic scenes, and ring games combining dance, rhythmic clapping, and songs and riddles (which sometimes incorporated veiled derision of the master and protest of slavery much as the church songs of their elders). Some games were probably unique to the quarter, such as "anti-over," often played at night when children grouped on opposite sides of a cabin and tossed a beanbag over the roof to allow the child who caught it to round the cabin and hit someone in the throwing group. Much of their play naturally took place outdoors where they could freely use fields and often nearby woods. For many children, hunting and fishing and trapping in the woods and streams were play activities that also served to supplement the family food supply. Such activities were remembered with fondness by former slaves, probably because these skills were usually taught by the parents or others in the quarter and allowed the children to obtain their first admiration and recognition from adults. Older teenaged children engaged in games of skill and prowess such as riding, jumping, wrestling, and dancing, which sometimes led to their being "sponsored" by groups of slaves or by owners for challenge matches or contests that pitted the best of one farm, quarter community, or plantation against the best of another.

Play provided slave children opportunities to win at competitions, to gain self-esteem, and perhaps most important, to establish the fellowship with their slave peers that would later help them blend into and contribute to the sense of community in whatever quarter they found themselves. This socialization to the behavior of the quarter was furthered by the tendency of slave children in their role-enactment play to emulate the social events they witnessed in the slave community and not those of the owner's family.[23] For instance, they played "church," which included preaching, shouting, and baptisms, and "funeral," complete with hymn singing, processionals, and graveside ceremonies. Through such enactments of the rituals of the slave community and rehearsals of the role behaviors, forms of address, social manners, and mock sentiments of adults, slave children had their group identities confirmed and strengthened. Yet either through the discomfort of the children themselves or the disapproval from the elders, there may have been an equalitarian emphasis in slave children's play that found them less likely than their white peers to engage in central-person games in which a single member had unlimited authority over the group or in elimination games that required the successive removal of participants.[24]

Children's play frequently seeks to neutralize their fears or anticipates significant or pivotal roles they will fill as adults, and slave children's play often internalized and forecast the world that was in store for them. Some slave children played games of "auction" and "master and slave," in which a child would pretend to be an auctioneer at a slave sale while others played the roles of slaves crying and begging not to be sold or traded.

At other times, one child would wield a simulated whip as an owner or overseer while the others would do his or her bidding. How such play was viewed by elders in the quarter, what the thoughts and characters were of children who refrained from such play, and to what degree the occurrence of such play reflected the tenor of master-slave relations in a given slaveholding are fascinating questions that need further research.

In many holdings slave children played on a relatively equal footing with the children of the owner, and the question of the role of such play in the socialization and accommodation to slavery of both the black and the white child also needs exploration. In instances where the play relationships did not repeat the caste positions of the elders, slave children developed perceptions, confidence, and possibly some interpersonal sensitivities in relating to whites that at some point could enable them to negotiate or ingratiate themselves with later owners to their advantage.

❖ ❖ ❖

WORK AND THE SLAVE CHILD

The slave child's acculturation to slavery was achieved as much through direct early work experiences as through any other means. Children age six or younger had no responsibilities within the system of slavery—that is, no demands were placed on them or contributions expected of them by the owner. Generally, all slave children between six and ten performed miscellaneous chores such as cleaning yards, gathering brush, carrying water and supplies to the field hands, chasing birds from newly seeded fields, shelling corn, assisting in the gardening in the slave quarters, and helping in meal preparation. Children of domestics, artisans, and skilled workers spent time during the day with or near their parents, assisting them in their tasks. These efforts were expected—but not necessarily assigned—by the owners and were done under the supervision and authority of the parent. Since 95 percent of slaves were slated to be field hands, however, the central issue in the socialization of slave children to work concerns the age at which growing children were required to do heavy manual labor.

A number of contemporary accounts, most defenders of slavery, and some narratives confirm that some owners advocated and followed a practice of exempting slave children from heavy physical work before they reached their early teens, choosing to defer production from children dur-ing what was seen as a protected period.[25] However, other accounts indi-cate that many (perhaps most) slave children did perform work that was coerced, drudging, and constant long before puberty. Whether and how much young children were required to work depended on the interests of the owner, the size of the slaveholding, local custom to some extent, and the predominant crop (virtually all of a slave force had roles in cotton production). The indications are that for most slave children childhood was not defined or remembered as a time when they were not expected to do some work; that there was a gradual increase in the work that was re-quired of them; that they and the cohort of children around them moved (and were expected to progress) in a steady transition from work that simply assisted others to work based on physical strength and taxing work quotas; and that as children they were defined as much by their physical sizes and production potentials as by their ages. Children heard them-selves referred to as quarter strainers, half-strainers, and three-quarter strainers long before that point in their early teens when they became "full hands."[26] Slave children were many times in the fields well before puberty, often under the direction of an older, experienced field hand, and working at tasks that though less exacting than those of adults were nevertheless compulsory. "Slaves started to work by de time dey was old enough to tote water and pick up chips to start fires wid. Some of dem started to work in de fields when dey about ten, but most of 'em was older."[27]

As a child, Andrew Moss was given a small hoe the length of his arm and was taught to stack it each day just like the grownups.

> I've walked many a mile, when I was a little feller, up and down de rows, followin' de grown folks, and chopping with de hoe round de corners where de earth was soft so de little 'uns could hoe easily.[28]
> I weren't nothin' but a child endurin' slavery, but I had to work de same as any man. I went to de field and hoed cotton, pulled fodder and picked cotton with de rest of de hands. I kept up, too, to keep from gettin' any lashes dat night when us got home.[29]

For many slave children, then, work was a constant, and they may not have experienced changes in the work they did as mileposts in their lives. Work filled the adult slaves' days, and work would fill the children's days well before their midteens and become the focal point of their lives. The type of work and even the toil involved was secondary to the fact that their lives and their time were defined by work. In their psychological experience of work, many slave children slipped from childhood into adulthood not through stages that flowed from any developmental experience but seamlessly through the "steady lengthening" of workloads until they had become full hands.[30]

Some slaves recollected a precise time when they were assigned to the heavy work of the fields and were designated as mature or full hands. These may have been those children who had never felt a strong sense of coercion in the work and tasks that all slave children performed but who were now expected to work at tasks and levels set by the owner, the overseer, or the black driver and, probably more important, who were now subject to being treated or whipped as mature hands if they balked or failed to perform. If the assignment represented a reality that had been denied by the young slave, that isolated the young slave from his family or cohort, or that met with some silent but shared objection by those in the quarter (because of age or physical frailty), the child may have been traumatized. Some were crushed emotionally and thereafter would have recurrent physical or psychological illnesses that rendered them useless to the slaveholder. Others became violent and rebellious; they would start the patterns of resistance, overt defiance, or running away that would lead to whippings, maiming, sale, or death. For all, however, a psychological divide had been reached. Lunsford Lane remembers his experience:

> When I began to work . . . I discovered the difference between myself and my master's white children. They began to order me about, and were told to do so by my master and mistress. . . . Indeed all things now made me *feel*, what I had before known only in words, *that I was a slave*. Deep was this feeling, and it preyed upon my heart like a never dying worm.[31]

Yet dramatic initiation to the fields was not the typical pattern for slave children. Most seem to have been subject to increasing tasks, increasing demands, and increasing coercion that permitted little real distinction between childhood and adulthood.

The blur between childhood and adulthood with regard to work was furthered by the lack of clear gender treatment for boys and girls. Just as both wore until puberty the same coarse, knee-length, long-sleeved smocks split up the side (called shirts for boys and dresses for girls), they were assigned equally to any of the tasks desired by the mistress or by the old nurse. The children who served in the big house as personal servants and the children who spent much of the day around parents who were domestic workers were more likely to have had tasks divided by gender.[32] But the bulk of the chores in the yards, in the vicinity of the fields, in tending animals, and in gathering and preparing foodstuffs was done by either sex, especially in the smaller holdings where the few children available made size and the amount of sense a child showed more important than sex in what the child was asked to do. Boys and girls were likely to have seen and experienced an equality in their early chores and activities that prepared them for the equal treatment and expectations that would pertain when they were adult field hands. Adulthood simply continued the patterns of work assignments that they had as children, with the one difference that the tune was now called by the overseer or driver.

❖ ❖ ❖

PUBERTY AND SEXUAL MATURITY

We would wonder what slave children had to look forward to as they moved through puberty and approached adulthood. It could hardly have been anticipated as a time of greater privileges, a time of greater personal and social choices, or a period when one could direct the course of one's life free of the constraints and limitations of childhood. Adulthood would bring increased status in the quarters since it would permit one to contribute and to share in shaping the life of the quarter. But slave children might have foreseen that adulthood would not bring any significant changes in the slaves' relationship to the master, that in fact it subjected more of their lives to the sun-up-to-sun-down scrutiny of the owner, and that in many respects it would provide even less autonomy than was the case during their childhoods.

The prospect of parenthood also would have created considerable ambivalence for young slaves as they passed puberty. Young males anticipating fatherhood had to accept the curtailed role as father that slavery permitted them. Even when allowed to marry and live in the same holding as his wife, a slave father could perform the roles of protector, nurturer, or teacher only at the times and within the limits set by the owner. Prospective mothers realized that while they could provide some teaching, guidance, and nurturing for their child, much of the daily care would be performed by others in the quarter. Parents could not project themselves as principal providers for their children since that role was preempted by the owner through the allotments of food, supplies, and shelter to the slave force. Adolescent slaves may also have foreseen that once they bore children they were bound more tightly to the owner and more dependent on the owner's good graces and protective treatment than ever before since as parents, the threats of sale and separation took on new meaning. Again, it might have appeared to the young slaves that the adult world they were entering offered no greater promises or choices than the childhood they were leaving.

Clouding prospective parenthood more immediately for adolescent slaves was the realization that their children would be the property of the owner and that the owner's interest in their own growing physical maturity and enhanced value as labor was matched by an equal interest in their sexual and reproductive maturity and the attendant increase in the slave force. If they were fortunate in owners, the interest in slave babies as wealth would have been disguised, and slaves would have been permitted to feel that they could control the circumstances of their unions with mates and the bearing of children (even though some owners provided incentives such as separate cabins for married couples, outright gifts of provisions or cash for newborns, or praise and privileges for women who had many children). Where owners were less guileful, the new ability to produce children raised the degrading and frightening prospect, particularly for young women, that one would be used to breed more slaves. Former slave Mollie Dawson, who, when interviewed, claimed that there was little in her life that would interest anybody and a lot that she would like to forget, expressed her bitterness about slave breeding:

> Co'se mah mother and father was slavery time married darkies. Dat didn't mean nuthin' dem days, but jest raisin' mo' darkies, and every slave darkie woman had ter do dat whether she wanted to or not. Dey would let her pick out a man, or a man pick him out a woman, and dey was married, and if de woman wouldn't have de man dat picks her, dey would take her ter a big stout high husky nigger somewhere and leave her a few days, jest lak dey do stock now'days, and she bettah begin raisin' chillins, too. If she didn't, dey would works her to death; dey say dat she no 'count and dey soon sells her.[33]

For young females coming into sexual maturity there was the additional prospect of being sexually exploited by the white males from the owner's family and family friends. This sexual abuse of young slave girls, particularly those who worked in the big house, was prevalent during slavery; there is evidence that forced sex was more common than the more patent forms of slave breeding.[34] The large numbers of mulatto children scattered throughout holdings suggest that many young females had to anticipate that parenthood would mean that at least some of their children would be fathered by white men in forced liaisons.

Any explanation of chattel slavery in the United States is lacking without some picture of the psychology of individual slaves and the ways the system shaped their development. The slave childhood is clearly the starting point, and the inquiry into how slave children grew and developed should help us begin to understand how slaves adapted to and survived the system and should also extend our appreciation of the variety and the elasticity in childhoods. We need to continue the effort to reconstruct the slave child's experience, and the use made here of developmental stages and concepts is simply one approach for achieving that. Within slave childhoods there were differences that need to be illuminated, especially the differences between the experience of children in extremely small holdings—for instance, a slave child and a parent held by a couple—and those in holdings large enough to provide some sense of community. Also to be explored are the differences between slave children reared in the more common plantation holdings in isolated rural areas and slave children reared in the cities, where the economics of slaveholding permitted more autonomy and even some enterprise for slaves and where the slave families were more likely to be held by merchants, professionals, or manufacturers. Studies of these differences would require other assumptions and research methodologies but would allow us to link modal patterns in childhoods to the variations we find in the experiences and accounts of adult slaves.

10

Golden Girls

Female Socialization among the Middle Class

of Los Angeles, 1880–1910

VICTORIA BISSELL BROWN

Growing up in Los Angeles early in the twentieth century, Susanna Bixby Bryant Dakin had wanted to be a doctor or, as she later recalled, "at least a nurse." So she was "transported with joy" when her father, the city's police surgeon, gave her a medical chart unfolding into a cardboard man for her sixth birthday. The chart had removable parts upon which she could "operate," and according to Dakin's memory of those days,

> when not in use, the naked man hung above my narrow brass bed where Mother had planned a gilt-framed painting of pretty children by Jessie Wilcox Smith. Gory red veins, organs and muscles crudely colored—these were in strange contrast to the little-girl pink predominant in moss rose wallpaper, dotted Swiss curtains, quilted bed coverlet. . . . But Mother never banished "That Man." Although he spoiled her color scheme, he hung there for years.[1]

That Susanna Dakin lived amid pink and dotted swiss but saved her admiration for the naked masculine figure from the medical world that hung above her bed reflects quite well the complex nature of female social-

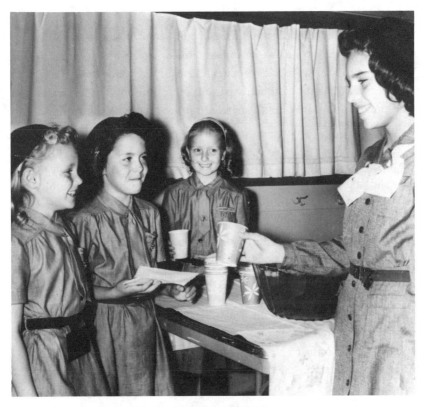

Girl Scouts, ca. 1964.
(Museum of New Mexico, neg. no. 29316)

ization in middle-class homes in cities like Los Angeles in the years between 1880 and 1910. The process involved both the preparation of girls
for a feminine, domestic future and the inculcation of respect for and
interest in that which was masculine.

Because of the contemporary attitudes about gender, parents did not
worry too much about their daughters' slight flirtations with masculine
interests. Many childrearing experts at the time believed that childhood
exposure to such interests would actually improve girls, making them
more rational and vigorous. Similar assurances were not given to the parents of boys who dabbled in girlish activities, which were thought merely
to sissify and weaken. According to the androcentric values of Americans
at this time, girls' desire to mimic boys was understandable; the reverse
was peculiar. Moreover, girls' participation in some masculine activities

could be regarded as good preparation for their later role as helpmeets; boys' interest in female activities did not seem to have similar value. Finally, the need to believe in innate female nature was so great in this period—and the "scientific" propaganda testifying to the power of female instinct so insistent—that many parents felt confident that Nature would win out and their little tomboys would instinctively be transformed into little ladies.[2]

In Susanna Bryant Dakin's case, this confidence was apparently rewarded. She did not become a doctor like her father or even a nurse. Nor did she become the director of the Placentia Citrus Cooperative as her mother, Susan Bixby Bryant, had been. Instead, Susanna's brother, Ernest, assumed that position and, like his male cousins in the extended Bixby family of southern California, he maintained the Bixbys' prominence in regional agribusiness. Susanna, on the other hand, married and had several children, published a local history of elite Californio women, and wrote an unpublished account of her childhood in pre–World War I Los Angeles.[3] In that account, Dakin never mentioned sex-role socialization, per se. She recorded no consciousness of being treated differently from her brother or of chafing at the restrictions on her sex. For Dakin, as for many others of her generation, the sex role she grew into was too obvious to be noticed. Yet evidence from her recollections, from the recollections of others growing up in Los Angeles in these years, and from data collected by researchers involved in the child-study movement at the time indicates that the development of femininity depended on much more than natural instinct. Despite the contemporary scientific view that girls acquired feminine characteristics through an innate process of biological development, the evidence reveals that girls in Los Angeles, like girls throughout the nation, were being thoroughly socialized for their female role. The evidence also reveals that because of the androcentric context in which they were allowed to sample masculine pursuits those opportunities served more to increase girls' awe of males than to encourage female independence.

Los Angeles was not unique in this regard. Indeed, the most notable aspect of Los Angeles in these years is its cultural similarity to other white, middle-class, native-born communities in the north and the east. This is hardly surprising since the remarkable population growth in Los Angeles during these years—from 11,000 residents in 1880 to 320,000 in 1910—was fueled primarily by white native-born migrants from cities like

Des Moines, Grand Rapids, Indianapolis, Milwaukee, and Omaha. These settlers brought their midwestern values with them; their intent was to change their environment, not their culture. They were attracted by Los Angeles' (carefully packaged) image as a metropolis that offered urban modernity amid semirural countryside. As one satisfied citizen bragged to a reporter for *Sunset* magazine in 1913, Los Angeles allowed him to "go to sleep with the mockingbird singing to me" and still attend the theater two nights a week. "I couldn't do those seemingly inconsistent things anywhere else in America."[4] For those who could afford to purchase a piece of the Los Angeles dream—and these are the Angelenos who left the best record of childhood socialization—the city offered a delightful mix of the progressive and the pastoral. As the fastest growing civic entity in the country at the turn of the century, Los Angeles was the first American city to be lit entirely with electricity, to have more telephone subscribers than any city in the world, and to boast of an electric railway system that tied the city to the outlying suburbs with over one thousand miles of track.[5] Still, crooned one Los Angeles enthusiast, there was "no crowding of doorsill upon doorsill, with the stench of the gutter and the glare of the pavement coming in. . . . Each house [was] set back from the street and surrounded by cypress and geranium hedges, with roses climbing over doors and windows, and figs and oranges growing on the lawns."[6] As Susanna Dakin recalled, hers was a world of "tree-shaded streets of shingled houses with front lawns and back gardens, lived-on porches and large attics."[7] It was a city that bragged of its devotion to domestic life, a city where boosters promised that "the ideal home can be made." The Los Angeles vision, wrote urban historian Robert Fogelson, was "epitomized by the residential suburb—spacious, affluent, clean, decent, permanent, predictable, and homogeneous."[8] The residents of Los Angeles in the 1880-to-1910 period who left a record of childhood were not social rebels; Elaine Tyler May observed in her book on divorce in Los Angeles in these years that the region "was settled by Victorians who endeavored to create a city that would keep their traditions intact."[9]

As a result, children growing up in Los Angeles at the turn of the century enjoyed a temperate climate and a unique suburban lifestyle but were still exposed to the same patterns of sex-role socialization as were their counterparts in other American cities at the time. This meant that girls were busy and active but more closely supervised by adults than boys were. Their opportunities to roam and to explore the public world of adults were more limited than boys' opportunities, and their adoption of feminine characteristics was due more to early social influences than theorists of child development at the time could recognize—or admit. So strong was contemporary faith in the scientific gospel that sexual differentiation was a product of biological evolution, not cultural tradition, that most people ignored evidence of the ways in which subtle pressures from friends and families served to shape girls—like Susanna Bixby Bryant Dakin—quite early in life.

The most important socializing force in girls' lives was, of course, the family. Parents are children's primary role models, and girls in Los Angeles learned their basic lessons about sex roles from observing the roles their mothers and fathers played in the family. Generally speaking, the mothers of Los Angeles girls stayed at home and the fathers went off to work. Caroline Meyberg Sichel, who grew up in Los Angeles during these years, recalled that "women were not supposed to work in the early days if they were supported by their husbands or even their fathers. So when a woman worked it denoted that her income was needed to augment her husband's." Sichel observed that "most women preferred to scrimp rather than admit the failure of their men-folks."[10] Nor was there much support in the community for those wives and mothers who had to work. The city's school nurse reported quite proudly to the Board of Education in 1907 that when immigrant mothers complained about having to take time from their jobs to tend sick children, "I tell them . . . in America, the mothers stay home and care for their children or pay someone else to do it."[11]

Only a minority of wealthy mothers in Los Angeles at the turn of the century paid someone else to care for their children. Susanna Bryant Dakin's black nurse, Effie Vermillion, was "the most important female" in her childhood, but Dakin's situation appears to have been atypical.[12] Families employed maids to do housework but not to care for children. Marshall Stimson grew up in an upper-middle-class neighborhood in Los Angeles in the 1890s; he recalled that when mothers wanted to attend matinees or afternoon social events, one mother in the neighborhood would stay home with all the children, and this responsibility revolved from mother to mother.[13] This suggests that daughters in Los Angeles learned from their mothers that childrearing was far too complex and serious a task to leave in the hands of servants. Mothers who became involved with the Child-Study Circles that proliferated around Los Angeles at this time certainly supported this view. Mattie Day Murphy, the Los Angeles–based president of the California Congress of Mothers and Child-Study Circles, described the organization's work as "a postgraduate course" in child development, and one history of the Los Angeles Child-Study Circles noted that members "felt the need for further study to fit themselves for their new profession—parenthood." [14]

It is doubtful that mothers and daughters in Los Angeles talked frequently or at great length about motherhood as a profession, but it is likely that when the subject arose, mothers conveyed the contemporary view that, although femininity was supposed to be instinctive, motherhood had moved beyond primitive biological duty. In modern America, it was work for which women needed to prepare. If Los Angeles mothers told their daughters what they themselves were being told, then daughters heard that motherhood was a high calling that required education as well as instinct. [15] This progressive view of motherhood did not replace the nineteenth-century emphasis on intuitive, moral motherhood, however; it simply augmented it. For example, in most families living in Los Angeles at the turn of the century, mothers still held primary responsibility for their children's moral education. Daughters and sons grew up knowing, at some level, that morality, ethics, and ideals were the province of women. Writing in one of the era's most popular books on life near the Pacific, Horace Vachell reported in 1901 that West Coast churches were filled with women but that men were conspicuously absent. "I often wonder," mused Vachell, "what the children who are sent to Sunday School and church think of the father who never accompanies them." [16]

Children probably did not think much of anything about their fathers' absence on Sunday mornings. If children regarded church as any sort of spiritual experience, they probably assumed that women were in charge of all matters of the spirit. If they looked upon church as just one more tedious chore, then fathers' absence was consistent with their absence from most tedious chores around the house. By all contemporary reports, American fathers were typically removed from the daily business of life at home. William Shearer, whose syndicted column on childrearing appeared in the *Los Angeles Times*, explained to his readers that "of necessity, the father must be away from home most of the time. When he returns," said Shearer, the father would be "wearied by the endless cares and work of the day," so mother should try to manage the family's interpersonal crises herself and call upon the father for assistance only "when absolutely necessary." [17]

Daughters growing up in this period would thus have quickly if unconsciously learned that women were the world's source of emotional nurturance and moral idealism as well as of food, clothing, and medical care. Men, on the other hand, were the source of financial security—and recreation. Where fathers do appear in recollections of childhood in Los Angeles, it is almost always in the context of special outings and family play. Over fifty years after the event occurred, Susanna Dakin vividly recalled the Saturday when her father gave up his weekly golf game to accompany the family to the theater to see Maud Adams as Peter Pan.[18] In his reminiscence of family life in Los Angeles, Marshall Stimson described his neighbor, George Rowan, who "put his whole family [of five boys and two girls] on horseback and later on bicycles. It was quite a sight to see Father and Mother Rowan and seven children pedaling along the highway."[19] Stimson became a father himself after World War I and admitted that he was an absentee father when his children were young, "but when they grew up so I could enjoy them I resigned from my golf club and I always spent every Saturday with them."[20] Los Angeles seems to have offered a pleasant environment in which fathers could play with their children; indeed, fathers who wanted to play may have been particularly drawn to the city. One anonymous father, who was describing the delights of Los Angeles in 1913, told a reporter for *Sunset* magazine that when he had returned from work that day the whole family had played "a lively hour of tennis before dinner [and] tonight we came to the show."[21] Blanche Gray recalled, too, that though her husband was busy as a lawyer during the week, on the weekends he piled the children into the car for picnics and excursions.[22]

Susanna Dakin's uncle, Fred Bixby, took his three daughters and Susanna on a rather extraordinary fourteen-day horseback ride from Oakland to Los Angeles in 1916. Anxious to prove themselves worthy of the time and effort Bixby was expending on them, none of the girls ever confessed to fatigue, but when they rendezvoused with their mothers at the halfway point they renewed their flagging spirits with maternal praise and encouragement. Here again, the father was a source of recreation, even challenge; the mothers provided solace for daily aches and pains.[23]

Adults in this era perceived one problem with putting mothers in charge of the daily business of children's lives: Boys might become feminized by too much contact with mother and too little contact with father. There was concern that without the voice of masculine authority in the home, boys would grow soft and comfortable.[24] A corollary concern was that the sons of absentee fathers would not know enough about the world they were to inherit. One of the key ways in which fathers in Los Angeles responded to this concern was by providing sons with opportunities for employment in the adult-male world. There is no evidence of girls in Los Angeles working alongside their fathers, but there is evidence that this was a common experience for boys.[25] Recollections suggest that Los Angeles boys at the turn of the century had regular contact with the rugged world of men's work. Harry Bixby, another member of the Bixby clan, was allowed to leave school in Los Angeles for a week at a time to work on the family's ranch in Long Beach. Harry's cousin, Sarah, who was the same age, was never included in this ranch work.[26] Similarly, Harold Story's male friends in rural San Dimas were excused from classes during irrigation season, but their sisters were not.[27] Later on, when Story moved into Los Angeles, he and his brother occasionally sold newspapers when there was an "extra" edition to hawk on the streets, but girls did not sell papers.[28] Harry Carr and Harry Bixby also found newspaper work. Carr got a job as a stringer for the *Times* before he was sixteen, and though Bixby's family was quite wealthy, Harry Bixby took on a paper route at age eleven, which required that he be up at three o'clock in the morning.[29] Thomas Talbert of Long Beach had to be up at five o'clock every morning to help with milking and to drive his father's milk truck, and Maynard McFie was driving the delivery wagon for his father's oil supply company by the age of ten.[30] Fathers in Los Angeles gave their school-age sons genuine responsibility. As a teenager Harold Story worked in his father's drugstore where he was registered as an apprentice pharmacist.[31] Marshall Stimson did not exactly apprentice in his father's bank, but he did remember being called out of school during the 1893 run on the banks and being handed a gun to guard the bank while his father went to get money with which to pay depositors.[32]

Girls in this period were largely excluded from these worldly activities with fathers. When they did engage in any sort of adult work, it was either housework or club work with their mothers. One researcher for the *Pedagogical Seminary*, for example, asked high-school girls to name their daily activities, besides studying. Eighty-three percent of the respondents cited "general housework" or sewing. These domestic duties required about an hour a day during the week and more time on Saturdays to aid with baking and mending.[33] Noteworthy here is not the amount of housekeeping girls engaged in, for that was not excessive; rather, it is that housekeeping was the only work cited. In this particular study, none of the girls mentioned working for pay outside the home, nor did they mention club work. Other child-study researchers at this time did find that daughters sometimes served an apprenticeship in moral reform and charity work by belonging to benevolent clubs organized by their mothers. In contrast, boys' clubs were more often formed by the boys themselves and devoted to adventure and fraternity.[34] In Los Angeles, this pattern showed up in the Annual Report of the Hospital Society of Los Angeles for 1904–1905, where membership in five of the six children's clubs was entirely female.[35] Although involvement with organizations such as the Hospital Society did give girls some contact with the world beyond the home, it did not give them experience with the world of independent, remunerative work the way boys' experiences alongside their fathers did.

Anna Kohler provided more evidence on differences in boys' and girls' work opportunities in 1897 when she conducted a study on "Children's Sense of Money" among four thousand California children between the ages of seven and seventeen.[36] Kohler learned that 74 percent of the California boys and 69 percent of the California girls earned their own money, but she found distinct gender differences in the ways in which they earned it. Among the girls, 17 percent named "working in fruit"—a distinctly rural occupation not open to most Los Angeles girls. Only 12 percent of California boys were dependent on fruit-picking as a source of income. Twenty-five percent of the girls earned money from doing housework, a minority, but a high percentage when compared to only 4 percent of the boys who earned money that way. Interestingly, more girls than boys earned money from "running errands"—19 percent of the girls compared to 14 percent of the boys—but this may indicate that girls were more available to their mothers' call than boys. Four percent of Kohler's girls reported earning money "for being good," but only 1 percent of the boys reported such earnings, and 7 percent of the boys but only 3 percent of the girls listed "selling things." The biggest difference in boys' and girls' paid occupations showed up in the vague "miscellaneous" category, where 54 percent of the boys but only 17 percent of the girls were grouped. This probably means that boys simply reported a much greater variety of paid jobs than girls did. Indeed, Kohler concluded from her figures, "girls' occupations are those which are suited to their more passive life, and which call into play a feeling of responsibility, while the boys' occupations are more active and varied, like their lives." [37] Kohler was not surprised to learn that more boys than girls were given a regular allowance—10 percent of boys compared to 7 percent of girls—since she observed that boys' more active lives put them in greater need of money. Nor was she surprised to find that boys were more likely to find money than girls were. "This we would expect as the boys live their lives more in public than girls do." [38]

Kohler's study not only provided evidence about California children's earning opportunities and boys' greater contact with the world but also shed light on boys' and girls' conformity to the sex roles they saw manifest in their parents' behavior. For example, when asked what they would do with $1,000, 40 percent of the boys said they would put it in the bank. Only 25 percent of the girls mentioned banking it, and the majority of that group said they would "have papa put it in the bank for me." [39] Kohler also found several interesting differences in the kinds of things for which boys and girls said they would save or spend their money. Both boys and girls would save for clothes, but girls wanted to save for luxuries like gloves, handkerchiefs, belts, and ribbons; boys listed shoes, hats, or a suit. Some boys claimed they would save money to buy "wood, coal, food or useful things," and though none of the girls thought of saving for those items, several girls did want to save to buy gifts for other people—a goal not shared by any of the boys. [40]

In regard to spending money, the California boys in Kohler's study were more likely than the girls to use it on pleasurable outings such as "renting wheels," "going to see tame bears," or "going to the swimming tanks." Girls, on the other hand, were more likely to spend it on other people (or at least to tell a researcher that they would). Kohler concluded that these differences in spending patterns reflected that girls were "not allowed to go about as freely as boys." In an analysis that was unusually cognizant of socialization, Kohler argued girls' more "altruistic" spending plans were "due in large part to the training given each from their earliest years." Where most of her colleagues in child study would have attributed these sex differences in spending to heredity, Kohler observed that "the daily life of girls, spent mostly in the home circle, has tended to make thought for others habitual, while boys, allowed freedom both in play and work, have naturally developed the egoistic side of their natures."[41]

Whether the California girls in Kohler's study were actually more altruistic and less egoistic than the boys is unknown, but her results do suggest that California children between the ages of seven and seventeen knew the appropriate response to put on a questionnaire. Similar evidence of this awareness of and conformity to sex roles appears in the results of another California study conducted by Katherine Chandler in 1897. Chandler asked five hundred schoolchildren around the state to respond to the question "John's father gave him a piece of ground for a garden and said he might plant three plants. Guess what he planted. Why?"[42] In evaluating the responses, Chandler found that boys' interest in the garden was consistently more "materialistic" and that girls' interest was consistently more "aesthetic." Chandler based these characterizations on the finding that boys were more likely to name food plants because they could be sold and girls were more likely to name flowers because they were pretty. And even among the girls who recommended planting food, a high percentage said it should be given away to poor people and to missionaries instead of sold. Chandler concluded her report with a mixture of cultural and hereditarian explanations. On the one hand, she suggested that boys' and girls' responses differed because "boys, from an early age, understand that they must earn a living, so have their eyes open to the relative value of things, while few girls have the idea of self-support thrust upon them and so are not so keen to utilitarian ideas." On the other hand, she claimed that her evidence of male materialism and female altruism supported the contemporary theory that these qualities were "inherent" in boys' and girls' different natures.[43]

Here again, Chandler's study—like Kohler's—cannot be taken as proof of boys' and girls' actual behavior. Rather, it offers evidence that boys and girls knew what behavior was appropriate to their sex role. One thirteen-year-old girl in Chandler's study demonstrated her sharp awareness of the expected differences between boys' behavior and girls' when she wrote

> I think if I were in John's place I would plant something that would be useful, either flowers or vegetables. If I lived in the city I would be certain to plant flowers, as I think the sick and crippled would be very

much pleased to receive them. John is a boy, and I hardly think I have a boy's thoughts. I think he would plant vegetables or something that would be of profit.[44]

Along with the adults of this period, girls and boys shared a set of assumptions about male and female nature that simultaneously reflected and shaped their experience. Girls were expected to "behave" or at least to be passive in their misbehavior—and typically they were. Boys were expected to act out in physical ways, and usually they did. In 1897 Earl Barnes, the respected child-study researcher at Stanford University, provided additional evidence of children's conformity to these expectations and of adults' role in shaping that conformity when he published his findings on "Discipline at Home and in the School." The results of Barnes's survey of nine hundred California boys and girls showed that boys were more likely to be disciplined for fighting and girls for "talking or whispering" or for "neglected work." Equal shares of girls and boys were disciplined for "destroying things," for "taking things," and for "running away," but the punishments for such misbehavior differed significantly. Almost half of the boys but only a little over one quarter of the girls reported being whipped, while only 6 percent of the boys and 17 percent of the girls reported being scolded. Girls were somewhat more likely than boys to be confined as a punishment or given extra work or a bad mark; boys were more likely to be sent to bed or denied a meal.[45]

The evidence on girls' daily experiences with their parents, with paid work, housework, and clubwork, and with punishment suggests that in Los Angeles as elsewhere they were learning a fairly standard set of rules about women's role. Implicit in these daily experiences was the message that girls were more spiritual, more moral, more domestic, more private, more compliant, less egotistical, less materialistic, less physical, and less aggressive than boys. Indirect lessons in these gender characteristics were accompanied by direct advice from parents and teachers alike. One woman, who grew up in southern California around the turn of the century, recalled at the age of seventy-two that her most powerful lesson in womanhood was her mother's example; she could picture her mother at home in a starched apron waiting for the children to return from school and serving them milk and cookies. Accompanying that image, however, was a vivid recollection of her mother scolding her—at age seven—in a disappointed voice, "I'd like to think you were a little lady." [46] Arcadia

Brennan, who lived in Los Angeles in the 1880s and spent her vacations at the family's Guajome Rancho, could also recall that directives about her behavior were linked to her sex. "Pumpkin, you must behave like a little lady," warned Brennan's aunt, "and not run every step you take." [47] Mothers were ultimately responsible for turning their daughters into ladies. Alice Birney, for example, told the readers of her childrearing manual in 1905 that mothers should have tea parties with little girls so they could "acquire niceties of speech and manner," and the *North American Review* noted in 1906 that the use of slang (while "unavoidable" in boys) was "simply odious" in girls and a "direct reflection upon the attention and tastes of their mother." [48]

It is impossible to measure precisely the effect of all these influences on girls growing up in Los Angeles. Common sense and a knowledge of women's history suggest that the effect was significant; the vast majority of American girls who grew up between 1880 and 1910 did, as adult women, adopt the concept if not the exact rules of ladylike behavior. More important, they adopted the assumption that women were—or should be—more moral, less materialistic, more selfless, and less aggressive than men. Even those who later took on a public role did so in the name of self-sacrifice to some greater cause. Rare was the girl who emerged from this era's upbringing with a secure sense of her own independence or an unbridled eagerness to pursue her own interests. Although evidence from young girls' play life in Los Angeles indicates that growing females at the turn of the century had opportunities to be rough, to get dirty, to escape adult supervision, to experiment with masculine behaviors, evidence also shows that girls knew (or were regularly reminded) of the limits to this freedom. Perhaps most important, evidence confirms that boys' freedom always exceeded girls', which made the condition of masculinity far more desirable than femininity to the average child of either sex. Boys might have been "a nofful lot of trouble" as one little girl in Los Angeles wrote, but a look at children's play experiences makes clear that from the point of view of energetic, inquisitive youngsters, boys' freedom to romp, explore, and move about made them the aristocrats of child society.[49]

Any discussion of girls' informal play must focus on the years before adolescence. During this supposedly neutered stage of development girls were allowed to run and tumble. These were the years when tomboyism was acceptable, when, according to the then popular theory of child development, boys and girls were still basically alike; thus it was appropriate to let girls act like boys (though potentially dangerous to let boys act like girls). As a result, girls in Los Angeles experienced a rather unsystematic mix of freedom and confinement that alternately exposed them to masculine liberty and screened them from it.[50]

The climate in Los Angeles may have contributed to the physical freedom. Susanna Dakin recalled that "after our earliest infancy, our daily life flowed out of doors as regularly as the ocean tide."[51] Dakin shared her childhood with her younger brother, Ernest; such sharing seems to have been a factor in the degree of freedom for girls. The presence of male relatives enhanced girls' opportunities for adventure. Recollections of childhood in Los Angeles indicate that girls had their most exciting outings when they were with boys. Boys, by contrast, recalled their playtime with girls as quiet interludes, as respite from the rough and tumble challenge of boys' separate play.

One way of comparing girls' experiences with boys' in this period is by looking at the childhood recollections of Sarah Bixby and her cousin, Harry Bixby. Members of the wealthy Bixby family who owned Rancho Los Cerritos and Rancho Los Alamitos in Long Beach, they both spent their youth living and going to school in Los Angeles and vacationing on the ranchos in Long Beach. Harry was born a year before Sarah, in 1870, and they were just two of a clan of eight Bixby cousins that included Susanna Dakin's mother, Susan. Sarah Bixby published her recollections of childhood life in *Adobe Days*; and though Harry died as a young man, his boyhood is preserved in an unpublished diary that he kept in 1884 and 1885.[52] The first impression upon reading these two works is that Sarah recalled playing with Harry far more than Harry recorded playing with Sarah. It is clear from his diary that Harry was fond of Sarah; he frequently recorded having dinner at "Sarah's house" in Los Angeles, but he never mentioned actually doing anything with her. Sarah, on the other hand, writing forty-five years later, could vividly recall conducting an "essence factory" with Harry, "collecting old bottles and filling them with different colored liquids obtained by soaking leaves and flowers."[53] Perhaps Harry had abandoned such feminine play by the time he started keeping a diary, or perhaps he did not think it as important as the baseball games and boxing matches he recorded daily. He certainly did not mention playing dolls with Sarah, but Sarah remembered "Hab"—at age eight or nine—doing the "doll family washing" while she "papered the doll house."[54] According to Sarah, boys and girls did not usually play dolls together. Sarah remembered hide and seek and prisoner's base as the only two games that were typically sex integrated. Otherwise, the girls played hop scotch, school, jacks, marbles, tag, "an adaptation of Peck's Bad Boy, and, between whiles, dolls." Doll play with Sarah Bixby was not for the squeamish. She remembered skinning and dressing rabbits and boiling the meat for her doll Isabel, but as adventuresome as that sounds, it was not attractive enough to engage cousin Harry on a regular basis. Doll play mostly involved staging "marriages, deaths, parties" and tailoring—Sarah had a "talent for [making] trousers"—and these dramas were apparently not as satisfying as the hiking and competitive sports that absorbed Harry after school in Los Angeles.[55]

At one point in her reminiscence, Sarah Bixby remarked that as a child she could "do almost anything the boys could"—a comparison that probably never would have occurred to Harry to make and one that may reveal more wishful thinking on Sarah's part than actual reality.[56] Sarah could remember vacations at Rancho Los Cerritos when she and Harry "romped in the barn or garden, visited the corrals or gathered eggs . . . played in the old stage or worked with tools in the blacksmith shop."[57] She recalled picking apples and pears from the orchard with Harry, building houses and gardens in the mud and sand with him, playing in the local river barefoot, even skinny-dipping in the river with Harry and their other cousins, Fred and Nan.[58] Harry, on the other hand, never named Sarah in his reports on recreation at Los Cerritos and made only two general references to "the girls." One day, when he was "tired," he spent the afternoon "in the garden and played with the girls"; another evening he "staid in the parlor and played games with the girls."[59] On one occasion, Harry mentioned that he and cousins Fred and Susie had gone to the river to spear carp, but his report that "Fred speared three and I speared three" suggested that Susie was merely a spectator.[60] The difference in Harry's record of life at Los Cerritos and Sarah's recollection may be a function of age. Sarah's fond memories of adventure with Harry may have been in her preadolescent years, but most of Harry's diary entries at the rancho were made when he was fourteen and Sarah was thirteen, just at the age when she would have "retired" to the garden. Even if age is the reason for the difference, it is still interesting that Sarah remembers so much more about her childhood years than about her adolescent years and in that sense quite possible that Sarah's experiences with Harry were more significant for her than for him. His activities at the rancho—working with the sheep and cattle, riding horses, going hunting and fishing and swimming with cousin Fred—overshadowed his comparatively tame experiences with Sarah. Her most exciting times measured up only to his most quiescent ones.

Twenty years after Sarah and Harry were children in Los Angeles and at Rancho Los Cerritos, their niece, Susanna Dakin, enjoyed similar opportunities for play with her younger brother, Ernest. The record here is not as informative, but it suggests the typical mixture of freedom and limits for girls. Interestingly, Dakin's strongest memories are of early childhood, when she was between six and ten and spending most of her afternoons with Ernest, "free to play in the street with our friends, to do some fancy roller-skating, ride our bicycles, and walk on stilts."[61] Her memories of early adolescence are a much more vague blur of art lessons, music lessons, dance lessons, and schoolwork. It was in early childhood that Dakin tried to fly "like Peter Pan"—sailing off the top of the stairs with wings cut out of the morning's *Los Angeles Times*.[62] In early childhood, too, she and Ernest liked to float down the irrigation ditches at her mother's Santa Ana Ranch and get into mischief with their "most spectacular" friend, Alice Hicks. According to Dakin, Alice Hicks not only had "long golden ringlets and an expression wise beyond her years" but also "had an advantage over us in being brought up Catholic." In Dakin's memory, young Alice went to confession every Sunday morning and afterward "felt free to sin." As a result, "she led us into extraordinary activities, ending in punishment for us but only another confession for her."[63] Dakin did not describe these "extraordinary activities" with Alice Hicks, but she did recall catching mice with her brother and his friends and "doing surgery" on them. Even though Susanna wanted to be a doctor, the actual surgery was always performed by one of the boys.[64]

At the same time that Susanna Dakin was playing with her younger brother in Los Angeles, Frances Cooper Kroll was playing with her younger brother in Santa Barbara. Here again the recollections published in her book, *Memories of Rancho Santa Rosa and Santa Barbara*, included vivid memories of physical play and adventurous outings in early childhood and a distinct sense of retirement after the age of thirteen.[65] In the relatively rural atmosphere of turn-of-the-century Santa Barbara, Kroll and her brother, Tommy, were free to "go almost anywhere alone" by the age of six or seven.[66] On one of their unsupervised afternoons, young Frances and Tommy were part of a small gang of boys and girls who offered to pay a little boy five cents if he ate five caterpillars. The proposition cost the group only two cents and a measure of guilty fear as the boy turned green with the third caterpillar. Kroll claimed never to have forgotten the look on his face as he raced home.[67] Usually, Kroll and her brother spent their time on horseback, taking picnics to the beach or exploring up in the hills. Unlike Susanna Dakin, who had proper riding lessons in Los Angeles, Frances Cooper Kroll was simply placed upon a horse (with a saddle) at age four and told to ride.[68] As a youngster, Kroll regarded a mounting block for horses as "sissyfied," but she seemed to feel it was perfectly appropriate when her teenage sisters switched from horseback riding to driving a horse and buggy.[69] She also considered it natural when the older girls gave up tumbling in the neighbor's haystack; and though as youngsters Frances and Tommy loved to explore Fern Falls, which made a pool in the Santa Barbara hills, she recorded without comment that when they were teenagers only Tommy dove and swam in the Fern Falls pool.[70]

Girls in southern California swam, of course. Harry Bixby recorded swims with his friend, Sarah Blanchard, at Los Cerritos, and a variety of scattered references suggest that girls frequently went on outings to the beach and customarily played along the shore and in the shallow waves.[71] Pearl Chase, who grew up in Santa Barbara around 1900, recalled in later years "jumping feet first from the pier."[72] Daredevil exploits in the water were not common among females, however. In his biography, Marshall Stimson made a special note that Marion Jones, who was later to become a champion tennis player, "was never afraid to go out in the deep water."[73] Boys, on the other hand, customarily did so. Stimson recalled how he "used to go with the other boys to San Pedro to swim." Once there, they would swim out to fishing boats and go aboard.[74] Even when Annette Kellerman was all the rage, it is doubtful that many girls in Los Angeles would have or—given their flannel bathing suits and woolen tights—could have swum out to fishing boats.

The same sorts of constraints applied to horseback riding. Visitors to southern California in this period commented on women's enthusiasm for riding and noted that some women in Los Angeles had even adopted the straddle position.[75] Girls did not enjoy the same freedom with horses as boys did, however. By the age of ten, Marshall Stimson had his own "riding horse," but his older and younger sisters shared a Shetland pony.[76] As a boy, Stimson was free to "ride all over the country" with three or four other boys. "We carried a skillet, coffee pot, bacon and bread," remembered Stimson, "and for the rest we depended on whatever we could get from vegetable gardens or orchards, camping wherever night found us."[77] Frances Cooper Kroll described a different sort of freedom for girls on horseback; she remembered riding from Rancho Santa Rosa to the Santa Ynez Valley one day when she was about fourteen and having a "gracious exchange" with a Mexican man on the way. "I did not realize nor appreciate how wonderful it was that a girl of my age could go anywhere without fear, even in the most isolated of places."[78] For boys, then, freedom meant living off the land; for girls, it meant protection from assault.

When the Bixby cousins rode with Fred Bixby from Oakland to Los Angeles in 1916, they did not camp out along the way nor were they free of the social constraints on their sex. The very first page of Katherine Bixby Hotchkis's book about the trip dealt with the girls' fight to persuade their parents to let them wear riding pants instead of divided skirts. Fred Bixby regarded pants as "immodest, unbecoming, and unfeminine" and conceded only when his wife finally sided with the girls.[79] Along with the riding pants the girls wore middy blouses and "floppy hats of white duck." They were "feeling pretty stylish" until they stopped for lunch at a restaurant their first day on the road and met the silent stares of other diners. "In our upbringing," recalled Hotchkis, "it was considered a sin to be conspicuous, especially for girls. Now here we were already attracting notice for having worn the unmaidenly riding pants that Father was so against."[80] Even on an adventure as challenging as this ride down the California coast, young females were not free of standards for femininity. The Bixby girls got used to the lunchtime looks but avoided embarrassment at dinner because their mothers had insisted that they take silk dresses and pumps in their knapsacks.[81]

In trying to envision girls' play life in Los Angeles in this period, it is essential to balance this feminine confinement with the childhood activity. An advertisement in *Land of Sunshine* in 1900 neatly captured the duality. "Healthy girls like healthy boys are rough on clothes," read the caption beneath a photo of a decidedly sturdy young girl in overalls. "Protect your little girl's clothing with a pair of American Girl overalls and let her have a good time." In smaller print the ad assured customers that the girls' overalls were cut especially wide "to accommodate the skirts."[82] There was undoubtedly a market for such playclothes in Los Angeles, for girls were out on the streets with their hoops and jacks and hop-scotch lagers; and girls, like boys, were caught up in the new fads like roller-skating and bicycling. At the height of the bicycle craze in 1895 the *Los Angeles Times* ran a story on Dr. A. S. Shorb's daughter, Lillian, who had been thrown from her bicycle "while swiftly rounding the corner at Main and 25th." When her front wheel struck a stone, young Lillian was thrown against the curb and sprained her ankle. According to the *Times*, Officer Mike Long helped the injured cyclist into a buggy that took her to her home in the exclusive West Adams Street neighborhood.[83]

Roller-skating was equally popular with the girls and the boys. Catherine Dace, who grew up in the San Fernando Valley in the 1890s, recalled "if anybody had roller skates they had to go to Pacoima because they had the only piece of cement in the entire valley. We used to ride bicycles across the bridge to get there."[84] Nellie McGraw Hedgepeth was growing up in San Francisco at the same time and also recalled the difficulty of skating on wooden planks. Hedgepeth remembered when her neighbor, Mayor James D. Phelan, paved the street in front of his house and she, along with "about fifty other children," would congregate there every day to skate on the smooth surface.[85]

Still, even when the activities were identical, there was generally a sense of restraint associated with girls' play that was not associated with boys'. When the *Los Angeles Times* complained in 1883 about the safety threat posed by roller-skating on the streets and sidewalks, it singled out the "swarms of Los Angeles boys" who were endangering citizens' lives and limbs.[86] Girls probably skated closer to home and in smaller groups. The evidence indicates that girls' play, though energetic, was more cautious and more confined than boys'. Nellie Hedgepeth provided a tempting metaphor for the condition of girls when she recalled that girls' tops in the 1880s had strings attached to them, but boys' tops did not. The tops with strings were "not very exciting," noted Hedgepeth. "We preferred the boys' tops."[87]

Like Hedgepeth's top, girls had strings tying them down; they simply could not move about the city as boys could. It is unlikely, for example, that Sarah Bixby would have been allowed out of the house alone at night, and yet when a fire broke out at the Boyle Heights Hotel at 9:30 P.M. on February 7, 1885, Harry Bixby reported in his diary that he "ran all the way over there without stopping once." Two of Bixby's friends went with him, but no adults, and the boys did not return home until 11:30 that night.[88] In a similar vein, Ervin King recalled "boys' thrills in Los Angeles" during the late nineteenth century. He remembered boys' freedom to roam at will, to have contact with nature, to deal with foreigners, to get into trouble.[89] Edwin Bingham corroborated King's story in his study of the Chinese community in Los Angeles. There, Bingham remarked, "for many years Chinatown was the only place where firecrackers might be obtained. This fact endeared the Chinese section to white boys."[90] Native-born white girls in Los Angeles were usually screened from contact with the city's foreign element, but their brothers were not. L. J. Rose, Jr., employed large numbers of Mexicans on his ranch outside of Los Angeles in the 1890s and boasted in his biography that his daughters' governess brought the girls out for a "glimpse" of the Mexican camp "occasionally" but that his sons "had free run, ate tortillas and frijoles with the Mexican children and learned to speak Spanish with them."[91]

Here again the contrasts between Harry and Sarah Bixby are illustrative. On the Fourth of July, 1885—when Harry was fifteen and Sarah was fourteen—Harry recorded in his diary that he had spent part of the day celebrating at a picnic with all the cousins. In the afternoon, however, Harry and the other male cousins joined the ranch hands for some horse races.[92] Sarah commented in *Adobe Days* that the girls did not often go to horse races because the mothers "frowned upon" them as being "unsuitable for Christians and girls."[93] Presumably, Sarah went home to an early bed on that Fourth of July, but Harry went on from the horse races to a Mexican dance in the barrio where he drank beer and stayed out until one in the morning.[94] Sarah did not mention this particular escapade in her book, but she did tell about the time that the women allowed the "menfolk" to take the children to the circus and Harry was his grandfather's "lucky escort" to every last sideshow.[95]

The anecdotal evidence from Los Angeles suggesting that girls enjoyed an active play life but were more confined than boys and simply excluded from certain activities is supported by child-study research conducted at the time. Typically, studies on children's play found that girls were getting outside and running around but their active play was segregated from that of the boys. Boys preferred baseball and football; girls preferred hide and seek, hop scotch, and jackstones. When girls did mention ballgames, they named handball, croquet, and baseball as their favorites. Three percent of the children in one study specified that their favorite games were those that were not "rough," and all the subjects in that three percent were girls. "Many of the boys" in that same study "distinctly stated that they prefer vigorous, active, rough games."[96] Girls in the play studies often named a wider variety of favorite activities than boys because boys' favorites were almost exclusively physical; girls named "imitative games, indoor games, games involving mental effort, and rhythmic games" as well as physical games.[97]

Genevra Sisson reported much the same results when she observed the free play of kindergarten children in Santa Cruz, California, in 1896.[98] The boys ran, wrestled, and played roughly. Their games of make-believe involved "boisterous" stories of "policemen, hunters, storekeepers, electric light men," and other masculine characters.[99] Girls, on the other hand, "conducted their play very quietly" in the sandpile or in the woodshed. Their make-believe revolved around playing house or school, and rather than being boisterous the girls were "domestic and motherly."[100] Indeed, housekeeping was such a universal favorite among girls that one young woman told a researcher in 1896 that she had frequently been left out of her girlfriends' games as a child because "housekeeping was a favorite" with them and she "could not be induced to play housekeeping."[101]

Despite such evidence of occasional rebellions against sex-role prescriptions, the overwhelming impression from the child-study data and from personal recollections is that the majority of girls on the West Coast at the turn of the century shaped their desire for childhood activity to the dictates of femininity; and according to those dictates, girls had fewer degrees of freedom in their range and level of activity than did boys. This is an important if not a surprising conclusion, but it is not the only conclusion to be drawn. Equally important is the conclusion that boys' greater freedom meant not only sex difference but also sex hierarchy. Boys' freedom to romp and explore made them—from a child's perspective—the aristocrats of child society. Thus from an early age, females learned to admire males and males learned to disdain females. Girls were conscious of not being allowed to do what boys could do, and boys consistently stated that they did not want to do what girls did.

Illustrative of this disparity in attitude toward masculinity and femininity are the studies done at the time on children's reading tastes. These studies make clear that girls' admiration for the male world of adventure was not reciprocated by any male admiration for the female world of domesticity. Clara Vostrovsky found this to be true when she conducted a reading study in 1899 among six hundred boys and six hundred girls in the Stockton, California, public schools. In reporting her findings at the annual meeting of the California Teachers' Association, Vostrovsky noted that none of the boys confessed to liking a "purely girl's story," and most boys regarded books about human emotions as "silly." [102] Girls were not so put off by boys' stories; about 10 percent of them listed adventure stories among their favorites, though Vostrovsky noted that "the exciting stories mentioned by the girls are very quiet compared to those mentioned by the boys." [103] Still, girls' willingness to read adventure stories compared to boys' unwillingness to read domestic stories caused Vostrovsky to ask rhetorically, "Are girls more interested in their brothers than boys are in their sisters?" [104]

Anna Kohler might well have asked the same question when she wrote her study on "How Children Judge Character." Kohler used the book *Little Men* to elicit a discussion of ethics among schoolchildren in Oakland, California. [105] Emerging most distinctly was the boys' lack of interest in female characters (the boys, said Kohler, waited "restlessly" for the boys in the story to reappear) and their aversion to any "pathos" in the story. "While the girls listened as attentively to the pathetic parts as they did to the gayer ones," reported Kohler, "several boys asked to 'skip that part' when we were reading about Dan's misfortunes or John Brook's death." [106] In contrast, Kohler found that "the interest of the girls was more sustained through the whole book"; they were equally interested in the exploits of the male and the female characters. [107] Male qualities and activities simply did not have the negative connotations for girls that female qualities and activities had for boys. In fact, the girls in Kohler's study preferred the tomboyish character, Nan, in *Little Men* over the ladylike character, Daisy. One little girl who especially identified with Nan wrote, "I like mischievous people, because I am so bad myself. I never am happy unless I am into some scrape." This same little girl added, as a postscript, "I think that when we are older it is time to settle down." [108] So even a self-described tomboy felt a time limit on her adventurousness, knowing that her masculine make-believe would have to end sooner rather than later. Indeed, when she did a study on "Children's Ideas of Lady and Gentleman," Kohler was informed by one young girl that "after the age of thirteen, a lady should not climb trees unless to get away from a dog." [109]

Taken together, the results of the child-study research on play and the recollections of childhood in Los Angeles indicate that preadolescent girls were allowed their opportunities for childish cavorting but were well aware that boys' opportunities were broader and that boys' futures were different. When Loretta Berner was growing up on the old Bean Ranch near Long Beach, she liked to help the local blacksmith and to listen to the men talk about their adventures. Berner recalled almost seventy years later, "At the age of nine, I was sorry I was a girl because I too wanted to roam the world free as a bird!" [110]

This wistful sense of regret over her femaleness, which was hardly unique to Loretta Berner, serves as a useful reminder of the double-edged nature of female socialization in these years. For as thorough and successful as that socialization was in behavioral terms and as vigorously and "naturally" as girls opted for feminine pursuits, they never forgot that their portion of life's activities was second-best, that what boys had and what boys did was more exciting and potentially more powerful. For some females this knowledge sparked a lifetime of conscious rebellion, but for the vast majority who were socialized at the turn of the century the result was conformity to the rules of femininity accompanied by an envy of and deference to masculinity that would make it difficult for women—especially the comfortable middle-class women who dominated Los Angeles—to challenge the gender hierarchy that had so shaped them as girls.

11

"Ties That Bind and Bonds That Break"

Children's Attitudes toward Fathers, 1900–1930

ROBERT L. GRISWOLD

Sometime in the late 1920s, four-year-old Harry White startled his mother while she visited him in the hospital: "Say, Mama," he asked, "is my daddy drunk yet?" Unnerved, she replied, "Harry, what did you say that for?" Not surprisingly, Harry had his reasons: "Because I don't want my daddy to drink. I want him to get a job." Much to her dismay, his mother later overheard little Harry confront his unemployed, hard-drinking father directly: "You dirty bum you, why don't you get out and get to work?"[1] Another, much older child from a different family expressed animosity toward both his father and mother: "All that I ever felt toward my parents was fear and dislike. . . . In addition to being misunderstood, I feel that I was not recognized as a personality."[2]

For every child like these two, however, there was probably a son like W. O. Saunders, who lauded his father's willingness to sacrifice for his family, to work "twelve to sixteen hours a day to keep a roof over the heads of the rest of us. . . . It is an inconspicuous part that fathers seem to play in life. Yet how unselfishly, how resolutely they set their faces to the task of building and maintaining homes that families may be raised."[3] Other children highlighted not their fathers' sacrifices but their companionship, affection, and care: "I always confided in my parents," recalled one youth, "especially my father. We would even discuss the words that

*Gonzalla Sullivan and son, Marion County, West Virginia, June 13, 1946.
(Russell Lee, photographer. National Archives, Records of the Solid Fuels
Administration for War [245-MS-1136])*

I picked up from the street. I loved to talk confidentially with my father because he seemed to know so much and because of the wholesome easy manner in which he explained things."[4]

Yet children's sentiments for fathers did not match their affection for mothers. When investigators asked youngsters in the 1920s and 1930s which parent they preferred, children favored their mothers. In one study, for example, 10 percent of nine-year-old boys preferred their fathers, 76 percent their mothers. The figures were much the same for nine-year-old girls: 14 percent preferred their fathers, 68 percent their mothers.[5] When researchers asked adolescents the degree "to which they tell their mother and father their joys and troubles," eighth- through tenth-grade boys and girls made it clear that they confided far more often in their mothers than in their fathers, a preference likewise voiced by three thousand young adults in another study done as the twenties came to a close.[6]

Children not only had their preferences but also thought about their parents in quite different ways. When a psychologist in the early 1930s asked 150 St. Louis children (average age twelve) to say the first ten things that came to mind when they heard the words "father" and "mother," a clear pattern emerged. Children tended to describe their fathers in instrumental terms; for example, "plays with me" was mentioned 121 times in regard to fathers, only 49 times in association with mothers. The children associated fathers with "outdoor games" 38 times, mothers not at all. In contrast, the youngsters more frequently associated affective terms with their mothers; 69 expressions of "love," "like," and "loyalty" went to mothers, only 27 to fathers.[7]

These scattered bits of information are interesting, but the key question, of course, is how to interpret them. Why did Harry White turn against his father while W. O. Saunders spoke so respectfully of his? Why did children prefer their mothers, and how do we interpret the meaning of this preference? If children confided in their mothers rather than in their fathers, what inferences can be made about children's place within the family and within society? What speculations, if any, can we make from these data about children's psychological development? More broadly, in what ways did important social transformations structure children's attitudes toward their fathers? What implications do these attitudes have for our understanding of patriarchy and the social construction of gender relations?[8] In this essay I cannot begin to answer the many questions these examples pose. Its aim is a more modest one: We have given little systematic thought to the subject of children's attitudes toward either parent, an omission I hope to address here by exploring key elements that shaped children's feelings about their fathers in the first third of this century.

Fathers' moral rectitude, particularly if linked to their success or failure as breadwinners, was one such element. Although children played a vital role in the economic strategies of working-class families, fathers remained identified as the principal breadwinners. This responsibility was central to men's sense of standing, dignity, and self-respect. Even those who failed economically more often than not received sympathy from their children. One fourteen-year-old daughter of an unemployed Russian immigrant, for example, defended her father and understood his psychological trauma: "In my estimation," she wrote, "it is a crime that a person physically well and seeking work should be so humiliated by not being able to supply the needs of his family."[9] Thousands of other youngsters went dutifully off to work to supplement their fathers' earnings. As Amoskeag textile worker Richard Laroche remembered, "There was no question. . . . It stands to reason that the father expected, when there was nine or ten children, that they're all gonna start working and pitch in."[10]

Such support was expected. It made survival possible, but it was assistance that was in some sense earned. Children could be keen critics of their fathers' moral shortcomings: Their perception that moral and economic failure were interrelated appeared repeatedly in case records from welfare agencies. In short, although little Harry White may have been more blunt than most, he was not unique. Other children made similar judgments. As an unemployed Boston plumber, for example, slipped into a state of despondency and discouragement and began spending more and more time in saloons, his son's affection evaporated and "as time went on, he began to lose all respect for his father and actually ran to hide at the latter's appearance in the home."[11] An Italian immigrant laborer from Pittsburgh shared the same fate. Unable to find work, he began to drink incessantly and became abusive toward his seven children. In response the children "seem very ashamed of him. . . . One of the children said she wished that her father would die so that her mother could marry the boarder, and they'd have things nice!"[12]

Other children expressed their resentment in more direct ways. The children of unemployed autoworker Paul Lombetti "no longer showed any respect for their parents and were rude and disobedient. We knew of no bootlegging, or gambling—but in juvenile delinquency, two of the boys, within the past two years, have come under the ban of the law." [13] Similar woes befell the family of a thirty-seven-year-old father of five who responded to underemployment by drinking and abusing his wife and children. Ultimately the parents separated and the children lost all respect for their father, referring to him as "the old man." The youngest daughter, age ten, began to "run the streets" and, like her sixteen-year-old brother, became a discipline problem at home, school, and the settlement house.[14]

Far more research is needed on the attitudes of children toward hard-pressed fathers. As these examples suggest, some children rallied behind their fathers but others became embittered and contemptuous. Children's emotional and psychological reactions to their father's class position and economic difficulties were by no means uniform and consistent: Feelings of guilt, devotion, shame, duty, love, sacrifice, and selfishness were hopelessly entangled as the young responded with a mixture of emotions to the plight of their fathers. It is fair to say, however, that the structure of urban industrial life lent itself to father-child conflict. After all, poverty, long working hours, cramped living quarters, and leisure patterns that took men away from the home reduced the ability of immigrant working-class fathers to shape the lives of their offspring.

The immigrant origins of these men worked to heighten their children's alienation from them. Reared in traditional European societies, immigrant fathers found it difficult to assert authority over their progeny or to resist the incursions of an American culture that came from every direction. Whether on the streets or at the movies, in stores or at school, immigrant children began to pick up the trappings of a culture very different from that of their fathers. Many writers have described the attraction of America to immigrant youth but none more succinctly than Hutchins Hapgood in his 1902 book, *The Spirit of the Ghetto*:

> In America, even before he begins to go to our public schools, the little Jewish boy finds himself in contact with a new world which stands in violent contrast with the orthodox environment of his first few years. Insensibly—at the beginning—from his playmates in streets, from his older brother or sister, he picks up a little English, a little American slang, hears older boys boast of prize-fighter Bernstein, and learns vaguely to feel that there is a strange and fascinating life on the street.[15]

Once these children reached working age, this process only accelerated. The availability of wage work for working-class youth put them beyond the observation of their parents, placed some money in their hands, and introduced them to a youth culture that played a critical role in pulling immigrant children out of the orbit of their parents' traditional culture.

As many immigrant children began to find the streets more congenial than their homes, they sometimes turned against their own people. The Americanized Jewish youth might well laugh "at the foreign Jew with as much heartiness as at the 'dago'; for he feels that he himself is almost as remote from the one as from the other." Nor could parents escape such condescension. Writing of Jewish boys, Hapgood noted that "the growing sense of superiority on the part of the boy to the Hebraic part of his environment extends itself soon to the home. He learns to feel that his parents, too, are 'greenhorns.' " [16] To Lincoln Steffens, the generational split in the ghetto was "an abyss of many generations; it was between parents out of the Middle Ages, sometimes out of the Old Testament days hundreds of years B.C., and the children of the streets of New York today." This abyss could create contempt among the young toward their fathers, contempt that Steffens described as ubiquitous:

> We saw it everywhere all the time. . . . we would pass a synagogue where a score or more of boys were sitting hatless in their old clothes, smoking cigarettes on the steps outside, and their fathers, all dressed in black, with their high hats, uncut beards, and temple curls, were going into the synagogues, tearing their hair and rending their garments. . . . It was a revolution. Their sons were rebels against the law of Moses; they were lost souls, lost to God, the family, and to Israel of old. [17]

Children found the Old World ways of their fathers restrictive, sometimes incomprehensible. Grace Grimaldi squirmed under the watchful eye of her suspicious father who refused to let her go out with girlfriends and carefully regulated her romantic life. Although she did meet her boyfriend on the sly, her father's threats were never far from her consciousness: "If I catch you walking around," she remembered him saying, "I'll break your neck." [18] Elizabeth Stern's and Rose Cohen's difficulties with their fathers involved education. Stern complained that "my father did not approve of my continuing high school. It was time for me to think of marrying a pious man." Rose Cohen recalled her horror when her father threw a library book out the window in which her brother had found the word "Christ": "When I looked out and saw the covers torn off and the pages lying scattered in the yard, I . . . wept aloud that I had a right to know, to learn, to understand . . . that I was horribly ignorant; that I had been put into the world but had been denied a chance to learn."[19]

Stories by Budd Shulberg and Anzia Yezierska vividly captured the split between immigrant fathers and their children. A brief exchange in Shulberg's novel *What Makes Sammy Run* explored the cultural chasm that sometimes divided fathers and sons:

> "I hadda chance to make a dollar," Sammy said.
> "Sammy!" his father bellowed. "Touching money on the Sabbath! God should strike you dead!"
> The old man snatched the money and flung it down the stairs. . . .
> "You big dope!" Sammy screamed at him, his voice shrill with rage. "You lazy son-of-a-bitch."
> The old man did not respond. His eyes were closed and his lips were moving. He looked as if he had had a stroke. He was praying.[20]

This cultural chasm was not restricted to father-son relations. Anzia Yezierska described the anguish of a young Jewish woman who took pride in her worldly success, only to find that her father's values lay elsewhere. Upset with her father's accusations that she neglected him, the young woman reminded the old man that she had given him one hundred dollars she had earned as a writer. Unimpressed, he shot back, "Can your money make up for your duty as a daughter? In America, money takes the place of God." Hoping that her father might take pride in her economic success, she began telling him of the ten thousand dollars she received from her publishers, but he had heard enough: "Can you touch pitch without being defiled? Neither can you hold on to all that money without losing your soul."[21]

These generational tensions were augmented by the rise of a distinctive youth culture that developed at the workplace itself. Young men and women, drawn into the workforce to help supplement their fathers' inadequate incomes, increasingly labored not in domestic or small-shop isolation but in the large factories, offices, and department stores of the expanding corporate economy. Thrown together in workrooms and department stores, young men and women staked out a measure of personal and generational autonomy for themselves by enforcing informal work rules, adhering to the "stint," and socializing new workers to the culture of the shop floor. Here the young affirmed their allegiance to the fads, styles, habits, and curiosities of their co-workers. Gossip, slang, clothing, hair styles, songs, and social rituals distinctively marked the work culture of the young. Frank discussions of sexuality, spiced with ribald jokes and sexual advice, punctuated the conversations of young females in ways that would have appalled their parents.[22]

This culture and these interests extended beyond the factory, office, or department-store doors. Unlike their fathers, who spent much of their leisure time in saloons and fraternal organizations, or their mothers, whose leisure was oriented to the home and kin, working-class youth found themselves drawn to heterosexual, pleasure-oriented commercial amusements. After a hard day of work, girls put on their finery and promenaded in the streets or headed for movie theaters or the ubiquitous dance halls to engage in "tough dancing" with boys of the same class. More exciting still was a trip to Coney Island and the bizarre amusement-park rides that promiscuously, and literally, threw young men and women together.

Relentlessly heterosexual, shaped by commercialized recreation and the burgeoning culture of consumption, the culture of the young eroded paternal prerogatives and the salience of traditional immigrant cultures. City streets, dance halls, amusement parks, and movie theaters offered immigrant youth social space for sexual experimentation, personal asser-tion, and the renegotiation of cultural mores. Compared to the excitement of a sexually charged dance hall with its "promiscuous interaction of strangers," ribald language, and general bawdiness, a quiet night at home with parents or a chaperoned evening with a beau seemed impossibly dull and old-fashioned to the working girl just off a ten-hour shift.[23]

Nor were some girls willing to acquiesce to parental demands when such demands interfered with their pursuit of pleasure. Antoinette Paluz-zi's father refused to allow her to date, but with the permission of her mother the young Italian walked to a park with a friend where she met her boyfriend, always certain to return home before her father's work day ended. Bolder still, Maureen Connelly decided that if she were going to violate her parents' curfew, she might as well do it royally: "If I went out and I knew I'd get hit if I came in at twelve . . . I'd stay out till one." Another wrote to the *Jewish Daily Forward*'s advice column, hoping to find an answer more in line with her own sentiments than those supplied by her father: "Is it a sin to use face powder? Shouldn't a girl look beautiful? My father does not want me to use face powder. Is it a sin?"[24] Clearly, she had her doubts.

Different factors shaped children's attitudes toward fathers in the middle class. In burgeoning suburbs, thousands of men finally had the income and the leisure time to construct a new vision of fatherhood that reflected the values of an emerging therapeutic culture dedicated to "growth," "personality," and "self-realization." As providers, men underwrote a consumer culture that equated the purchase of goods with happiness and self-expression; as nurturers, men tried, albeit with mixed success and considerable ambivalence, to become more involved in the development of their offsprings' personalities and individual growth. Love and involvement, not discipline and dominance, were the hallmarks of the modern middle-class father.

Consequently, children's attitudes toward fathers developed in different ways. Absent was the clash between New World children and Old World fathers. This issue, which resonated so strongly in the lives of immigrant children and colored their perception of their parents in both negative and positive ways, was not important to the WASP middle class. Nor did children harbor resentments stemming from their fathers' failures in the working world: These men were, after all, in various degrees successful. We do find among middle-class children a distinct tendency to see their fathers less as breadwinners and more as companions. When a St. Louis psychologist compared the attitudes of lower-, middle-, and upper-class children to their fathers, he found that the two more wealthy groups of children tended to view their fathers as "[someone who] takes me places" and who "plays with me," but children of working-class fathers placed far more emphasis on their fathers' role in discipline. Middle-class children frequently described their fathers as someone who "does things for you"; working-class youth described fathers as someone who "takes care of you."[25] After categorizing the responses, the investigator concluded that "children from the lowest economic level outrank the children from the other two groups in the frequency with which they think of their parents in terms that are either economic, manual or physical."[26]

The psychologist teased other findings of interest from his data. Children from working-class parents tended to feel less psychologically secure in their emotional relationships with their fathers: Their dependence upon them was more forced, less free.[27] Working-class youth also tended to see their fathers as more repressive than did middle-class youth—though no more so than upper-class children—and as substitutes for God. They shared with middle-class youth a vision of their fathers as "models and guides" and showed the highest level of "appreciation" for their fathers. Conversely, working-class youth fell well behind their more wealthy counterparts in their tendency to associate fathers with "companions." Summarizing the results, the psychologist concluded that economic security was associated with emotional security. Middle-class youth had the least repressive relationship, the most healthy degree of dependence, attachment, and acceptance, and the least conflict and hostility with their fathers.[28] In all these areas, working-class youth fared the worst and upper-class youth occupied the middle ground.

What one can make of this evidence is, of course, questionable. The psychologists of the 1920s and 1930s were fixated on the question of "personality formation," and it should come as no surprise that these middle-class ideologues extolled the virtues of middle-class childrearing. Nevertheless, much of the data and interpretation is in keeping with other evidence. Middle-class fathers did have more leisure time than men from the working class. They did play with their children more frequently, took them more places, read them more stories, and spent more time with them than did their hard-pressed working-class compatriots.[29] The son of a dentist recalled that he did not "read a great deal myself but my father read aloud to me almost every evening. . . . For many years my father and I took long walks at daybreak. We naturally observed and became interested in birds."[30] Another remembered that "he has always appreciated and realized a child's desires, and he has done everything for us—though not so lavishly as to make us unappreciative of it. He built toboggans for us in the winter, hung up swings and hammocks in the summer, and was always contriving some new and fascinating toy. He gave us everything he could."[31] Such companionship was precisely what children wanted from fathers: When Robert and Helen Lynd asked Middletown youth what they considered the most desirable traits in a father, over 60 percent of both boys and girls mentioned "spending time with his children, reading, talking, playing with them, etc.," a response that far outdistanced any other.[32]

Children identified by psychologists as "well-adjusted" invariably described their own fathers as men who demonstrated sharing, harmony, understanding, respect, and rational discipline. Young men and women drew attention to their fathers' involvement, fairness, and nurture. The college-age daughter of a skilled tradesman fondly reminisced how her father "would romp and tussle for hours while mother sat by laughing or adding a word of caution if things were getting too rough for me. . . . Our family was rather an affectionate one. Father especially was demonstrative. I liked this, for I felt I was getting lots of attention and that he must care a great deal for me."[33] Others also emphasized the closeness and companionship they felt with their fathers, the interest their fathers took in their activities and recreation, and the security they found in being able to confide in their parents: "Mother, father and I always have confided in one another," wrote one student, "and I find now when I do really have problems that the old feeling of wanting to tell mother and father is a blessing."[34] In the best of families, according to the White House report, the frontiers of father-child confidentiality extended into the realm of sexuality. Among college boys who confided in their fathers "very much," 73 percent received sex education within the family; among boys who confided "very little," only 38 percent received sexual instruction at home.[35]

Those with complaints about their fathers shared the same assumptions as those who praised them. One college woman admitted, for example, that her parents provided well for her but "they have never given me the affection I always wanted." Another criticized her father's aloof, harsh, and suspicious manner: "He makes no effort whatsoever to understand either my brother or me. . . . He was forbidding and harsh as far back as I remember, though I really think that he is rather proud of us when he's talking with other people."[36] Still a third had particular disdain for his father's unwillingness to speak frankly about sex: "He also told me that if I thought too much about matters pertaining to sex I might go crazy, for a very large percentage of the inmates in feeble-minded institutions were there for that reason."[37]

Despite children's desires for companionship with their fathers, other forces pulled children away from their homes and ultimately shaped their attitudes toward their fathers. Leisure time, for example, became increasingly segmented. Parents and children in the middle class had considerable leisure time each day, but rarely did they spend it together. Suburban children spent less of their leisure time at home than either their fathers or mothers and when at home read, studied, or listened to the radio much of the time, all activities of a solitary nature. Fathers and children might in fact spend considerable time in the same house and yet scarcely see one another. As a young suburban daughter put it, "Oh, yes, I've been home, and so has Father, but I haven't seen him for three days." Her experience was not atypical: Out of some 800 suburban girls in one study, only 37 percent played with any family member during the course of one day. Nor did meal times offer much chance for family togetherness. Only 16 of every 100 suburban families ate three meals a day together; almost 40 percent, by contrast, managed only one meal together per day. The crucial variable was the income of the father and whether he commuted. Those who commuted often left for work before their children were awake and returned from the city after they were in bed.[38]

These men left early and stayed late to fulfill their obligations as breadwinners, but in the early twentieth century a culture of consumption emerged that gave new meaning to this obligation. Fathers' wages and salaries continued to provide food and shelter, to be sure, but they also provided access to a cornucopia of goods that was transforming the very nature of American culture. Material goods promised not just sustenance but vitality, experience, and life itself, and it was up to middle-class fathers to make these goods available to their families.[39] As a pervasive consumer culture began to take shape in the 1920s, middle-class fathers found themselves put to the test: If family experts clamored for fathers' time, their wives, children, and the wider culture clamored for their time and for their money.[40]

Consumption, after all, promised to fill the void created by changes in community life, work, religion, and family by offering a new source of vitality, reality, and "personal growth."[41] It was, as Robert Lynd put it, a key element in "the increasing secularization of spending and the growing pleasure basis of living," part of "a new gospel which encourages liberal spending to make the wheels of industry turn as a duty of the citizen." Ultimately, Lynd argued, America was undergoing a seismic shift: The older values of thrift, saving, hard work, and struggle were being replaced by an emphasis on leisure, consumption and, in the last analysis, money. Faced with "the increasingly baffling conflict between living and making money in order to buy a living," Americans showed "the tendency, public and private, to simplify this issue by concentration on the making of money."[42]

This emphasis on money certainly colored children's views of their fathers, but to what extent is as yet unknown. Children were clearly affected by the consumer culture. Although middle-class fathers underwrote the purchases of their families, purchasing became increasingly individuated. Robert Lynd's description of this development was apt: "A rising standard of living, coupled with new ideas as to equality of marital partners and in parent-child relationships, and an increased degree of mobility and independence among women and children have all operated apparently to distribute the family's spending money more generally through the several members of the family. Merchants testify that children are buying more things today unassisted by their parents." [43]

Children's purchases were shaped in large degree by the emergence of dating and by the peer culture that developed in the burgeoning high schools and colleges in the opening decades of the twentieth century. Both required money; both had the power to undercut paternal authority. By the mid-1920s dating had replaced the older system of calling. No longer subject to parental chaperonage, dating couples spent their time in public places of amusement—restaurants, dance halls, movie houses, and amusement parks. [44] Anonymity, freedom, and even "slumming" were central to the appeal of dating to urban youth. One young, well-heeled woman informed the *Ladies' Home Journal*: "Nowadays it is considered 'smart' to go to the low order of dance halls, and not only be a looker-on, but also to dance among all sorts and conditions of men and women. . . . Nowadays when we enter a restaurant and dance place it is hard to know who is who." But achieving this anonymity and freedom, as Beth Bailey has explained, required money: "Money—men's money—became the basis of the dating system and, thus, of courtship." [45]

For high-school boys and college men, to date was to spend. To be popular in the competitive dating arena of the interwar years, boys needed access to an automobile, the right clothing, and ample spending money for the food, drinks, flowers, and movie and dance-hall admissions required of the successful date. [46] Girls, too, needed fashionable clothes, club memberships, and grooming aids in order to attract the all-important male escort. As early as 1930, the American cosmetics industry reported sales of $180 million, and throughout the 1920s and 1930s advertising directed at women linked personality, popularity, and consumption. [47]

This consumption, as Paula Fass has noted, was mediated by the peer culture that developed in high schools and colleges in the early twentieth century. Spending much of their young lives in each others' company, high-school and college youth developed a complex culture that pushed against the moral boundaries of adult America while simultaneously fostering conformist behavior among the young. And conformity required money. To be a part of the peer culture meant spending money on things of importance in the peer culture: "In placing emphasis on the externals of appearance and the accessories of sociability and in demanding constant and careful conformity to all its subtleties," writes Fass, "the peer society promoted and enforced an ethos of consumerism."[48]

The consumerism of the peer culture engendered parent-child tensions and challenged the power of parents. As Fass explained, "The high school, by occupying the largest portion of the individual's time and dominating his daily attention, oriented youth largely to each other and cut the young off from the influences of adult patterns."[49] Nowhere was this alienation of the young from the old clearer than in matters of consumption. Children used their fathers' money to keep pace with fast-changing fads, to buy goods that would ensure popularity, and to forge an identity separate from and often in conflict with that of their parents. It was a situation rife with irony and conflict; in essence, fathers financially underwrote children's alienation from paternal authority.

A study of a small Iowa town in the early 1930s, for example, found that parent-child conflict took shape around two issues—use of the family automobile and spending money. Both were intimately connected with a peer culture characterized by distinctive ideas about leisure and dating. "The early sexual development and sophistication of the young," wrote Earl Bell, "combined with the prolongation of their economic dependence upon their parents, together with the new high cost of courtship, brings the children and parents into sharp conflict."[50] Children tended to see their parents as "tyrannical old fogies" who were "just jealous because we have good times," and parents often characterized their children as demanding, unappreciative, and overly acquisitive.

For these Iowa children, the recreation favored by their parents—church socials, lawn parties, debates, singing and literary societies, coasting and sleighing parties—had little appeal. Despite parents' hearty approval of such innocent amusements, children had other ideas: "The only ones who go to Church parties," one girl told Bell, "are those who aren't in on anything else."[51] In place of church parties, children wanted access to the family automobile, access parents gave grudgingly. As Bell put it, "Each boy is certain that his family will not, out of sheer perversity, allow him the use of the car for a date." [52] Indiana youth shared the same desires and frustrations. The Lynds found that 36 percent of high-school boys and 30 percent of high-school girls had disagreements with their parents over the use of the family car. [53]

Money was even more basic to the disputes between fathers and children. Although only 12 percent of Middletown boys and 11 percent of the girls checked "making plenty of money" as the "most desirable trait in a father"—to their credit, they valued companionship far more—arguments about spending money were very common. Almost 40 percent of the boys and 30 percent of the girls cited spending money as a source of disagreement with their parents. Other sources of conflict included the number of evenings children were away from home on school nights, the hour children returned at night, school grades, and the use of the automobile. All, perhaps even school grades, involved children's connection to the youth culture and the culture of consumption of the early twentieth century. [54]

Iowa youth reported the same tension with their parents. Without regular allowances, children's spending money came from whatever they could cajole and coax out of their parents and what they could make performing service work for friends and neighbors. It was a situation meant for conflict: "Although the parents are opposed," observed Bell, "they give in to their children's demands, after much coaxing and temper tantrums on each side, and are the gullible subjects for persuasion, lying, and deceit on the part of their children." [55]

Bell's portrait of these Iowa youths was hardly flattering. According to his observations, the children paid little attention to parental wishes and constantly ignored or subverted their parents' authority. Although Bell acknowledged that some parents tried to restrict their children's hours, friendships, and excursions, children rendered such efforts futile: "If the parents' half-hearted permission cannot finally be gained by persuasion, argument, or temper tantrums, they may be deceived very easily." Nor were children likely to turn against each other to dispel parental deception: "There has grown up among the young people a close-mouthed loyalty to each other, which does not allow them to tell the old folks anything concerning the conduct of one of their age group even if they themselves do not approve." Such loyalty extended even to sexual matters. Children evidently viewed their parents as gatekeepers of a sexual morality the young no longer subscribed to, a fact demonstrated by the Iowa adolescents' unwillingness to turn against a young girl who was romantically involved with an older man of poor reputation. Although the children knew about the liaison, "not a word ever came out through one of the young people, and this in the face of the fact that many mothers held before their daughters the miscreant girl as an example of perfection."[56]

If Bell's observations were accurate, even small Iowa towns in the early 1930s developed a youth culture based upon automobiles and money that undermined paternal authority. Children regularly deceived their parents and ran roughshod over their wishes. To Bell, the reasons for this generational inversion stemmed from deep-seated changes in the social structure of rural America. Fathers who had once passed vital knowledge to sons had now fallen behind modern technological developments. The consequences of such paternal backwardness had been graphically exposed by the onset of the depression and the ensuing ruin of thousands of farm families. To these sons, their fathers were primitives, out of step with the world of youth and with modern economic developments.[57] Long-developing trends coupled with the immediate devastation of the depression had rendered the authority of these fathers suspect. Children increasingly gravitated toward each other and found a home of sorts within a youth culture characterized by consumerism, automobiles, movies, and sexual experimentation.

Men who commuted to work from the suburbs or who toiled in factories profited from the gender-based division of labor. This division was, after all, crucial to men's domination of women, crucial, in other words, to patriarchy. Yet the division may not have redounded to men's benefit as fathers. In fact, evidence from the 1920s and 1930s reveals unequivocally that children preferred their mothers to their fathers. In one study of 500 children ages five to nine, 70 percent of the girls and 61 percent of the boys preferred their mothers to their fathers while only 22 percent of the boys and 28 percent of the girls favored their fathers.[58] Nor did the age of the children make much difference in their attitudes; except for five-year-old girls who showed an anomolous preference for their fathers, children of different ages preferred their mothers over their fathers to roughly the same degree. Another study of 400 children between the ages of five and twelve reported that children showed more consideration for their mothers than for their fathers and more frequently associated the "best happenings" of their lives with their mothers.[59]

By the time children reached adolescence, these preferences shaped the nature and depth of parent-child contact. Asked the degree "to which they tell their mother and father their joys and troubles," eighth- through tenth-grade boys and girls made it clear that they far more often confided in their mothers than in their fathers. Forty-one percent of urban white boys and 62 percent of urban white girls "almost always" confided in their mothers. In contrast, only 27 percent of the boys and 23 percent of the girls "almost always" confided in their fathers. Among rural youth, the disparities were similar save for rural white boys who seldom confided on a regular basis with either their mothers or their fathers.

This pattern of maternal preference continued among young adults. A 1928 study of almost three thousand men and women in their late teens and twenties (1,336 males and the same number of females) found that "fathers do not secure as much willing obedience from either their sons or daughters as do mothers." Moreover, only one-half as many sons and one-fifth as many daughters confided as completely in their fathers as in their mothers. Sixty percent of the sons confided "certain things only" to their fathers and 6 percent nothing at all. More remarkably, 45 percent of the young men noted that they would willingly attend a place of amusement with their mother but only 31 percent would do so with their fathers, evidence that led the study's author to argue that "the fathers of this study enjoy the companionship of their children,—so far as common, willing attendance at places of amusement is concerned,—rarely or not at all."[60]

To the social scientists who authored these studies, the implications of this data underscored the importance of studying mother-child rather than father-child relationships. "For both boys and girls," wrote Ernest Burgess, "the key to a confidential relation with the children lies in the hands of the mother. For this reason, the relation of mother and child was studied more intensively than that of father and child." This relationship held the key to successful "social compliance, emotional stability, desirable character traits and obedience in the classroom." Fathers were certainly important—after all, good personality adjustment correlated with father-child intimacy—but they were of secondary significance compared to mothers.[61]

Other studies, each with its own samples, methodologies, anomolies, and idiosyncracies, could be cited. Yet some speculation is needed as to the meaning of these parental-preference studies in light of the evidence examined earlier regarding working- and middle-class children's attitudes toward their fathers. Clearly the study of children's attitudes toward parents cannot be understood without understanding structural and cultural developments within the wider society. Working-class children who dutifully helped support their families also experienced frustration when these obligations collided with their own desires. Meanwhile, their immersion in a vibrant youth culture pulled them away from the authority of their fathers, authority further undermined by the father's marginal success as a breadwinner in a rapidly expanding consumer society. Fathers' absence from home while at work coupled with leisure spent outside the home also eroded their influence over their offspring. The impact of these factors was heightened within immigrant homes by the cultural divide separating Old World parents and New World children.

Different factors obviously shaped the attitudes of middle-class children toward their fathers. Because of their fathers' success as breadwinners, these children were not part of the family economy; instead they were part of a growing youth culture with standards and values often at odds with those of their parents. Segmented leisure, school activities, the ubiquitous automobile, and consumerism marked the lives of these children. Thus, despite widespread calls that fathers spend more time with their children, there were forces at work that muted the strength of such calls. So far as work would permit, fathers might try to be playmates and pals with their younger children; but as the children grew older, the influence of fathers steadily waned.

To understand working-class and middle-class children's attitudes toward fathers, then, is to understand the interplay of these factors. Men's and women's work and leisure patterns, children's role within the family economy, maternal and paternal involvement with children, the growth of a youth culture, the Americanization process, and burgeoning consumerism must be examined if we are to comprehend the issue. As historians begin to comb through the many types of documents that will yield insight into such attitudes, the findings will undoubtedly help explain why children of all classes invariably preferred their mothers to their fathers and the meaning of that preference.

For now, some speculations on the last point are in order. The family is an arena of power and sentiment. In an arena of power, children's sentiments toward their fathers may be irrelevant to the matter—after all, male domination is founded on power, not on affection—or they may in fact have been a perfect expression of patriarchy at work. So long as fathers identified themselves primarily as breadwinners, being the "second parent" in the eyes of their children was of little consequence. Indeed their children's sentiments may have only confirmed the cultural significance of contemporary gender ideology: Mothers were crucial to the affective dimensions of family life and fathers were central to its instrumental dimensions. In other words, the children's emotional allegiances and choices reinforced the father's power by perpetuating the identification of women with the domestic realm and of men with the public realm.

There is much to this argument. Children's preferences for their mothers undoubtedly heightened the identification of children with women, an identification in turn that could enhance the power of men over women and children. Yet the story is surely more complicated. The family is not only an arena of power, it is also one of sentiment, affection, and love. A crucial aspect of such companionate relationships is the bond between parents and children, and yet children felt much closer to their mothers than they did to their fathers. This disparity occurred, moreover, at a time when men, at least in the middle class, hoped to establish closer ties with their children. As work became more alienating and the private realm more enticing, personal relationships within the family became ever more important, but now it was children who exercised a new and strange power over their fathers. If fathers wanted the affection of their children—and apparently many did so—they would have to become more nurturant, more committed, more willing to spend time with their offspring.

They had to make this commitment and at the same time honor their obligation to earn the family bread. And it was just this dual responsibility that put fathers at a relative disadvantage: Children needed and wanted both love and money; mothers supplied healthy doses of the former, but fathers by and large were the sole suppliers of the latter. Consequently, children looked to their mothers as emotional caretakers and to their fathers as combination playmates and bankers. Without major changes in family life, without a major challenge to the gender-based division of labor at the core of modern economic life, children would remain in many ways alienated from their fathers. Men could be breadwinners for their children and companions to their children. They would and still do find it hard to be both.

12

"The Only Thing I Wanted Was Freedom"

Wayward Girls in New York, 1900–1930

RUTH M. ALEXANDER

❖　❖　❖　❖　❖　❖　❖　❖　❖　❖　❖　❖　❖　❖　❖

In the summer of 1916 sixteen-year-old Ella Waldstein started "going around with a bad crowd of girls," often staying away from her Brooklyn home until one or two o'clock in the morning. Ella, the daughter of Russian Orthodox Jews, had never before given her parents any trouble; in fact, since the age of fourteen she had worked without complaint as a factory operative, helping to support a family of six. But apparently the girl had changed, and fearing for her safety and sexual virtue, Ella's mother and father "talked to her and begged and pleaded with her to come home earlier." Ella listened to their pleas in stony silence: "When they asked her where she had been she would say she had been with a girl friend or simply would not answer. No matter how they scolded her she never talked back."

Throughout the following year, tension within the Waldstein home mounted, peaking in the summer of 1917 when Ella's relatives learned that she was spending her evenings on Coney Island, usually in the company of a handsome married Irishman who "was not of our kind . . . and not very respectable." The man gave Ella expensive gifts and the young woman's parents suspected that she was prostituting herself for him. Mrs. Waldstein approached Ella and "threatened to send [her] away if she would not stay at home in the evenings." Ella would not listen

Wayward girl in New York, Hudson School for Girls
Reformatory, New York State, 1946–1949.
(Marion Palfi, photographer. Spencer Museum of Art,
University of Kansas. Gift of the artist)

and finally her desperate parents took her to court; she was convicted of "wilful disobedience" and committed to the New York State Reformatory for Women at Bedford Hills. Her three-year sentence was the standard term meted out to all female reformatory inmates.[1]

Ella was committed to Bedford Hills at a time of rapid and disconcerting change in the cultural and experiential construction of female adolescence, particularly within the working class. With the vast expansion of the nation's industrial economy in the late nineteenth and early twentieth centuries, millions of immigrant and native-born young women and girls were drawn into the urban workforce as unskilled factory workers, retail clerks, and waitresses. Most adolescent girls took up wage labor to help their struggling families, but employment also exposed them to a new world of experience and values. At work, previously sheltered teenage girls met young people who shared modern ideas about fashion, recreation, and sex. At night, putting these ideas into practice, working girls flocked to commercial dance halls, nickelodeon theaters, amusement parks, and other "cheap amusements," engaging in social rituals that celebrated feminine allure and heterosexual romance, the autonomy of youth, and the purchase of fun. Substituting an "up-to-date" lifestyle for Victorian and Old World standards of girlhood decorum, the daughters of the working class produced a distinctly modern rendering of female adolescence, one that was enthusiastically taken up by middle-class young women during and after World War I.[2]

Surely we can appreciate the Waldsteins' astonishment and alarm as they witnessed the social transformation of their formerly dutiful daughter. Yet most early twentieth-century working-class parents did not take their daughters to court and ask for a reformatory commitment.[3] Why in this instance were communication and compromise so elusive, and why was New York State so willing to uphold the Waldsteins' right to filial obedience? Just as important, what became of Ella during her incarceration and after her release from Bedford Hills? Did Bedford succeed in "reforming" her and, if so, in a manner agreeable to her family? Or did Ella reject the reformative efforts of family and state, convinced even after her incarceration that self-assertion was a valid and productive path?

Drawing on the inmate case files of two New York State reformatories, I have analyzed the experience of twenty-two young women whose attempts to participate in the remaking of female adolescence met with bitter family opposition and severe legal sanction.[4] All of the "wayward girls" were the daughters of immigrant or working-class parents, committed at the request of family members either to the New York State Reformatory for Women at Bedford Hills or to the Western House of Refuge for Women in Albion, New York.[5] With only three exceptions, the girls served standard three-year sentences, usually spending one or two years of that time on parole.[6]

The experience of New York's wayward girls simultaneously affirms and departs from recent work on early twentieth-century working women. The splendid scholarship of Kathy Peiss and Joanne Meyerowitz generally emphasizes the agency and inventiveness of America's early twentieth-century working women, acclaiming their break with social and sexual convention. According to these historians, working-class young women "pioneered new manners and mores," displacing traditional models of female adolescence and young womanhood as they participated in the construction of modern heterosocial culture. Certainly, as both Peiss and Meyerowitz recognize, low wages, a persistent sexual double standard, and a new ethic of material consumption prevented young women from translating sexualized values and behavior into real social autonomy. Nonetheless, through their lively use of leisure and bold explorations of individuality and heterosexuality, America's working women and girls "helped forge the modern sexual expression that replaced Victorian reticence."[7]

Although not denying the agency of young working women or the newness of their lifestyle, I shall shift the focus away from the cultural values they helped to invent and look instead at their sometimes pained and thwarted efforts to construct a new sense of self. This essay is an investigation of the subjective experience and emerging social identities of young women who, in embracing the "modern," collided with tradition and with the limits of cultural and familial change. In contending with the coercive tactics of reformatories, wayward girls were atypical adolescent females. Their unique ordeal was only a variation on a common theme, however. Just as other working- and middle-class young women in early twentieth-century America, wayward girls struggled to construct social identities from competing models and ideals of female adolescence. We shall examine how they fared in the contest between modernity and tradition.

The wayward girls at Bedford Hills and Albion came from working-class families that were unusually precarious, economically and socially. Insecurity and hardship tended to make the homes of the wayward girls depressing and unpleasant; misfortune also precluded parents from reacting to cultural change with favor or good will. Indeed, the wayward girls' mothers and fathers experienced female adolescent rebellion as a threat to their own survival, and they resorted to legal action to protect their families from further peril.

Although only a few of the wayward girls lived in truly destitute circumstances, nearly all came from families that struggled to remain economically stable. Twenty of the wayward girls were the daughters of men of very modest economic standing; their fathers were factory workers, carpenters, machinists, drivers, house painters, and janitors.[8] Often the incomes of the girls' fathers were inadequate to meet family expenses, and five of the wayward girls had mothers who worked for wages. In addition, all but three of the girls had themselves worked to add to their families' meager earnings, usually leaving school by the age of fourteen to do so.[9]

Economic insecurity was not all that troubled these families. Eighteen of the twenty-two wayward girls came from homes impaired by daunting tragedy or dysfunction: the death of one or both parents, desertion, separation, divorce, alcoholism, disabling illness, pronounced marital discord, wife and child battering, or incest. Moreover, only seven of the young women had American parents; the rest were the daughters of immigrants who daily confronted the trials of cultural dislocation and assimilation. Finally, four of the wayward girls were black and thus came from families forced to contend with racism as well as with economic insecurity and domestic calamity.[10]

Struggle as they must to withstand economic and social adversity, the parents, guardians, and older siblings of New York's wayward girls were unprepared to tolerate the rebellion and sexual experimentation of their daughters or young sisters. These adults depended on their girls to support and uphold the good name of their families; traditional forms of filial obedience and girlhood virtue provided a semblance of security, assuring them of their ability to endure in a difficult world. In this context, a young woman's assertion of self was far more than the ingenuous proclamation of a modern sensibility; it represented an unbearable threat to the survival of an already precarious family unit.

Self-assertion was equally meaningful to the wayward girls, yet to them it represented not danger but an essential route to happiness. The dispiriting atmosphere in the wayward girls' homes compared unfavorably with the buoyant mood and lively companions to be found in city streets, dance halls, and amusement parks. And feeling helpless to change their families, the young women sought friends and recreation that offered respite, hope, and entertainment. They longed for a life different from the one their families could offer, and many saw in New York's urban youth and "cheap amusements" the means to attain it.

Invariably, the wayward girls' explorations of autonomy led to bitter familial conflict; when the strain of generational controversy became unbearable, parents and guardians turned to the courts for assistance and relief. Conflict usually began well before the girls evinced an interest in heterosexual romance, first arising instead over their attraction to the dress, manners, and companionship of urban youth. Few mothers or fathers actually went to court because of their daughters' efforts to find friends or recreation outside of the family setting; rather, parents waited until they saw evidence of sexual misconduct. However, there were exceptions. For example, Louisa Parsons, the daughter of a Utica, New York, insurance agent, wanted to choose and enjoy her friends without paternal interference and occasionally resorted to subterfuge to gain what she desired. Mr. Parsons, a strict disciplinarian with a drinking problem, responded with threats and verbal abuse. When he became convinced that Louisa could be taught to respect his authority in no other way, Mr. Parsons asked for her commitment to Albion.[11]

In other cases, conflict reached intolerable levels when wayward girls tried to avoid (or expose) physical abuse or sexual assault within the family. As with the girls' quests for social independence, attempts to escape severe or violent chastisement produced intense controversy because they signaled adolescent females' unwillingness to shape themselves to the needs and values of an unstable family unit. Rae Rabinowitz was the target of frequent beatings by an older brother who had fashioned himself the family patriarch after Mr. Rabinowitz deserted the household. When Rae tried to make friends on her own and complained that her siblings and mother were " 'sticks' [who] want to sit in the house [all evening while] the neighbors sit on their front stoops and visit," her brother responded with insults and physical assaults. Resolving to escape her brother's brutal treatment, Rae ran away from home; but at her family's request, she was pursued, arrested, and committed to Bedford Hills.[12]

Still, for the great majority of the wayward girls, adolescent sexual expression paved the most direct route to court. Sexual virtue was a critical symbol of feminine selflessness and, for the parents of wayward girls, its absence signified disorder and dangerous individualism. Mothers and fathers worried that sexually active daughters had ruined all their chances of finding good husbands and becoming respectable wives and mothers. Just as important, parents worried that girls with sexual experience might damage the reputation of their fragile families. Familial distress and humiliation were particularly acute when the sexual relations of adolescent girls resulted in pregnancy or violated racial, religious, or ethnic boundaries.[13]

Thus when twenty-year-old Evelyn Blackwell became pregnant in 1926 "after running out nights with different men," her father, a well-respected black mechanic, "absolutely refused to have the girl at home." Relations between Evelyn and her parents had been severely strained by two earlier pregnancies, and the girl had been pushed into a hasty and disastrous marriage while awaiting the birth of her second child. Now, Evelyn's father, a recent widower, could not stand the dishonor of yet a third illegitimate child. If Evelyn's mother had been alive, the matter might have been handled differently, but Evelyn's father took his daughter to court and "asked to have the girl sent away."[14]

In a similar case, Lena Meyerhoff stunned her Russian immigrant parents by keeping company with a "colored man," sometimes staying out late at night, some nights "not [coming] home at all," and finally leaving her parents' home to live with her lover. Mr. and Mrs. Meyerhoff initially reacted to their daughter's conduct with incomprehension and ineffectual protests, but when Lena gave birth, apparently to a mulatto infant, her mother decided that she must act to protect her daughter and her family from utter ruin. Mrs. Meyerhoff turned to the Jewish Board of Guardians, a social agency that worked with unmarried mothers and, following the board's advice, took Lena to court. There she asked for a reformatory sentence on the grounds that the girl "habitually associates with dissolute persons . . . left her home in Woodbridge [N.Y.] . . . and came to New York City where she lived with J. Smith to whom she is not married and bore an illegitimate child to him."[15]

Undoubtedly the wayward girls were a spirited lot, eager to be free of restraint and fascinated with the youth culture and amusements beyond their doors. Lena stood up to her parents, playing the confusion and hesitation of her mother against that of her father to win the sexual and social autonomy she desired. Rae Rabinowitz ran away from home, heading straight for Coney Island, after deciding that she had had enough of her brother's abuse. In another case, Sophie Polentz left home to take an apartment with a girlfriend after growing impatient with her father's demand that "first time she met a fellow to bring him up to the house."[16]

The wayward girls' mettle pales next to their vulnerability, however. Some of these young women had been physically abused by members of their family; others had experienced distress over their parents' distrust and withdrawal of affection. Moreover, despite their bold manner, most of the wayward girls were unsophisticated and susceptible to sexual exploitation and abuse. When Rae Rabinowitz ran away to Coney Island, she was raped by two soldiers who had generously paid for a night's entertainment and lodging. Rae allowed the men to pay for a hotel room for her, not understanding that they expected sexual favors in return. As she later told Bedford's psychiatrist, Dr. Cornelia Shorer, "I will never forget that day. . . . You never want to do such a thing only I did not want to stay on the street all night. . . . [The sailor said] 'If you don't let us do it you won't have no place to sleep tonight'. . . . That's when I gave myself away. . . . I didn't think they would do such a thing. You know some fellows have pity." Ella Waldstein also had to cope with sexual exploitation and manipulation, although of a less overt sort. When the young woman gave up trying to communicate with her parents, she was left on her own to decipher her Irish boyfriend's intentions. Most important, she did not know if he was telling the truth when he said that he would someday divorce his wife to marry her.[17]

In addition, sexually active (or exploited) wayward girls risked contracting venereal disease or becoming pregnant. A young woman with knowledgeable friends might find a doctor without too much difficulty who was willing to treat her for V.D., although payment of the doctor was another problem. Pregnancy could not be concealed from family members as easily as illness; wayward girls who became pregnant were at once dependent upon their families for care and helpless to resist their families' reproof.

Finally, the wayward girls' status as legal dependents made them vulnerable to state coercion. In requesting reformatory commitments, the working-class parents and guardians of wayward girls took advantage of a novel provision of New York's criminal law, one that permitted a partnership between the criminal-justice system and the parents of disobedient or "immoral" adolescent girls. That partnership began in 1886 when New York City amended a statute concerning the reform of prostitutes so that parents or the police might request a reformatory commitment for any girl over the age of twelve "[who] is found in a reputed house of prostitution or assignation; or is willfully disobedient to parent or guardian and is in danger of becoming morally depraved." [18]

The 1886 law was amended several times, and under the so-called "incorrigible girl" statutes, many working-class young women were sent to Bedford Hills. The laws did not apply to adolescent females beyond the boundaries of New York City, but by the late nineteenth and early twentieth centuries, upstate parents were making creative use of the state's vagrancy and disorderly conduct statutes to secure the commitment of rebellious daughters to the Western House of Refuge for Women in Albion. Thus, Millicent Potter was committed to Albion in 1900 after her father went to court complaining that "for six months past, [she] has been frequenting disorderly houses against the wishes of her parents and becoming an inmate of such houses." [19]

In 1923 New York passed the Wayward Minor Act, giving formal recognition to the legal rights of upstate parents. Under the Wayward Minor Law, the main provisions of the old "incorrigible girl" statutes were extended statewide to aid in the control of adolescent females. [20] By this time mental health professionals were beginning to protest the punitive treatment of young delinquents, arguing that juvenile or adolescent misconduct was usually the outcome of improper parenting and should be treated in a clinical setting. Mental-health professionals also had begun to abandon Victorian thinking about girlhood, asserting that adolescent girls must have social autonomy and sexual freedom if they were to achieve psychosexual maturity. [21] However, the clinicians' challenges to parental authority and Victorian ideology had little effect on the state's partnership with desperate working-class mothers and fathers. Both the criminal-court system and the working-class parents continued to hold disadvantaged young women and girls to Victorian standards of sexual morality, not trusting their ability to explore heterosexuality without drifting into immorality and prostitution. Targeting young women in late adolescence, the Wayward Minor Law affirmed that disobedient or immoral females between the ages of sixteen and twenty-one could be convicted solely upon the testimony of their parents or guardians. It gave parents the option of having their daughters remain at home under the supervision of a probation officer but allowed them to request institutional commitment for any girl who "is not a fit subject for probation."[22]

The wayward girls who were sent to Bedford Hills and Albion were viewed by their parents and the courts as self-conscious rebels in need of reform. These adults did not realize that few of the girls demonstrated genuine loyalty either to immoral behavior or to the values of urban youth subcultures. True, the wayward girls had been defiant at home and often sexually active on the streets, but frequently their defiance was closely bound up with "ill treatment" or some other family crisis. Similarly, the pleasures of sex had often been clouded by sexual ignorance, physical danger, and economic need. The wayward girls had confronted hazards and obstacles to their safety, autonomy, and happiness whether they were with their families or with their peers. When they entered the gates of the reformatories, most of these young women were still searching for a satisfying lifestyle or social identity and had yet to find it.

Bedford Hills and Albion did little to ease the difficulty of their search, although over time the reformatories profoundly affected the wayward girls' sense of self. Presenting the matter of female adolescent identity in stark moral terms, Albion and Bedford Hills demanded that the wayward girls adopt a Victorian model of girlhood virtue, abandoning social and sexual expression for deference and sexual control. To hasten the wayward girls' compliance, the reformatories presented them with both positive and negative inducements to reform. Under the watchful eye of morally upright matrons and female teachers, the girls were offered rich opportunities for "self-improvement." Housed separately from the institutions' older and more hardened inmates (usually prostitutes), they were given comfortable rooms in homelike cottages. In addition, the wayward girls were afforded academic and vocational training, recreational activities in a campus setting, and religious instruction. These "opportunities" had been incorporated into the reformatories' programs at the turn of the century by middle-class female reformers who wanted the state to "rescue" impoverished and ignorant young women from lives of immorality and crime.[23]

Thus afforded a wide range of opportunities and privileges, Bedford and Albion expected "their girls" to be ready for lives of honest employment, sexual virtue, and deference to the family claim by the time they were paroled. However, if kindness, education, and moral suasion proved to be working too slowly, coercion could be relied on as an additional prod. Strict surveillance, the censoring of mail, and a formidable array of punishments, including the postponement of parole, made resistance to reform difficult and unpleasant.

There is little evidence to suggest that while they remained inmates the wayward girls found much appeal in the social identity their female keepers held before them. Instead, acutely sensitive to their lack of freedom and privacy, the wayward girls spent much of their time engaged in struggle with reformatory officers, matrons, and teachers. True, nearly half of the young women in my sample were generally well behaved, knowing that to be otherwise was to risk punishment and postponement of parole. Still, even among this "good" group, it is possible to detect signs of discontent and resentment. Althea Davies, an eighteen-year-old West Indian who was committed to Bedford after becoming pregnant, was generally reliable but often "sulky" or "noisy." Deborah Herman, another young black woman committed because of an illegitimate pregnancy, was an "excellent" worker, and yet she threw occasional temper tantrums.[24]

Moreover, twelve of the wayward girls were openly defiant. Their acts of misconduct included "lewd" talk, smoking, insolence, attempted escape, and innumerable other offenses. Often the troublesome girls acted as individuals, but they also misbehaved together. Acting in pairs or groups, wayward girls revealed something more than a rejection of authority or a willingness to risk punishment; they announced their identification with a distinctive inmate subculture, one that legitimated the right of young women to define their own values and to oppose as irrelevant the genteel model of young womanhood upheld by their keepers.

The lesbian relationships between inmates are a particularly significant example of this inmate subculture. Although no record exists of lesbian attachments at Albion, they were a well-recognized problem at Bedford; among the wayward girls in my sample were two young women who had engaged in homoerotic relationships.[25] Rae Rabinowitz, the seventeen-year-old who was sent to Bedford as an "incorrigible girl" after being beaten by her brother and raped by two sailors, was "more or less trouble about colored girls all the time." Similarly, Melanie Burkis, a wayward minor who began her sentence at Bedford in 1924, was much criticized for her "distasteful and demoralizing . . . obsession" with a "colored" inmate.[26]

These homoerotic relationships were a form of behavior through which young inmates tried to give evidence of their own power; that is, they used sexual desire and the capacity to shock as ways to deny their defenselessness against the demands of the reformatory staff. Melanie Burkis deliberately made her "obsession" for Valerie Revere obvious, causing one Bedford teacher to remark, "If thwarted in any undesirable action toward Valerie Revere she showed plainly that her affection for her teacher or desire to improve was assumed in order to continue her obsession for the colored pupil."[27]

In addition, the homosexual or homoerotic relationships between inmates at Bedford Hills reveal young women's interest in bending and testing the normative meanings of gender and race that dominated conventional society and urban-youth subcultures. The wayward girls in these relationships did not altogether reject the gender roles that were part of contemporary youth cultures, but they insisted on manipulating the meanings of both masculinity and femininity. Similarly, by crossing racial boundaries and playing with race as though it were entirely a social construct, young women defied the deep-seated segregationist sentiments of both their keepers and of the society beyond the institution's gates.

Thus when Jewel Foster, one of Rae's black girlfriends, wrote Rae a love letter, she adopted the persona of a white woman and became "Mama Blondie." Rae was addressed as "my own loving Daddy," and "Mama Blondie" devoted much of her letter to showing that she was worthy of her "Daddy's" love and intended "to be a good true mama to you now and out in the big world." As "Mama Blondie" Jewel emphasized the seductive and aggressive masculinity of her lover and reveled in fantasies of her "beautiful daddy . . . teasing and trying to fuck me and do everything that goes with." Yet she also slipped into speaking of Rae (five feet, two inches tall, 101 pounds) as a "pretty doll" with "cute little arms."[28]

Despite their obvious contempt for the reformatories, even some of the most defiant wayward girls were eventually persuaded to modify their conduct. Although the reformatories' preferred model of young womanhood may have had little appeal, severe and frequent punishment compelled defiant inmates to question the merit of their conduct and to acknowledge the dangers of self-assertion and sexual expression. For example, Ella Waldstein was "childish" and difficult, but only during her first year at Bedford; after that her behavior showed "marked improvement." Numerous minor punishments and confinement for eight days in the reformatory's dilapidated "prison building" were unpleasant enough to cure Ella of her disobedient outbursts. Rae Rabinowitz also showed a definite improvement in behavior. Rae was at various times punished for passing love letters, "being impertinent," and calling others "vile names." She lost recreational privileges, had her parole date postponed, and was at least once placed for two weeks in Bedford's "disciplinary building," a cell block with triple doors on every cell that was used to house the reformatory's most disturbed or troublesome inmates. The weight of these punishments may have eventually induced Rae to heed the reformatory's rules, for when she came up for parole consideration she was judged a good and obedient inmate. She had even "given up colored girls."[29]

Other quite defiant wayward girls made some effort to improve, but not fully understanding or accepting what their keepers were asking of them, they continued to display an unacceptable lack of deference. Melanie Burkis, for example, wrote frequent notes to Bedford's superintendent, trying to persuade him that she was not as bad as others thought her to be:

> I am writing in reference to a little trouble which occurred a few days ago in the cottage. Most likely you have already heard about me doing some thing. Tuesday when Miss Furniss was on duty I Thought I'd be doing myself some Good by behaving myself but it seems as though things have gone against me. While in my room reading Miss Furniss heard someone whistle to another girl on campus and immediately thought I was guilty . . . then a note was thrown out of my window (but not by me) and Miss Furniss figured I was guilty again which I was not. then when Miss Mace spoke to me I tried to defend myself. . . . Of course she thought I was trying to be impudent by defending myself. Now Dr. Baker, I wish you would kindly look into this matter as it means quite alot to me for I am trying my level best to do what is right and no wrong. If you think it best to speak to Miss Furniss about this kindly do so at your earliest convenience as I think it high time for me to be getting affair chance on going out soon.[30]

Of course, there were a few wayward girls who willingly risked punishment throughout their stay at the reformatories, refusing to bow to their keepers and exhibiting delight when they fooled the system. Sophie

Polentz apparently boasted within earshot of Bedford's parole officer to the effect that "no girl had been more disorderly than she and that she had been given her parole in eight months. Even though she ran away, was impudent and saucy to the matrons and never hesitated to tell an officer just what she thought of her in impolite language."[31]

We can assume in Sophie's case that the reformatory had given her no reason to be good; the same thing is probably true of her family. Bedford and Albion often turned to parents and guardians for help in securing the inmates' reform, urging them, for example, to write encouraging letters to their daughters.[32] However, not wanting family members to take a free hand in the reform process, Bedford and Albion strictly controlled all contact between the wayward girls and their families, opening and censoring all correspondence, chastising parents who wrote highly critical letters to their girls, and permitting family visitors at infrequent intervals.[33] These measures ensured the reformatories of the control they desired but ironically also subverted their reformist goals. Prevented from communicating openly, the wayward girls and their relatives could not easily resolve their conflicts or modify their expectations of one another. If inmates and their families managed to reconstruct or reforge the ties that bound them, they got little aid from Albion or Bedford Hills.[34]

Moreover, though parents might be prevented from conveying openly hostile or intolerant attitudes to their daughters, by reading between the lines or contemplating a dearth of mail, the wayward girls probably sensed how their parents felt. Sophie, for example, received frequent missives from her father and probably realized that he felt victimized by his troublesome daughter. Mr. Polentz was disabled and had depended upon his daughter's income until she became so disobedient that he was forced to send her to Bedford. In one letter, written from the sanatorium where he had been sent by a Jewish charity, Sophie's father wrote, "the Doctor of the Society has forbidden me to think too much and to worry, . . . but I cannot help it. So I want you to pray to God that I will be home again soon, but there is a strong doubt in my mind whether I will be able ever to feed my wife and children again. . . . I remain with best greetings as ever, your suffering father." In another letter, Mr. Polentz wrote of his sorrow that Bedford's parole board had refused to grant Sophie her parole, noting that Bedford's superintendent understood how badly Sophie's misconduct hurt her father, even if she did not. "I can write you that Dr. Baker is one of the finest men that I ever met in my life, a true

Gentleman. He feels sorry for you, and he also feels more bad for me than my own children. . . . Your Parole come up before the Parole of Manager [again] next month, and I hope that next month you surely will come home." Mr. Polentz wanted his daughter to recognize that she was partially responsible for his suffering, but instead of prompting her reform his attitude may well have annoyed Sophie and redoubled her rebellious intent.[35]

Exceptions like Sophie notwithstanding, by the time of their release on parole most of the wayward girls well understood the hazards of individualism and self-assertion. However, while teaching the wayward girls to cultivate caution the reformatories had not offered them a convincing role model or given them the tools with which to repair troubled relations with their families. Young women who begged to be forgiven by their families or who swore that they had learned their lesson took the chance of being reunited with parents who themselves had not made any attempt to reform and were still ill prepared to understand or to cope with their daughters.[36] Thus, even as they faced the real world many of the wayward girls must have been uncertain of who they were and wary of their ability to steer a beneficial course between the rules of parole, the demands of their families or employers, and the lure of urban youth and city streets.

As parolees, most wayward girls were sent home to their families with the understanding that they would take jobs or do housework as their parents or guardians required. Those who were not sent home were usually placed in domestic positions with reputable middle-class families, although a few wayward girls were paroled to kitchen or laundry positions in hospitals with dormitory facilities.[37] Regardless of where they lived and worked, the parolees were expected to be obedient and dependable young women. They were not permitted to make friends, take any recreation, or go out at night without the explicit approval of their parents or employers. In addition, in monthly letters to the superintendents of Bedford or Albion, parolees were supposed to describe their work, account for their free time, and mention any efforts they might have made to save money or to plan for the future.

Neither reformatory could be entirely certain that the wayward girls were fulfilling their directives. Throughout the period from 1900 to 1930, Bedford and Albion struggled along with fewer parole officers than they needed; and although Bedford was assisted by social workers from Catholic Charities, the Jewish Board of Guardians, and the (Episcopal) Church

Mission of Help, the wayward girls were visited by parole officers or social workers on an irregular and infrequent basis.[38] Still, most of the girls who violated parole found it impossible to escape oversight or to avoid punishment altogether. Complaints from parents or employers often came later than the reformatory superintendents would have liked, but nonetheless they provided a critical link between parolees and the reformatories. The New York City Police Department also took a hand in locating Bedford parole violators.

More important, the records of wayward girls on parole demonstrate that most of these young women were persuaded to make truly conservative choices about their lives and identities. In the confinement of the reformatories, the wayward girls' limited powers of resistance had been outweighed by the authority of their keepers, and they had learned to value obedience as an expedient. In the world beyond the gates, the authority of the reformatories was relatively diffuse; wayward girls were exposed simultaneously to the values and expectations of reformatory, family, and urban youth. Peer friendships, heterosexual expression, and urban amusements were once again within reach. As they struggled to situate themselves amid these competing social claims, however, the wayward girls discovered that, pleasure notwithstanding, urban youth subcultures lacked social authority and were unable to shield them from the power of family and reformatory. More consequential still, they learned that conformity to convention offered its own kind of freedom, lessening their vulnerability to familial rejection, social ostracism, and state surveillance. There were of course exceptions among the parolees. But as the final phase of a reformatory sentence, parole generally had a conservative and inhibiting impact on working-class wayward girls.

The lessons of parole were surely decisive; surprisingly, for some girls they were relatively uncomplicated. Fully half of the wayward girls realized rather quickly that the protection and approval offered by reformatory or family were worth more than the company of their peers. Three of the young women in this group found socially conservative choices particularly easy to make. Each of the girls had been badly abused or mistreated by their own kin (sometimes by male lovers as well), and instead of being sent home to their families they were paroled to domestic positions. Ilene Sterling's background, for example, included verbal abuse by an alcoholic stepfather, sexual exploitation by an older boyfriend, and an illegitimate pregnancy. Susanna Nedersen, another Bedford girl, had been committed to the reformatory after being sexually assaulted by her father and raped by a neighbor. The illegitimate infant born as a consequence of the rape was taken from Susanna by her mother and probably killed, for Susanna never saw it again. Although Susanna's parents escaped legal action, their daughter was convicted of perjury (and sent to Bedford) after bringing charges against her father for assault and then, under considerable pressure from her family, dropping them.[39]

Good behavior on parole and deference to a genteel model of female adolescence seemed an obvious choice for these young women, determined largely by the severity of their former mistreatment and unhappiness. Wanting protection and security more than anything else, they looked to reformatory superintendents, parole officers, or domestic employers as surrogate mothers and did all in their power to please them. Thus, after being paroled as a domestic to the home of a middle-class couple in Tuckahoe, New York, Susanna wrote to Bedford's parole officer, "I will never forget what you have done for me and want to now thank you. I could not find anyone so good to me as Mr. and Mrs. Jackson. . . . Mrs. Jackson is my . . . guiding angle [*sic*] for she tells me all the things that I want to know & she is teaching me how to read the newspaper & to talk better than I did." Similarly, Ilene wrote to Bedford's superintendent Alice Cobb to tell her how pleased she was with her new domestic position and with the guidance the reformatory had provided. "I am so happy where I am. . . . Please Miss Cobb give my regards to all the Cowdin [cottage] girls and tell them it pays to be good, if they only knew how happy I am they would realize what I am saying is true."[40]

For the other wayward girls who quickly accepted conservative social values, familial reconciliation was the key to reform. Welcomed and forgiven by their parents, eight young women reasoned that conformity to working-class family and gender-role expectations was preferable to the excitement, independence, and danger previously found on the streets. Yet the wayward girls in this group were not always fully content with their new lives. As a parolee, Ella Waldstein was thankful for her family's affection but regretted that life was not as interesting as it had been when she spent every spare moment at Coney Island. In one parole letter she remarked, "I would write you more often but there is really nothing to write it is the same thing over and over again. I'm always home and go out very little so you can see Bedford has changed me quite a bit."[41] Nonetheless, Ella and the others like her were convinced that security and long-term happiness lay with conventional family life.

In contrast, other wayward girls found the lessons of parole difficult and painful. Most of these young women had been "troublesome" as reformatory inmates, and they were not particularly anxious to be "good girls" on parole. Some were eager to rejoin urban-youth subcultures, and the likelihood of their succeeding on parole was also diminished by the inflexibility of their parents. Eventually, however, the majority of the women in this group decided that it "paid" to be good.

In several cases, all involving single mothers, eventual success on parole was achieved only after the wayward girls recognized that they could not survive without the support and approval of their kin. Reconciliation with family members was often difficult, but it seemed their only choice, socially and economically. For example, Althea Davies was at odds with the married sister and aunt to whom she was paroled for nearly two years. She complained that they treated her as an "outcast"; they, on the other hand, complained that Althea was "pert and saucy," did not take proper care of her baby, and stayed out late at night with unknown men. But after voluntarily returning to Bedford three times to escape their criticism and enduring over and over again the constraints and deprivations of reformatory life, Althea finally returned to her family and, relying on her sister for childcare, settled into a regular job and a conventional hardworking life.[42]

In other cases, success on parole was achieved in spite of the wayward girls' steadfast refusal to reconcile themselves to the demands of their kin. Nanette Wilkins, after being sent to a domestic position, was returned to Bedford for impertinence and staying out all night. When Bedford's superintendent asked her if she would be willing to go to her family when she was again paroled, Nanette refused: "Do you think it any pleasure for a girl to go to ther pople when there will never be any peice in the Home? [sic]" However, by this time Nanette knew that "the only thing I wanted was freedom," and when she was once again sent to a domestic position, she willingly conformed to the demands and expectations of both Bedford and her employer. After her final discharge, Nanette took another job as a domestic servant.[43]

Only five wayward girls show evidence of long-term reinvolvement or identification with urban-youth or delinquent subcultures. The young women in this group had often been among the most unruly inmates at the reformatory, and they were certainly Bedford's and Albion's worst parole violators. To the historian they appear as iconoclasts, unwilling to compromise their individuality or independence as other inmates and parolees did. They proved unwilling to bow to the demands or expectations of their families and had little interest in or regard for conventional notions of female sexual morality. Nor did they display any respect for or fear of the authority and power of the reformatories. Although some of these women were punished for violating parole, they still refused to "learn a lesson."

All but one of these young women were paroled to their parents, and usually they made an effort to keep to the terms of their parole, at least for a while. Thus, despite Sophie Polentz's boast that she had been one of the worst girls at the reformatory, the new parolee lost no time in finding employment as a factory worker, writing to Superintendent Baker that she was "doing all in my will power to keep my parole." However, Sophie's resolve did not last. Three months after her parole began the young woman "left her home and employment. . . . It is suspected that she went away with a young man who was interested in her." Sophie's file only hints at what may have caused her to run away; the young man may have tempted her to violate her parole. It is likely, however, that relations within Sophie's home were extremely strained. Her immigrant father expected absolute obedience and he was capable of laying a heavy burden of guilt on his children. In a letter sent to Sophie after she was returned to Bedford as a parole violator Mr. Polentz wrote, "Yes dear Daughter I am still in a Sanatarium and I am very sick. God knows if I shall be able to stand so much suffering. you children make me sick and you will also be responsible for my dying soon. you are ungrateful children who have no feelings for my heart and thoughts. You don't know what the word Father means. you have disgraced me at every step and I am paying for it now with my life."[44]

Janine Rosen, another Bedford parolee, also tried to do well for the first several months on parole, but she could not satisfy her father. Mr. Rosen complained about her "secretive ways" and the "snappy answers" she gave when asked about how she spent her time in the evenings after work. Janine, in turn, insisted that she was maintaining high standards of behavior despite the oppressive conditions in her father's house. Eventually, eager to escape the petty restrictions and confining moral codes of her family, Janine ran away from home.[45]

There is little likelihood that any of the women in this group ever achieved the independence they so evidently wanted. Four of the young women disappeared while they were still on parole, but as parole violators they had good reason to be afraid of the law. They also had good reason to stay away from their families, who might have reported them. However, having little education, few job skills, and small hope of being able to support themselves on the income earned from legal employment, these young women had little choice but to allow prostitution and the risk of arrest to define their lives. Indeed, three of the parole violators were eventually arrested for earning money illegally and were taken back to Bedford.[46]

Sophie Polentz returned to Bedford once but disappeared again when she was reparoled. Although she was never retaken, the institution did hear occasional reports of her, and her experience may be similar to that of others in this group. Sophie became a streetwalker, and once having taken refuge from her family and the reformatory in New York City's street life, the young woman found it difficult to disengage herself from her underworld associates. She married after working for nearly two years as a prostitute and was forced to pay hush money to the couple she had worked for lest her husband be told of her past life. When Sophie missed a few payments her husband was confronted with information about her former career, and as her marriage fell apart Sophie discovered just how relentlessly her "immorality" could haunt her.[47]

Although urban America offered working-class young women opportunity for social invention and heterosexual experimentation during the early twentieth century, it could not protect adolescent females from parental denunciation or legal sanction. Of course, most assertive and sexually active adolescent girls did not become wayward girls. Some defiant young women undoubtedly came from families that found ways to cope with adolescent rebellion. Others may have deliberately (and successfully) concealed their self-expression, knowing that New York's law-enforcement system was prepared to work with working-class parents to limit the rebellion of adolescent daughters. Using a variety of strategies, the great majority of adolescent girls and young women must have negotiated America's urban terrain in relative safety, enjoying and inventing a sexualized lifestyle while acknowledging the limits of their freedom and acting to protect themselves from social stigma or state action.

New York's wayward girls had a different experience; they were unable to avoid getting into trouble. Domestic misfortune prompted these young women to attach particular importance to the social and cultural landscape beyond their own front doors; they viewed sexualized urban-youth cultures as a critical source of amusement, companionship, and relief from family turmoil. Unfortunately, modern youth cultures also exposed them to new forms of sexual exploitation and manipulation. Moreover, adverse conditions at home made it difficult for their parents to tolerate cultural change and filial disobedience. When New York's wayward girls failed to be the daughters their families wanted or needed, the reformatories at Albion and Bedford Hills attempted to remold their character and social identity, urging them to abandon their interest in lively peer groups and cleave once again to old-fashioned values.

As the history of the wayward girls so clearly shows, to a large extent the reformatories succeeded in their goals. Inside the walls of the reformatories and on parole most wayward girls became convinced that self-assertion was a dangerous enterprise: It did not guarantee independence from unhappy or oppressive home conditions, and it made them vulnerable to sexual exploitation, social ostracism, and state control. Having been caught in their attempts at independence, the wayward girls learned to attach new value to safety and to social acceptability, and they worked hard to remove the stigma on their names. By becoming cautious and conventional, the wayward girls may not have found comfort or contentment. However, having experienced grief, abuse, and disappointment as wayward girls, these young women reasoned that conformity was the best option they had.

Part Five

❖ ❖ ❖ ❖ ❖ ❖ ❖ ❖ ❖ ❖ ❖ ❖ ❖ ❖ ❖ ❖

Looking Backward

REMEMBERING CHILDHOOD

Tom and Ma and Pa got into the front seat. Tom let the truck roll and started on compression. And the heavy truck moved, snorting and jerking and popping down the hill. The sun was behind them, and the valley golden and green before them. Ma shook her head slowly from side to side. "It's purty," she said. "I wisht they could have saw it."

"I wisht so too," said Pa.

Tom patted the steering wheel under his hand. "They was too old," he said. "They wouldn't have saw nothin' that's here. Grampa would a been a-seein' the Injuns an' the prairie country when he was a young fella. And Grandma would a remembered an' seen the first home she lived in. They was too ol'. Who's really seein' it is Ruthie an' Winfiel'."

– John Steinbeck, The Grapes of Wrath

As a biological condition, childhood ends about the age of thirteen, adolescence about seven or eight years later. The actual events of those early years are fixed and unchanging. Yet in another sense we never really put childhood behind us; as an influence on our lives, it lingers. Lingers—and evolves. For childhood, in this sense, exists through recollection, which, as everyone eventually discovers, is an exceedingly tricky enterprise. No memory, not even one from a moment in the past, is absolutely accurate, and the farther we grow from remembered events, the more loosely our memories hang on the facts. Every family has stories and jokes about its elders remaking experiences and returning over and over to favorite moments, worn by retelling into comfortable shapes. Memory, Claude Houghton has written, is "a nursery in which children who have grown old play with their broken toys."

And yet these memories are also cultural treasures. Among the acknowledged classic works on American life are Henry Adams's *Education*, the *Narrative* of Frederick Douglass, and Benjamin Franklin's *Autobiography*. Other immensely popular memoirs span the diversity of the national experience, from Elizabeth Cady Stanton's *Eighty Years and More* to Russell Baker's *Growing Up*. Every year scores more appear in print, mostly from small private presses. Besides all these, archives bulge with thousands of unpublished reminiscences about life in an earlier America. In all of them, the authors' youthful memories offer invaluable insights from the child's unique perspective into the details and larger patterns of life over nearly three centuries of American history.

These memoirs, as historical documents, are doubly troublesome and doubly revealing. What we read on the surface must be tested with special rigor to decide where the authors, in Marquis James's fine phrase, "elevate the truth above the range of the familiar." Memoirists tend to sift through their recollections—eliminating, emphasizing, remolding—to revise their individual pasts to fit psychological needs of the present. At work here is a compelling human urge, something like a conversation each of us has with ourselves, an ongoing discussion that continuously redraws the fuzzy boundary between who we are and who we wish to have been. This same distortion, however, gives these memoirs a richness and resonance not found in diaries, letters, and other documents closer in time to the events described. Memoirs tell something about past fact and present myth, both personal and collective.

In the final essay in *Small Worlds*, Liahna Babener explores some of the complexities of this reminiscent literature. The scene is the Middle West during the late nineteenth and early twentieth centuries, a time and place that produced a remarkable number of memoirs from those who grew up on the region's homesteads. Babener finds in these recollections a contradiction between explicit memories and implicit emotions, a contradiction that helps in capturing what midwestern childhood was truly like. But just as important it suggests another level of experience—the power of myth, in this case the persistent American belief in the uplifting force of an idyllic agrarian life. In a larger sense, Babener is suggesting how the perception of childhood, as much as the actuality of it, becomes an essential part of the adult identity.

That in turn brings us back to the paradox running throughout most of these essays. In so many ways—in how they think, how they behave, how they respond to what is put before them—children are fundamentally different from adults. And yet, ultimately, children and adults cannot be understood separately. Neither can childhood and adulthood. The young form their characters partly by watching their elders; parents change through the trials and pleasantries of childrearing; maturing women and men edit the scripts of their early lives; adults' changing perceptions of their own childhoods help shape their evolving characters.

13

Bitter Nostalgia

Recollections of Childhood on the Midwestern Frontier

LIAHNA BABENER

Like many frontier dwellers in nineteenth-century America, midwestern homesteaders had been attracted to the region by the promise of personal betterment that resettlement to the west was said to offer. Lured by visions of open spaces and free land, fertile soil and abundant productivity, settlers established themselves in the rural heartland with fervent hopes. Although men and women approached agrarian life with differing expectations and their experiences on the land produced separate responses, both were compelled by the national ideal of independent yeomanry and attracted to the moral rewards of work. In spite of the hardships they faced, these early farmers were sustained through difficult times by the romantic power of their idealism, and they tended to look on their homesteading endeavor—however successful—with a measure of pride and satisfaction.

Yet the children of these settlers and their children, writing narratives of growing up on prairie farms and villages in the late nineteenth and early twentieth centuries, record a more ambivalent view of their experience, less steeped in the affirmation that had drawn their parents and grandparents to the land. Their childhood reminiscences, written in adult life, are riddled with conflicting feelings, at once nostalgic celebrations of the contentments of rural life and grim chronicles of the adversity borne by

Washday.
(Museum of New Mexico, neg. no. 71144)

pioneer families. Even the most sentimental recollections, penned in the rosy glow of retrospection and meant to recount the joys of agrarian life— close family bonds, traditional homespun values, fiscal independence, community attachments, and the organic pleasures of cultivation and hus- bandry—diverge unwittingly into complaint, even rancor. Often against their declared intentions, these midwestern autobiographers reveal an incipient strain of animosity toward their regional heritage.

The recognition that life on the farms and in the hamlets of the middle border, despite the prevalence of utopian myths about country living, could be harrowing is hardly news to readers of Hamlin Garland, Sinclair Lewis, Sherwood Anderson, Susan Glaspell, Ruth Suckow, Edgar Lee Masters, and other familiar chroniclers of the downside of the midwest- ern experience. Such writers were deliberate refugees from their places of origin, artists, journalists, and social observers who fled the backwater towns of their childhood to cultural meccas east and west, where they made careers dramatizing the bleakness of the heartland, producing a literature of "revolt from the village."[1] The collective vexation with their rural past conveyed by these commentators was potent enough to prompt literary critics of the early twentieth century to coin the phrase "Middle

Westishness" to characterize the shrill disillusionment pervading works by émigrés from the farm belt. In a biting retrospective of his native Wisconsin, Glenway Wescott, one of those fugitive writers, defined the region as "the state of mind of people born where they do not like to live."[2]

Perhaps surprisingly, the same acrimony is detectable in the sunnier reminiscences of a whole generation of midwesterners—few of whom were professional writers or public figures—who remained by choice in the domain of their youth. Raised by parents immersed in the Jeffersonian gospel of agrarian virtue still prominent at the end of the nineteenth century,[3] these unpretentious authors—people like Idella Alderman Anderson, who grew up on a farm in Atchison County, Kansas, in the 1870s; or Minnie Ellingson Tapping, who wrote *The Saga of a Minnesota Pioneer* to commemorate her midwestern girlhood during the decades following the Civil War; or Victor Hass, whose "Looking Homeward" is a memoir of small-town life in Wisconsin at the turn of the century; or Fern Crehan, who summons forth *The Days before Yesterday* spent on her family's Ohio farmstead—sought to record, order, and preserve through narrative a way of life they saw threatened by the advent of industrialization, materialism, and urban growth.[4]

Regardless of their nostalgic purposes, most of these narrators convey vividly if inadvertently a deeply felt tension between fondness for and resentment of their rustic life. Indeed, buried under layers of idealized recollection of pastoral childhood, suppressed beneath accolades to a bygone era sits a quiet indignation about the deprivations that attend a midwestern upbringing. The disparity between the acclamatory motive behind such remembrances and the underlying bitterness that surfaces in many of them derives partly from the shaping impact of a national culture that had tended to glorify westward expansion and the domestication of the prairie. These memoirists, imbued from childhood with the romance of homesteading, are disposed to rehearse the familiar dogma even if their own experience contradicts it. Not surprisingly, their having outlasted hardships to achieve comfortable lives constitutes for most of them a form of individual triumph, charted retrospectively through autobiography. Hence, they seem often to be constructing for themselves a kind of personal myth, a chronicle that serves to justify and validate their life history and is thus driven toward affirmation, even at the expense of incisive self-knowledge or emotional honesty.[5]

To argue that the authors of such remembrances disclose unintentionally a vein of suppressed aggravation about their midwestern upbringing is not to say that they devalue their past experiences or begrudge their growing up. Indeed, the opposite is often true: Most give utterance to the belief that their rural childhoods endowed them with lifelong values and functional skills that equipped them to make their way in the world. Certainly, a reading of these materials that credits at face value the agreeable memories and positive judgments offered up by the authors is plausible. I argue, however, that in spite of the proverbial optimism reflected in these accounts, undercurrents of resentment lurk beneath. To discover such ambivalent attitudes, the scrutinizing reader must understand the narrative strategies that govern these texts, since the writers' divided feelings about their past lives are imparted indirectly in the manner of storytelling rather than through express pronouncement.

Because of the limited readership for which these modest narratives were generally written—sons, daughters, grandchildren, neighbors, community members, and others who would inherit and revere the familial and regional traditions they were meant to preserve—they differ materially from the more public and artistically self-conscious autobiographies by established writers. Where the latter are inclined to underscore their individual presence in a panoramic historical tableau, these relatively private memoirs are more caught up in the habitual business of living, less interested in the grand sweep than in the diurnal routine, and markedly less centered in the ego of the subject. While professional writers are usually reflective about their world, gravitating to the abstract and metaphorical to convey their insights, these utilitarian autobiographies focus on close-range experience conveyed through concrete details. The narrational mode is itemization rather than introspection. As Elizabeth Hampsten argues in *Read This Only to Yourself,* this functional, prosaic reportage produces meaning, but it is a kind of immediate and literal revelation rather than the imaginative magnitude that metaphor allows.[6]

Nonetheless, despite their pedestrian character, such accounts of daily life in the rural Midwest are powerfully affecting.[7] The authors of these workaday texts recreate their childhood world by cataloging its mundane data; they convey strength of conviction and intensity of feeling through quantification rather than in declaration, by piling on particulars. Recollection is translated into story by means of the pervasive device of the list: A typical account enumerates the day-to-day activities of pastoral life, tabulates the articles of domesticity, and charts the vicissitudes of land, weather, provisions, crops, the market, and life's rites of passage. In the absence of contemplative or analytical commentary, such listings have a cumulative force that is unconsciously revealing, adumbrating for the reader the otherwise unspoken tribulations of the homestead.

Thus, the arresting quality about midwestern growing-up narratives is that for all their lovingly rendered detail it is the adversity of the rural world that sticks, despite the insistent nostalgia of the memoirists. This "bitter nostalgia" as I have called it is consistent with the double-mindedness that attends most of the residual values traditionally associated with the Midwest—the tendency of the region's myths and ideals to spill over into their dark obverse conditions. Such ironic reversal is apparent in a whole spate of cultural contradictions: What is celebrated, for example, as midwestern pragmatism has an unpalatable underside, a kind of "soul shrinking" anti-intellectualism as Wallace Stegner called it;[8] or what is idealized as midwestern rootedness can double back onto itself as entrapment. Similarly, the region's characteristic moderation may become mediocrity, openness seem like emptiness, thrift convert to niggardliness, and local pride turn into Babbittry. This same play of oppositions gives distinctive character to the reminiscences of middle western natives who mean to lionize—but often lambast—their cultural traditions. In romanticizing their past lives, these narrators disclose, ironically and inadvertently, a resentment of their childhood worlds that registers more keenly than their deliberate validation.[9]

There are, of course, occasions when discontent is directly and purposefully asserted. Such expressions are common in the ruminant personal histories of career artists who fled the Midwest for more fertile creative terrain. Autobiographies by Herbert Quick and Hamlin Garland articulate the counterfable of prairie life that expatriate writers advanced against the myth of agrarian happiness so prevalent in the new century. Writing about his pioneering boyhood in Iowa, Quick provides in *One Man's Life* the representative overview: "Upon us [homesteaders] rested the burdens of poverty, exhausting labor and frequent illness; and all about us the life seemed narrow, sordid, circumscribed, repressive. Ours was a prosy and uninteresting world."[10] Garland upholds the paradigm in *A Son of the Middle Border*: "I grew up on a farm and I am determined once and for all to put the essential ugliness of its life into print. . . . A proper portion of the sweat, flies, heat, dirt, and drudgery of it all shall go in."[11]

Although we might expect such bitterness from Quick and Garland, we may be surprised to discover the same disaffection latently present in more sentimental reminiscences by unheralded authors. Intermittently, even the more idealized accounts slip from approbation into condemnation, as does Ernest Venable Sutton's narrative that begins as a felicitous account of his upbringing in the Dakotas but culminates in a kind of jeremiad against the frontier:

> The rosy dreams of those overzealous [pioneers] . . . were at an end. The grasshoppers had left them in poverty, the epidemic had brought them sorrow and suffering; their spirits were broken and they were discouraged. A prominent . . . member of the [community] absconded with funds sorely needed, a woman hanged herself, while one man killed his wife and children and then committed suicide. A brother of the engineer in the mill went crazy and killed his whole family, and when committed to the insane asylum at St. Peter, set that building afire and burned many of the patients, including himself. A national panic added to their distress.[12]

And so on, as the chronicle comes to sound like the story of Job retold and relocated to the Great Plains. And this from a memoirist who titles his narrative *A Life Worth Living* and describes his migration west as a "trek into wonderland."

The same litany of grievances incorporated into an otherwise laudatory tale is reiterated again and again. "The labor was monotonous, the board was poor, my lips were blistered by the sun, my feet were sore, and I was thoroughly unhappy," writes Gurdon Wattles in his *Autobiography*, a remembrance of life in an Iowa prairie town, which the author somewhat unconvincingly refers to as "our new Utopia."[13] Anna Lathrop Clary begins her *Reminiscence* with the blithe recreation of an unfettered girlhood on the Minnesota prairie, praising the togetherness of the family on the homestead but slipping midsentence into the language of alienation and loneliness as "weeks, . . . months would go by without our seeing anyone from the outside world." Though claiming to be "gloriously happy" in that isolated terrain, her recollection of the "endless" and "tedious" winters, "laborious" tasks, "monotonous" days, and "fatiguing" duties amounts to fixation, and she sums up her childhood experience as enduring "a five-year exile."[14]

This pattern of involuntary recrimination, wherein the writer intends to render a memory favorably but falls off into an expression of dissatisfaction, serves as a structural model for most midwestern autobiographies. Pleasurable experience, no matter how pungently it may have been lived in youth, is generally relayed to the reader by means of hazy (and trite) abstractions ("I had a happy childhood in a happy family"; "Altogether it seems as if these Indiana years were beautiful and complete"; "I tasted such ineffable happiness that in my tale of twenty-five thousand days it stands out like a star");[15] hardships are called up in sharply etched particulars, enhancing their pejorative power. Hence, positive recollections are dimmed against the darker shadow of adversity. Since these narratives rely primarily on the cataloging of minutiae and the clustering of anecdotes rather than on studied assertion to characterize the remembered world, the discerning reader must learn to ferret out the author's muffled complaints from beneath a heap of details.

For example, many accounts extol the ingenuity of homely nostrums devised by pioneer mothers to combat illness. But stories intended as complimentary memories of maternal solicitude and the efficacy of folk medicine on the frontier ultimately serve contrary purposes as they highlight instead the rampant and chronic maladies that plagued nineteenth-century rural dwellers. Assiduous lists of home remedies (swamp-cabbage root mixed with honey for whooping cough; cold water wraps for scarlet fever; beef's gall sliced in alcohol and rubbed on limbs for polio victims; quinine or port wine for ague; salt pork and boric acid for mouth cankers; lard and sulfur ointment for scabies) are finally more illuminating for the suffering and persistent pathology they unmindfully disclose. Preventative practices were often onerous and unpleasant for children. As one memoirist recalls: "During epidemics of children's contagious diseases we often wore small bags of assofoetida next to the skin, suspended around our necks by a string. The close, ill-ventilated schoolrooms must have been odiforous."[16] Such oppressions were often endured in vain, however. The same narrator subsequently describes how her neighborhood playmate died anyway from the infectious diphtheria she was being armored against. She herself was spared only to confront a savage epidemic of dysentery, which systematically incapacitated her entire family.

Certainly most autobiographers regard the tenacious infirmity of pioneer life with resignation, but the pain of illness and loss is repeatedly registered in the omnipresent itemizations of symptoms and the tabulations of victims. Families were decimated by the untimely deaths of offspring, and children were prematurely sobered by funeral customs that commanded their participation; most accounts contain fastidiously detailed recitations of the dressing and "laying out" of corpses, the "viewing" of the dead, the sending of "funeral cards," and the marching in graveside processions to hear burial sermons. Descriptions of pioneer health practices devolve unconsciously into lengthy tallies of afflictions: malaria, diptheria, pneumonia, measles, smallpox, rheumatism, influenza, bronchitis, prickly heat, tuberculosis, typhoid, meningitis, goiter, cholera, trichinosis, appendicitis. Small ailments are the focus of endless discomfort: festering sores from bare feet on the burnt-over prairie, chilblains from exposure to glacial cold, sunstroke from field labor, puncture wounds from stray pitchforks, bruises and broken bones from livestock hooves. What may begin as acclaim for the resiliency of rural dwellers often culminates in a scathing inventory of the daily dangers of homestead life, as the list of accidents recalled in just one memoir attests: loss of a hand from a malfunctioning band cutter; contusions from a flying hammerhead; cracked limbs resulting from falls from a hay-loft, a horse, a threshing machine, a tree, and a wagon, and into a river, a well, and a quicksand marsh.[17]

To the pioneering mind, the disparity between everyday mishap and dire calamity is often slight; indeed, prairie memoirs constitute a kind of hardship docket, itemizing annoyances and disasters with equal dispassion. Eliza St. John Brophy records in *Twice a Pioneer* the overturning of a haywagon in impassive prose: "One night in October of '96, my husband accidently fell out of the wagon on the way home from town."[18] The same unperturbed tone is used to describe a bridge collapse where several victims, including a blind man, his young son, and two teams of horses are maimed and killed. Salient for the reader is the sheer ordinariness of catastrophe in Brophy's 1870 Dakota. One might expect a sense of horror from the adult author looking back on the tragedy she had witnessed as an impressionable child, but none is offered. The very absence of outrage attests to the way in which people became conditioned to adversity. Of course, their expectation of it did not lessen their suffering; rather it allowed them to cloak pain behind a mantle of resignation.

Hamlin Garland is more forthcoming about the oppressions of a frontier childhood that he characterizes in retrospect as "the sordid monotony of farm life. . . . I perceived now the tragic value of scenes which had hitherto appeared merely dull or petty. My eyes were opened to the enforced misery of the pioneer."[19] Casting off the numbing stoicism of his midwestern upbringing, he is "beset with a desire to record" the austerity and affliction of rural subsistence. And yet the same autobiography is paradoxically laden with celebrations of bucolic life and ends with Garland's problematical tribute to the world he has vilified: "I acknowledged myself at home and for all time. Beneath my feet lay the rugged country rock of my nativity. It pleased me to discover my mental characteristics striking so deep into this typically American soil."[20]

Garland's fierce ambivalence about the value and meaning of his childhood in the hinterlands is reinforced at a more prosaic level in the memoirs of innumerable grass-roots authors recounting farm life on the midwestern frontier. Reverent depictions of the prairie landscape, for example, exalting its vast contours, undulating grasses, dramatic horizons, and opulent productivity revert unawares into disquieting images of barren expanses bleached and scorched by summer heat, pummeled by winter blizzards, and severed from communal contact.

Autobiographical accounts report with little variance the feelings of isolation and imprisonment experienced periodically by prairie residents, calling to mind the dementia brought on by open spaces that afflicted Beryl Hansa in O. E. Rolvaag's archetypal novel of Midwest settlement, *Giants in the Earth*. As autobiographer Faye Lewis recalls, on the prairie there was "nothing to make a shadow,"[21] the source of a pervasive, deep-seated phobia among settlers who had forsaken the cozy domesticity of eastern backyards for the treeless western horizon. Gurdon Wattles describes the anxiety of exposure one felt out on the borderland as a predatory "sickness" that eventually debilitated those who did not escape the land.[22]

Even for children, who were not bound by memories of New England neighborhoods, the place seemed barren of life. Eliza Brophy's first sighting of prairie country made her feel as if she were on the moon, surveying a parched terrain where "there was not a single tree or shrub to be seen, just miles and miles of prairie."[23] Ironically, the expansiveness of the flatlands could be incarcerating; as one memoirist recalls, "Although my new home was in the wide-open spaces, I lost my freedom to run and play outside. . . . I could not leave the swept area in front of the house unless one of my grandparents was with me; and I was not allowed in the garden because of the danger of rattlesnakes."[24]

Hervey White's portrait of his family's farmstead in frontier Iowa, recounted in *Childhood Fancies*, illustrates the mixture of aversion and affection that autobiographers register about Midwest geography: "There was a dry bed of a dry creek near the house where a few scrubby cottonwoods grew desolately; the landscape was barren, unattractive, but in no way had it depressed the spirits of the family. All were alert, optimistic, enthusiastic, boasting gaily of the hardships of the past seasons, of the grasshoppers and the hot winds and the blizzards."[25] White's stinging language of dessication and devitalization belies the cheerful affirmation contained in the passage and offers his readers unintentional insight into the characteristic conflict between attachment to and alienation from the home place that typifies midland memoirs.

Similarly, autobiographical accounts of the daunting natural events that accompanied prairie life slip easily from childish wonderment into horror, as the writers' sense of the grandeur of ecological forces shifts unwittingly to exasperation about the futility of settlement in such a volatile region. Nearly every example of the genre contains a report of a prairie fire, a locust plague, a tornado "touchdown," a lightning death, a killing frost, a mosquito infestation, a "gully-wash," and a legion of other such alarming natural visitations. This insistent drive to register and take the measure of nature's fury serves as an index to the sustained frustration of those forced to adapt to circumstances and to endure misfortunes beyond their control.

Weather details deluge the narratives: wind storms, dust storms, hail storms, snow storms, and ice storms; heat and humidity, freezing and thawing, flooding and drought. The cataloging midwestern mentality goads memoirists to delineate standout disasters, such as the Grasshopper Years of 1874, 1876, 1881, or the Drought Years of 1884, 1885, 1894, or the Big Winter Years of 1871–1872, 1880–1881, 1888–1889. Though adult writers attempt to recapture the sense of the marvelous they felt as children witnessing such colossal events, a feeling of helpless battering by nature is voiced instead. Periodic assertions of the splendor of the regional climate sound contrived against the meticulous registry of hard times.

Most frontier autobiographers reserve special adulation for the ethos of hard work they inherited from their pioneer parents, who in turn reflected the Puritan precepts of earlier generations. Perhaps the paramount theme of midwestern narratives is what Irene Hardy calls "the good fun of good work" in her memoir, *An Ohio Schoolmistress.*"[26] But just as every other conventional ideal is effectively undermined by these writers as their conflicting impulses are inadvertently betrayed, assertions of the moral rewards of labor are transmuted into a kind of martyrology of saints. Chore routines, detailed with compulsive particularity, show not merely the weighty burden of responsibility that pressed the homesteading family but also the dreary and deadening impact of sameness.

Household activities were staggering in their repetitiousness—clothes to be sewn, mended, laundered, ironed, folded, and sorted; dishes to be scraped, stacked, washed, dried, and polished; ashes to be drained, boiled, poured, and leached for soft soap; fabric to be spun, carded, loomed, and dyed; candles to be molded, rugs to be woven, and hides to be tanned; hogs to be butchered, scalded, smoked, cured, and ground for sausage; sheep to be sheared and wool to be fleeced. Food preparation was an interminable process of reenactment; Della Lutes in *Country Kitchen* describes what her mother did with corn: husking, hulling, shelling, grinding, boiling, baking, sifting, chopping, pickling, popping, and frying.[27] Despite the genial tone adopted by most autobiographers as they record such tasks, the regimental quality of the work and the reduplication of the activities attest to a grimmer reality, acknowledged at least subconsciously by narrators compelled to quantify their memories in ever more exhaustive tallies.

Female autobiographers, conditioned by established expectations of gender, report matter of factly the unremitting household exercises that occupied their mothers and claimed their own girlhood energies; males, less acclimated to kitchen and parlor and coached in Victorian gallantry, write of the feminine domain with more pronounced sentimental veneration. Yet in both cases the magnitude of the burden and the tedium of the labor stand out. Clara Erlich means to commend frontier thrift when she tells of the many uses for flour sacks, but her summary alerts us instead to the exacting and versatile sewing skills demanded of women: The sacks could be hemmed and made into dishcloths, recut and sewn into underwear, subdivided and finished into handkerchiefs, or pieced together in fours and converted to tablecloths.[28]

Housecleaning was a perpetual occupation that required strong mettle. Victor Hass recollects in "Looking Homeward" the pride his mother demonstrated in her spotless Wisconsin home, but in spite of the filial compliment he means to deliver about her conscientious housework, the penalties of domestic prudence stand out for the reader: her roughened fingers, sore back, and aching limbs after a typical workday. With a naive complacency, he catalogs the tasks she performed (moving furniture, swabbing floors, dusting surfaces, beating rugs, and scrubbing wood and coal dust from walls). Noting that "she would be up at 4 A.M." to haul the wood and heat the wash water on the stove "because there was an unspoken challenge to any woman in town to get her wash on the lines first," he aims to pay homage to his mother's competitive gusto, but already we discern the long hours and physical stresses of laundry day. "She . . . laboriously carried [the water] from stove to bench. She used Fels Naptha and a scrub board, an instrument of the Devil that left hands scratched and raw." Reflexively, the paragraph shifts from a glib expression of the Yankee work ethic into a lament for the drudgery of women's toil.[29]

Outdoor activity on the farm was equally routinized. The farmer's unending cycle of cultivation—terracing, furrowing, and plowing the soil, planting, seeding, cradling, tasseling, threshing, pitching, raking, tramping out, cleaning, separating, binding, stacking, storing, and selling the grain—is altered somewhere in the process of retelling by these writers from an organic ritual into a suffocating ordeal. The growing fields become the killing fields, as this contradictory account from Cyrenus Cole in *I Remember, I Remember* suggests:

> I have little patience . . . with those who . . . write so dolefully about [farm labor]. . . . I would rather marvel at the beauty of life. . . . My parents bore many burdens and endured many sorrows. . . . [but] not from hard work, (for even such work was a joy to them). For that pittance [fifteen cents a bushel for potatoes] we had planted and plowed, pulled weeds and picked beetles from the vines . . . and scratched them out of the dirt with our own bare fingers. And for all that fifteen cents a bushel! That was my father's sigh of sorrow and the burden that bent his back.[30]

Cole's avowal of the pleasures of labor rings hollow against his caustic portrayal of the travails of cultivation and the cruel whimsy of the marketplace.

Though agriculture was a seasonal occupation, farm work was ceaseless. Autobiographers emphasize not only the arduousness of the endeavor but also the compulsive drive of its practitioners to do ever more. Bertha Van Hoosen provides in her Michigan memoir a lengthy list of the various exertions necessary to sustain her parents' small enterprise and the tireless efforts of her father to attend to the many routine demands of husbandry and tillage. Beginning as an admiring portrait of her father's industriousness, it instead becomes an unwitting critique of his obsessive work habits: She explains how, when the chores were complete at the end of the day or the crops in at harvest time, he was unable to rest or recreate but was impelled to fill leisure hours with new tasks. "When the farm work was a little slack, we pulled stumps"; when the seeds were in the ground in spring, it was time to construct a water system for the house; the hay was hardly mown before the pipes were to be extended to the barn. Then a new barn had to be built and a new fence to surround it. When neighbors teased him about his unflagging zeal, he chastised them with moral apothegms.[31] Mildred Renaud was schooled in the work ethic by her driven grandmother: "She lost no time in teaching me to be helpful. She said, 'Idleness is sinful.' The only time she was idle was when she was sleeping." Forced to obey her grandmother's dictum, she had to forgo girlhood amusements in favor of tasks such as drying dishes, peeling potatoes, and shaving off the calluses and corns that grew on the older woman's overtaxed feet, a graphic example of the unsavory side of pioneer existence.[32]

Children confronted their chores with a predictable blend of readiness and disinclination, as one autobiographer's retelling of his assignment demonstrates: "To have to milk two or three cows morning and evening is to be a slave to them, I know, but I felt my slavery less than my pride in being the eldest brother and bearing this responsibility. And I enjoyed milking, even the cantankerous, tough-uddered old Shorthorn and the Jersey that kicked like a horse."[33] In spite of the author's declaration that he liked his task, the disagreeable cameo of the cows and the slave imagery leave a more disparaging impression on the reader. Minnie Tapping reports that "Poppy had an idea that to be happy we must have work to do," a sentiment she tries to endorse, but her grueling inventory of duties— filling the woodbox, sweeping the steps, watering the calves, bringing home the livestock, chopping the kindling, shelling corn for the chickens, pulling vegetables for the pigs, filling the fuel basket with chips, picking up and sorting fruit from the orchard ground, collecting the eggs, scaring the blackbirds from the cornfields, weeding the cornrows—seems hardly to evoke gladness. As the author recognizes, the moral gratifications of labor had to be shored up with tangible rewards for workers (a stick of candy, a ride in the wagon, a dime to spend at the local confectionary), and she and her siblings were punished if they failed to execute their tasks with a "cheerful spirit."[34]

Religion is another facet of experience that brings out the same double-mindedness about midwestern living. A strong religiosity undergirds most heartland reminiscences. Inculcated with the Christian pieties of their parents, ingrained with an earthy faith born of their rustic way of life, well schooled in scripture, and nurtured by the social offices and cordial communalism of rural churches, most memoirists recall with felicity the religious practices of their childhoods. But as their stories often unwittingly reveal, devout sentiments can be squelching as well as uplifting.

Most accounts reflect a tacit conflict between validation of and disaffection for the straitlaced mores of rural religious culture. Bruce Bliven professes to admire the moral earnestness of his Protestant upbringing, but his enumeration of the diversions "frowned upon" by the church—"drinking, smoking, dancing, the theater, and card-playing"—suggests that he chafed under the taboos, especially since in the same recollection he applauds his mother's surreptitious defiance; she produced amateur musicals and hosted convivial gatherings of the local whist club where play continued until the daring hour of eleven o'clock.[35] Irene Hardy adds sewing on the Sabbath and playing the fiddle to the roster of prohibitions, noting with visible regret that her father, a skillful violinist, had forsworn the instrument in deference to the opinion of fellow churchgoers who considered it "wicked and worldly."[36] Ernest Venable Sutton lists Sunday picnics, the skating rink, thought to be "the haunt of Satan," and the local saloon, described as "the front door to perdition" by the townsfolk, among the bans. Although he claims to appreciate the necessity behind such moral regulations, his faith in the legitimacy of them is called into question when, having investigated the saloon on his own, he concludes that "it was just as respectable a place as the church, and much more friendly."[37]

Conditioned by established concepts of upstanding behavior, frontier children generally venerated the traditional virtues, but their adult reminiscences suggest that they often squirmed beneath such constraints. Ernest Sutton maintains that the enforced Bible readings and prayer sessions at school and at home were "all to the good," but he admits that he learned the recited texts by heart so he could tell when they were going to end. Though taught to maintain proper decorum during the two hours of religious instruction in Sunday school, he sorely envied the mischievous boys who "could shoot paper wads and throw spit balls" with impunity.[38] He frequently hails functional prairie ethics, but he also criticizes the "failure . . . of forced morality" that curtailed the vital spirits of frontier children.[39] Another author recalls his ingenuous dismay when the local Iowa opera company staged *The Pirates of Penzance*, featuring solo performances by members of the church choir; the minister, overcome with the profanation he saw in such music, preached a fiery sermon on the text of Revelation 19:2: "For he hath judged the great whore which did corrupt the earth with her fornications," causing several choir members to react "as if they had been called dreadful names" and alienating the narrator by his "inflexible rectitude."[40]

Although these autobiographers generally begin with an endorsement of such proscriptions of error, their implicit complaint about the self-abnegating mentality of midwestern Protestantism eventually shows. Hervey White's portrait of the denominational upheavals in his family is illustrative of a similar ambivalence. His memoir is replete with respectful remembrances of his favorite Uncle Bart, whose transformation from buoyant good humor to the staunch probity of Seventh Day Adventism won the boy's admiration but lost his affection. In spite of White's concession that his reformed uncle's passage to the afterlife was more probable, his distaste for the new moralist is everywhere apparent.[41]

Hellfire and damnation, endemic to much frontier Protestantism, could have drastic effects on impressionable children. Most memoirists register a mixture of captivation and bewilderment over the mysterious miracles in which they were instructed; revelation could be spellbinding, but frequently it cast a pall on youthful peace of mind as the after effects of the frenzied revival meetings, a staple feature of nineteenth-century rural life, demonstrate. In spite of their adult credence, these writers often reveal lasting emotional misgivings about Christianity's campaign against perdition. White remembers the chilling power of domestic worship: "This baleful influence of religion was always shadowing him . . . always the winds of Death across his play-time! . . . Then at the breakfast table, another gloomy 'Blessing' to take away the cheer of homely living."[42] Though they applaud the devotional exercises they remember from childhood—Bible recitations, mealtime prayers, evening hymns, singing the Doxology, memorizing moral maxims, reading didactic children's stories, receiving the local pastor—autobiographers tend to tabulate such observances with the same doggedness exhibited in their tally sheets of ailments and chores.

Farm children often found it difficult to reconcile the organic literalism of their daily venue with the metaphorical tenets of Christianity. In spite of their childhood instruction in theology, memoirists record a kind of pragmatic skepticism about the supernatural; too, they are less inclined to interpret their own experience through the glass of scriptural allegory as their parents were wont to do. Jerusalem—and heaven—seemed far distant from their quotidian worlds. It was a struggle to correlate the stern invective of the prophets with the trifling vices of their siblings. Mary Austin remembers her confusion and anxiety when she could not make out the connection between "the God-of-the-Bible" she had heard about at her Presbyterian Sunday school and the "God the little bird sang about," whose spiritual presence she had sensed when she wandered in the walnut orchard.[43] This preadolescent contradiction brimmed over in later life to a more pronounced disillusionment with farm-belt pietism and an abiding sense of betrayal over the fact that the convictions of sin and salvation to which her sectarian relatives so earnestly clung were inaccessible to her.[44]

Prophecies of doom and parables of divine wrath that gave moral structure to their parents' worldview sometimes assumed a terrifying credibility to children raised on the prairie and accustomed to awesome natural forces. Edward Ross recalls a summer he spent timorously awaiting the apocalypse on the Illinois flatland, "going out and looking anxiously for the lightning 'that cometh out of the east and shineth even unto the west.'" It is unclear whether his later disengagement from religion came from his sense of having been duped by false divination, but he confesses in his memoir that "eventually I came to feel stern over this end-of-the-world nonsense."[45]

By a parallel process of inversion, other hallowed institutions are subtly subverted by midwestern autobiographers even in the midst of deliberate affirmation. Contrary to the popular assumptions about kinship that most of these writers consciously accept, family often emerges as a strangulating rather than a strengthening bond in their narratives. Taught to esteem their forebears and to honor their roots, the authors of these memoirs provide admiring portraits of their parents and obliging transcriptions of family history, but underlying many of them is a suppressed yearning for deliverance from the constrictions of blood ties.

Victor Hass sums up the credo that governed midwestern circles: "And what had been most attractive to townsmen and farmers alike during the golden era was the celebration of family. We were so close-knit that often three generations . . . lived together in the same house."[46] But Hass's encomium to intergenerational solidarity comes in the midst of a protracted complaint about the poverty and privations that attended large rural families. With so many mouths to feed, "there was scarcely enough money for necessities, much less frills." Christmas gifts had to be homemade; though taught to exclaim over handwrought items like cornhusk dolls or carved wooden keepsakes, farm children like Hass were rarely free of envy and disappointment on such occasions, emotions that resonate through recollections intended instead to extol the virtues of self-sacrifice.

Many of these authors illustrate unwittingly the psychic penalties of parental expectation and filial loyalty. Bertha Van Hoosen strove to win the approval of her punctilious father, and her chronicle discloses the anguish she experienced trying to free herself from a deferential pattern: "From early childhood, my ambition had been to please my father, to hear him say, 'That's right. . . .' After his death the breaking of all these connecting threads consumed years."[47] Similar revelations appear in most such remembrances. Written by authors counseled in the domestic ideals of the age, these memoirs nonetheless demonstrate that familial affiliations could be suffocating. Though disposed to endorse, even to sentimentalize the patriarchal family model, many autobiographers divulge its oppressive effects. Della Lutes writes humorously of her headstrong father in *Country Kitchen*, but it is clear that his overbearing nature stifled his wife and children, however endearing her rendition of his foibles. Norman Hapgood reports the same paternal shackling, though his tone betrays more vitriol: "The highest authority I knew, in those days, was my father,—my mother assisting in the process of putting him first."[48]

Homesteading conditions, of course, exacerbated family stresses. The isolation of prairie farms, the long, frigid winters that kept inhabitants indoors in confined spaces, the economic and climatological uncertainties of agriculture that contributed to tensions, and the rural conservatism that preached acceptance of one's lot in life—augmented the silent suffering that many experienced in their domestic spheres. Growing up in such

conditions, regional autobiographers were not unmindful of their meager allotments, and a consciousness of deprivation resides under their
nostalgic renditions of the cheery dwellings in which they were raised.

James Norman Hall, whose account is typical, describes his home in
rural Iowa, which sat

> on its exposed hilltop where it took the buffetings of the bitter mid-
> winter winds sweeping down from Canada. . . . The only water faucet
> in the house was in the cellar, for this was believed to lessen the risk
> of the pipe freezing in winter, but it froze nevertheless. All water was
> carried up to the kitchen. On a small back porch we had an icebox;
> but Iowa summers were as hot as the winters were cold, and those
> precious blocks of ice would vanish before the day was done. But
> that old frame house was a home in the best sense of the word. Com-
> forts and conveniences there were none, but they were not missed
> because we had never known them.[49]

Whatever the naive complacency of the child who had grown up in such
a habitation, the adult remembrance is rife with a feeling of destitu-
tion. Concrete details like battering winds, frozen pipes, subterranean
faucets, sweltering summers, and inoperative refrigeration pile up ruin-
ously against quaint abstractions about domestic contentment.

Not surprisingly, home could seem like detention even for those who
wished to look on it as a haven. Regional memoirs provide abundant
details about houses: their design, size, construction, layout, spatial organization, temperature, decor, and ambience; chroniclers record compul-
sively what was done in particular rooms, when, how, why, and by
whom. Yet even in their complacent accounts of dwelling spaces, autobiographers reveal again the familiar ambivalence. What begins as a loving
recreation of daily rituals often deviates into a humdrum memorandum
of enforced regimens. Household objects—ash hoppers, coal scuttles,
candle molds, pork barrels, rug beaters, dash churns, watering pots, seed
bags, grindstones, wash basins, sewing baskets, and a hundred other
serviceable implements—are named and explicated, calling attention unconsciously to the round-the-clock labor that supported rural homes.

Appurtenances serve the reader as inadvertent reminders of a make-
do existence: tin-can footstools, patchwork cushions, rag rugs, quilts for
doors, crates for chairs, goosegrease for shoe polish, asparagus branches
for insect decoys, toilet paper vamped from the pages of mail-order cata-

logs. As the tone of stifled yearning in these narratives suggests, decorative artifacts come to stand as much for prohibitions as they do for embellishments: the antimacassars that shielded chairs from dirty fingers, the fragrant sachets hidden in mother's drawer to veil the adult world of sensation and sexuality, the fragile "air castles" that danced from walls and ceilings well above the reach of children, the Brussels carpet and velvet drapes in the parlor, that forbidden zone where no one could traffic. Displayed on a center table in the entry way, the family Bible becomes an icon, not merely of the venerable Christian ethos of small town life but also of the constraints under which middle western households operated.

Community life is subject to the same retrospective ambivalence. Despite their immersion in the parochial boosterism of rural America and the traditional esteem for village life that had prompted their parents' settlement ventures, regional annalists hold up a darkened lens to hometown history. Though they mean to celebrate the social occasions and entertainments of small prairie towns, they unintentionally document how such organized affairs could impose contrived fellowship and conformist pressures upon participants and drive the nonjoiners to despair. Since most such activities revolved around moral edification, fun usually had a didactic edge to it. With notably subdued enthusiasm, autobiographers report on attending lectures by circuit preachers, political orators, temperance advocates, and the literati. Competitive impulses were channeled into self-improving outlets like spelling bees, public debates, rivalries at the county fair, and piece-speaking contests; imaginative curiosity was corralled into the arenas of local lyceums and traveling chautauquas.

School and church governed most adolescent exchanges between the sexes, and tellingly, the chief form of group fraternizing was the "work social," where community residents combined conviviality with industry at husking or quilting bees, apple parings, nut shellings, barn raisings, log rollings, geese pluckings, maple sugarings, hog stickings, and pound parties. Even Decoration Day and Fourth of July picnics, the highlight of the year for most midland country-town dwellers, were homiletic occasions at which patriotic speeches by war heroes and the ritualistic reading of the Declaration of Independence dominated the activity. In spite of the sentimental averments in these memoirs, the persistent narrational strategy of list-making tells a different story: Activities are recounted in plodding inventories and deadpan chronologies that invite the incisive reader to recognize the undertone of boredom and discontent. After just such an index of the amusements available in her back-country Iowa locale, Hannah Hawke writes that "although in this 'far away out west' part we were debarred from much that the older and more cultivated districts enjoyed, we were not without pleasure and advantages,"[50] a quintessentially revealing statement of midwestern ambivalence.

As a body, the childhood remembrances of pioneer midwesterners undercut the romance of agrarian life. Collectively, these life histories demonstrate that beneath the proverbial pleasures of rural existence lies a buried discontent that surfaces forcefully albeit covertly in the narrative practices of the authors. Even the most rosy-hued memoirs reveal a darker strain of experience. Ultimately, the vision of growing up on the middle border that these autobiographies afford is more clouded and more anguished than previous recognition has allowed.

When Hamlin Garland sums up his family's homesteading saga as a "bitter mockery" but returns obsessively to reprise that dire venture again and again, we are struck by the urgency of his paradoxical feelings but hardly surprised because Garland is the spokesman for a well-publicized coterie of renegade midwesterners caught in the same contradictory cycle of affection for and alienation from the land of their roots. In the words of one critic, "The relationship between the Midwestern expatriate and his home region is a complex mixture of pride and regret, of love and denial, of necessary dependence and inevitable rejection."[51] Yet when lifetime resident Clara Lenroot begins her uncelebrated memoir *Long, Long Ago* with the wistful evocation of her hometown, Hudson, Wisconsin, pining for the simpler yesterdays of her rural upbringing and then leads readers through a grim tale of withering poverty, dispiriting routine, and personal entrapment, we are confronted with the need to revise our national myths about the agrarian heartland and the American dream.

In a larger sense, Lenroot and her fellow regional autobiographers remind us how complex a task we face in reconstructing the lives of children in an earlier America. All of us revise and reshape our childhoods as we grow older, looking back at youth through the refracting glass of cultural expectations and rooted traditions. Sorting through the disparities between experience and remembrance in the narratives of these pioneer writers, and uncovering the strategies by which they reveal covert feelings about the past, we gain insight not only into the history of our precursors but also into the formative patterns and psychic processes of our own lives.

Notes

❖ ❖ ❖ ❖ ❖ ❖ ❖

CHAPTER 1.
Children and Commercial Culture

1. Edward Chandler, "How Much Children Attend the Theatre, the Quality of the Entertainment They Choose and Its Effect upon Them," *Proceedings of the Children's Conference for Research and Welfare* (New York, 1909), 1:56.

2. Charles Matthew Feldman, "The National Board of Censorship (Review) of Motion Pictures, 1909–1922" (Ph.D. diss., University of Michigan, 1975), 43; Robert O. Bartholomew, "Report of Censorship of Motion Pictures and of Investigation of Motion Picture Theatres of Cleveland, 1913" (Cleveland, 1913), 56; Juvenile Protective Association (JPA) of Chicago, "Five and Ten Cent Theatres—Two Investigations" (Chicago: JPA, 1911), n.p.; Edward de Grazia and Roger K. Newman, *Banned Films: Movies, Censors and the First Amendment* (New York: Bowker, 1982), 179.

3. Vice Commission of Chicago, *The Social Evil in Chicago* (Chicago: 1911), 247–51; New York Society for the Prevention of Cruelty to Children, *Thirty-fourth Annual Report* (1909), 23–24.

4. For a list of cities with such ordinances, see Lucius H. Cannon, "Motion Pictures: Laws, Ordinances, and Regulations on Censorship, Minors and Other Related Subjects," St. Louis Public Library, *Monthly Bulletin* (July 1920).

5. John Collier, "The Motion Picture," *Proceedings of the Child Conference for Research and Welfare* (1910), 2:108; Michael M. Davis, Jr., *The Exploitation of Pleasure: A Study of Commercial Recreations in New York City* (New York: Russell Sage Foundation, n.d.), 34; Bartholomew, "Report of Censorship," 26; Rev. J. J. Phelan, *Motion Pictures as a Phase of Commercialized Amusement in Toledo, Ohio* (Toledo, 1919), 53.

6. See, for example, letter to Mayor Gaynor from president, Board of Education, May 31, 1910, in Mayor's Papers, William J. Gaynor, box WJG 80, Subjects File: Censorship: Motion Pictures, Municipal Archives, New York City; *New York Times*, Nov. 12, 1911, 8; John Collier, " 'Movies' and the Law," *Survey* 27 (Jan. 20, 1912), 1629; final quotation is from "Moving Picture Houses," Nov. 23, 1913, 36, in Magnes Papers, Hebrew University, Jerusalem, Israel.

7. Maurice Wertheim to Commissioner Raymond B. Fosdick, "Suggestions for Legislation for the Improvement of the Condition of the Moving Picture Shows in the City of New York," Sept. 19, 1910, in National Board of Review papers, box 170, Subjects Papers: Papers Relating to the Formation and Subsequent History of the National Board of Review, Special Collections, New York Public Library. See also president of Board of Education to Mayor Gaynor, May 31, 1910, in Mayor's Papers, William J. Gaynor, box WJG 80, Subjects File: Censorship: Motion Pictures, Municipal Archives; John Collier, " 'Movies' and the Law," 1629.

8. Raymond B. Fosdick, "Report on *Moving Picture Shows* in the City of New York," Mar. 22, 1911, 11–12, in Mayor's Papers, William J. Gaynor, box GWJ 22: Department Correspondence: Account Commissioner, 1911, Municipal Archives.

9. Bartholomew, "Report of Censorship," 10, 27–28.

10. Maurice Willows, "The Nickel Theatre," in National Children Labor Committee, Seventh Annual Meeting, *Annals* (Philadelphia, 1911), 96.

11. Jane Addams, *The Spirit of Youth and the City Streets* (New York: Macmillan, 1909), 5–6; Research Department, School of Social Economy of Washington University, "The Newsboy of Saint Louis" (St. Louis, n.d.), 9; William Hard, "De Kid wot works at night," in David Nasaw, *Children of the City: At Work and at Play* (New York: Oxford University Press, 1985), 125.

12. "A Visitor's Experience in a Penny Arcade," City Club of Chicago Records, box 9, folder 5, Chicago Historical Society, Chicago, Ill. I have corrected the grammar.

13. On children and "stools," see "Extract from New York World," March 30, 1906, in City Club of Chicago Records, box 9, folder 5. This article, though here labeled "New York World" was in fact published in the *New York Globe*. A clipping of the published article can be found in Community Service Society papers, box 180, "Theatre Investigation" folder, Rare Book and Manuscript Library, Columbia University, New York City. See also Lewis to Kingsley, April 5, 1907, City Club of Chicago Records, box 9, folder 5.

14. "A Visitor's Experience in a Penny Arcade," City Club of Chicago Records, box 9, folder 5.

15. On signs advertising peep-show machines, see Walter S. Ufford to O. F. Lewis, April 5, 1906, in Community Service Society papers, box 180, "Theatre Investigation."

16. "Extract from New York World, March 30, 1906," City Club of Chicago Records, box 9, folder 5.

17. Lewis to Kingsley, April 5, 1907, Community Service Society papers.

18. See letters to Lewis in Community Service Society papers; to Kingsley in City Club of Chicago papers; on Boston investigations, see S. H. Stone to Kingsley, April 4, 1907, and Frederick B. Allen to Lewis, March 23, 1906, in City Club of Chicago papers, box 9, folder 5.

19. Nasaw, *Children of the City*, 124.

20. *Moving Picture World* 1 (June 27, 1907): 262–63.

21. Phelan, *Motion Pictures in Toledo*, 50–55; Bartholomew, "Report of Censorship," 22–26; JPA, "Five and Ten Cent Theatres." n.p.

22. The list of banned subjects comes from Pennsylvania State Board of Censors, *Rules and Standards* (Harrisburg, 1918).

23. Collier, "Motion Picture," 116.

24. See, for example, the twelve volumes of the Payne Fund studies, all published by Macmillan in 1933 and summarized and popularized in Henry James Forman's *Our Movie-Made Children* (New York: Macmillan, 1933). For more on these and other studies of youth and the movies, see Garth Jowett, *Film: The Democratic Art* (Boston: Little, Brown, 1976).

25. John Collier, "Cheap Amusements," *Charities and the Commons* 20 (April 11, 1908): 75.

CHAPTER 2.
Children on the Plains Frontier

1. Frances I. S. Fulton, *To and through Nebraska* (Lincoln, Nebr.: Journal Co., 1884), 42.

2. Linnaeus B. Rauck interview, 41/158–59, Indian-Pioneer Collection, Oklahoma Historical Society (OHS), Oklahoma City; Hiram M. Drache, *The Challenge of the Prairie* (Fargo: N. Dak. Institute for Regional Studies, 1970), 195; Percy G. Ebbutt, *Emigrant Life in Kansas* (London: Swan Sonnenschein, 1886), 90.

3. Anne Jones Davies diary, June 2, 6, 13, 14, 16, 1888, Kansas

State Historical Society (KSHS), Topeka; Glen R. Durrell, "Homesteading in Colorado," *Colorado Magazine* 51, 2 (Spring 1974): 98–101; Hub Jones interview, Oral History Collection, Southwest Collection, Texas Tech University (SWC, TTU), Lubbock; Ellison Orr, "Reminiscences of a Pioneer Boy," *Annals of Iowa* 40, 7 (Winter 1971): 551.

4. Edna Matthews Clifton reminiscence, pt. 1, 12, SWC, TTU.

5. Ralla B. Pinkerton, "Pioneer Days in Beaver Creek Community," reminiscence, R. J. Bradley Collection, SWC, TTU; Maggie L. B. Holden reminiscence, Maggie Lee Bullion Papers, SWC, TTU; Oello Ingraham Martin, "Father Came West," reminiscence, 21–22, KSHS; Sadye Drew autobiography, SC1532, Montana Historical Society (MHS); Orr, "Reminiscences," 594–95; Samuel Evans Boys, *My Boyhood in the Flint Hills of Kansas, 1873–1893* (Plymouth, Ind.: by the author, 1958), 32–34.

6. Frank Albert Waugh, "Pioneering in Kansas," reminiscence, 114–15, KSHS; Christopher J. Huggard, "The Role of the Family in Settling the Cherokee Outlet" (M.A. thesis, University of Arkansas, 1987), 68–69; J. S. Bird, *Prairies and Pioneers* (Hays, Kans.: McWhirter-Ammons Press, 1931), 34; Holden reminiscence; Charles O'Kieffe, *Western Story: The Recollections of Charley O'Kieffe, 1884–1898* (Lincoln: University of Nebraska Press, 1960), 36–37.

7. William Holden, James W. Mayfield, Sam Crawford, James E. Black, C. M. Randal, Sr., interviews,

Oral History Collection, SWC, TTU; Lucy H. Stocking diary, Nov. 20, 1873, SC142, MHS; Charles W. Wells, *A Frontier Life* (Cincinnati, Ohio: Jennings and Pye, 1902), 31–32; Orr, "Reminiscences," 616–24; Vallie McKee, "Passing of the West," reminiscence, 8, and George Cork reminiscence, Jessie K. Snell Collection, KSHS; Venola Lewis Bivens, ed., "The Diary of Luna E. Warner, A Kansas Teenager of the Early 1870s," *Kansas Historical Quarterly* 35, 3 (Autumn 1969): 283, 294, 308.

8. John T. Norton diary, July 22, 28, Aug. 5, 15, 19, Sept. 12, Nov. 7, 16, 1877, Jan. 2, 26, Feb. 6, 12, 27, Mar. 6, 12, 13, 23, May 2, June 16, 1878, Feb. 15, 1879, KSHS.

9. Curt Norton diary, Oct. 2, 1877; Norton family diaries, May 20, 22, July 14, Nov. 2, 1880, KSHS.

10. Gerald W. McFarland, *A Scattered People: An American Family Moves West* (New York: Pantheon Books, 1985); Lillian Schlissel, Byrd Gibbens, and Elizabeth Hampsten, *Far from Home: Families of the Westward Journey* (New York: Schocken Books, 1989).

11. Roberta R. Collard, "Exploration and Play," in *Play and Learning*, ed. Brian Sutton-Smith (New York: Gardner Press, 1979), 45–68; Irene Athey, "Contributions of Play to Development," in *Child's Play: Developmental and Applied*, ed. Thomas D. Yawkey and Anthony D. Pellegrini (Hillsdale, N.J.: Lawrence Earlbaum Associates, 1984), 9–28; David Elkind, *The Child's Reality: Three Developmental Themes* (Hillsdale, N.J.: Lawrence Earlbaum Associates, 1978).

12. Diane Ackerman, *A Natural History of the Senses* (New York: Random House, 1990), 289.

13. Josephine Moorman Reiley, " 'I Think I Will Like Kansas': The Letters of Flora Moorman Heston, 1885–1886," *Kansas History* 6, 2 (Summer 1983): 78; Craig Miner, *West of Wichita: Settling the High Plains of Kansas, 1865–1890* (Lawrence: University Press of Kansas, 1986), 51; Allie B. Wallace, *Frontier Life in Oklahoma* (Washington, D.C.: Public Affairs Press, 1964), 79; Frank Dean, "Pioneering in Nebraska, 1872–1879," *Nebraska History* 36 (June 1955): 113.

14. Ella Irvine Mountjoy reminiscence, Wiley and Ella Mountjoy Collection, SC545, MHS.

15. Pinkerton, "Pioneer Days in Beaver Creek Community," 16; O'Keiffe, *Western Story*, 25–26, 36–38, 44–57; Mrs. W. H. Hathaway reminiscence, Arizona Historical Society.

16. Bivens, "Diary of Luna Warner," 283, 288; Lillian Miller, "I Remember Montana," reminiscence, 21–25, SC1404, MHS; Orr, "Reminiscences of a Pioneer Boy," 556–57, 600–614.

17. Waugh, "Pioneering in Kansas," 65–71, 80–85.

18. Wallace A. Wood reminiscence, 3, KSHS; Agnes Morley Cleaveland, *No Life for a Lady* (Lincoln: University of Nebraska Press, 1977), 47–49; Marvin Powe interview, Pioneer Foundations Collection, University of New Mexico Library, Albuquerque; Wallace, *Frontier Life*, 13.

19. Cliff Newland interview, Oral

History Collection, SWC, TTU.

20. Clifton reminiscence, pt. 1, 21–22; Susie Crocket interview, 21/221–29, Indian-Pioneer Collection, OHS.

21. Barbara Finkelstein, "Casting Networks of Good Influence: The Reconstruction of Childhood in the United States, 1790–1870," in *American Childhood: A Research Guide and Historical Handbook*, ed. Joseph M. Hawes and N. Ray Hiner (Westport, Conn.: Greenwood Press, 1985), 111–52; Robert McGlone, "Suffer the Children: The Emergence of Modern Middle-Class Family Life, 1820–1870" (Ph.D. diss., University of California, Los Angeles, 1971); Carl Degler, *At Odds: Women and the Family in America from the Revolution to the Present* (New York: Oxford University Press, 1980); Joseph Kett, *Rites of Passage: Adolescence in America: 1790 to the Present* (New York: Basic Books, 1977); Viviana A. Zelizer, *Pricing the Priceless Child: The Changing Social Value of Children* (New York: Basic Books, 1985).

CHAPTER 3.
Immigrant Children at School, 1880–1940

1. Selma Berrol, *Immigrants at School* (New York: Arno Press, 1978); Stephan Brumberg, *Going to America, Going to School* (New York: Praeger, 1986); David Tyack, *The One Best System* (Cambridge, Mass.: Harvard University Press, 1974); Lawrence Cremin, *The Transformation of the School* (New York: Alfred A. Knopf, 1961).

2. Ewa Morawska, *For Bread and Butter* (New York: Cambridge University Press, 1985), 132.

3. In 1905, 63 percent of the New York City elementary schools were on part-time schedules; all were located in immigrant districts. Berrol, *Immigrants*, 143–44; Ruth Schwartz Cowan and Neil Cowan, *Our Parents' Lives* (New York: Basic Books, 1989), 86. I have used two different methods for citing the memoirs of immigrant children. If the source is an autobiography, I have used the full name, but if an interview, either with me or with another historian, I have followed the lead of the authors of the various collections cited in these notes and used only the given name and first initial of the surname.

4. Irving Howe and Kenneth Libo, *How We Lived* (New York: Richard Marek, 1979), 201.

5. Selma Berrol, "Education and Economic Mobility," *American Jewish History* 55 (Mar. 1976): 261.

6. New York City, Department of Education, United States of America, *Public Schools of the City of New York*, eighteen unpaged volumes containing examples of children's work separated by grade levels with ages and some first names listed, prepared for the Paris Exposition of 1900. In the Special Collections of Teachers College Library, Columbia University, New York.

7. Berrol, *Immigrants*, 217–19; author's interview with Isidor B., Feb. 11, 1990; Edward Bok, *The Americanization of Edward Bok* (New York: Charles Scribner's, 1920), 21; Leonard Covello, *The Social Background of the Italo-American School*

Child (Totowa, N.J.: Rowan and Littlefield, 1972), 303, 344.

8. Berrol, *Immigrants*, 87.

9. Colleen Johnson, *Growing Up and Growing Old* (New Brunswick, N.J.: Rutgers University Press, 1985), 34; Harry Roskolenko, *When I Was Last on Cherry Street* (New York: Stein and Day, 1965), 8.

10. June Namias, *First Generation* (Boston: Beacon Press, 1978), 33.

11. David Nasaw, *Children of the City* (Garden City, N.Y.: Doubleday, 1985), 26; Morawska, *Bread and Butter*, 268.

12. Hasia Diner, *Erin's Daughters in America* (Baltimore: Johns Hopkins Press, 1983), 97.

13. Alfred Kazin, *A Walker in the City* (New York: Harcourt Brace Jovanovich, 1951), 17; Howe and Libo, *How We Lived*, 196, 197; Cowan and Cowan, *Our Parents' Lives*, 101.

14. John Bodnar, *Lives of Their Own* (Urbana: University of Illinois Press, 1982), 96; Selma Berrol, "Ethnicity and Childhood," in *American Childhood*, ed. Ray Hiner and Joseph Hawes (Westport, Conn.: Greenwood Press, 1985), 360.

15. Sydney Stahl Weinberg, "Longing to Learn," *Journal of American Ethnic History* 8 (Spring 1989): 11.

16. Covello, *Italo-American Child*, 339.

17. Cowan and Cowan, *Our Parents' Lives*, 88.

18. Kazin, *Walker*, 17; Bok, *Americanization*, 5; Cowan and Cowan, *Our Parents' Lives*, 87, 88; Roskolenko, "America the Thief," in Thomas Wheeler, *Immigrant Experience* (New York: Dial Press, 1971), 166; Leonard Covello, *The Heart Is*

the Teacher (Totowa, N.J.: Littlefield, Adams, 1970), 25; Jerre Mangione, *Mount Allegro* (Boston: Houghton Mifflin, 1942) 210.

19. Richard Gambino, *Blood of My Blood* (Garden City, N.Y.: Doubleday, 1974), 237; Paul Wrobel, *Our Way* (Notre Dame, Ind.: University of Notre Dame Press, 1977), 117.

20. Mary Antin, *Promised Land* (Boston: Houghton Mifflin, 1969), 207, 208, 209, 210; Cowan and Cowan, *Our Parents' Lives*, 96.

21. Cowan and Cowan, *Our Parents' Lives*, 97, 98; Covello, *Heart*, 24; Jeffrey Kisseloff, *You Must Remember Me* (New York: Harcourt Brace Jovanovich, 1989), 559.

22. Jade Snow Wong, "Puritans from the Orient," in Wheeler, *Immigrant Experience*, 119; Gambino, *Blood*, 236; Roskolenko, *Cherry Street*, 8.

23. Sydney Stahl Weinberg, *The World of Our Mothers* (Chapel Hill: University of North Carolina Press, 1988), 180.

24. Cowan and Cowan, *Our Parents' Lives*, 96, 97, 98; Howe and Libo, *How We Lived*, 197, 201; Kate Simon, *Bronx Primitive* (New York: Viking Press, 1982), 44.

25. Brumberg, *Going to America*, 111.

26. Ibid., 130; John Briggs, *An Italian Passage* (New Haven, Conn.: Yale University Press, 1978), 242; Berrol, *Immigrants*, 244.

27. Covello, *Heart*, 26; Bok, *Americanization*, 5; *Public Schools of the City of New York*.

28. *Public Schools of the City of New York*.

29. Interview with Isidor B.;

Brumberg, *Going to America*, 129.

30. Cowan and Cowan, *Our Parents' Lives*, 87.

31. Covello, *Heart*, 25, 41; Abraham Karp, *Golden Door to America* (New York: Penguin Books, 1977), 182.

32. Henry Klein, *My Last Fifty Years* (New York: Isaac Goldman, 1935), 11; Kazin, *Walker*, 17; Simon, *Bronx*, 44; Covello, *Heart*, 26.

33. Selma Berrol, "Julia Richman, Agent of Change," *Urban Education* 11 (Jan. 1977): 368.

34. Interview with Shirley K., Aug. 29, 1989.

35. Cowan and Cowan, *Our Parents' Lives*, 102, 101; Catherine Brody, "A New York Childhood," *American Mercury* 14 (May 1928): 63.

36. Mangione, *Mount Allegro*, 1; Brumberg, *Going to America*, 127, 126.

37. Maxine Hong Kingston, "Song for A Barbarian Reed Pipe," in *Immigrant Women*, ed. Maxine Seller (Philadelphia: Temple University Press, 1981), 292; Jade Snow Wong, "Puritans," 119–20.

38. Harriet Pawlowska, "The Lessons Which Most Influenced My Life . . .," in Seller, *Immigrant Women*, 216–17; Mangione, *Mount Allegro*, 1.

39. Nasaw, *Children*, 26; Rosemary Prosen, "Looking Back," in *Growing Up Slavic*, ed. Michael Novak (EMPAC!), 1976, 3.

40. Brumberg, *Going to America*, 132.

41. Covello, *Italo-American Child*, 337, 338, 343, 344.

42. Pawlowska, "Lessons," 219.

43. Covello, *Italo-American Child*, 344; Pawlowska, "Lessons," 219; Thomas Napierkowski, "Growing Up Polish," in Novak, *Growing Up Slavic*, 13.

44. Gambino, *Blood*, 235.

45. Interview with Isidor B.; Cowan and Cowan, *Our Parents' Lives*, 90.

46. Cowan and Cowan, *Our Parents' Lives*, 89; Brumberg, *Going to America*, 130–31; William V. D'Antonio, "Confessions of a Third Generation Italian American," *Society* 13 (Nov.–Dec. 1975): 57; Cary Goodman, *Choosing Sides* (New York: Schocken Books, 1978), 46.

47. Napierkowski, "Growing Up Polish," 13; interview with Shirley K.

CHAPTER 4.
"Star Struck"

I gratefully acknowledge the research assistance of Amagda Pérez and Christine Marin. I appreciate the generosity and long-standing support of Sherna Gluck, who has given me permission to quote from eight volumes of the Rosie the Riveter Revisited Oral History Collection housed at California State University, Long Beach. I also wish to thank the American Council of Learned Societies and the Committee on Research, University of California, Davis, for financial support of this project. Roland Marchand, Ramon Gutiérrez, and Howard Shorr provided incisive comments on earlier drafts, and I appreciate their interest in my work.

1. Oscar Handlin, *The Uprooted* (New York: Grosset and Dunlap,

1951); Alfred Kazin, *A Walker in the City* (New York: Harcourt Brace Jovanovich, 1951).

2. Examples of this rich literature include John Bodnar, *The Transplanted* (Bloomington: University of Indiana Press, 1985); Kathy Peiss, *Cheap Amusements: Working Women and Leisure in Turn-of-the-Century New York* (Philadelphia: Temple University Press, 1986); Paula S. Fass, *The Damned and the Beautiful: American Youth in the 1920's* (New York: Oxford University Press, 1977); and John D'Emilio and Estelle B. Freedman, *Intimate Matters* (New York: Harper and Row, 1988).

3. Albert Camarillo, *Chicanos in a Changing Society: From Mexican Pueblos to American Barrios in Santa Barbara and Southern California, 1848–1930* (Cambridge, Mass.: Harvard University Press, 1979), 200–201; Ricardo Romo, *East Los Angeles: History of a Barrio* (Austin: University of Texas Press, 1983), 61; T. Wilson Longmore and Homer L. Hitt, "A Demographic Analysis of First and Second Generation Mexican Population of the United States: 1930," *Southwestern Social Science Quarterly* 24 (Sept. 1943): 140.

4. Manuel Gamio, *Mexican Immigration to the United States. A Study of Human Migration and Adjustment* (1930; reprint, New York: Arno Press, 1969); Paul S. Taylor, *Mexican Labor in the United States*, 2 vols. (Berkeley: University of California Press, 1928, 1932); Emory S. Bogardus, *The Mexican in the United States* (Los Angeles: University of Southern California Press, 1934). Mauricio Mazón's *The Zoot Suit Riots: The Psychology of Symbolic Annihilation* (Austin: University of Texas Press, 1984) and the Luis Valdez play and feature film *Zoot Suit* provide examples of the literature on *pachucos*.

5. Works that focus on Mexican women during this period include Rosalinda M. González, "Chicanas and Mexican Immigrant Families 1920–1940: Women's Subordination and Family Exploitation," in *Decades of Discontent: The Women's Movement, 1920–1940*, ed. Lois Scharf and Joan Jensen (Westport, Conn.: Greenwood Press, 1983), 59–83, and Vicki L. Ruiz, *Cannery Women, Cannery Lives: Mexican Women, Unionization, and the California Food Processing Industry, 1930–1950* (Albuquerque: University of New Mexico Press, 1987).

6. Ruth Zambrana, "A Walk in Two Worlds," *Social Welfare* 1 (Spring 1986): 12.

7. The age breakdown for the thirteen interviewees is as follows: two women were born between 1910 and 1912; six between 1913 and 1919; four between 1920 and 1929; and one after 1930.

8. Adelina Otero, "My People," *Survey* 63 (May 31, 1931), in *Aspects of the Mexican American Experience*, ed. Carlos Cortés (New York: Arno Press, 1976), 150; Ruth Tuck, *Not with the Fist* (1946; reprint, New York: Arno Press, 1974), 185–88; Vicki L. Ruiz, "Oral History and La Mujer: The Rosa Guerrero Story," in *Women on the United States–Mexico Border: Responses to Change*, ed. Vicki L. Ruiz and Susan Tiano (Boston: Allen and Unwin, 1987), 226–

27; interview with Belen Martínez Mason, Rosie the Riveter Revisited: Women and the World War II Work Experience, ed. Sherna Berger Gluck, 43 vols. (Long Beach, Calif.: CSULB Foundation, 1983), 23: 24–25.

9. Ruby Estrada interview by María Hernández, Aug. 4, 1981, The Lives of Arizona Women, Oral History Project, Special Collections, Hayden Library, Arizona State University, Tempe, 6.

10. Mary Luna interview, Rosie the Riveter, 20: 10. During the 1940s, bilingual education appeared as an exciting experiment in curriculum reform. See "First Regional Conference on the Education of Spanish-Speaking People in the Southwest," ed. George I. Sanchez (Dec. 1945), reprint, in *Aspects of the Mexican American Experience*.

11. Margarita B. Melville, "Selective Acculturation of Female Mexican Migrants," in *Twice a Minority: Mexican American Women*, ed. Margarita B. Melville (St. Louis: C. V. Mosby, 1980), 161; Ruiz, "Oral History and La Mujer," 222.

12. Rose Escheverria Mulligan interview, Rosie the Riveter, 27: 16–17, 24; Ruiz, "Oral History and La Mujer," 227–28; Taylor, *Mexican Labor*, 1: 79, 205–6.

13. Tuck, *Not with the Fist*, 162–63, 190–91; Paul S. Taylor, "Women in Industry," field notes for *Mexican Labor*, Bancroft Library, University of California, box 1; Estrada interview, 10–15; Escheverria Mulligan interview, 40; Taylor, *Mexican Labor*, 1: 205. A synthesis of the Taylor study has been published. See Paul S. Taylor, "Mexican Women in Los Angeles Industry in 1928," *Aztlan* 11 (Spring 1980): 99–131.

14. Lois Rita Helmbold, "The Work of Chicanas in the United States: Wage Labor and Work in the Home, 1930 to the Present" (seminar paper, Stanford University, 1977), 53; Taylor, notes; Tuck, *Not with the Fist*, 190–91; Julia Luna Mount interview with the author, Nov. 17, 1983.

15. John Bodnar, "Immigration, Kinship and the Rise of Working-Class Realism in Industrial America," *Journal of Social History* 14 (Fall 1980): 53–55; Tamara K. Hareven, "Family Time and Industrial Time: Family and Work in a Planned Corporation Town, 1900–1924," in *Family and Kin in Urban Communities*, ed. Tamara K. Hareven (New York: New Viewpoints, 1977), 202; Taylor, notes; U.S. Department of Labor, Bureau of Labor Statistics, "Labor and Social Conditions of Mexicans in California," *Monthly Labor Review* 32 (Jan.–June 1931): 89.

16. Mario Barrera, *Race and Class in the Southwest* (Notre Dame, Ind.: University of Notre Dame Press, 1979), 131; Taylor, notes. The percentage of Mexican women workers employed in industry was comparable to the participation of European immigrant women in Eastern industry where one-third of the ethnic women who worked outside the home labored as blue-collar employees (Alice Kessler-Harris, *Out to Work: A History of Wage Earning Women in the United States* [New York: Oxford University Press, 1982], 127).

17. Heller Committee for Research

in Social Economics of the University of California and Constantine Panuzio, *How Mexicans Earn and Live*, University of California Publications in Economics 13, 1, Cost of Living Studies (Berkeley: University of California, 1933), 5: 11, 14–17; Taylor, notes; Luna Mount interview; Alicia Shelit interview, Rosie the Riveter, 37: 9. For further delineation of the family wage and the consumer wage economy, see Louise A. Tilly and Joan W. Scott, *Women, Work and Family* (New York: Holt, Rinehart, and Winston, 1978).

18. Taylor, notes; Helmbold, "Work of Chicanas," 15, 30–31, 36; Douglas Monroy, "An Essay on Understanding the Work Experience of Mexicans in Southern California, 1900–1939," *Aztlan* 12 (Spring 1981): 70; González, "Chicanas and Mexican Immigrant Families," 72.

19. Discussing popular magazines and movies helped build important cross-cultural bridges—bridges that would facilitate union-organizing drives among southern California food processing workers during the late 1930s and early 1940s. See Ruiz, *Cannery Women, Cannery Lives*.

20. Roland Marchand, *Advertising the American Dream: Making Way for Modernity, 1920–1940* (Berkeley: University of California Press, 1985), 197–99, 219; D'Emilio and Freedman, *Intimate Matters*, 278.

21. Taylor, notes; Richard G. Thurston, "Urbanization and Sociocultural Change in a Mexican-American Enclave" (Ph.D. diss., University of California, Los Angeles, 1957; reprint, San Francisco: R

and E Research Associates, 1974), 128; Helmbold, "Work of Chicanas," 42–44; Carmen Bernal Escobar interview with the author, June 15, 1986.

22. Elizabeth Fuller, *The Mexican Housing Problem in Los Angeles*, Studies in Sociology, Sociological Monograph 5, 17 (1920; reprint, New York: Arno Press, 1974), 4–5.

23. Ruiz, "Oral History and La Mujer," 226.

24. Shelit interview, 4; Adele Hernández Milligan interview, Rosie the Riveter, 26: 14; Martínez Mason interview, 59–60; Luna interview, 18, 26; Clint C. Wilson II and Felix Gutiérrez, *Minorities and Media* (Beverly Hills: Sage Publications, 1985), 85–86.

25. For examples, see *La Opinion*, Sept. 16, 1926, Sept. 18, 1926, May 13, 1927, May 15, 1927, June 3, 1927, June 4, 1927.

26. Ibid., Sept. 23, 1926, Sept. 24, 1926, Sept. 27, 1926, Sept. 30, 1926.

27. Ibid., Mar. 2, 1927.

28. Taylor, notes. Referring to Los Angeles, two historians have argued that "Mexicans experienced segregation in housing in nearly every section of the city and its outlying areas" (Antonio Ríos-Bustamante and Pedro Castillo, *An Illustrated History of Mexican Los Angeles 1781–1985* [Los Angeles: Chicano Studies Research Center/University of California, 1986], 135). Ruth Tuck noted that Anglo-Americans also employed the term "Spanish" in order to distinguish individuals "of superior background or achievement" (Tuck, *Not with the Fist*, 142–43).

29. Shelit interview, 32; Mulligan

interview, 14; Melville, "Selective Acculturation," 155, 162.

30. Tuck, *Not with the Fist*, 133.

31. Gamio, *Mexican Immigration*, 172–73; Bogardus, *Mexican in the United States*, 75; Romo, *East Los Angeles*, 142; Ruiz, "Oral History and La Mujer," 224. "Some adolescents are stimulated to play the dual roles of being good Mexicans at home and good 'Americans' at school" (Bogardus, 75).

32. Ruiz, "Oral History and La Mujer," 221, 224–25; Margaret Clark, *Health in the Mexican American Culture* (Berkeley: University of California Press, 1959), 21.

33. Clark, *Health*, 21.

34. Tuck, *Not with the Fist*, 108.

35. Ríos-Bustamante and Castillo, *Illustrated History*, 139; George Sanchez, "The Rise of the Second Generation: The Mexican American Movement," unpublished paper, courtesy of the author, 26–27; Luisa Moreno interview with Albert Camarillo, Aug. 12–13, 1977.

36. Sociologist Norma Williams contends that contemporary Mexican Americans view the Catholic church almost solely in terms of social, life-cycle functions, such as baptisms and funerals. See Norma Williams, *The Mexican American Family: Tradition and Change* (New York: G. K. Hall, 1990).

37. Vicki L. Ruiz, "Dead Ends or Gold Mines?! Using Missionary Records in Mexican American Women's History," *Frontiers* 12 (June 1991): 33–56; Mulligan interview, 24. For an interesting collection of Protestant missionary reports for

this period, see Carlos Cortés, ed., *Church Views of the Mexican American* (New York: Arno Press, 1974).

38. Luna interview, 9.

39. George Sanchez, "'Go after the Women': Americanization and the Mexican Immigrant Woman 1915–1929," Stanford Center for Chicano Research, Working Paper no. 6, 2.

40. Bogardus, *Mexican in the United States*, 74; Martínez Mason interview, 44. During the 1920s, Mexican parents were not atypical in voicing their concerns over the attitudes and appearance of their "flapper adolescents." A general atmosphere of tension between youth and their elders existed—a generation gap that cut across class, race, ethnicity, and region. See Fass, *Damned and Beautiful*.

41. Shelit interview, 18; Taylor, *Mexican Labor*, 2: 199–200; María Fierro interview, Rosie the Riveter, 12: 10.

42. Gamio, *Mexican Immigration*, 89; the verse is taken from "Las Pelonas" in the original Spanish:
Los paños colorados
Los tengo aborrecidos
Ya hora las pelonas
Los usan de vestidos.
Las muchachas de S. Antonio
Son flojas pa'l metate
Quieren andar pelonas
Con sombreros de petate.
Se acabaron las pizcas,
Se acabó el algodón
Ya andan las pelonas
De puro vacilón.

43. Taylor, *Mexican Labor* 2: vi–vii.

44. *La Opinion*, Sept. 18, 1926,

May 3, 1927, June 5, 1927. Using endorsements from famous people was a common advertising technique. See Marchand, *Advertising the American Dream*, 96–102.

45. Rodolfo F. Acuña, *A Community under Siege: A Chronicle of Chicanos East of the Los Angeles River 1945–1975* (Los Angeles: UCLA Chicano Studies Research Center Publications, 1984), 278, 407–8, 413–14, 418, 422; *FTA News*, May 1, 1945; Escobar interview. For an example of the promotion of a beauty pageant, see issues of *La Opinion*, June–July 1927.

46. Escobar interview.

47. Sherna B. Gluck, *Rosie the Riveter Revisited: Women, the War and Social Change* (Boston: Twayne, 1987), 81, 85.

48. *Chisme* means gossip.

49. Letter from Carey McWilliams dated Oct. 3, 1937, to Louis Adamic, *Adamic File*, carton 1, Carey McWilliams Collection, Special Collections, University of California, Los Angeles.

50. Martínez Mason interview, 29–30; Escobar interview; Fierro interview, 15; Estrada interview, 11–12. Chaperonage was also common in Italian immigrant communities. Indeed, many of the same conflicts between parents and daughters had surfaced a generation earlier among Italian families on the East Coast (Peiss, *Cheap Amusements*, 69–70, 152).

51. Hernández Milligan interview, 17.

52. Evangeline Hymer, "A Study of the Social Attitudes of Adult Mexican Immigrants in Los Angeles and Vicinity: 1923" (M.A. thesis, University of Southern California, 1924; rpt. San Francisco: R and E Research Associates, 1971), 24–25.

53. Escobar interview; Estrada interview, 11, 13.

54. Estrada interview, 12; Shelit interview, 9; Ríos-Bustamante and Castillo, *Illustrated History*, 153.

55. Taylor, notes; Thurston, "Urbanization," 118; Bogardus, *Mexican in the United States*, 28–29, 57–58.

56. Martínez Mason interview, 30; Beatrice Morales Clifton interview, Rosie the Riveter, 8: 14–15.

57. Shelit interview, 9, 24, 30; Escobar interview; Martínez Mason interview, 30; Hernández Milligan interview, 27–28; Taylor, notes.

58. Luna Mount interview; Fierro interview, 18; Luna interview, 29; Gregorita Rodriguez, *Singing for My Echo* (Santa Fe, N. Mex.: Cota Editions, 1987), 52; Martínez Mason interview, 62.

59. "Elisa Morales," Manuel Gamio field notes, Bancroft Library, University of California.

60. Taylor notes; Taylor, *Mexican Labor*, 2: vi–vii; Gamio, *Mexican Immigration*, 89. The Corrido "Enganchado" in vol. 2 offers an intriguing glimpse into attitudes toward women and americanization.

61. Wilson and Gutiérrez, *Minorities and Media*, 86.

62. Tuck, *Not with the Fist*, 115; Shelit interview, 26.

63. Tuck, *Not with the Fist*, 115.

64. Taylor, *Mexican Labor*, 1: 205–6; Ruiz, "Oral History and La Mujer," 227–28; Sanchez, "Mexican Ameri-

can Movement," 7–10, 12; Escheverria Mulligan interview, 17.

65. Kenneth L. Roberts, "The
Docile Mexican," *Saturday Evening
Post*, Mar. 10, 1928, as quoted in
Sanchez, " 'Go After the Women,' " 8.

66. Rodolfo F. Acuña, *Occupied
America: A History of Chicanos*, 2d
ed. (New York: Harper and Row,
1981), 138, 140–41; Albert Cama-
rillo, *Chicanos in California* (San
Francisco: Boyd and Fraser, 1984),
48–49; Abraham Hoffman, *Unwanted
Mexican Americans in the Great Depres-
sion* (Tucson: University of Arizona
Press, 1974), 43–66; Francisco E.
Balderrama, *In Defense of La Raza:
The Los Angeles Mexican Consulate
and the Mexican Community, 1929–
1936* (Tucson: University of Arizona
Press, 1982), 16–20; Neil Betten and
Raymond A. Mohl, "From Discrimi-
nation to Repatriation: Mexican
Life in Gary, Indiana, during the
Great Depression," in *The Chicano*,
ed. Norris Hundley (Santa Barbara:
ABC-Clio Press, 1975), 132, 138–39.

67. Sanchez, "Mexican American
Movement," 10.

68. Albert Camarillo, "Mexican
American Urban History in Comparative Ethnic Perspective," Distinguished Speakers Series, University
of California, Davis (Jan. 26, 1987);
Acuña, *Occupied America*, 310, 318,
323, 330–31; Romo, *East Los Angeles*
139; Tuck, *Not with the Fist*, 51, 53;
Shelit interview, 15.

69. Taylor, *Mexican Labor*, 1: 221–
24; María Arredondo interview with
Carolyn Arredondo, Mar. 19, 1986.

70. Heller Committee Study, *How
Mexicans Earn and Live*, 68–69, 72;

Camarillo, *Chicanos in a Changing
Society*, 215.

71. Tuck, *Not with the Fist*, 209–10.

72. Barrera, *Race and Class*, 82–91;
Mario T. García, *Desert Immigrants:
The Mexicans of El Paso, 1880–1920*
(New Haven, Conn.: Yale Univer-
sity Press, 1981), 110–26; Gilbert
González, "Racism, Education,
and the Mexican Community in
Los Angeles, 1920–30," *Societas* 4
(Autumn 1974): 287–300.

73. González, "Chicanas and
Mexican Immigrant Families," 63–
66; Taylor, *Mexican Labor*, 1: 162–66,
176–79, 190–91, 217, 220, 227–28
(quote from 220).

74. Melville, "Selective Acculturation," 159–60; John García,
"Ethnicity and Chicanos," *Hispanic
Journal of Behavioral Sciences* 4 (1982):
310–11.

75. Sanchez, "Mexican American
Movement," 7–9; Guadalupe San
Miguel, Jr., "Culture and Education
in the American Southwest: Towards
an Explanation of Chicano School
Attendance," *Journal of American
Ethnic History* 7 (Spring 1988): 15, 17;
La Opinion, June 5, 1927.

76. "Sra——," Manuel Gamio,
field notes.

77. Clark, *Health*, 92.

78. Ruiz, *Cannery Women, Cannery
Lives*; Shelit interview, 52–55; Sherna
Berger Gluck, "Interlude or Change:
Women and the World War II Work
Experience," 14, 32–34 (rev. version
originally published in *International
Journal of Oral History* 3 (1982), cour-
tesy of author); see also Gluck, *Rosie
the Riveter Revisited* (1987).

79. William H. Chafe, *The Ameri-*

can Woman: Her Changing Social,
Economic, and Political Roles, 1920–
1970 (New York: Oxford University
Press, 1972), 137–43, 146; Barrera,
Race and Class, 131, 140–45.

80. Shelit interview, 32; Esche-
verria Mulligan interview, 14;
Richard Griswold del Castillo, *La
Familia: Chicano Families in the Urban
Southwest, 1848 to the Present* (Notre
Dame, Ind.: University of Notre
Dame Press, 1984), 120–22.

81. Many of the husbands were
skilled workers in the aerospace
industry. The most prestigious occupation for a spouse was firefighter.

82. Clark, *Health*, 20.

83. Tuck, *Not with the Fist*, 134.
According to historian Richard Griswold del Castillo, "present-day Chicano families are a bridge between
the social and cultural heritages
of Anglo and Latin America" (*La
Familia*, 126).

CHAPTER 5.
Made, Bought, and Stolen

1. Samuel G. Goodrich, *Recollec-
tions of a Lifetime*, 2 vols. (New York:
Miller, Orton & Mulligan, 1856), I:
92–93; Caryl Rivers, *Aphrodite at Mid-
Century: Growing-Up Catholic and
Female in Post-War America* (Garden
City, N.Y.: Doubleday, 1973), 20.

2. Dorothy Howard, *Dorothy's
World: Childhood in Sabine Bottom
1902–1910* (Englewood Cliffs, N.J.:
Prentice-Hall, 1977), 181.

3. In 1989 a panel of three federal
judges ruled that G.I. Joe is a doll,
although the industry defines action
figure as one lacking removable

clothes. See the Associated Press
story, "Say It Ain't So, G.I. Joe,"
Washington Post, July 26, 1989, B1.

4. Hasbro Industries, Inc., which
has manufactured G.I. Joe since
1964, reduced his size in 1976 and
1982 while increasing the number
of accessories such as weapons,
vehicles, and other paraphernalia. His original size made him a
fit companion for Barbie; his later
incarnations are in scale with the figures mentioned from the *Star Wars*
motion pictures, TV cartoons, and
Ninja Turtle toys. In their actual
play with toys, children do not seem
concerned with scale.

5. Brian Sutton-Smith, *Toys
as Culture* (New York: Gardner
Press, 1986).

6. Karin Lee Fishbeck Calvert,
"To Be a Child: An Analysis of the
Artifacts of Childhood," (Ph.D.
diss., University of Delaware, 1984),
146–47.

7. See Bernard Mergen, "Children's Play in American Autobiographies, 1820–1914," in *American Play*,
ed. Kathryn Grover (Amherst: University of Massachusetts Press, in
press), and Mihaly Csikszentmihalyi
and Eugene Rochberg-Halton, *The
Meaning of Things: Domestic Symbols
and the Self* (New York: Cambridge
University Press, 1981). I found that
homemade toys are mentioned by
32 percent of the male autobiographers (N=54) and 57 percent of
the female (N=24). Manufactured
toys are mentioned by 35 percent
of the males and 48 percent of the
females. Csikszentmihalyi asked
members of eighty-two families
in the Chicago area to list objects

that were "special" to them in some way. Children mentioned "bed" and "refrigerator" more frequently than "toys." "Stuffed animals" were mentioned as often as refrigerators, and the TV was mentioned more frequently than anything else. I have argued elsewhere that toys are closely linked to the development in children of a sense of the American economic system and that becoming a consumer is a step toward citizenship. As this happens, toys become more important and children are on their way to becoming adults. See Bernard Mergen, "Red, White, Blue, and Green: Citizenship and Prosperity," in *Red, White and Blue: Childhood and Citizenship* (Philadelphia: Please Touch Museum, 1987), 14–16.

8. For a pioneering reading of autobiographies of childhood, see Edith Cobb, *The Ecology of Imagination in Childhood* (New York: Columbia University Press, 1977). I used Cobb's bibliography supplemented by Louis Kaplan, *A Bibliography of American Autobiographies* (Madison: University of Wisconsin Press, 1961), and Mary Louise Briscoe, *American Autobiographies, 1945–1980* (Madison: University of Wisconsin Press, 1982). For a useful discussion of autobiographies in general and an analysis of William Dean Howells's *A Boy's Town* in particular, see Thomas Cooley, *Educated Lives: The Rise of Modern Autobiography in America* (Columbus: Ohio State University Press), 1976.

9. Edward Everett Hale, *A New England Boyhood* (1893; reprint, Boston: Little, Brown, 1964), 37–38.

10. Robert Coles, *The Moral Life of Children* (Boston: Atlantic Monthly Press, 1986), and Jerome Kagan and Sharon Lamb, eds., *The Emergence of Morality in Young Children* (Chicago: University of Chicago Press), 1989.

11. Hale, *New England Boyhood*, 57, 70; Sutton-Smith, *Toys as Culture*, 207.

12. Lucy Larcom, *A New England Girlhood* (Boston: Houghton Mifflin, 1889), 33, 110.

13. Emily Wilson, *The Forgotten Girl* (New York: Alphabet Press), 1937, 23; Caroline Richards, *Village Life in America* (New York: Holt, 1913), 25; Laura Elizabeth Howe Richards, *When I Was Your Age* (Boston: Estes and Lauriat, 1894), 23, 28–35.

14. Samuel Clagett Busey, *An Autobiographical Sketch of Early Life* (Washington, D.C.: n.p., 1896); John Albee, *Confessions of a Boyhood* (Boston: Badger, 1910); Thomas Bailey Aldrich, *The Story of a Bad Boy* (Boston: Houghton Mifflin, 1870); William Dean Howells, *A Boy's Town* (New York: Harper and Bros., 1890); Edward Eugene Schermerhorn, *Letters to Phil: Memoirs of a New York Boyhood, 1848–1856* (New York: Kampmann, 1982); H. W. DeLong, *Boyhood Reminiscences* (Dansville, N.Y.: F. A. Owen, 1913), 14, 51. I want to thank Dr. Katherine C. Grier for the DeLong reference.

15. James Landgon Hill, *My First Years as a Boy* (Andover: Andover Press, 1928), 309, 316–26. The opinion of "boughten toys" comes from Thomas Ripley, *A Vermont Boyhood* (New York: Appleton-Century, 1937), 84.

16. Walter Brooks, *A Child and a Boy* (New York: Brentano's 1915), 17–18, 29, 44–49, 62–63, 85–88; Lincoln Steffens, *The Autobiography of Lincoln Steffens*, 2 vols. (New York: Harcourt Brace and World, 1931), 1: 9; Meta Stern Lilienthal, *Dear Remembered World: Childhood Memories of an Old New Yorker* (New York: Richard Smith, 1947), 13.

17. Margaret Wade Campbell Deland, *If This Be I, As I Suppose It Be* (New York: Appleton Century, 1935), 77–83; Hamlin Garland, *A Son of the Middle Border* (New York: Macmillan, 1917), 1–3, 11, 68–70, 144. Schermerhorn recalled "something we called Base Ball" in New York City in the 1840s, and James Baldwin mentions "town ball" as played in Indiana in the same decade. Schermerhorn, *Letters to Phil*, 16; Baldwin, *In My Youth: From the Posthumous Papers of Robert Dudley*, pseud. (Indianapolis: Bobbs-Merrill, 1914), 342.

18. The Inman and Comegys paintings may be seen in the Philadelphia Academy of Fine Arts as well as in many histories of American art. Spencer's painting hangs in the Newark Museum. For Brown, see Philip N. Grime, *John George Brown 1831–1913: A Reappraisal* (Burlington, Vt.: Robert Hull Fleming Museum), 1975. Three interesting studies of children in nineteenth-century American painting are Lois Fink, "Children as Innocence from Cole to Cassatt," *Nineteenth Century* (Winter 1977); 71–75, Jadviga M. Da Costa Nunes, "The Naughty Child in Nineteenth-Century American Art," *Journal of American Studies* 21 (Aug. 1987): 225–47, and Sarah Burns, "Barefoot Boys and Other Country Children: Sentiment and Ideology in Nineteenth-Century American Art," *American Art Journal* 20, 1 (1988): 25–50.

19. Olive Thorne, "Playthings," *St. Nicholas Magazine*, November 1879, 20, 16.

20. William Allen White, *The Autobiography of William Allen White* (1946, 27, 42, 44–47, 80; reprint, University of Kansas Press, 1990).

21. Mary Alves Long, *High Time to Tell It* (Durham, N.C.: Duke University Press, 1950), 22–23, 31; Katherine Stauffer Krebs, *Back Home in Pennsylvania* (Philadelphia: Dorrance, 1937), 52–53; Zona Gale, *When I Was a Little Girl* (New York: Macmillan, 1925), 35–37, 194, 204.

22. Eleanor Abbott, *Being Little in Cambridge When Everyone Else Was Big* (New York: Appleton Century, 1936), 77–78; Una Atherton Clarke Hunt Drage, *Una Mary: The Inner Life of a Child* (New York: Scribner's, 1914), 152–53; Estilline Bennett, *Old Deadwood Days* (New York: J. H. Sears, 1928), 13.

23. H. L. Mencken, *Happy Days, 1880–1892* (New York: Knopf, 1946), 17, 130; Philip Goodman, *Franklin Street* (New York: Knopf, 1942), 188–90; Stewart Culin, "Street Games of Boys in Brooklyn, N.Y.," *Journal of American Folklore* 4, 14 (July–Sept. 1891): 237.

24. Daniel C. Beard, *The American Boys Handy Book: What to Do and How to Do It* (1882; 1966; reprint, Boston: David Godine, 1983); Lina Beard and Adelina Beard, *American Girls Handy Book: How to Amuse Yourself and Others* (1888; reprint, Rutland, Vt.:

Tuttle, 1969; and Boston: Godine, 1987); John D. Champlin and Arthur E. Bostwick, *The Young Folks' Cyclopaedia of Games and Sports* (New York: Holt, 1890). Mencken mentions being influenced by *Boys' Useful Pastimes*; and Robert Lawson, in *At That Time* (New York: Viking, 1947), a memoir of childhood near New York City in the 1890s, describes digging a cave hideout inspired by *The American Boys Handy Book*.

The promotion and acceptance of the yo-yo by children is an interesting case study in the interplay of adult-child ideas about toys. Years after the bandalore failed to catch on, an article in *Playthings*, June 5 and 6, 1907, 71, described a yo-yo that it called a "spinereno." This too failed to sell. Twenty years later a Philippine immigrant, Pedro Flores, began manufacturing yo-yos, the Tagalog name. Flores sold his company to Donald Duncan, who promoted yo-yos through the Hearst newspapers and with contests in major cities. He was so successful that boys began making their own, and the yo-yo reentered the category of folk-toy. Frank Conroy devotes an entire chapter of his autobiography, *Stop Time* (New York: Viking, 1967), to the yo-yo he had in Chula Vista, Florida, in the late 1940s. It is a brilliant evocation of the sexual pleasure yo-yoing gave a pubescent boy. See also D. W. Gould, *The Top: Universal Toy, Enduring Pastime* (New York: Clarkson Potter, 1973); George Malko, *The One and Only Yo-Yo Book* (New York: Avon, 1978); John O'Dell and Richard Loehl, *The Great Depression Era Book of Fun* (New York:

Harper and Row, 1981); and Francis Edward Abernethy, ed., *Texas Toys and Games* (Dallas: Southern Methodist University Press, 1989).

25. Harvey Fergusson, *Home in the West: An Inquiry into My Origins* (New York: Duell, Sloan, Pearce, 1945), 88; Marquis James, *The Cherokee Strip: A Tale of an Oklahoma Boyhood* (New York: Viking, 1945), 50, 96–97; S. N. Behrman, *Worcester Account* (New York: Random House, 1954), 220–23; Taylor Gordon, *Born to Be* (1929; reprint, Seattle: University of Washington Press, 1975), 38–40; Michael Gold, *Jews without Money* (New York: Liveright, 1930), 48; Jimmy Savo, *I Bow to the Stones: Memories of a New York Childhood* (New York: Howard Frisch, 1963), 18. For commentary on the rising homicide rate from 1900 to 1930, see Hugh Davis Graham and Ted Robert Gurr, eds., *Violence in America: Historical and Comparative Perspectives* (New York: Bantam Books), 1969.

26. Richard Wright, *Black Boy: A Record of Childhood and Youth* (New York: Harper Bros., 1945), 17–19, 23–25, 49–53, 93; Woody Guthrie, *Bound for Glory* (1943; reprint, New York: Signet, 1970), 103; Flannery Lewis, *Brooks Too Broad for Leaping: A Chronicle from Childhood* (New York: Macmillan, 1938), 257; Robert Paul Smith, *"Where Did You Go?" "Out" "What Did You Do?" "Nothing"* (New York: Norton, 1957), 81; Cass S. Hough, *It's a Daisy!* (Rogers, Ark.: Victor Comptometer Corp., 1976); O'Dell and Loehl, *Depression Era Book of Fun*, 2–13; Bill Tate, *Growing Up in New Mexico* (Truches, N. Mex.: Tate Gallery Publication, 1970), 18;

Fielding Dawson, *Tiger Lilies: An American Childhood* (Durham, N.C.: Duke University Press, 1984), 34–54.

27. T. S. Croswell, "Amusements of Worcester School Children," *Pedagogical Seminary* 6, 3 (Sept. 1899): 314–71.

28. Zach McGhee, "A Study of the Play Life of Some South Carolina Children," *Pedagogical Seminary* 7, 4 (Dec. 1900): 459–78; Croswell, "Amusements," 353–54.

29. George E. Johnson, *Education through Recreation* (Cleveland, Ohio: Survey Committee of the Cleveland Foundation, 1916), 48–51.

30. Brian Sutton-Smith and B. G. Rosenberg, "Sixty Years of Historical Change in the Game Preferences of American Children," *Journal of American Folklore* 74, 291 (1961): 17–46.

31. Eda Lord, *Childsplay* (New York: Simon & Schuster, 1961), 27.

32. "Children as Toy Designers," *Playthings*, Jan. 1920, 230–31; "The Toy and the Teacher," ibid., May 1920, 88–90; "Americanizing Children of Foreign Born by Means of Toys," ibid., Nov. 1920, 75–77; *Playthings Supplement*, April 1940, 2–7.

33. Estha Briscoe Stowe, *Oil Field Child* (Fort Worth: Texas Christian University Press, 1989), 11, 29, 94; O'Dell and Loehl, *Depression Era Book of Fun*, 55.

34. The collection was donated by Katharine Parker Taylor Frysinger (1917–1991) and contains some of her toys and some belonging to her father and mother, Ralph Savery Taylor (1888–1957) and M. Margaret Brown Taylor (1884–1983), her husband, Daniel Chappell Frysinger (b. 1915), and their children, William (b. 1944), Robert (b. 1946), Margaret (b. 1949), and Howard (b. 1953). Although the objects have yet to be documented by oral histories and although the collection is limited to what Katharine Taylor Frysinger saved and what her family was willing to part with, its usefulness is archeological, a record of the play life of a middle-class Quaker family who in a sense excavated their home and presented their artifacts to the museum. There is no way to know what percentage of the Frysinger and Taylor families' total accumulation this sample represents. Toys long lost or forgotten are not here, nor are those considered too valuable to give away. The third generation of the family is far better represented than the first or second. In the 1940s and 1950s, each of the four children probably received dozens of new toys each year, counting both gifts and their own purchases. A conservative estimate of fifteen toys per year for each child over a fifteen-year period yields a total of nine hundred different toys. Even though parents and grandparents probably had fewer manufactured playthings, the family's total easily exceeded one thousand.

I want to thank Nancy D. Kolb, executive director, and Dona W. Horowitz, curator of collections, Please Touch Museum, Philadelphia, for allowing me access to the collection for this study. Special thanks to Ms. Horowitz for valuable comments on an early draft of this paper.

35. Susan Allen Toth, *Blooming: A*

Small-Town Girlhood (Boston: Little Brown, 1981), 73; Annie Dillard, *An American Childhood* (New York: Harper & Row, 1987), 45–49.

36. Joyce Maynard, *Looking Back: A Chronicle of Growing Up Old in the Sixties* (Garden City, N.Y.: Doubleday, 1973), 27.

37. Stephen Kline and Debra Pentecost, "The Characterization of Play: Marketing Children's Toys," *Play & Culture* 3, 3 (Aug. 1990), 235–55.

CHAPTER 6.
Sugar and Spite

My special thanks to Claude Brunell, Perry Marten Brunell, T. J. Jackson Lears, Martha Hoades, Lisa Tiersten, and the participants and commentators at the Seventh Berkshire Conference on Women's History.

1. Mary Lawrence, "Dolls: Logically Considered," *Babyhood*, Oct. 1895, 330–31.

2. Catharine E. Beecher and Harriet Beecher Stowe, *American Woman's Home* (1869; reprint, Watkins Glen, N.Y.: Library of Victorian Culture, 1979), 298.

3. On children and the American family see John Demos, *A Little Commonwealth: The Family in a Plymouth Colony* (New York: Oxford University Press, 1970); Bernard Wishy, *The Child and the Republic: The Dawn of Modern American Child Nurture* (Philadelphia: University of Pennsylvania Press, 1968); Joseph Kett, *The Rites of Passage: Adolescence in America, 1790 to the Present* (New York: Basic Books, 1977); Philip

Greven, *The Protestant Temperament: Patterns of Child-Rearing, Religious Experience and the Self in Early America* (New York: New American Library, 1977); Michael Gordon, ed., *The American Family in Relationship: Parents and Children over Three Centuries* (Hanover and London: University of New England Press, 1987); N. Ray Hiner and Joseph M. Hawes, eds., *Growing Up in America: Children in Historical Perspective* (Chicago: University of Illinois Press, 1985); Steven Mintz and Susan Kellogg, *Domestic Revolutions: A Social History of Family Life* (New York: Macmillan, 1988); Mary Stevens Heininger, "Children, Childhood, and Change in America, 1820–1920," in Heininger et al., *Centuries of Childhood, 1820–1920* (Rochester, N.Y.: Margaret Woodbury Strong Museum, 1984), 6.

4. Childrearing literature included Theodore Dwight, *The Father's Book* (1834), Dr. John Abbott, *The Mother's Book* (1844), and Catharine Beecher, *Treatice on Domestic Economy* (1847); see Mary P. Ryan, *The Empire of the Mother: American Writing about Domesticity, 1830–1860* (New Haven, Conn.: Yale University Press, Institute for Research in History, and Hawthorn Press, 1982), especially ch. 2.

5. Beecher and Stowe, *American Woman's Home*, 299.

6. Miss Eliza Leslie, *The American Girl's Book or Occupations for Play Hours* (New York: C. S. Francis, 1831), intro. This book, which appeared one year after the very popular *American Boy's Book*, went through fourteen editions, the last published in 1849.

7. Mary Sewell, quoted in Linda Pollock, *A Lasting Relationship: Parents and Children over Three Centuries* (Hanover and London: University of New England Press, 1987), 103–4.

8. Lydia Maria Child, *Girl's Own Book* (New York: Clark Austin & Co. 1833), iii, iv.

9. Mary P. Ryan, *Cradle of the Middle Class: The Family in Oneida County, N.Y., 1790–1865* (Cambridge: Cambridge University Press, 1981), 161; *Mothers' Monthly Journal*, July 1837, 127; Richard Meckel, "Education a Ministry of Mothers: Evangelical Maternal Associations, 1815–1860," *Journal of the Early Republic* 2, 4 (Winter 1982): 402–23.

10. Nancy F. Cott, *Bonds of Womanhood: Woman's Sphere in New England, 1780–1835* (New Haven, Conn.: Yale University Press, 1977), 43.

11. Paula Petrik, "The Paraphernalia of Childhood: New Toys for Old and Selchow & Righter Co., 1830–1870" (work in progress).

12. Cott, *Bonds of Womanhood*, 43; Susan Strasser, *Never Done: A History of American Housework* (New York: Pantheon, 1982); Ruth Schwartz Cowan, *More Work for Mother: The Ironies of Household Technology from the Open Hearth to the Microwave* (New York: Basic Books, 1983), 63, 66, 201.

13. Beecher and Stowe, *American Woman's Home*, 298.

14. Lucy Larcom, *A New England Girlhood* (Boston: Northeastern University Press, 1986), 29.

15. Jean M. Thompson, "The Story of Rosamond," *Harper's Bazaar*, May 1906, 474.

16. Child, *Girl's Own Book* iii, iv.

17. Larcom, *New England Girlhood*, 29.

18. Paintings in the National Gallery of Art, Smithsonian Institution, Washington, D.C.; Ineze Marshall McClintock, *Toys in America* (Washington, D.C.: Public Affairs Press, 1961), 68.

19. "Two Sisters," reprinted in *Children's Stories of the 1850's* (Americana Review).

20. Emily Wilson, *The Forgotten Girl*, (New York: Alphabet Press, 1937), 7.

21. Wilson, *Forgotten Girl*, 14–15. I am grateful to Bernard Mergen for sharing his research on girls' autobiographies with me.

22. Suzanne Lebsock, *The Free Women of Petersburg: Status and Culture in a Southern Town, 1794–1860* (New York: W. W. Norton, 1984), 64.

23. Larcom, *New England Girlhood*, 29.

24. Leslie, *American Girls' Book*, 287–88; see also Maria Edgeworth and Richard Lowell Edgeworth, *Practical Education* (New York: Harper, 1835), 16–17.

25. Larcom, *New England Girlhood*, ch. 1.

26. Kathryn Kish Sklar, *Catharine Beecher: A Study in American Domesticity* (New Haven, Conn.: W. W. Norton, 1973), 9. See also Wilson, *Forgotten Girl*, 14–15. In fact, mothers were also advised to permit their middle-class daughters, most of whom still lived in rural areas, to participate in outdoor games. In *The Mother's Assistant and Young Lady's Friend*, Mrs. Sarah S. Ellis advocated

"exercise in open air" as an antidote to "artificial habits" causing a "host of numerous maladies" in genteel daughters. Anne Scott MacLeod, "The Caddie Woodlawn Syndrome: American Girlhood in the Nineteenth Century," in Heininger et al., *Century of Childhood*, 105 (includes quote from Frances Willard, *Glimpses of Fifty Years*).

27. Bernard Mergen, *Play and Playthings: A Reference Guide* (Westport, Conn.: Greenwood Press, 1982), 25.

28. MacLeod, "The Caddie Woodlawn Syndrome," 97–120.

29. *Ridleys' Fashion Magazine*, cited in Jan Foulke, "Dolls of the 1880's," *Doll Reader*, Nov. 1988, 103.

30. Ibid., 98.

31. "A Doll's Story," *Doll's Dressmaker* (DD), May 1893, 103.

32. J. E. Jeuck, *Catalogues and Counters: A History of Sears, Roebuck & Co.* (Chicago: University of Chicago Press, 1950).

33. Joseph J. Schroeder, Jr., ed., *The Wonderful World of Toys, Games, and Dolls* (Northfield, Ill.: DBI Books, 1971), intro.

34. Susan Porter Bensen, *Counter Cultures* (Urbana and Chicago: University of Illinois Press, 1988).

35. On Macy's 1874 window see McClintock, *Toys in America*, 266–67. According to *Playthings*, Oct. 1903, 6, Macy's "was one of the first, if not the first, to sell toys in a department store."

36. Philip G. Hubert, Jr., "Some Notes as to Christmas Toys," *Babyhood*, Dec. 1893, 15.

37. Ibid., 15–16.

38. William Leach, "Transformations in a Culture of Consumption: Women and Department Stores, 1890–1925," *Journal of American History* 71 (Sept. 1984): 319–42.

39. *Harper's Bazaar* (1881) cited in Foulke, "Dolls of the 1880's," 94.

40. "A Doll's Story, Told by Herself," DD, Jan. 1891, 5.

41. Ibid., 101–2.

42. Elizabeth Eggleston Seelye, "Suggestions Concerning Toys and Amusements," *Babyhood*, Dec. 1890, 17; "Toys for Children," DD, Nov. 1892, 283.

43. Meta Lilienthal, *Dear Remembered World: Childhood Memories of Old New York* (New York: R. R. Smith, 1947), 283.

44. One researcher of Polish children found that doll play ceased at age ten—earlier than among American children. See Madam Anna Grudzinska, "A Study of Dolls among Polish Children," *Pedagogical Seminary* 14, 6 (Sept. 1907): 385–90.

45. L. Emmett Holt, "Infant Feeding," part of an address given before the Cleveland Medical Society, 26 Oct. 1900, 10; *The Diseases of Infancy and Childhood* (New York, 1897), 158, cited in Kathleen W. Jones, "Sentiment and Science: The Late Nineteenth-Century Pediatrician as Mother's Advisor," *Journal of Social History* 17 (Fall 1983): 86; Janet Golden, "Trouble in the Nursery: Physicians, Families and Wet Nurses at the End of the Nineteenth Century," in *"To Toil the Livelong Day," America's Women at Work, 1790–1980,* ed. Carol Groneman and Mary Beth Norton (Ithaca, N.Y., and London: Cornell University Press, 1987), 126.

46. H. Coyle, "Papa's Weary Head," DD, May 1891, 98.

47. Wishy, *Child and the Republic*, 16; Heininger, "Children, Childhood," 19–20.

48. DD, May 1891, 100.

49. *Babyhood*, Jan. 1891, 5.

50. Louisa May Alcott, *A Doll's Journey* (Boston: Little, Brown, 1873), 5.

51. *Youth's Companion* was founded in 1827, *St. Nicholas* in 1873, *Children's Magazine* in 1879. Other children's magazines include *Harper's Young People* and *Frank Leslie's Chatterbox*.

52. Mintz and Kellogg, *Domestic Revolutions*, xix; Daniel Scott Smith, "Family Limitation, Sexual Control and Domestic Feminism in Victorian America, *Feminist Studies* 1 (Winter–Spring 1973): 40–57.

53. *A Tribute to Margaret Woodbury Strong* (Rochester, N.Y.: Margaret Woodbury Strong Museum, 1986), 7.

54. "A Doll's Story, Told by Herself," 5.

55. J. M. Barrie, *Peter Pan* (1911; reprint, Toronto: Bantam, 1985).

56. Victorian juvenile furniture, Domestic Life Division, National Museum of American History, Smithsonian Institution.

57. My thanks to John Gillis for bringing this out.

58. *Pretty Pursuits for Children* (London and New York: Butterick, 1897), 61.

59. *The Doll's Tea Party* (Boston: Lothrop, 1895).

60. T. R. Croswell, "Amusements of Worcester School Children," Pedagogical Seminary 6, 3 (Spring 1899): 347.

61. "Dressing Dolls," Doll Reader (DR), June 1892, 145.

62. Ibid., 144.

63. Evelyn Jane Coleman, *Carte de Visite; Album de la Poupee*, 1978 reproduction.

64. *Pretty Pursuits*, 78.

65. "Styles for Dolls," *Delineator*, Nov. 1897, 558.

66. Mrs. H. W. Beecher, *Monthly Talks with Young Homemakers* (New York: J. B. Ford, 1873), 293.

67. McClintock, *Toys in America*, 78; Barbara Pickering, "In Loving Memory—Dolls and Death," DR, Nov. 1988, 132.

68. Harvey Green, *The Light of the Home* (New York: Pantheon, 1983), 165. "Mourning etiquette for men was less vigorously defined, and their actions less circumscribed, in part because of the demands of the middle-class commercial world" (ibid., 173). John Gillis, "Ritualization of Family Life in 19th and 20th Century Britain," paper, Woodrow Wilson Colloquium, Spring, 1988, 33; Karen Halttunen, *Confidence Men and Painted Ladies: A Study of Middle-Class Culture in America, 1830–1870* (New Haven, Conn.: Yale University Press, 1982), ch. 5; Ann Douglas, *The Feminization of American Culture* (New York: Avon, 1978), ch. 5.

69. C. Kurt Dewhurst, Betty MacDowell, and Martha MacDowell, *Artists in Aprons* (New York: E. P. Dutton and the Museum of American Fold Art, 1979), 60–62, 66–70.

70. Kate Douglas Wiggin, *Rebecca of Sunnybrook Farm* (1903; rev. ed., Middlesex, UK: Puffin, 1985), 63.

71. Mary Alves Long, *High Time to Tell It* (Durham, N.C.: Duke University Press, 1950), 23. Slave children

staged funerals as well, according to David K. Wiggins, "The Play of Slave Children in the Plantation Communities of the Old South, 1820–1860," in Hiner and Hawes, *Growing Up in America*, 178.

72. Mrs. Fairstair (Richard Henry Horne), *Memoirs of a London Doll, Written by Herself* (London: 1846; rpt. N.Y., 1967), 9.

73. *The Doll's Own Book* (Ohio: n.p., 1882); many also had large print, such as *Twilight Stories* (New York, London, Manchester, Glasgow: n.d.).

74. See issues of the *Doll's Dressmaker* for other installments by doll author.

75. Reynale Smith Pickering, "Christmas in Song and Story" and "The New Christmas Doll Complains," (poems), Ladies Home Journal (LHJ), Dec. 1908, 126. See also the poem by Laura Starr, *The Doll Book* (N.Y.: Outing Co., 1908), 199.

76. S. K. Simons, "The Happy Doll," DD, April 1893, 90; C. S. Valentine, "Coquette's Story," DD, Oct. 1891, 227. "So I like to just stay up here in the attic, out of sight of the gay, fashionable dolls, and dream of the dear old times of the maid who loved me just for myself, tenderly, devotedly" (Thompson, "Rosamond," 475).

77. It also laid the basis for inevitable frustration when girls got older. Among middle-class Americans and the British, love had been "feminized"—caring and loving had become the work of women, support and protection of men. Gillis, "Ritualization," 15; Francesca Cancian, *Love in America: Gender and Self-*

Development (Cambridge: Cambridge University Press, 1987).

78. "Dolls: Logically Considered," *Babyhood*, Oct. 1895, 330–1.

79. In stereographs and illustrations, boys often played the role of doctor as well.

80. Thompson, "Rosamond," 474.

81. Heininger, "Children, Childhood," 26–27; see also Anita Schorsch, *Images of Childhood: An Illustrated Social History* (Pittstown, N.J.: Main Street Press, 1985), ch. 6.

82. "The Tragical-Comical Tale of Mrs. Kennedy and Punch," *Frank Leslie's Chatterbox*, 1885–1886, 10.

83. Anna Clark, *Women's Silence Men's Violence: Sexual Assault in England 1770–1845* (London and New York: Pandora, 1987).

84. For an example of a taunting monkey, see "Naughty Jacko" in *Dolly in Town*. In "The Little Doll," a poem by Charles Kingsley in *The Water Babies*, a wooden doll's arms are "troddened off by cows." See "Kate Douglas Wiggin's Poetry for Children," LHJ, Oct. 1907, 50.

85. Aunt Laura [pseud.], *The Dolls' Surprise Party* (Buffalo, N.Y.: Breed, Butler, 1863).

86. Beatrix Potter, *The Tale of Two Bad Mice* (New York: F. Warne, 1904), 46.

87. Ibid., 59.

88. Hubert, "Some Notes as to Christmas Toys," *Babyhood*, Dec. 1893, 14.

89. Emily Kimbrough, *How Dear to My Heart* (N.Y.: Dodd, Mead, 1944), 76–77.

90. "The Doll of the Colored Children," *Babyhood*, Oct. 1894, 351.

91. Una Atherton Hunt, *Una*

Mary: The Inner Life of a Child (New York: Scribners, 1914), 20; A. C. Ellis and G. Stanley Hall, "Study of Dolls," *Pedagogical Seminary* 1, 2 (Dec. 1896): 134.

92. "Home-Made Rag Doll," *Babyhood*, Sept. 1908, 417.

93. David Katzman, *Seven Days a Week* (Urbana, Chicago, London: University of Illinois Press, 1981).

94. Ellis and Hall, "Study of Dolls," 141.

95. "Of average city school children below 6 years, 82% of boys . . . played with dolls; between 6 and 12 yrs., 76% of boys." Ibid., 155.

96. *Maiden America and Friends: Parade of Playthings* (Yankee Doodle Dollers of Massachusetts, UFDC Regton 15, Nov. 9–11, 1984), 51.

97. Dorothy Washburn, "Report: Preliminary Results, Doll Oral History Project," 2, Margaret Woodbury Strong Museum, doll 79.9962.

98. M. H. Jones, "Dolls for Boys," *Babyhood*, June 1896, 216.

99. Ellis and Hall, "Study of Dolls," 145.

100. According to one ten-year-old boy, "My doll used to get angry and I would grab her by the hair and throu her down stairs but afterward give her a nice piece of mud cake with raspberries on it." Ibid., 149, 150–51.

101. Jones, "Dolls for Boys," 216.

102. Ellis and Hall, "Study of Dolls," 147.

103. Croswell, "Amusements," 347.

104. Ibid., 5; Brian Sutton-Smith, "The Play of Girls," in *Becoming Female*, ed. Clare B. Knopp (New York: Plenum, 1979) 229–30.

105. Eleanor Hallowell Abbott, "Being Little in Cambridge When Everyone Else Was Big," in Mergen, *Play and Playthings*, 186–87.

106. Lawrence, "Dolls: Logically Considered," 330–31.

107. "The Natural Instincts of Boys and Girls," *Babyhood*, April 1905, 143.

108. Ellis and Hall, "Study of Dolls," 140.

109. Ibid., 141.

110. Carolyn Wells, "A Dolly's Dialogue," *St. Nicholas*, Dec. 1906, 156–57; Lucy Foster, "Little Mothers," ibid., Aug. 1908, 933–35. Rather than lacking empathy, however, they were probably expressing anger.

111. Ellis and Hall, "A Study of Dolls," 146–47. Death and burial were the subjects of late nineteenth-century school-girls' ring games. See Sutton-Smith, "Play of Girls," in Knopp and Kirkpatrick, *Becoming Female*, 232.

112. "Burying Baby Dolls," *Doll's Dressmaker*, Nov. 1891, 240.

113. Ethel Spencer, *The Spencers of Amberson Avenue: A Turn of the Century Memoir*, ed. Michael P. Weber and Peter N. Stearns (Pittsburgh, Pa.: Pittsburgh University Press, 1983), 65.

114. Alice Kent Trimpey, *Becky My First Love* (Wis.: Whitman, 1949), 1–2. According to one nine-year-old, "Doll broken, funeral just for fun" (Ellis and Hall, "Study of Dolls," 146).

115. James Sully, *Children's Ways* (New York: Appleton, 1897), 492.

116. Lilienthal, *Dear Remembered World*, 20–21.

117. Hunt, *Una Mary*, 14.

118. Zona Gale, *When I Was a Little Girl* (New York: Macmillan, 1913), 196.

119. Croswell, "Amusements," 354.

120. Hunt, *Una Mary*, 163–65.

121. Ibid., 20.

CHAPTER 7.
The Youngest Fourth Estate

The major collections for this paper are contained at the American Antiquarian Society in Worcester, Massachusetts, and in the Library of Amateur Journalism, American Private Press Association, 112 E. Brunett Street, Stayton, Oregon. I wish to acknowledge a Hall James and Kate B. Peterson Fellowship at the American Antiquarian Society that introduced me to these documents (some twenty thousand pieces) and a Montana State Research and Creativity Grant that provided me with funding to visit the Library of Amateur Journalism. I would also wish to thank Martin Horvat, the curator of the Library of Amateur Journalism, who allowed me access to the extensive collection (some thirty thousand pieces) of the former Fossils Association. His help and interest have proven invaluable.

1. Mary P. Ryan, *Cradle of the Middle Class* (New York: Cambridge University Press, 1981), 164–65, 184–85; Joseph F. Kett, *Rites of Passage, Adolescence in America, 1790 to the Present* (New York: Basic Books, 1977), 111–210.

2. *The Post Boy* (Cambridge, Mass.), Dec. 7, 1850; *The Rising Sun* (Mill River, Mass.), Oct. 14, 1919 facsimile of 1855 edition.

3. *Germ* (Boston), Mar. 16, 1846.

4. *National Eagle* (Boston), Aug. 1870. In any month there were approximately 500 amateur papers. With an average run of 500 copies per paper, the amateur press put 250,000 pieces into circulation each month. Although most issues were exchanged among editors, others found their way into general circulation as editors sold issues to schoolmates and friends.

5. *Oliver Optic's Magazine*, April 1874, 318–19; June 1874, 477–79.

6. *Oliver Optic's Magazine*, Oct. 5, 1867, Dec. 21, 1867, Jan. 11, 1868, Feb. 1, 1868, Feb. 22, 1868, Feb. 29, 1868, April 4, 1868, May 9, 1868, July 18, 1868.

7. Truman J. Spencer, *The History of Amateur Journalism* (New York: Fossils, 1957), 21; *Oliver Optic's Magazine*, Sept. 19, 1868.

8. *Oliver Optic's Magazine*, Dec. 1874, 950.

9. William Taylor Adams, *Desk and Debit* (Boston: Lee and Shepard, 1872).

10. See Fred E. Case, *Bob the Bootblack, or Street Life in New York* (Ipswich, N.H., 1876), for an example of a juvenile literary theft taken from Horatio Alger's *Ragged Dick*. See also *Literary Gems* (New Haven, Conn.: English & Hall, 1875), 7, for an example of the writers' awareness of the situation. In the latter, William H. Dennis's review of Charles McColm's *The Young Tar* spoke to the phenomenon of plagiarism when he wrote, "What little plot the book possesses is stolen,

and spoiled in the stealing, from Oliver Optic. This is impossible to disguise."

11. *Our Album* (Boston), June 15, 1872.

12. William Taylor Adams, *A Soldier Boy, a Story of the Great Rebellion* (Boston: Lee and Shepard, 1864), 15–17, 89, 91, 116–17, 144–51, 152–232, 258–59, 261–333, *Boy's Advertiser* (Birmingham, Conn.), Jan. 1871, Mar. 1871, April 1871, Aug. 1871, Sept. 1871, Nov. 1871, Dec. 1871.

13. Richard "Humpty Dumpty" Gerner, *The Lord of Monteith, or the Secret of the Red Chamber* (Haverhill, Mass.: R. C. Smith, 1873), 1.

14. Richard "Humpty Dumpty" Gerner, *"?", a Tale of Baden-Baden* (Dubuque, Iowa: Glenn M. Farley, 1876), n.p.

15. For examples, see Charles "Skiff" McColm, "A Hundred-Fold," *Schoolmate* (Cleveland), July 1872; J. Fred "Red Cross" Demarest, *Tim, the Fox* (New York: Rutherford Press, 1872).

16. *Boy's Advertiser*, Aug. 1871.

17. Will H. "Gaston Folnay" Dennis, *Dick Marlowe, a Story of School Life* (Jersey City, N.J.: Henri Gerard, 1872), 25.

18. Thomas G. Harrison, *The Career and Reminiscences of an Amateur Journalist and a History of Amateur Journalism* (Indianapolis: Thomas G. Harrison, 1883), 284–85.

19. Reprinted in *Le Bijou* (Cincinnati, Ohio), Sept. 1879; see also *North Carolina Amateur* (Rose Hill, N.C.), Sept. 1879.

20. *Le Bijou*, Sept. 1879.

21. Ibid., Oct. 1879.

22. Ibid., Feb./Mar. 1880.

23. Ibid., Nov. 1879.

24. Both Benjamin Pelham and his brother, twenty-year-old Robert, were involved with the *Venture*, although Robert's participation in the civil rights debate lessened as he moved toward adulthood. He apparently attended the 1879 NAPA convention with his brother and then disappeared from the ranks of amateur journalism to manage the Pelhams' fledgling printing business.

25. *Venture* (Detroit), Feb. 1880.

26. Ibid., Dec. 1882.

27. *Egyptian Star* (Cairo, Ill.), Jan. 1880.

28. *Le Bijou* (Cincinnati, Ohio), Feb. 1880.

29. *Venture*, Mar. 1882.

30. Ibid., Feb. 1882; see also June 1882 and Jan. 1882. In many ways the *Venture's* criticism of Eva Britton's candidacy anticipated the next consuming controversy among the amateur journalists—women's rights.

31. Gerner, *A Tale of Baden-Baden*, n.p.

32. A. N. Demarest, *Edith, the Girl Detective* (Chicago: R. E. Haver, 1876), 24–28.

33. *Boy's Journal* (Martinsburg, N.Y.), Feb. 1871.

34. *The Yankee Land* (Detroit), May 1872.

35. J. A. Fynes, *Love's Discovery* (Ansonia, Conn.: Stoddard & Phelps, 1876), n.p.

36. *Little Things* (Brinton, Pa.), Aug. 1872.

37. *Pen* (Springfield, Mass.), July 15, 1879.

38. *Dreamer* (Jackson, Mich.), May 1875.

39. *Hurricane* (Charleston, S.C.), July 1882.

40. *North Carolina Amateur* (Lenoir, N.C.), Oct. 1883.

41. *Welcome Visitor* (La Fayette, Ind.), Jan. 1877.

42. *Violet* (Cincinnati, Ohio), Sept. 1884, Dec./Jan. 1884/85, Feb. 1885, June 1885.

43. *Violet* (Cincinnati, Ohio), Oct. 1885.

44. *Mirror* (San Francisco), Oct. 1886.

45. Ibid.; *Little Acorn* (Kansas City, Mo.), Aug. 1885. Leslie Warren of the latter paper early on defended Arlington's appearance in the fraternity: "Hal Bixby and M. G. Jonas are evidently 'woman haters' of the first degree. Their ungallant attacks of Miss Arlington and the young ladies in general are entirely un-called for and brand them as, well we hardly know what,—certainly not gentlemen."

46. John Travis Nixon, comp, *History of the National Amateur Press Association* (Crowley, La.: John T. Nixon, 1900), 58–62.

47. *Le Bijou* (Cincinnati, Ohio), Oct. 1878; *Fossil*, April 1905, June 1906. It seems likely that, although Herbert Clarke was very young, he taught in a Freedman's Bureau school in Rodney, Mississippi, during his adolescence. Such an eventuality was not unknown. The *Fossil* was the alumni newspaper of the Fossils, the group that came together to remember their junior journalistic experience and to encourage others. One of the oldest hobby organizations in the United States the group still meets annually under the name of the American Private Press Association. At this writing I have not been able to trace further Herbert A. Clarke's career or his Oklahoma paper.

48. Rayford N. Logan and Michael R. Winston, eds., *Dictionary of American Negro Biography* (New York: W. W. Norton, 1982), 486–87.

49. *Boy's Advertiser* (Birmingham, Conn.), Dec. 1872. It would be beneficial to trace the young female editors in the same fashion that it is possible to track the young men, but that has proven beyond the scope of the essay. Did the young women carry their feminist ideology into their adult lives? Two clues suggest that they did. First, Zelda Arlington Swift ultimately divorced her husband and married a fellow amateur journalist. Maud May Frye, a prolific contributor to the women's amateur press became a leading women's-rights activist in Nova Scotia. The career of Eva Britton, the youngest feminist of the group, remains a mystery.

CHAPTER 8.
The Homefront Children's Popular Culture

The letters referred to in the notes were written to the author by two thousand homefront children in response to an appeal for wartime recollections that I had made in letters to the editors of a variety of newspapers and magazines. In 1990, with the support of a Projects Research Grant from the Interpretive Research Division of the National Endowment for the Humanities, I wrote the one hundred largest newspapers in the United States (by circulation) as well as seventy-five African American, Hispanic American, and Jewish American newspapers and magazines. The hundreds of letters received dealt with an amazing variety of topics ranging from adultery, air raids, and alcoholism to V-J Day, War Bonds, and war-boom communities.

With the help of Kathryn N. Kretschmer, I coded 175 different topics with which these letters deal and thus have been able to access the material that I need. The letters have proved to be invaluable in writing *Their War, Too* (forthcoming). Moreover, I believe that this method, which I have used to capture the experiences of people who have no historical record of their childhood other than their memories, can be used in pursuing a host of other topics that can be fully researched in no other way.

I also wish to thank David M. Katzman and Burton Peretti for their careful reading of this chapter and their suggestions for its improvement.

1. Letters no. 114, 236, 408; "Jack the Nazi Killer," *Newsweek*, Aug. 23, 1943, 80; Robert C. Ferguson, "Americanism in Late Afternoon Radio Adventure Serials, 1940–1945" (unpublished paper), 4–8; J. Fred MacDonald, *Don't Touch That Dial: Radio Programming in American Life, 1920–1960* (Chicago: Nelson-Hall, 1980), 68–69, 203–4; Thomas White-

side, "Up, Up and Awa-a-y," *New Republic*, Mar. 3, 1947, 15–17; Jim Harmon, *The Great Radio Heroes* (Garden City, N.Y.: Doubleday, 1967), 49–51.

2. "Jack the Nazi Killer," 80; MacDonald, *Don't Touch That Dial*, 257–71; Raymond William Stedman, *The Serials: Suspense and Drama by Installment* (Norman: University of Oklahoma Press, 1977), 329–39.

3. MacDonald, *Don't Touch That Dial*, 68–69, 203–4; "Jack the Nazi Killer," 80.

4. See the discussion in Roy De Verl Willey and Helen Ann Young, *Radio in Elementary Education* (Boston: D. C. Heath, 1948), 10–13.

5. Letters no. 114, 166, 192, 228, 229, 278, 300, 408, 413; Willey and Young, *Radio in Elementary Education*, 3–4; Weston R. Clark, "Radio Listening Habits of Children," *Journal of Social Psychology* 12 (Aug. 1940): 131–49; "Mack and the Beanstalk," *Newsweek*, June 28, 1943, 108; *New York Times*, April 26, Oct. 18, Nov. 1, 8, 15, 1942; May 27, 1945; John K. Hutchens, "Tracy, Superman et al. Go to War," *New York Times Magazine*, Nov. 21, 1943; "Radio Programs for Children," *Child Study* 21 (Fall 1943): 28–29; "Radio Programs for Children," *Child Study* 22 (Winter 1944–1945): 53; "Something for the Boys & Girls," *Time*, Sept. 24, 1945, 78; "It's Superfight," *Newsweek*, April 29, 1946, 61; Albert N. Williams, "And a Little Child Shall Lead Them," *Saturday Review of Literature*, Feb. 8, 1947, 26–27; Whiteside, "Up, Up and Awa-a-y," 15–17; Ferguson, "Americanism in Late Afternoon Radio Adventure Seri-

als," 9–11; Arthur Frank Wertheim, *Radio Comedy* (New York: Oxford University Press, 1979), 263–82; MacDonald, *Don't Touch That Dial*, 43–44, 140–41, 257–71; Harmon, *Great Radio Heroes*, 85, 107, 231–33; George A. Willey, "The Soap Operas and the War," *Journal of Broadcasting* 7 (Fall 1963): 339–52; Paul A. Lazarsfeld and Frank N. Stanton, eds., *Radio Research 1942–1943* (New York: Duell, Sloan and Pearce, 1944), 34–69; Erik Barnouw, *The Golden Web: A History of Broadcasting in the United States, 1933 to 1953*, 3 vols. (New York: Oxford University Press, 1968), 2: 94–97.

6. Letters no. 43, 44, 53, 59, 97K, 131, 146, 171, 195, 206K, 208, 241, 246, 276, 323, 394, 408, 440; Clara Savage Littledale, "Radio Interprets the War to Children," *Parents' Magazine*, Mar. 1943, 17; MacDonald, *Don't Touch That Dial*, 288, 291–310.

7. Marie Winn, "Why Has Radio Tuned Out Children?" *New York Times*, Sept. 25, 1983.

8. Newman F. Baker, ed., "Current Notes: Radio Crime Programs," *Journal of Criminal Law and Criminology* 31, 2 (1940–1941): 222–23; Azriel L. Eisenberg, *Children and Radio Programs* (New York: Columbia University Press, 1936), 185–90; *New York Times*, Oct. 5, 1941; June 27, 1945; Willey and Young, *Radio in Elementary Education*, 8–9; Erle Kenney and Harriet E. Neall, "His Ear to the Radio," *Parents' Magazine*, Mar. 1944, 88; "Howard Rowland, "Radio Crime Dramas," *Educational Research Bulletin* 23 (Nov. 15, 1944): 210–11; Sara Ann Fay, "Are Children's Radio Programs a Good Influence?" *Library*

Journal 70 (Feb. 15, 1945): 175–76; Dorothy Gordon, *All Children Listen* (New York: George W. Stewart, 1942), 44–49, 52–61; Child Study Association, "Children in Wartime: Parents' Questions," in *The Family in a World at War*, ed. Sidonie Matsner Gruenberg (New York: Harper, 1942), 261–62; MacDonald, *Don't Touch That Dial*, 43–46, 68–70.

9. Dorothea English Murphy, "A Survey of the Radio Interests and Listening Habits of 358 Elementary School Students" (M.A. thesis, Fordham University, 1946), 60–68; Jane Ferguson Porter, "Radio Interests of the Children in Mason County, West Virginia" (M.A. thesis, Marshall College, 1945), 10–17; Colleen Kelly Gery, "An Historical Study of American Radio's Role in Informing Children in the United States about World War II, 1941–1945" (M.A. thesis, Indiana University, 1968), 18–82.

10. Raymond Rubicam, "Advertising," in *While You Were Gone: A Report on Wartime Life in the United States*, ed. Jack Goodman (New York: Simon and Schuster, 1946), 421–46.

11. Harold T. Christensen and Doyle L. Green, "The Commercialization of Patriotism in World War II," *Sociology and Social Research* 27 (July–Aug. 1943): 447–52; Theodore S. Repplier, "Advertising Dons Long Pants," *Public Opinion Quarterly* 9 (Fall 1945): 269–78.

12. Letters no. 15, 25, 97D, 166, 203, 335, 385, 390, 426; War Finance Division, Department of the Treasury, *New Songs for Schools at War* (Washington, D.C.: GPO, 1943); Joe Bookman, "The Truth about Silly

War Songs," *Collier's*, July 24, 1943, 20, 42–43; Robert Fyne, " 'You're a Sap, Mr. Jap': Tin Pan Alley Fights the Axis" (unpublished paper), 1–6.

13. Margaret Mead quoted in *Newsweek*, Nov. 27, 1978, 75–76; Joshua Meyrowitz, "The Adult-like Child and the Childlike Adult: Socialization in an Electronic Age," *Daedalus* 113 (Summer 1984): 19–48; Joshua Meyrowitz, *No Sense of Place: The Impact of Electronic Media on Social Behavior* (New York: Oxford University Press, 1985), 226–67. For related books, see Kenneth Keniston and the Carnegie Council on Children, *All Our Children: The American Family under Pressure* (New York: Harcourt Brace Jovanovich, 1977); David Elkind, *The Hurried Child: Growing Up Too Fast Too Soon* (Reading, Mass.: Addison-Wesley, 1981); Alice Miller, *Prisoners of Childhood: How Narcissistic Parents Form and Deform the Emotional Lives of Their Gifted Children* (New York: Basic Books, 1981); Valerie Polakow Suransky, *The Erosion of Childhood* (Chicago: University of Chicago Press, 1982); Neil Postman, *The Disappearance of Childhood* (New York: Delacorte, 1982); Marie Winn, *Children without Childhood* (New York: Pantheon, 1983); Vance Packard, *Our Endangered Children: Growing Up in a Changing World* (Boston: Little, Brown, 1983); Richard Louv, *Childhood's Future: New Hope for the American Family* (Boston: Houghton Mifflin, 1990).

14. Letters no. 12B, 187, 276, 316, 405.

15. Letters no. 97E, 442B.

16. Letters no. 150, 312, 318, 350, 435; Raymond Fielding, *The American Newsreel, 1911–1967* (Norman: University of Oklahoma Press, 1972), 288–95; *Kansas City Star*, April 21, 1986; Roger Manvell, *Films and the Second World War* (South Brunswick, N.J.: A. S. Barnes, 1974), 122–23, 183–85.

17. Letters no. 42, 150, 222; Fielding, *American Newsreel*, 295; interview with Frances Degen Horowitz, Feb. 9, 1984.

18. See Allen L. Woll, *The Hollywood Musical Goes to War* (Chicago: Nelson-Hall, 1983); John H. Lenihan, *Showdown: Confronting Modern America in the Western Film* (Urbana: University of Illinois Press, 1980); *New York Times*, May 19, 1943.

19. David Culbert, " 'Why We Fight': Social Engineering for a Democratic Society at War," in *Film & Radio Propaganda in World War II*, ed. K. R. M. Short (London: Croon Helm, 1983), 173–91; Erik Barnouw, *Documentary: A History of the Non-Fiction Film* (New York: Oxford University Press, 1983), 139–64; Manvell, *Films and the Second World War*, 167–83; "War Films Available to School and Adult Audiences," *School Review* 51 (April 1943): 205; Harold Putnam, "The War against War Movies," *Educational Screen* 22 (May 1943): 162–63, 175; Thornton Delehanty, "The Disney Studio at War," *Theater Arts* 27 (Jan. 1943): 31–33; Richard Schickel, *The Disney Version: The Life, Times, Art, and Commerce of Walt Disney* (New York: Simon and Schuster, 1968), 270–71; Leonard Maltin, *The Disney Films* (New York: Bonanza, 1973), 16, 60–64; Leonard

Maltin, *Of Mice and Magic: A History of American Animated Cartoons* (New York: McGraw-Hill, 1980), 70–71.

20. Garth Jowett, *Film: The Democratic Art* (Boston: Little, Brown, 1976), 316, 473–75, 483; "Big Movie Year," *Business Week*, Feb. 13, 1943, 37–38; Peter A. Soderbergh, "The Grand Illusion: Hollywood and World War II, 1930–1945," *University of Dayton Review* 5 (Winter 1968–1969): 18.

21. Letters no. 228, 229, 254, 300, 312, 350, 408; Willie Morris, *North toward Home* (Boston: Houghton Mifflin, 1967), 34–35; "How to Run a Theater," *Time*, Nov. 22, 1943, 94.

22. Gladys Denny Shultz, "Comics—Radio—Movies," *Better Homes and Gardens*, Nov. 1945, 22–23, 73–75, 108; Jim Harmon and Donald F. Glut, *The Great Movie Serials: Their Sound and Fury* (Garden City, N.Y.: Doubleday, 1972), 217–19, 235–41, 244–61, 273–81; Stedman, *Serials*, 330.

23. "The Production Code, 1930–1968," in *Children and Youth in America: A Documentary History*, ed. Robert H. Bremner et al., 3 vols. (Cambridge, Mass.: Harvard University Press, 1974), 3 (1933–1973): 891–93; Catherine MacKenzie, "Movies—and Superman," *New York Times Magazine*, Oct. 12, 1941; Catherine C. Edwards, "Let's Talk about the Movies," *Parents' Magazine*, Oct. 1945, 31ff.

Some of the best studies of the wartime feature films are Jowett, *Film: Democratic Art*, 293–332; Manvell, *Films and the Second World War*, 176–203; Dorothy B. Jones,

"The Hollywood War Film: 1942–1944," *Hollywood Quarterly* 1 (Oct. 1945): 1–19; Bosley Crowther, "The Movies," in Goodman, *While You Were Gone*, 511–32; Lewis Jacobs, "World War II and the American Film," *Cinema Journal* 7 (Winter 1967–1968): 1–21; Soderbergh, "Grand Illusion," 13–22; Colin Shindler, *Hollywood Goes to War: Films and American Society, 1939–1952* (London: Routledge & Kegan Paul, 1979); Robert B. Ray, *A Certain Tendency of the Hollywood Cinema, 1930–1980* (Princeton, N.J.: Princeton University Press, 1985), 113–25; Bernard F. Dick, *The Star-Spangled Screen: The American World War II Film* (Lexington: University of Kentucky Press, 1985); Otto Friedrich, *City of Nets: A Portrait of Hollywood in the 1940s* (New York: Harper & Row, 1986); Jeanine Basinger, *The World War II Combat Film* (New York: Columbia University Press, 1986); Clayton R. Koppes and Gregory D. Black, *Hollywood Goes to War: How Politics, Profits, and Propaganda Shaped World War II Movies* (New York: Free Press, 1987); Terry Christensen, *Reel Politics: American Political Movies from "Birth of a Nation" to "Platoon"* (London: Basil Blackwell, 1987), 63–101.

24. Scott Momaday, *The Names: A Memoir* (New York: Harper & Row, 1976), 89; letters no. 32, 228, 443; Florene M. Young, "Psychological Effects of War on Young Children," *American Journal of Orthopsychiatry* 17 (July 1947): 507; Josette Frank, "Chills and Thrills in Radio, Movies and Comics," *Child Study* 25 (Spring 1948): 42–46, 48; Manvell, *Films and*

the Second World War, 199; *New York Times*, Oct. 24, 1943; Ken D. Jones and Arthur F. McClure, *Hollywood at War: The American Motion Picture and World War II* (New York: Castle, 1973), 198–99.

For a summary of prewar studies done on the psychological impact of films, see Franklin Fearing, "Influence of the Movies on Attitude and Behavior," *Annals of the American Academy of Political and Social Science* 254 (Nov. 1947): 70–79. A study of postwar films released between late 1945 and 1949 is Martha Wolfenstein and Nathan Leites, *Movies: A Psychological Study* (Glencoe, Ill.: Free Press, 1950).

25. Letter no. 219; Ruth Weeden Stewart, "The Year's New Books for Boys and Girls Over Ten," *Library Journal* 68 (Oct. 15, 1943): 824–25; Lena Barksdale, "A Selected List of Children's Books," *Nation*, Nov. 20, 1943, 591–93; Margaret C. Scoggin, "Young People in a World at War, *Horn Book* 19 (Nov. 1943): 394–400; "Books: Hints to Santa," *Newsweek*, Dec. 13, 1943, 105; "Children's Books of 1943–1944" and "Children's Books of 1944–45," both in *Journal of the National Educational Association* 33 (Nov. 1944): 195–96, and 34 (Nov. 1945): 167–68; "Most Widely Used Children's Books of 1939–1943," *Chicago Schools Journal* 27 (Sept.–Dec. 1945): 33; Jane Cobb and Helen Dore Boylston, "What's Your Child Reading?" *Atlantic*, Nov. 1946, 160ff.; U.S. Children's Bureau Publication no. 304, *For the Children's Bookshelf: A Booklist for Parents* (Washington, D.C.: GPO, 1946).

26. John J. DeBoer, "Children's Books in Wartime," *Chicago Schools Journal* 24 (Sept.–Dec. 1942): 40–42; Marie Nelson Taylor, "Facing the War with Our Young People," *Wilson Library Bulletin* 17 (April 1943): 656–58; Vernon Ives, "Children's Books and the War," *Publishers Weekly*, Oct. 23, 1943, 1592–93; letter no. 220.

27. Bobbie Ann Mason, *The Girl Sleuth: A Feminist Guide* (Old Westbury, N.Y.: Feminist Press, 1975), 6, 8–12; Carol Billman, *The Secret of the Stratemeyer Syndicate: Nancy Drew, the Hardy Boys, and the Million Dollar Fiction Factory* (New York: Ungar, 1986).

28. John R. Tunis, *Keystone Kids* (New York; Harcourt, Brace, 1943), 149–61, 188, 208; Stewart, "The Year's New Books for Boys and Girls Over Ten," 823; Alice Dalgliesh, " 'To Light a Candle,' " *Publishers Weekly*, April 28, 1945, 1736; Toby Smith, "The Writer Who Taught Generations How to Play the Game," *Wall Street Journal*, Jan. 2, 1990.

29. Maltin, *Of Mice and Magic*, 116–17, 137–39, 163–67, 172, 246–47, 250–52, 284–85.

30. Carl A. Posey, "The Strange Case of Carter Hall," *Air & Space*, Nov. 1989, 69; Catherine MacKenzie, "Children and the Comics," *New York Times Magazine*, July 11, 1943; *New York Times*, Feb. 2, Mar. 25, Dec. 15, 1944; Jan. 13, Dec. 16, 25, 1945; Harvey Zorbaugh, "Comics—Food for Half-Wits?" *Science Digest* 17 (April 1945): 79–82; Elliot M. Rosenberg, "Winning the War with Captain Marvel," *New York Times Magazine*, Sept. 3, 1985; "Up, Up and Awaaay!!!" *Time*, Mar. 14, 1988, 68;

"The Comic Book (Gulp!) Grows Up," *Newsweek*, Jan. 18, 1988, 70–71; Laurance F. Shaffer, *Children's Interpretations of Cartoons* (New York: Bureau of Publications, Teachers College, Columbia University, 1930), 1–5, 21–41.

For the importance of the home-front comics, see "Let Children Read Comics," *Science News Letter* 40 (Aug. 23, 1941): 12–25; "Regarding Comic Magazines," *Recreation* 35 (Feb. 1942): 689; Gweneira Williams and Jane Wilson, "They Like It Rough: In Defense of Comics," *Library Journal* 67 (Mar. 1, 1942): 204–6; "The Comics and Their Audience," *Publishers Weekly*, April 18, 1942, 1476–79; "Issues Relating to the Comics," *Elementary School Journal* 42 (May 1942): 641–44; "Profitable Reading Pleasure," *Parents' Magazine*, Nov. 1942, 44; Sister M. Katharine McCarthy and Marion W. Smith, "The Much Discussed Comics," *Elementary School Journal* 44 (Oct. 1943): 97–101; Milton Caniff, "The Comics," in Goodman, *While You Were Gone*, 488–510; Ruth Hartley and Robert M. Goldenson, *The Complete Book of Children's Play* (New York: Crowell, 1957), 139; Steve M. Barkin, "Fighting the Cartoon War: Information Strategies in World War II," *Journal of American Culture* 7 (Summer 1984): 113–17; Michael Uslan, ed., *America at War: The Best of DC War Comics* (New York: Simon and Schuster, 1979), 5–12.

31. Gloria Steinem, *Wonder Woman* (New York: Holt, Rinehart and Winston, 1972), "Introduction"; Ger-hart Saenger, "Male and Female Relations in the American Comic Strip," *Public Opinion Quarterly* 19 (Summer 1955): 195–205.

32. Letters no. 74, 270.

33. Kathryn Weibel, *Mirror Mirror: Images of Women Reflected in Popular Culture* (Garden City, N.Y.: Anchor, 1977), 116–19; M. Joyce Baker, *Images of Women in Film: The War Years, 1941–1945* (Ann Arbor, Mich.: UMI Research Press, 1981); Dick, *Star-Spangled Screen*, 174–87; Leo A. Handel, *Hollywood Looks at Its Audience: A Report of Film Audience Research* (Urbana: University of Illinois Press, 1950), 120–24; Carol Trayner Williams, *The Dream beside Me: The Movies and the Children of the Forties* (Rutherford, N.J.: Fairleigh Dickinson University Press, 1980), 41–80.

34. This dialogue is quoted in Barbara Deming, *Running Away from Myself: A Dream Portrait of America Drawn from the Films of the Forties* (New York: Grossman, 1969), 8–10.

35. Letter no. 120; Peter A. Soderbergh, "The War Films," *Discourse* 11 (Winter 1968): 87–91; Peter A. Soderbergh, "On War and the Movies: A Reappraisal," *Centennial Review* 11 (Summer 1967): 405–18; Peter Roffman and Jim Purdy, *The Hollywood Social Problem Film: Madness, Despair, and Politics from the Depression to the Fifties* (Bloomington: Indiana University Press, 1981), 227–35; Dick, *Star-Spangled Screen*, 324–27.

36. Jean Bethke Elshtain, *Women and War* (New York: Basic Books, 1987), xii, 14–17; Walter Goodman, "Romance Narrows the Generation

Gap," *New York Times*, Aug. 10, 1986.

37. Lawrence W. Levine, *Highbrow/Lowbrow: The Emergence of Cultural Hierarchy in America* (Cambridge, Mass.: Harvard University Press, 1988), especially 243–56; Godfrey Hodgson, *America in Our Time: From World War II to Nixon* (Garden City, N.Y.: Doubleday, 1976), 12–16.

PART 3.
Seen but Not Heard

The following persons provided valuable assistance to the author in selecting photographs for this essay: Oliver Olivas and Richard Rudisill of the Museum of New Mexico; Ann Marvin and Nancy Sherbert of the Kansas State Historical Society; Nicolette Bromberg and L. E. James Helyar of the Kenneth Spencer Research Library, University of Kansas.

1. For a review of the recent historiography of children, see the following two works edited by Joseph M. Hawes and N. Ray Hiner: *Children in Comparative and Historical Perspective: An International Handbook and Research Guide* (Westport, Conn.: Greenwood Press, 1991) and *American Childhood: A Research Guide and Historical Handbook* (Westport, Conn.: Greenwood Press, 1985).

2. U.S. Bureau of the Census, *Historical Statistics of the United States, Colonial Times to 1957* (Washington, D.C.: GPO, 1960), 10–11; Robert Wells, *Revolutions in Americans' Lives: A Demographic Perspective on the History of Americans, Their Families,*

and Their Society (Westport, Conn.: Greenwood Press, 1982).

3. Susan Kismaric, *American Children: Photographs from the Collection of the Museum of Modern Art* (New York: Museum of Modern Art), 5.

4. After completing the introduction to this essay, I was able to contact and visit with Frank Chapman (b. Santa Fe, 1916), now a retired teacher and school administrator living in Albuquerque, New Mexico. He and his wife Jennie have two grown children, Pamela and Kenneth. His sister Helen (b. 1918) married Robert Potter, a career military officer, and was the mother of six children. She died in 1944. Frank does not recall the specific occasion of the photograph reproduced here, but he believes that it was taken by his father, Kenneth Chapman, (1875–1968), an artist, writer, and expert on Native American Art of the Southwest.

5. National Archives, *The American Image: Photographs from the National Archives* (New York: Pantheon Books, 1979), xxi.

6. Beaumont Newhall, *The Daguerreotype in America*, 3d ed. (New York: Dover Publications, 1976), 36. See also Richard Rudisill, *Mirror Image: The Influence of the Daguerreotype on American Society* (Albuquerque: University of New Mexico Press, 1971).

7. Beaumont Newhall, *The History of Photography from 1839 to the Present*, rev. ed. (New York: Museum of Modern Art, 1982), 30.

8. Cited in Newhall, *History of Photography*, 129.

9. Susan Sontag, *On Photogra-*

phy (New York: Farrar, Straus, and Giroux, 1973), 8.

10. Michael Lesy, *Bearing Witness: A Photographic Chronicle of American Life 1860–1945* (New York: Pantheon Books, 1982), xiv.

Selected Bibliography

Akmakjian, Hiag. *The Years of Bitterness and Pride: Farm Security Administration FSA Photographs, 1935–1943*. New York: McGraw-Hill, 1975.

Challinor, Joan R. et al. "Family Photo Interpretation." In *Kin and Communities: Families in America*, 239–63. Edited by Allan J. Lichtman and Joan Challinor. Washington, D.C.: Smithsonian Institution Press, 1979.

The Children's Aid Society. *New York Street Kids: 136 Photographs Selected by the Children's Aid Society*. New York: Dover Publications, 1978.

Conrat, Maisie, and Conrat, Richard. *The American Farm: A Photographic History*. Boston: Houghton Mifflin, 1977.

Collier, John. *Visual Anthropology: Photography as Research Method*. Rev. ed. New York: Holt, Rinehart, and Winston, 1986.

Corkin, Jane, and Dault, Gary Michael. *Children in Photography: 150 years*. Willowdale, Ontario, Canada: Firefly Books, 1990.

Crew, Spencer. *Field to Factory: Afro-American Migration, 1915–1940*. Washington, D.C.: Smithsonian Institution, 1987.

Curtis, James. "Documentary Photographs as Texts." *American Quarterly* 40 (June 1988): 246–52.

Darrah, William Culp. *Stereo Views: A History of Stereographs in America and Their Collection*. Gettysburg, Pa.: Times and News Publishing, 1964.

Eakle, Arlene H. *Photographic Analysis*. Salt Lake City, Utah: Family History World, 1976.

Fleischhauer, Carl, and Brannan, Beverly W., eds. *Documenting America, 1935–1943*. Berkeley: University of California Press, 1988.

Gifford, Don. *The Farther Shore: A Natural History of Perception, 1798–1984*. New York: Atlantic Monthly Press, 1990.

Gilbert, George. *Photography: The Early Years, A Historical Guide for Collectors*. New York: Harper and Row, 1980.

Goldstein, Ruth M., and Zornow, Edith. *The Screen Image of Youth: Movies about Children and Adolescents*. Metuchen, N.J.: Scarecrow Press, 1980.

Graves, Ken, and Payne, Mitchell. *American Snapshots*. Oakland, Calif.: Scrimshaw Press, 1977.

Gutman, Judith Mara. *Lewis W. Hine, 1874–1940: Two Perspectives*. New York: Grossman Publishers, 1974.

Hurley, F. Jack. *Portrait of a Decade: Roy Stryker and the Development of Documentary Photography in the Thirties*. New York: De Capo Press, 1972.

Jackson, Kathy Merlock. *Images of Children in American Film: A Sociocultural Analysis*. Metuchen, N.J.: Scarecrow Press, 1986.

Jacobs, David L. "Domestic Snapshots: Toward a Grammar of Motives." *Journal of American Culture* 4 (Spring 1981): 93–105.

Jareckie, Stephen B. *American Photog-*

raphy, 1840–1900. Worcester, Mass.: Worcester Art Museum, 1976.

Kismaric, Susan. *American Children: Photographs from the Collection of the Museum of Modern Art*. New York: Museum of Modern Art, 1980.

Lemann, Nicholas. *Out of the Forties*. New York: Simon & Schuster, 1981.

Lesy, Michael. *Bearing Witness: A Photographic Chronicle of American Life, 1860–1945*. New York: Pantheon Books, 1982.

———. *Time Frames: The Meaning of Family Pictures*. New York: Pantheon Books, 1980.

———. *Wisconsin Death Trip*. New York: Pantheon Books, 1973.

Library of Congress. *Image of America: Early Photography, 1839–1900, a Catalog*. Washington, D.C.: Library of Congress, 1957.

Macdonald, Gus. *Camera Victorian Eyewitness: A History of Photography, 1826–1913*. New York: Viking Press, 1979.

Motz, Marilyn. "Visual Autobiography: Photograph Albums of Turn-of-the Century Midwestern Women." *American Quarterly* 41 (Mar. 1989): 63–92.

National Archives. *The American Image: Photographs from the National Archives, 1860–1960*. New York: Pantheon Books, 1979.

Newhall, Beaumont. *The Daguerreotype in America*. 2d ed. New York: Dover Publications, 1976.

———. *The History of Photography from 1839 to the Present*. Rev. ed. New York: Museum of Modern Art, 1982.

Norfleet, Barbara. *The Champion Pig:*

Great Moments in American Life. New York: Penguin Books, 1980.

Peters, Marsha, and Mergen, Bernard. " 'Doing the Rest': The Uses of Photographs in American Studies." *American Quarterly* 39 (Bibliography Issue, 1977): 280–303.

Riis, Jacob. *How the Other Half Lives: Studies among the Tenements of New York*. 1890; reprint, New York: Dover Publications, 1971.

Rinhart, Floyd, and Rinhart, Marion. *American Daguerreian Art*. New York: Clarkson N. Potter, 1976.

Rothstein, Arthur. *The Depression Years as Photographed by Arthur Rothstein*. New York: Dover Publications, 1978.

Rudisill, Richard. *Mirror Image: The Influence of the Daguerreotype on American Society*. Albuquerque: University of New Mexico Press, 1971.

Sandler, Martin W. *American Image: Photographing One-Hundred Fifty Years in the Life of a Nation*. Chicago: Contemporary Books, 1989.

Schlereth, Thomas J. "Historians and Material Culture." *OAH Newsletter* 13 (Nov. 1985): 3–5.

———. *Material Culture: A Research Guide*. Lawrence: University Press of Kansas, 1985.

Seixas, Peter. "Lewis Hine: From 'Social' to 'Interpretive' Photographer." *American Quarterly* 39 (Fall 1987): 381–409.

Shaw, Renata V. *A Century of Photographs Selected from the Collections of the Library of Congress*. Washington, D.C.: Library of Congress, 1980.

Simpson, Jerry, comp. *The Way*

Life Was: A Photographic Treasury of the American Past. New York: Praeger, 1974.

Sontag, Susan. *On Photography*. New York: Farrar, Straus, and Giroux, 1973.

Stange, Maren. *Symbols of Ideal Life: Social Documentary Photography in America, 1890–1950*. Cambridge: Cambridge University Press, 1989.

Stryker, Roy Emerson, and Wood, Nancy. *In This Proud Land: America 1935–1943 as Seen in the FSA Photographs*. New York: Galahad Books, 1973.

Taft, Robert. *Photography and the American Scene: A Social History, 1839–1889*. New York: Dover Publications, 1964.

Trachtenberg, Alan. *Reading American Photographs: Images as History, Mathew Brady to Walker Evans*. New York: Hill and Wang, 1989.

Wagner, Jon, ed. *Images of Information: Still Photography in the Social Sciences*. Beverly Hills, Calif.: Sage Publications, 1979.

Willing, William. *Photography in America: The Formative Years, 1839–1900*. Albuquerque: University of New Mexico Press, 1978.

White, Hayden. "Historiography and Historiophoty." *American Historical Review* 93 (Dec. 1988): 1193–1199.

CHAPTER 9.
Children as Chattel

1. By the start of the Civil War in 1861, 99 percent of U.S. slaves were native-born and most of them were fourth-, fifth-, and sixth-generation Americans. Robert W. Fogel and Stanley L. Engerman, *Time on the Cross: The Economics of American Negro Slavery* (Boston: Little, Brown, 1974), 23–24.

2. John W. Blassingame, *The Slave Community: Plantation Life in the Antebellum South* (New York: Oxford University Press, 1972), 94.

3. The nursing house in these large holdings allowed the owner to monitor the care given to slave babies and to free mothers as soon as possible for return to productive labor. Thomas L. Webber, *Deep like the Rivers: Education in the Slave Quarter Community, 1831–1865* (New York: W. W. Norton, 1978), 11. See also the narrative of John Crawford in *Bullwhip Days: The Slaves Remember—An Oral History*, ed. James Mellon (New York: Weidenfeld and Nicolson, 1988), 316.

4. The "old nurse," who could be appointed to the role either by the owner or by the slaves, appears to have been a salient figure in the lives of many slave children. Descriptions of the nurse, gleaned from narratives and biographies, are drawn with intense warmth and affection by some and with bitter scorn by others. She often emerges in these accounts as a much fuller, more completely drawn figure than the natural mother, with adjectives and emotionally toned characterizations applied to her that appear to be more varied than those applied to mothers. This would happen if interactions with the nurse had been more frequent, diverse, or meaningful than those with the natural mother.

5. The contemporary view is that

the initial parental bonding and the establishment of the mother as an attachment figure are primarily a function of, first, the time spent interacting with the child, and second, the quality of the interaction. Mary D. S. Ainsworth, "The Development of Infant-Mother Attachment," in *Review of Child Development Research*, ed. Bettye M. Caldwell and Henry N. Ricciuti, 3 vols. (Chicago: University of Chicago Press, 1973), vol. 3, and Mary D. S. Ainsworth, M. Blehar, Everett Waters, and S. Wall, *Patterns of Attachment* (Hillsdale, N.J.: Erlbaum, 1978). The issue of bonding arises from the discussion in some of the literature of a supposed indifference of many slave mothers to their babies—an attitude that if true would have curtailed the mother's emotional bonding to the child and might have prevented the child's attachment later. There is simply not enough evidence to indicate that, despite the restricted time spent with each other, anything other than normal bonding and attachment took place in the vast majority of slave mother-infant pairs. For a discussion of some reasons why observers may have detected an "indifference," see Eugene Genovese, *Roll, Jordan, Roll: The World the Slaves Made* (New York: Pantheon Books, 1974), 495–97.

6. David Ausubel, *Theory and Problems of Adolescent Development* (New York: Grune and Stratton, 1954). See also Marvin D. Wyne, Kinnard P. White, and Richard H. Coop, *The Black Self* (Englewood Cliffs, N.J.: 1974), 35–36.

7. Sarah Fitzpatrick, aged ninety, interviewed in 1938 by Thomas Campbell; John Blassingame, *Slave Testimony: Two Centuries of Letters, Speeches, Interviews, and Autobiographies* (Baton Rouge: Louisiana State University Press, 1977), 644.

8. The Federal Writers' Project interview with former slave Susan Hamlin is used by James West Davidson and Mark Hamilton Lytle to illustrate some cautions in valuing the differences in responses that were elicited by white and black interviewers. As Susan "Hamilton," she omitted this account in a subsequent interview with a black FWP interviewer. However, the selectivity does not obscure the psychological impact this experience had on the young slave, especially the pointed recollection that "he turn his back and laugh." James West Davidson and Mark Hamilton Lytle, "The View from the Bottom Rail," in *After the Fact: The Art of Historical Detection* (New York: Alfred A. Knopf, 1982), 169–204.

9. Leslie H. Owens, *This Species of Property: Slave Life and Culture in the Old South* (New York: Oxford University Press, 1977), 204.

10. Davidson and Lytle, *After the Fact*, 195.

11. Mellon, *Bullwhip Days*, 196.

12. Blassingame, *Slave Community*, 207.

13. Mellon, *Bullwhip Days*, 287–88.

14. Nathan I. Huggins, *Black Odyssey: The Afro-American Ordeal in Slavery* (New York: Vintage Books, 1979), 131.

15. The focus of the argument

has been the extent to which coresidential, two-parent families existed during slavery, with the major positions having been advanced by Ulrich B. Phillips, Kenneth M. Stampp, Eugene D. Genovese, and Herbert G. Gutman. I am persuaded by impressionistic evidence from slave narratives, slave testimony, and slave biography that the incidence of such families does not square with Gutman's conclusion that slave children characteristically lived in two-parent households. Some recent regional and longitudinal analyses of slave-family households and family slaveholdings, using estate records, plantation records, tax digests, bills of sale, county records, and Federal census schedules, suggest that both the size of the holding and the position of the holding in the developmental cycle were critical factors in determining slave-family composition. Carole Elaine Merritt writes that on units of twenty or fewer slaves, where about 50 percent of slaves resided, "two-parent households were demographically infeasible for most slave children." An analysis of the kinship and household structure of a moderate-sized family holding in two Georgia counties between 1820 and 1860 showed that more than 80 percent of the slave children did not live with both parents and that over 75 percent of slave adults did not live with mates. Carole Elaine Merritt, *Slave Family and Household Arrangements in Piedmont, Georgia* (Ph.D. diss., Emory University, 1986), 219. Ann Patton Malone

argues that the position of the slaveholding in the developmental cycle influenced household-prevalence patterns. Regardless of when they were inventoried, recently established holdings (brought about by disruptions and redistributions due to death, sale, purchase of significant portions, or by estate transfer) showed fewer coresident unions and more households consisting of mothers and children; older, more established holdings more often consisted of households and individuals spanning two or three generations. Ann Patton Malone, *The Nineteenth Century Slave Family in Rural Louisiana: Its Household and Community Structure* (Ph.D. diss., Tulane University, 1985).

16. In advising that the concept of family as applied to slaves be reconsidered, Leslie H. Owens suggested that even as it related to the ways blacks used it in the quarters, the term had several overlapping meanings (Owens, *This Species of Property*, 192).

17. Although the statements of loyalty and affection of former slaves for their masters were to some extent affected by the race of interviewers and the questions they asked, there is enough evidence to suggest that many slaveholdings represented more than units whose individuals were tied together by property laws and caste relationships and that *familial* relationships developed that in some ways helped them cohere. It appears that accounts of deep affection do not occur as frequently in the slave testimonies (published

by antebellum newspapers and magazines primarily to support the abolitionist cause), fugitive slave accounts, or biographies by former slaves.

18. The centrality of owner "Grandpappy" Jake as an emotionally bonded figure in this former slave's life is apparent throughout the narrative. Mellon, *Bullwhip Days*, 305–10.

19. Blassingame, *Slave Community*, 203–4.

20. The ability to portray the prescribed and apparently highly rewarded (by the slaveholder) role of the grinning, mindless, infantile flunky was an artfully honed act requiring a highly sophisticated "stage presence . . . that is the capacity to play his role convincingly before the master, even while he . . . sabotaged the effort in actuality." Charles H. Nichols, *Many Thousands Gone: The Ex-Slaves' Account of Their Bondage and Freedom* (Leiden, Netherlands: Brill, 1963), cited in Norman R. Yetman, *The Slave Personality: A Test of the "Sambo" Hypothesis* (Ph.D. diss., University of Pennsylvania, 1970).

21. James S. Jackson, Wayne R. McCullough, and Gerald Gurin, "Group Identity Development within Black Families." In *Black Families*, ed. Harriette P. McAdoo (Beverly Hills, Calif.: Sage Publications, 1981), 252–63.

22. Interview with Mingo White at age eighty-five–ninety. Norman R. Yetman, ed., *Voices from Slavery* (New York: Holt, Rinehart and Winston, 1970), 310–15.

23. David Kenneth Wiggins, *Sport and Popular Pastimes in the Plantation Community* (Ph.D. diss., University of Maryland, 1979), 62.

24. Ibid., 72–76.

25. Postponement of full production from prepubertal children was done for economic and not for humanitarian reasons. The (economic) reality was that many slaveholders believed that a slowed maturity during childhood guaranteed maximum productivity later, that work during childhood weakened the foundation for physical health in adulthood, and that a slow breaking-in reduced the trauma of going to the fields and facing the whip. Genovese, *Roll, Jordan, Roll*, 504–5.

26. Webber, *Deep like the Rivers*, 23.

27. Narrative by George Fleming in Mellon, *Bullwhip Days*, 259.

28. Norman Yetman, *Life under the "Peculiar Institution"*, 232, cited in Webber, *Deep like the Rivers*, 23.

29. Mingo White in Yetman, *Voices from Slavery*, 311.

30. James Axtell describes the passage of colonial children from child to adult as one that was unbroken but clearly marked by cultural signposts. James Axtell, *The School upon a Hill: Education and Society in Colonial New England* (New Haven, Conn.: Yale University Press, 1974), 98–100. Such signposts or milestones (except for categories defined by work) are difficult to find for slave children. Much of their work as children consisted of doing what their parents did—but probably less of it. Signposts based on expecta-

tions of maturity, the assumption of responsibility, and recognition of a time when personal or legal accountability was reached were only weakly applicable to slaves if at all. There were, however, strong moral standards and codes of behavior established for adults and to some extent for children in the quarters, but further research needs to be done to determine how such standards were incorporated as signposts of development.

31. Lunsford Lane, *The Narrative of Lunsford Lane, Formerly of Raleigh, North Carolina* (Boston: By the author, 1842), 13, cited in Webber, *Deep like the Rivers*, 24.

32. Jacqueline Jones, " 'My Mother Was Much of a Woman,' " *Feminist Studies* 8 (Summer 1982): 247, in *Articles on American Slavery*, ed. Paul Finkleman, 18 vols. (New York: Garland, 1989), 9: 195–229.

33. Mollie Dawson in Mellon, *Bullwhip Days*, 423.

34. Analysis of the reports of forced sex and sexual exploitation in the slave narratives indicates that, despite underreporting, forced sex occurred on 20 percent of the plantations. Catherine Clinton, "Caught in the Web of the Big House," in Finkleman, *Articles on American Slavery*, 9: 9–24.

CHAPTER 10.
Golden Girls

1. Susanna Bryant Dakin, "The Scent of Violets" (unpublished manuscript, 1966, Bancroft Library,

University of California, Berkeley), 45–46.

2. Victoria Bissell Brown, "Golden Girls: Female Socialization in Los Angeles, 1880–1910" (Ph.D. diss., University of California at San Diego, 1985. Chapter two, "Female Nature," discusses the theories of child development popular in this era and the ways in which these theories reinforced traditional American androcentrism and popular notions that femininity was innate, not socialized.

3. Biographical information on Susanna Bryant Dakin is available in her files at the Bancroft Library, University of California, Berkeley. Additional information on the Bixby family is available at Rancho Los Cerritos Museum, Long Beach, California.

4. Rufus Steele, "The Red Car of Empire," *Sunset* 31 (Oct. 1913): 710.

5. Frank Beach, "The Transformation of California, 1900–1920: The Effects of Westward Movement on California's Growth and Development in the Progressive Period" (Ph.D. diss, University of California, Berkeley, 1963), 207–8; J. E. Scott, "Los Angeles, the Old and the New," *Western Insurance News—Supplement* 8 (1911): 12; Steele, "Red Car of Empire," 712.

6. Ratcliffe Hicks, *Southern California, or, the Land of the Afternoon* (Springfield, Mass.: Springfield Printing and Binding Co., 1898), 23.

7. Dakin, "The Scent of Violets," 27.

8. Robert Fogelson, *The Fragmented Metropolis: Los Angeles, 1850–1930*

(Cambridge, Mass.: Harvard University Press, 1967), 145. For an expanded discussion of Los Angeles in this period, see Brown, "Golden Girls," ch. 1.

9. Elaine Tyler May, *Great Expectations: Marriage and Divorce in Post-Victorian America* (Chicago: University of Chicago Press, 1980), 15.

10. Carolyn Meyberg Sichel, "Los Angeles Memories," *Western States Jewish Historical Quarterly* 7 (Oct. 1974): 57.

11. Annual report of the school nurse to the Los Angeles Board of Education, *Los Angeles Board of Education Report, 1906–1907*, 132.

12. Dakin, "Scent of Violets," 4.

13. Marshall Stimson, "Fun, Fights, and Fiestas" (printed in Los Angeles in 1966 and available at the Los Angeles Public Library), 32.

14. Report of the President of the Federation of Child-Study Circles, *Los Angeles Board of Education Report, 1901–1902*, 133. "History—Los Angeles Tenth District," unpublished report by the California Congress of Parents and Teachers, n.d., 3, quoted in Margaret Deffterios, "History of the California Congress of Parents and Teachers" (Ph.D. diss., University of California, Berkeley, 1958), 13.

The child-study movement was both an academic research effort and a popular vehicle for parent education. Mothers would meet in child-study circles to read and discuss the research and theoretical writings of the academic leaders of the movement, especially G. Stanley Hall. California was second only to Massachusetts in the level of its academic commitment to child study, and Los Angeles was the center of the popular child-study movement. So great was the interest in child study in Los Angeles that the Board of Education even included reports from the president of the Federation of Child-Study Circles in its annual reports.

15. Childrearing books in this era typically extolled the "profession" of motherhood. For a discussion of this trend in the literature at the time, see Brown, "Golden Girls," ch. 2. For examples of this trend, see Jane Dearborn Mills, *The Mother Artist* (Chicago: Palmer Co., 1904); Elizabeth Harrison, *A Study of Child Nature* (Chicago: R. R. Donnelley and Sons, 1890); Susan E. Blow, *Letters to a Mother* (New York: D. Appleton, 1912); Barnetta Brown, "Mothers' Mistakes and Fathers' Failures," *Ladies' Home Journal*, Jan. 1900, 30; Nora A. Smith, "Training for Parenthood," *Outlook* 49 (Jan. 6, 1894): 24–25; "Are Mothers Fitted for Child Study?" *Child-Study Monthly* 3 (Feb. 1898): 460–61; "Desirable Reforms in Motherhood," *Arena* 28 (Nov. 1902): 499–505; Mrs. Julia Hallman, "The Mother's Work," *Child-Study Monthly* 5 (Mar. 1900): 431–32; Rosemary Baum, "Kindergarten Methods for Mothers," *Harper's Bazaar*, Dec. 1, 1900, 1998; Mrs. Frederick Schoff, "The Task of the American Mother," *Independent* 55 (Jan. 1, 1903): 35–37, and "The Purpose of the National Congress of Mothers," *Annals of the American Academy of Political and Social Science* 25 (Jan. 1905): 200–202; Anna Rogers, "Why American Mothers

Fail," *Atlantic Monthly*, Mar. 1908, 289–97; Sarah Comstock, "Mothercraft: A New Profession for Women," *Good Housekeeping* Dec. 1914, 672–78; Olivia R. Fernow, "Does Higher Education Unfit Women for Motherhood?" *Popular Science Monthly*, April 1905, 573–75. See also Jane S. Mulligan, "The Madonna and Child in American Culture, 1830–1916" (Ph.D. diss., University of California, Los Angeles, 1975).

16. Horace Vachell, *Life and Sport on the Pacific Slope* (New York: Dodd, Mead, 1901), 236.

Observers regularly noted that the majority of churchgoers in the City of Los Angeles were women and children. Pomona's female minister, Lila F. Sprague, speculated that this was because women were "more dependent upon the social life of the church for that contact with others which men get in following their ordinary pursuits." The more general view, however, was that women were by nature more concerned with moral and spiritual matters than were men. Rev. Lila F. Sprague, "Women's Work in the Church," in *Women's Parliament of Southern California: A Magazine of Papers Read at the Women's Parliament Held in Los Angeles, November 15–16, 1892* (Los Angeles: Unity Church Leage, 1893), n.p. Manuscript collection, University of California, Los Angeles Research Library.

17. William J. Shearer, *Management and Training of Children* (New York: Richardson, Smith, 1904), 123–24.

18. Dakin, "Scent of Violets," 53.

19. Stimson, "Fun, Fights, and Fiestas," 26.

20. Ibid., 130–31.

21. Rufus Steele, "Red Car of Empire," 710.

22. Blanche Gray, *Ruffled Petticoat Days* (Culver City, Calif.: Murray and Gee, 1953), 96–98.

23. Katharine Bixby Hotchkis, *Trip with Father* (San Francisco: California Historical Society, 1971), 10, 24, 1. In introducing the Bixby family at the beginning of her story, Hotchkis remarked that "naturally," her father had been "disappointed that his first three children were not boys."

24. C. P. Selden, "The Rule of the Mother," *North American Review* 161 (Nov. 1895): 160. In "The Suburban Child," Mrs. Samuel Lindsay expressed concern that suburbia would damage boys because it was so totally female and so comfortable. *Pedagogical Seminary* 16 (Dec. 1909): 499–500.

25. The examples listed here of boys' employment with fathers reflect the general problem with Los Angeles sources. The recollections available are from those in the middle and upper classes. There, the differences between sons' and daughters' employment with fathers is marked. It is possible that this difference was less notable among working class families; daughters there may have had more experiences working alongside fathers in the family store or at the small factory where the father was employed. We do not yet have a clear enough picture of the occupational structure in Los Angeles in these years to be able to speculate on the likelihood of such arrangements. The most we can say at this point is that middle-

and upper-class boys and girls were being socialized for the economic roles regarded as appropriate to their class.

26. Harry Bixby, diary, Jan. 1, 1885–Dec. 31, 1885 (unpublished manuscript, Rancho Los Cerritos Museum, Long Beach), 12–13, 22.

27. Harold Story, "Memoirs of Harold Story, 1901–1930," (unpublished manuscript, UCLA Oral History Project, 1967, University of California at Los Angeles Research Library, Special Collections), 120.

28. Ibid., 103.

29. Harry Carr, *Los Angeles: City of Dreams* (New York: D. Appleton-Century, 1935), 173. Bixby, diary, 22.

30. Thomas Talbert, *My Sixty Years in California* (Huntington Beach, Calif.: News Press, 1952), 13–15; Maynard McFie, *The Gay Nineties* (Los Angeles: Sunset Club, 1945), 13.

31. Story, "Memoirs," 121–22.

32. Stimson, "Fun, Fights, and Fiestas," 37.

33. Helen P. Kennedy, M.D., "Effect of High School Work upon Girls during Adolescence," *Pedagogical Seminary* 3 (June 1896): 478.

34. F. G. Bonser, "Chums: A Study in Youthful Friendships," *Pedagogical Seminary* 9 (June 1902): 221–36; William Forbush, "The Social Pedagogy of Boyhood," *Pedagogical Seminary* 7 (Oct. 1900): 307–45; Amy Tanner, *The Child: His Thinking, Feeling, and Doing* (Chicago: Rand, McNally, 1904), 409; Irving King, *The Psychology of Child Development* (Chicago: University of Chicago Press, 1903), 203.

35. Annual Report of the Hospital Society of Los Angeles, 1904–1905

(Los Angeles Municipal Library, Los Angeles City Hall), 28–31.

36. Anna Kohler, "Children's Sense of Money," *Studies in Education* 1 (Mar. 1897): 323–31.

37. Ibid., 327–28.

38. Ibid., 329.

39. Ibid., 330.

40. Ibid., 325.

41. Ibid., 326.

42. Katherine Chandler, "Children's Purposes," *Child Study Monthly* 3 (Sept. 1897): 130.

43. Ibid., 132.

44. Ibid., 130–31.

45. Earl Barnes, "Discipline at Home and in the School," *Studies in Education* 1 (Jan. 1897): 270–72.

46. Interview with "A Woman, Age 72," in *America's Families: A Documentary History*, ed. Donald M. Scott and Bernard Wishy (New York: Harper and Row, 1982), 434.

47. Arcadia Bandini Brennan, "Arcadian Memories of California: Childhood at Guajome Rancho," (unpublished, undated manuscript at Bancroft Library, University of California at Berkeley), 4.

48. Mrs. Theodore W. Birney, *Childhood* (New York: Frederick A. Stokes, 1905), 121. "The American Girl a Bore," *North American Review* 183 (Oct. 1906): 821.

Birney sent quite a different message to mothers about how to play with sons. The ideal mother, wrote Birney, knew "all the technical and slang terms descriptive of all the games that are the delight of boy nature." This mother was "ready with fresh marble bags for the marble season," could manufacture kites and thought baseball "a truly wonderful game." The felt need for mothers to be available to their sons in this way partially explains the tolerance for some play with boys during a female's childhood.

49. "School Days," *Vox Puellarum*, Westlake School newspaper, June 1911, 39. Westlake School Alumnae Office, Los Angeles.

50. The leader in the field of developmental psychology—or "child-study" as it was called at the time—was G. Stanley Hall of Clark University. According to Hall's theory of "recapitulation," stages in child development recapitulated the stages in human evolution. Since Hall and his colleagues regarded sex differentiation as a characteristic of advanced civilizations, their theory predicted few differences between boys and girls until adolescence, when puberty supposedly brought on the "dawn of civilization" in the individual. Even though all the findings of child-study research in this era showed sex differences in behavior long before adolescence, advocates of recapitulation resisted the implication that sex roles were the result of socialization rather than of biology. Hall himself dismissed as simplistic all attempts to explain children's behavior in terms of their environment. He and his colleagues insisted throughout the period between 1880 and 1910 that evidence of sex differences prior to puberty proved that a hereditary predisposition for certain sex-typed behaviors had been laid down very early in the evolutionary history of the species. For further discussion of recapitulation theory and

its relationship to gender-role attitudes in this period, see Brown, "Golden Girls," chs. 2 and 3. See also G. Stanley Hall, *Adolescence* (New York: D. Appleton, 1904); G. Stanley Hall, "Recent Advances in Child Study," *Pedagogical Seminary* 15 (Sept. 1908): 356–57; Richard Lowry, *The Evolution of Psychological Theory: 1600 to the Present* (Chicago: Aldine-Atherton, 1971), 124; Edwin G. Boring, "The Influence of Evolutionary Theory upon American Psychological Thought," in *Evolutionary Thought in America*, ed. Stowe Persons (New Haven, Conn.: Yale University Press, 1950), 279–80; Duane Schultz, *History of Modern Psychology*, 2d ed. (New York: Academic Press, 1975), 144.

51. Dakin, "Scent of Violets," 5.

52. Sarah Bixby-Smith, *Adobe Days* (Cedar Rapids, Iowa: Torch Press, 1925); Harry Bixby, diary. Though Harry Bixby's diary is that of an adolescent, many of his comments relate to issues of play rather than of social life.

53. Bixby-Smith, *Adobe Days*, 140.

54. Ibid., 141. In remembering her doll play with Harry, Sarah commented that "there was no sex distinction as to the work to be done," without noting that a fundamental sex distinction existed in that it was unusual to have Harry play with dolls at all.

55. Ibid.; Bixby, diary.

56. Bixby-Smith, *Adobe Days*, 118.

57. Ibid., 122.

58. Ibid.

59. Bixby, diary, 24, 54.

60. Ibid., 52.

61. Dakin, "Scent of Violets," 82.

62. Ibid., 49–50.

63. Ibid., 85.

64. Ibid., 13.

65. Frances Cooper Kroll, *Memories of Rancho Santa Rosa and Santa Barbara* (privately printed, 1961), 85.

66. Ibid., 83.

67. Ibid., 3.

68. Ibid., 35, 84–85.

69. Ibid., 5–6, 80.

70. Ibid., 80.

71. Bixby, diary, 54, 61.

72. Pearl Chase (unpublished interview with Gibbs Smith, UCSB Oral History Project, 1971, University of California at Santa Barbara Library, Special Collections), 25.

73. Stimson, "Fun, Fights, and Fiestas," 44.

74. Ibid., 28.

75. Mary Wills, *A Winter in California* (Norristown, Pa.: n.p., 1889), 63. Hicks, *Southern California*, 35–36.

76. Stimson, "Fun, Fights, and Fiestas," 33.

77. Ibid., 34.

78. Kroll, "Memories," 66.

79. Hotchkis, *Trip with Father*, 3.

80. Ibid., 1.

81. Ibid., 3.

82. "The American Girl Overalls," advertisement in *Land of Sunshine* 12 (April 1900): n.p.

83. "Bicycle Spill," *Los Angeles Times*, Jan. 11, 1895, 10. According to Henry W. Splitter, the number of bicycles in Los Angeles increased from fifty in 1890 to thirty thousand in 1899, and by the late 1890s, "more persons in southern California rode bicycles than horse-drawn vehicles." "Los Angeles Recreation, 1846–1900," *Historical Society of Southern California Quarterly* 43 (Mar. 1961): 57.

84. Catherine Egbert Dace, "Early San Fernando Memoirs," 42 (unpublished manuscript, UCLA Oral History Project, 1961. Manuscript collection, University of California, Los Angeles Research Library.)

85. Nellie McGraw Hedgepeth, "My Early Days in San Francisco," *Pacific Historian* 5 (Nov. 1961): 161–62.

86. Splitter, "Los Angeles Recreation," 57.

87. Hedgepeth, "My Early Days," 159.

88. Bixby, diary, 10.

89. Ervin King, "Boys' Thrills in Los Angeles of the '70's and '80's," *Historical Society of Southern California Quarterly* 30 (Dec. 1948): 303–16.

90. Edwin R. Bingham, "The Saga of the Los Angeles Chinese" (M.A. thesis, Occidental College, Los Angeles, 1942), 30.

91. L. J. Rose, Jr., *L. J. Rose of Sunny Slope, 1827–1899, California Pioneer, Fruit Grower, Wine Maker, Horse Breeder* (San Marino, Calif.: Huntington Library, 1959), 219.

92. Bixby, diary, 50.

93. Bixby-Smith, *Adobe Days*, 161.

94. Bixby, diary, 50–51.

95. Bixby-Smith, *Adobe Days*, 161.

96. Will S. Monroe, "Play Interests of Children," *National Education Association Proceedings* 43 (1899): 1088.

97. Ibid., 1086. Even in the less physical games, Monroe found sex segregation. For example, 28 percent of the boys in his sample but only 4 percent of the girls named "marbles" as a favorite game.

98. Genevra Sisson, "Children's Plays," *Studies in Education* 1 (Nov. 1896): 171–74.

99. Ibid., 172.

100. Ibid., 173.

101. Will S. Monroe, "Children's Ambitions," *Journal of Education* 43 (June 18, 1896): 414.

102. Clara Vostrovsky, "A Study of Children's Reading Tastes," *Addresses and Record of the Proceedings of the State Teachers' Association of California* (1899): 275–87.

103. Ibid., 283.

104. Ibid., 284.

105. Anna Kohler, "How Children Judge Character," *Studies in Education* 1 (Sept. 1896): 94–97.

106. Ibid., 94.

107. Ibid., 95.

108. Ibid., 97.

109. Anna Kohler Barnes, "Children's Ideas of Lady and Gentleman," *Studies in Education* 2 (June 1, 1902): 147.

110. Loretta Berner, "Sketches from 'Way Back," *Los Fierros* 7 (Spring 1970): 2.

CHAPTER 11.
"Ties That Bind and Bonds That Break"

1. Marion Elderton, ed., *Case Studies of Unemployment* (Philadelphia: University of Pennsylvania Press, 1931), 28–29.

2. White House Conference on Child Health and Protection (WHC), *The Adolescent in the Family: A Study of Personality Development in the Home Environment*, Ernest W. Burgess, chairman (New York: Appleton-Century, 1934), 246.

3. W. O. Saunders, "Getting Acquainted with Father: A Confession," *American Magazine*, (Feb. 1923), 39, 174, 177.

4. WHC, *Adolescent in the Family*, 210.

5. Margarete Simpson, *Parent Preferences of Young Children* (New York: Teachers College, Columbia University Contributions to Education, no. 652, 1935), 25.

6. WHC, *Adolescent in the Family*, 133. The figures on young adolescents appear later in the essay. In the study of young adults (1,336 males and an equal number of females), only about one-half the sons and only one-fifth as many daughters confided as completely in their fathers as in their mothers. See Meyer Nimkoff, "Parent-Child Intimacy," *Social Forces* 7 (1928): 244–49.

7. H. Meltzer, "Children's Attitudes to Parents," *American Journal of Orthopsychiatry* 5 (1935): 244–65.

8. The *Women's Studies Encyclopedia* offers succinct and useful definitions of both patriarchy and gender. "Patriarchy is the system of male dominance by which men as a group acquire and maintain power over women as a group." "Gender is a cultural construct: the distinction in roles, behavior, and mental and emotional characteristics between females and males developed by a society." See *Women's Studies Encyclopedia*, ed. Helen Tierney, 2 vols. (New York: Greenwood Press, 1989), 1:153, 265.

9. Elderton, *Case Studies of Unemployment*, 390.

10. Tamara Hareven, *Family Time and Industrial Time: The Relationship between the Family and Work in a New England Industrial Community* (Cambridge: Cambridge University Press, 1986), 189.

11. Elderton, *Case Studies of Unemployment*, 44.

12. Ibid., 104. For other examples of cases in which children lost respect for their father or in which fathers became irritable or abusive toward their children because of unemployment see 99, 104, 133, 175, 179, 258, 272, 363.

13. Ibid., 69.

14. Ibid., 158; for other examples of children's delinquency in the wake of their fathers' economic failure see 116–17, 208–9.

15. Hutchins Hapgood quoted in Abraham Karp, *Golden Door to America: The Jewish Immigrant Experience* (New York: Penguin, 1977), 141.

16. Irving Howe and Kenneth Libo, eds., *How We Lived: A Documentary History of Immigrant Jews in America, 1880–1930* (New York: Richard Marek, 1979), 45.

17. Steffens's autobiography quoted in Karp, *Golden Door to America*, 141.

18. Grace Grimaldi was interviewed by Elizabeth Ewen for the latter's book, *Immigrant Women in the Land of Dollars: Life and Culture on the Lower East Side, 1890–1925* (New York: Monthly Review Press, 1985), 190.

19. Ibid., 195; Howe and Libo, *How We Lived*, 130.

20. Budd Schulberg, *What Makes Sammy Run?* (New York: Random House, 1941), 237.

21. Howe and Libo, *How We Lived*, 130.

22. Kathy Peiss analyzes the origins and shape of working-class youth culture in *Cheap Amusements: Working Women and Leisure in Turn-of-the-Century New York* (Philadelphia: Temple University Press, 1986). Susan Porter Benson explores the work culture of saleswomen in *Counter Cultures: Saleswomen, Managers, and Customers in American Department Stores, 1890–1940* (Urbana: University of Illinois Press, 1986).

23. Peiss, *Cheap Amusements*, 38–49, 98, 101–3.

24. Quoted in ibid., 70, 72.

25. H. Meltzer, "Economic Security and Children's Attitudes to Parents," *American Journal of Orthopsychiatry* 6 (1936): 594–95.

26. Ibid., 597.

27. Ibid., 601.

28. Ibid., 602–5.

29. Middle-class fathers were more likely to attend PTA meetings and child-study groups than their working-class counterparts; moreover, they took a more active part in disciplining the children. See WHC, *The Young Child in the Home: A Survey of Three Thousand American Families* (New York: Appleton-Century, 1934) 210–21, 237.

30. WHC, *Adolescent in the Family*, 257–58.

31. Ibid., 145.

32. Robert S. Lynd and Helen Merrell Lynd, *Middletown: A Study in Modern American Culture* (1929;

reprint, New York: Harcourt, Brace and World, 1956), 522, 524. Asked the same question of mothers, students mentioned "being a good cook and housekeeper" first; "always having time to read, talk, go on picnics or play with her children" was second.

33. WHC, *Adolescent in the Family*, 264, 266.

34. Ibid., 147. Chester T. Crowell, whose oldest of five children was twelve and whose youngest was three, exemplified the modern father. "Above all," wrote Crowell, "I accept the children as equals and grown persons, so that they feel no embarrassment in telling me their own thoughts" ("Notes of an Amateur Father," *American Mercury*, Oct. 1924, 137–42).

35. WHC, *Adolescent in the Family*, 195–96.

36. Ibid., 151, 154.

37. Ibid., 205.

38. George A. Lundberg, Mirra Komarovsky, and Mary A. McInerny, *Leisure: A Suburban Study* (New York: Columbia University Press, 1934), 183–84; WHC, *Adolescent in the Family*, 163–65. After examining the pattern of leisure among American families, Ernest Burgess concluded that "social interaction between members of the family during almost the only time when the entire family is at home together is limited to whatever casual conversation interrupts the reading and studying carried on by the children" (*Adolescent in the Family*, 166). In a later study involving 1,500 high-school students, Melvin J. Williams

found that 43 percent viewed their home as "a place of little companionship and partnership." Yet 80 percent also described their home as "a place where I share life with people dear to me," 56 percent as "a place to which I return eagerly," and 50 percent as "a joyful place" ("Personal and Familial Problems of High School Youths and Their Bearing upon Family Education Needs," *Social Forces* 27 [1949]: 283).

39. T. J. Jackson Lears, "From Salvation to Self-Realization: Advertising and the Therapeutic Roots of the Consumer Culture, 1880–1930," in *The Culture of Consumption: Critical Essays in American History, 1880–1980*, ed. T. J. Jackson Lears and Richard W. Fox (New York: Pantheon Books, 1983).

40. When four hundred members of five different Princeton graduating classes were asked why they had had fewer children than they ideally wanted to have, almost 60 percent listed "limited financial means" as the answer, a figure far outdistancing any other reasons to explain the disparity. See Charles P. Dennison, "Parenthood Attitudes of College Men," *Journal of Heredity* 31 (1940): 527–31.

41. Lears, "From Salvation to Self-Realization," 3–37.

42. Robert S. Lynd, "The People as Consumers," in *Recent Social Trends in the United States: Reports of the President's Research Committee on Social Trends*, 2 vols. (New York: McGraw-Hill, 1933), 2:866–67.

43. Ibid., 866.

44. Beth L. Bailey, *From Front Porch to Back Seat: Courtship in*

Twentieth-Century America (Baltimore: Johns Hopkins University Press, 1988), 13.

45. Bailey, *From Front Porch to Back Seat*, 18, 21.

46. In 1938 *Senior Scholastic* described an ideal high-school dinner date in depression America as costing over $5.50, this at a time when one-third of American families spent approximately $30.00 per year on leisure. See Bailey, *From Front Porch to Back Seat*, 60.

47. Bailey, *From Front Porch to Back Seat*, 71–73.

48. Paula Fass, *The Damned and the Beautiful: American Youth in the 1920s* (Oxford: Oxford University Press, 1977), 230.

50. Earl H. Bell, "Age Group Conflict and Our Changing Culture," *Social Forces* 12 (1933): 238.

51. Ibid., 239.

52. Ibid., 241.

53. Lynd and Lynd, *Middletown*, 522. Harold Punke's 1943 study of 7,000 high-school youth and Melvin J. Williams's post–World War II study of 1,500 high-school students contain a wealth of data on children's personal problems and their perceptions of their parents. As with the earlier investigators, Punke found that money and the social life of youth were the two most frequent sources of disagreement between parents and children. See Punke, "High-School Youth and Family Quarrels," *School and Society* 58 (Dec. 1943): 507–11 and Williams, "Personal and Familial Problems of High School Youths," 279–85. See also Marjorie T. Edwards, "What Is

Wrong with Parents," *Journal of Home Economics* 32 (Dec. 1940): 685–86.

54. Lynd and Lynd, *Middletown*, 522.

55. Bell, "Age Group Conflict and Our Changing Culture," 241.

56. Ibid., 242.

57. Ibid., 243. In Bell's judgment, mothers likewise had little substantive training to offer their daughters. Thanks to modern conveniences, packaged and prepared foods, and store-bought clothes, mothers' role in preparing daughters for housewifery had been rendered insignificant. Consequently, "the daughter is looking toward new endeavors for self-expression, endeavors even more foreign to her mother than to herself."

58. Simpson, *Parent Preferences of Young Children*, 25. Ralph Stogdill offers a useful overview of parental-preference literature in "Survey of Experiments of Children's Attitudes toward Parents: 1894–1936," *Journal of Genetic Psychology* 51 (1937): 293–303.

59. Arthur Jersild, Frances Markey, Catherine Jersild, *Children's Fears, Dreams, Wishes, Daydreams, Likes, Dislikes, Pleasant and Unpleasant Memories* (Child Development Monographs, no. 12: Bureau of Publications, Teachers College, Columbia University, New York, 1932). Meyer Nimkoff offers a brief survey of child-preference literature and an interpretation of child preference as evidenced in autobiographies in "The Child's Preference for Father or Mother," *American Sociological Review* 7 (1942): 517–24. John Anderson

found much the same patterns of preference in his analysis of 1,600 children. Although most of the children in this study registered no preference, when preference was shown it was overwhelmingly for the mother. Even among ten- to twelve-year-old boys—an age when identification with fathers would most likely be strong—only 10 percent listed their father as their favorite person in the home while 18 percent accorded their mother this status. Less surprisingly, between 3 and 4 percent of girls of this age listed their fathers as their favorite compared to 16 percent who so listed their mothers. See WHC, *Young Child in the Home*, 228–29.

60. Nimkoff, "Parent-Child Intimacy," 244–47, 249.

61. WHC, *Adolescent in the Family*, 134–35, 370. Fifty-two percent of boys and 65 percent of girls who "almost always" confided in their fathers had good personality adjustment compared to only 33 percent of boys and the same percentage of girls who "almost never" told their fathers their "joys and troubles." A later study of 1,500 high-school youth also found them much more willing to confide in their mothers than in their fathers. Seventy-one percent talked over their problems with their mothers; only 31 percent did so with their fathers. Melvin J. Williams, "Personal and Familial Problems of High School Youths," 279–85.

Certainly one does not have to be a psychohistorian to appreciate the role the sex of the child played in shaping the attitudes of the young toward their fathers; so too with the age of the child. Margarete Simpson found, for example, that although children of both sexes preferred their mothers, the tendency was slightly more marked in boys. This tendency to prefer mothers also increased with age. By the time boys were nine years old, only 10 percent preferred their fathers; 76 percent preferred their mothers. Five-year-old girls, however, confounded this pattern. Unlike all other children ages five to nine, five-year-old girls showed an overwhelming preference (60 percent) for their fathers; yet by the age of nine only 14 percent preferred their fathers. See Simpson, *Parent Preferences of Young Children*, 24–30.

This preference for mothers extended to the incidence of jealousy. Children reported being the most jealous when affection was shown by their mothers to another child. Half the children reporting jealousy noted that it occurred in this context. Thus, although 73 percent of five-year-old boys and 61 percent of five-year-old girls reported never being jealous, 14 percent of the boys and 21 percent of the girls mentioned being jealous when their mothers showed affection for another child. In contrast, only 9 percent of the boys and 14 percent of the girls felt such jealousy when their fathers showed affection for a sibling, a finding in keeping with children's preference for mothers in general. See WHC, *Young Child in the Home*, 228–33.

CHAPTER 12.
"The Only Thing I Wanted Was Freedom"

1. Ella Waldstein, inmate case file, New York State Reformatory for Women, Bedford Hills 00018, 1917, Records of the Department of Correctional Services, New York State Archives and Records Administration, State Education Department, Albany, New York 12230. Inmate case files and the names of wayward girls, family members, and friends have been changed in compliance with New York State regulations governing researchers' access to restricted documents.

2. For further examination of the impact of wage work on working-class young women in early twentieth-century America see Kathy Peiss, *Cheap Amusements: Working Women and Leisure in Turn-of-the Century New York* (Philadelphia: Temple University Press, 1985); Leslie Tentler, *Wage-Earning Women: Industrial Work and Family Life in the United States, 1900–1930* (New York: Oxford University Press, 1979); Elizabeth Ewen, *Immigrant Women in the Land of Dollars: Life and Culture on the Lower East Side, 1890–1925* (New York: Monthly Review Press, 1985; Alice Kessler-Harris, "Independence and Virtue in the Lives of Wage-Earning Women: The United States, 1870–1930," in *Women and Culture in Politics: A Century of Change*, eds. Judith Friedlander, Blanche Wiesen Cook, Alice Kessler-Harris, and Carroll Smith Rosenberg (Bloomington: Indiana University Press, 1986), 3–17. The transformation of female adolescence within the middle class is discussed in Ruth M. Alexander, " 'The Girl Problem': Class Inequity and Psychology in the Remaking of Female Adolescence, 1900–1930" (Ph.D. diss., Cornell University, 1990); John Modell, *Into One's Own: From Youth to Adulthood in the United States, 1920–1975* (Berkeley: University of California Press, 1989); Paula S. Fass, *The Damned and the Beautiful: American Youth in the 1920s* (New York: Oxford University Press, 1977).

3. For further discussion of parent-daughter conflict and the compromises attained in working-class households see Tentler, *Wage-Earning Women*, 107–14; Ewen, *Immigrant Women in the Land of Dollars*, 208–14; Peiss, *Cheap Amusements*, 67–72.

4. Nineteen of the twenty-two young women were convicted of summary or conduct offenses. Just three were convicted of minor criminal offenses. The twenty-two cases are part of a larger study of one hundred reformatory women, most committed to Bedford Hills or Albion following a police arrest (usually for solicitation) and without evidence of direct intervention by family members. My sample of twenty-two cases includes five young women committed to Albion and seventeen committed to Bedford Hills, all between the ages of sixteen and twenty-one at the time of sentencing. The sample used in this study is admittedly small and does not claim to be statistically representative. I deliberately selected cases that were richly documented, revealing the values and concerns of working-class female adoles-

cents and their families. The files include official reports documenting the inmates' families and criminal histories and their conduct at the reformatories and on parole. Many of the files also include correspondence to, from, and about individual inmates, including letters that did not pass the reformatory censors.

5. I have found no cases of young women from white middle-class, native-born families who were committed to the reformatories at the request of family members. Such families were undoubtedly unwilling to suffer the stigma of having a daughter in a reformatory and relied on methods of control that did less to disturb their social status and privacy. By the 1920s social workers and psychologists were urging both working- and middle-class parents to turn to out-patient mental-hygiene clinics for help with their adolescent daughters. See Alexander, " 'Girl Problem,' " ch. 4. One recent study suggests that mental-hygiene clinics were used by working-class parents more often than by middle-class parents (for treating problems of all kinds in children of all ages and both sexes), but the wayward girls are proof that working-class families also continued to make use of the criminal-court system. See Margo Horn, *Before It's Too Late: The Child Guidance Movement in the United States, 1922–45* (Philadelphia: Temple University Press, 1989). For a study that emphasizes middle-class use of mental-hygiene clinics see Kathleen W. Jones, "As the Twig Is Bent: American Psychiatry and

the Troublesome Child, 1890–1940," (Ph.D. diss., Rutgers, 1988).

6. The wayward girls who did not serve three-year sentences were recommitted from the regular reformatory at Bedford to its Division for Mentally Defective Delinquents. The young women in this division usually had IQs of less than 65 and their sentences were indefinite. Bedford had legal authority to keep the "mentally defective" inmates in the institution for life if necessary; however, the case files show that these young women actually followed the basic reformatory program, although at a slower pace than the other inmates. The "mentally defective" wayward girls in my sample served four-, five-, and seven-year sentences, including time spent on parole.

7. Peiss, *Cheap Amusements*, 8; Joanne J. Meyerowitz, *Women Adrift: Independent Wage Earners in Chicago, 1880–1930* (Chicago: University of Chicago Press, 1988), 141.

8. One of the fathers in this subgroup was an insurance agent and thus a white-collar rather than a manual worker. However, circumstantial evidence suggests that the man had been unable to achieve the social or economic stability that permitted entry into the middle class; he had a serious drinking problem and his wife supplemented the family income by doing piece work at home. Both of his adolescent daughters were factory workers. Only two young women in the larger group of twenty-two had fathers whose jobs placed them above the typical working-class man: one was

a rabbi, the other an owner of a silk-goods store.

9. The high percentage of working mothers in this group (23 percent) was well above the national average. In 1900 only 5.6 percent of all married women were in the labor force. That figure rose to 10.7 in 1910, dropped to 9.0 by 1920 and rose again to 11.7 by 1930. Nancy Woloch, *Women and the American Experience* (New York: Alfred A. Knopf, 1984), 544. New York's Compulsory Education Law of 1903 required all children between the ages of eight and fourteen to attend school during the months from October to June. Children between the ages of fourteen and sixteen were permitted to work as long as they obtained working papers that showed proof of their age and level of schooling. Sol Cohen, *Progressives and Urban School Reform: The Public Education Association of New York City, 1895–1954* (New York: Teachers College Press, 1964), 67–68.

10. Two young white women had emigrated to the United States with their parents as small children, one from Austria, the other from the West Indies. Two of the young black women were orphans who had been raised by relatives; one of these orphans was an immigrant from the West Indies. The third black woman lived with her mother, the father having deserted the family when she was very young. The fourth lived with a recently widowed father.

11. Louisa Parsons, Albion 00076, 1924.

12. Rae Rabinowitz, Bedford 00052, 1917.

13. In my sample, eighteen of twenty-two young women were taken to court over sexual misconduct. Of the eighteen, five were pregnant and two had just given birth at the time of their commitment to the reformatories. At least two of the wayward girls had been involved with men "outside of their faith"; one girl was involved in an interracial relationship.

14. Evelyn Blackwell, Bedford 00088, 1926.

15. Lena Meyerhoff, Bedford 00084, 1924.

16. Lena Meyerhoff, Bedford 00018, 1917; Rae Rabinowitz, Bedford 00052, 1917; Sophie Polentz, Bedford 00059, 1924.

17. Rae Rabinowitz, Bedford 00052, 1917; Ella Waldstein, Bedford 00018, 1917.

18. New York, *Laws of 1882*, ch. 410, sec. 1466; *Laws of 1886*, ch. 353; *Laws of 1903*, ch. 436; *Laws of 1914*, ch. 445. For a brief discussion of the laws see Paul W. Tappan, *Delinquent Girls in Court: A Study of the Wayward Minor Court of New York* (New York: Columbia University Press, 1947), 44–47.

19. Millicent Potter, Albion 00101, 1900.

20. Two years later the Wayward Minor Act was extended to apply to males as well as to females. New York, *Laws of 1925*, ch. 389.

21. Jessie Taft, "Mental Hygiene Problems of Normal Adolescence," *Mental Hygiene* 5 (Oct. 1921): 741–51; Gerald Pearson, "What the Adolescent Girl Needs in Her Home," *Mental Hygiene* 14 (Jan. 1930): 40–53; Winifred Richmond, *The Adolescent*

Girl (New York: Macmillan, 1926); Miriam Van Waters, *Youth in Conflict* (New York: Republic Publishing, 1926), ch. 2; Phyllis Blanchard, *New Girls for Old* (New York: Macauley, 1930), ch. 9; Helen Williston Brown, "The Deforming Influences of the Home," *Journal of Abnormal Psychology* 12 (April 1917): 49–57; Frankwood E. Williams, *Adolescence: Studies in Mental Hygiene* (New York: Farrar and Rinehart, 1930), ch. 3; E. Van Norman Emery, "Revising Our Attitude toward Sex," *Mental Hygiene* 11 (April 1927): 324–38; Ruth Kimball Gardiner, "Your Daughter's Mother," *Journal of Social Hygiene* 6 (Oct. 1920): 542; Alexander, " 'Girl Problem,' " ch. 4; Jones, "As the Twig Is Bent," 163–66, 215–47.

22. New York, *Laws of 1923*, ch. 868. Two years later the Wayward Minor Act was extended to apply to males as well as to females. New York, *Laws of 1925*, ch. 389. The passage of the Wayward Minor Act led to a dramatic increase in the number of young women committed to the reformatories at Bedford Hills and Albion for "wilful disobedience" or immorality. In the year ending June 30, 1921, only 7.69 percent of Bedford Hills' new inmates were "incorrigible girls," having been convicted of violating the New York City statute. However, by 1925, 23.6 percent of Bedford's new inmates were wayward minors; in 1928 the percentage was 26.6. Commitments to Albion under the new law were slow at first: In 1925 only 7.8 percent of the inmates admitted that year were wayward minors, yet in 1928, 28.6 percent were. Although

these statistics do not tell us who testified against the girls in court, it is probably safe to assume that parents, not police, acted as complainants in the majority of cases. New York State Reformatory for Women at Bedford Hills, *Twenty-first Annual Report* (Albany, N.Y., 1921), 16; New York State Reformatory for Women at Bedford Hills, *Twenty-fifth Annual Report* (Albany, N.Y., 1925), 14; Albion State Training School, *Annual Report* (Albany, N.Y., 1925), 16; State Commission of Correction, *Second Annual Report* (Albany, N.Y., 1928), 519.

23. As Albion's board of managers wrote in his annual report to the New York State legislature in 1919, the various "lines of training" at the reformatory were "intended to make the girl self-supporting, while the one thought which is kept in mind all the time is that she may be surrounded with influences that will tend to strengthen her character and awaken within her the desire to go back out into the world and live a good and useful life." Western House of Refuge for Women at Albion, New York, *Twenty-fifth Annual Report* (1919), 4. In the years from 1900 to 1930 Albion and Bedford responded to new trends in women's employment and popular amusements by making small modifications in their programs— Bedford, for example, showed movies and offered limited training in clerical skills during the 1920s— however, the basic goals and methods of the reformatories remained unchanged. For additional discussion of "protection and rescue" as

a mission of the women's reformatories see Estelle Freedman, *Their Sisters' Keepers: Women's Prison Reform in America, 1830–1930*, (Ann Arbor: University of Michigan Press, 1981) ch. 3.

24. Althea Davies, Bedford 00083, 1924; Deborah Herman, Mentally Defective Delinquent (MDD), Bedford 00093, 1926.

25. The reformatory was especially offended by cross-race lesbian relationships, which raised fears among staff members that the white girls involved would lose all respect for racial and sexual conventions. In 1915 staff members speculated that the white girls involved in lesbian relationships might "take up living in colored neighborhoods" once they were discharged from the reformatory. Believing that the "most undesirable sex relations grow out of [the] mingling of the two races," Bedford ended its experimentation with integrated housing and established segregated cottages in 1916. State Board of Charities, *Report of the Special Committee . . . to investigate charges made against the New York State Reformatory for Women at Bedford Hills, N.Y.* (Albany: J. B. Lyon, 1915), 18–19, 26–27. For additional discussion of homosexuality among female prison and reformatory inmates see Margaret Otis, "A Perversion Not Commonly Noted," *Journal of Abnormal Psychology* 8 (1913): 113–16; Charles A. Ford, "Homosexual Practices of Institutionalized Females," *Journal of Abnormal Psychology* 23 (1929): 442–48.

26. Rae Rabinowitz, Bedford 00052, 1917, 7; Melanie Burkis, Bedford 00087, 1928, 3.

27. Melanie Burkis, Bedford 00087, 1928, 3.

28. Rae Rabinowitz, Bedford 00052, 1917.

29. Ella Waldstein, Bedford 00018, 1917; Rae Rabinowitz, Bedford 00052, 1917.

30. Melanie Burkis, Bedford 00087, 1928.

31. Sophie Polentz, Bedford 00059, 1924.

32. For example in 1923 Bedford's superintendent Amos Baker wrote to ask Nanette Wilkins's aunt, the individual responsible for the wayward-minor charge against the sixteen-year-old black girl, to correspond with her niece. Baker did not mention Nanette's frequent misconduct, but he did point out that "your niece, Nanette Wilkins, tells me that she has not heard from any of her people in some time and she is somewhat discouraged and anxious. I think a line from you would cheer her up and encourage her" (Nanette Wilkins, Bedford 00017, 1923, 6).

33. A good example of the reformatories' chastisement of parents is in the file of Lena Meyerhoff, the young Jewish woman committed to Bedford as a wayward minor after giving birth to an illegitimate (mulatto) child. After reading a letter that Mrs. Meyerhoff sent to Lena, Bedford's Superintendent Baker wrote to her, saying "the statements which you made in your letter are true; nevertheless they were so upsetting to Lena that I doubt the wisdom of writing letters of this kind to her in her present situation. I know it is very difficult to decide

just what course to pursue in regard to her, but I think encouraging letters would be better than those that tend to depress and discourage" (Lena Meyerhoff, Bedford 00084, 1924, 5).

34. Many families were in fact acutely aware of the reformatories' efforts to limit their involvement in the reform process. It was not uncommon for parents or other relatives to write to the reformatory superintendents to give advice or to make special requests regarding the care of their girls. Requests for the early discharge or parole of a girl were especially frequent. Often, the request for early release was combined with or eventually evolved into a debate over the conditions of parole: Was the inmate to be sent to her families' home or to a domestic position, was the infant of an inmate to be adopted or sent home with the young woman, and so forth. Some families tried to add weight to their requests by hiring lawyers or by soliciting assistance from politicians, ministers, or community leaders. Families rarely succeeded in winning the early release of an inmate; their frustrating and often bitter campaigns thus offer further proof of the institutions' substantial authority. There were fifteen cases in my sample in which family members challenged the reformatory authorities or intervened in the handling of their daughters.

35. Sophie's father wrote frequently to his daughter and to Bedford's superintendent Amos Baker. Most of his letters were not censored, but because they were written in German, translations were always made before the letters were passed and those translations remain in Sophie's file. Sophie Polentz, Bedford 00059, 1924, 6, 7.

36. Althea Davies was one wayward girl who, while still an inmate, apparently promised her family that her "bad" days were behind her. In a letter to Bedford's superintendent Amos Baker, Althea's aunt noted, "Althea has promised me with eyes of tears that she will amend her ways. She is very sorry of her deeds and promised me that she will not be found in any such trouble again" (Althea Davies, Bedford 00083, 1924).

37. Of the twenty-two young women in my sample, thirteen were initially sent home, six were placed in domestic positions, and three were placed in hospital positions. Often, employment changed several times over the course of parole, some women changing jobs while they remained at home, other young women leaving a hospital position to live at home and take a factory job.

38. Amos Baker, Bedford's superintendent from 1921 to 1927, noted that the lack of adequate parole supervision made it "very difficult, well nigh impossible, to follow each girl a sufficient length of time to determine with absolute certainty what the institution has accomplished." New York State Reformatory for Women, *Twenty-fourth Annual Report* (Albany, N.Y.: J. B. Lyon, 1925), 9.

39. Susanna Nedersen, Bedford 00029, 1917; Ilene Sterling, Bedford 00024, 1917.

40. Susanna Nedersen, Bedford 00029, 1917; Ilene Sterling, Bedford 00024, 1917.

41. Ella Waldstein, Bedford 00018, 1917.

42. Althea Davies, Bedford 00083, 1924.

43. Nanette Wilkins, Bedford 00017, 1923.

44. Sophie Polentz, Bedford 00059, 1924.

45. In a letter to Bedford she wrote: "Upon the slightest provocation reference to Bedford is made with much threatening, etc. I am trying to redeem myself and do the right thing. Let me assure you that the inclination to do or be otherwise never enters my mind. All I want is a fair chance; in other words an 'even break.' If I were to say my parents are all wrong and I am in the right I don't doubt that I would sound like every girl that is guilty of breaking parole, but my parent's attitude makes life well nigh impossible at times" (Janine Rosen, Bedford 00025, 1926).

46. Janine Rosen, Melanie Burkis, and Sophie Polentz were all returned to Bedford for violating parole. Before being retaken, Janine Rosen had worked in a speakeasy and as a dance-hall teacher; the two others had worked as prostitutes. Janine Rosen, Bedford 00025, 1926; Melanie Burkis, Bedford 00087, 1928; Sophie Polentz, Bedford 00059, 1924.

47. Sophie Polentz, Bedford 00059, 1924.

CHAPTER 13.
Bitter Nostalgia

1. Carl Van Doren coined the phrase "revolt from the village," which appeared in his *Contemporary American Novelists, 1900–1920* (New York: Macmillan, 1922), 146.

2. The phrase "Middle Westishness" comes from English writer and editor Ford Madox Ford. Ford, along with Carl Van Doren, H. L. Mencken, Alfred Kazin, Frederick Hoffman, and other critics in the early decades of the century, called attention to the acute disillusionment visible in works about the midwestern country town. See Barry Gross, "In Another Country: The Revolt from the Village," in *Mid-America IV* (1977): 101–11, for a discussion of the critical history of the idea, along with John T. Flanagan, "Literary Protest in the Midwest," *Southwest Review* 34 (Spring 1949): 148–57. Glenway Wescott's autobiographical essay is *Goodbye Wisconsin* (New York: Harper & Brothers, 1928), 39.

3. For a discussion of the role of Jeffersonian agrarianism in the dreams and expectations of midwestern settlers, see David Anderson, "The Dimensions of the Midwest," *MidAmerica I* (1974): 7–15. Anderson's extensive work on the literary and cultural history of the region remains among the most informative and incisive.

4. Idella Alderman Anderson, *When You and I Were Young* (Holton, Kans.: Recorder Press, 1927); Minnie Ellingson Tapping, *Eighty Years at the Gopher Hole: The Saga of a Min-*

nesota Pioneer (New York: Exposition Press, 1958); Victor P. Hass, "Looking Homeward: A Memoir of Small-Town Life in Wisconsin," *Wisconsin Magazine of History* 65, 3 (1982): 176–94; Fern Crehan, *The Days before Yesterday* (New York: Dodd, Mead, 1958).

5. Recent critical studies of the genre of autobiography have shifted increasingly away from the more orthodox notion of personal history as a straightforward accounting of a life by an author who is the originator and the subject of the text. Poststructuralist analysts have called into question the traditional conception of a preexisting life that is recollected and recorded through narrative, arguing that autobiography may be understood instead as the act of inventing a life; the memoir is thus closer to fiction than to history, and the writer is not necessarily in control of his or her story.

As Sidonie Smith has recently summed up the argument, "Purporting to reflect upon or recreate the past through the processes of memory, autobiography is always . . . storytelling: memory leaves only a trace of an earlier experience that we adjust into story; experience itself is mediated by the ways we describe and interpret it to others and ourselves; cultural tropes and metaphors which structure autobiographical narrative are themselves fictive; and narrative is driven by its own fictive conventions about beginnings, middles, and ends. . . . The recent postmodern incursion on authority, legitimacy, origin, and meaning have all colluded in ren-

dering the old essential self and its myth of uniqueness, coherence, and imperial power, a fictive construct." From "Construing Truths in Lying Mouths: Truthtelling in Women's Autobiography," *Studies in the Literary Imagination* 23, 2 (Fall 1990): 145–46.

Although I have reservations about the full implications of this theoretical approach, I take from it the fundamental idea that memoirists may write against or in spite of their conscious intentions, and their documents reflect attitudes and assumptions that they may not have purposely articulated. I am also influenced in my examination of personal narrative by the insights of the new historicism, which emphasizes the notion that history is itself a construct, a narrated story that is rooted in the complex set of texts that are produced by and define a culture. In this sense, the events of the past do not exist apart from the way they are represented. Again, I employ these assumptions guardedly, but as a literary scholar I am convinced by the elemental notion that written documents are much more than the deliberately concocted, self-contained, and narrowly circumscribed statements of their authors.

Readers interested in retracing the new critical work on autobiography should start with the foundation piece, Charles Gusdorf's 1956 essay, "The Conditions and Limits of Autobiography," in *Autobiography: Essays Theoretical and Critical*, ed. James Olney (Princeton, N.J.: Princeton University Press, 1980), 28–48, along with Roy Pascal's hugely influential book, *Design and Truth in Autobiography* (Cambridge, Mass.: Harvard University Press, 1960) and James Olney's study, *Metaphors of Self: The Meaning of Autobiography* (Princeton, N.J.: Princeton University Press, 1975). A spate of theoretical and applied critical discussions of autobiography have appeared since the 1970s that employ poststructural and new historicist approaches. Three useful current studies are Timothy Dow Adams, *Telling Lies in Modern American Autobiography* (Chapel Hill: University of North Carolina Press, 1990), G. Thomas Couser, *Altered Egos: Authority in American Autobiography* (New York: Oxford University Press, 1989), and Paul John Eakin, *Fictions in Autobiography: Studies in the Art of Self-Invention* (Princeton, N.J.: Princeton University Press, 1985). James Olney's edited collection, *Studies in Autobiography* (New York: Oxford University Press, 1988), contains a number of useful essays, along with the Fall 1990 issue of *Studies in the Literary Imagination*, cited in n. 5.

6. Elizabeth Hampsten, *Read This Only to Yourself: The Private Writings of Midwestern Women, 1880–1910* (Bloomington: Indiana University Press, 1982). Scholarly examinations of private documents (letters, journals, diaries, intimate reminiscences, and so forth), particularly those written by women for whom the personal genre is a principal form, are considerable in recent years. In addition to Hampsten, see especially Lillian Schlissel, *Women's Diaries of the Westward Journey* (New York:

Schocken Books, 1982); Shari Benstock, ed., *The Private Self: Theory and Practice of Women's Autobiographical Writing* (Chapel Hill: University of North Carolina Press, 1988); Bella Brodzki and Celeste Schenck, eds., *Life/Lines: Theorizing Women's Autobiography* (Ithaca, N.Y.: Cornell University Press, 1988); Margo Culley, ed., *A Day at a Time: The Diary Literature of American Women from 1764 to the Present* (New York: Feminist Press, 1985); Leonore Hoffman and Margo Culley, eds., *Women's Personal Narratives: Essays in Criticism and Pedagogy* (New York: Modern Language Association, 1985); Estelle C. Jelinek, ed., *Women's Autobiography: Essays in Criticism* (Bloomington: Indiana University Press, 1980); Estelle C. Jelinek, *The Tradition of Women's Autobiography* (Boston: Twayne, 1986); and Judy Nolte Lensink, *"A Secret to be Burried": The Diary and Life of Emily Hawley Gillespie, 1858–1888* (Iowa City: University of Iowa Press, 1989). *Women's Studies International Forum* (10, 1) is a special number on women's autobiography.

David Lowenthal's 1985 book, *The Past Is a Foreign Country* (Cambridge: Cambridge University Press) provides important insights about the ways personal annalists exploit individual and shared memories. Clyde Milner offers provocative application of these ideas in "The Shared Memory of Montana Pioneers," *Montana Magazine of Western History* (Winter 1987): 2–13. Several sustained examinations of pioneer life as gleaned from personal narrative have appeared recently, all models of social-history analysis, particularly Paula M. Nelson's *After the West Was Won: Homesteaders and Townbuilders in Western South Dakota, 1900–1917* (Iowa City: University of Iowa Press, 1986), John Mack Faragher's *Sugar Creek: Life on the Illinois Prairie* (New Haven, Conn.: Yale University Press, 1987), and Elliott West's superb study *Growing Up with the Country: Childhood on the Far Western Frontier* (Albuquerque: University of New Mexico Press, 1989).

7. This essay is part of a larger study, *Bitter Nostalgia: Growing Up Midwestern*, for which I have examined over three hundred narratives by autobiographers from the region. In spite of the repetitiveness among such reminiscences, they continue to work a mundane magic on me.

8. Wallace Stegner, "Rediscovery: Wescott's *Goodbye Wisconsin*," *Southern Review* 6 (1970): 677.

9. Many studies of midwestern literature explore the characteristic double-mindedness of the regional ethos. Of particular value are Robert C. Bray, *Rediscoveries: Literature and Place in Illinois* (Urbana: University of Illinois Press, 1982); Margaret Stuhr, "The Middle West and the American Imagination," (Ph.D. diss., Northwestern University, 1983), and Catherine Raymond, "Down to Earth: Sense of Place in Midwestern Literature," (Ph.D. diss., University of Pennsylvania, 1979).

10. Herbert Quick, *One Man's Life* (Indianapolis, Ind.: Bobbs-Merrill, 1925), 175–76.

11. Hamlin Garland, *A Son of the Middle Border* (New York: Macmillan, 1923), 416.

12. Ernest Venable Sutton, *A Life Worth Living* (Pasadena, Calif.: Trail's End, 1948), 57.

13. Gurdon W. Wattles, *Autobiography of Gurdon Wattles* (New York: Scribner's, 1922), 29.

14. Anna Lathrop Clary, *Reminiscences of Anna Lathrop Clary* (Los Angeles: Bruce McCallister, 1937), 28ff.

15. Carl Van Doren, *Three Worlds* (New York: Harper & Brothers, 1936), 41; Frazier Hunt, *One American and His Attempt at Education* (New York: Simon and Schuster, 1938), 40; Edward A. Ross, *Seventy Years of It* (New York: D. Appleton-Century, 1936), 13.

16. Clara Clough Lenroot, *Long, Long Ago* (Appleton, Wis.: Bader Printing, 1929), 16.

17. Eliza St. John Brophy, *Twice a Pioneer* (New York: Exposition Press, 1972).

18. Brophy, *Twice a Pioneer*, 122.

19. Garland, *Son of the Middle Border*, 375.

20. Ibid., 467. Garland had earlier recreated his childhood in *Boy Life on the Prairie* (1899), a memoir with a thin fictional gloss that presents a more affirmative picture of his pioneering past than emerges from *A Son of the Middle Border*. It is perhaps significant that the more embittered portrait was written in later life, when he seems to have been freed from the Victorian impulse to write an uplifting narrative. Either he was more in tune with his truer feelings or he became increasingly acrimonious with age. Similar patterns are

visible in the successive autobiographical retellings by midwestern
writers William Dean Howells and
Sherwood Anderson.

21. Faye Cashatt Lewis, *Nothing
to Make a Shadow* (Ames: Iowa State
University Press, 1971).

22. Wattles, *Autobiography*, 19.

23. Brophy, *Twice a Pioneer*, 72.

24. Mildred A. Renaud, "Rattlesnakes and Tumbleweed: A Memoir
of South Dakota," *American Heritage*
26, 3 (April 1975): 56.

25. Hervey White, *Childhood Fancies* (Woodstock, N.Y.: Maverick
Press, 1927), 129.

26. Irene Hardy, *An Ohio Schoolmistress* (Kent, Ohio: Kent State
University Press, 1980), 79.

27. Della Lutes, *The Country
Kitchen* (Boston: Little, Brown, 1937).

28. Clara Erlich, "My Childhood
on the Prairie," *Colorado Magazine* 51,
12 (1974): 140.

29. Hass, "Looking Homeward,"
187.

30. Cyrenus Cole, *I Remember
I Remember: A Book of Recollections*
(Iowa City: State Historical Society
of Iowa, 1936), 72–73.

31. Bertha Van Hoosen, *Petticoat
Surgeon* (Chicago: People's Book
Club, 1947), 15–20.

32. Renaud, "Rattlesnakes and
Tumbleweed," 56.

33. Van Doren, *Three Worlds*, 42.

34. Tapping, *Eighty Years*, 17.

35. Bruce Bliven, "A Prairie Boyhood," *Palimpsest* 49 (1968): 329.

36. Hardy, *Ohio Schoolmistress*, 6.

37. Sutton, *Life Worth Living*, 185–
86.

38. Ibid., 5–6.

39. Ibid., 58.

40. Quick, *One Man's Life*, 345–47.

41. White, *Childhood Fancies*, 72.

42. Ibid., 60–61.

43. Mary Austin, *Earth Horizon:
Autobiography* (Boston: Houghton
Mifflin, 1932), 52.

44. Ibid., 185.

45. Ross, *Seventy Years*, 5.

46. Hass, "Looking Homeward,"
177.

47. Van Hoosen, *Petticoat Surgeon*, 305.

48. Norman Hapgood, *The Changing Years: The Reminiscences of Norman
Hapgood* (New York: Farr and Rinehart, 1930), 7.

49. James Norman Hall, *My Island
Home: An Autobiography* (Boston:
Little, Brown, 1952), 4.

50. Hannah Hawke, "Possessed
of a Restless Spirit: A Young Girl's
Memories of the Southern Iowa
Frontier," ed. Brian Birch, *Palimpsest*
66, 5 (Sept./Oct. 1985): 180.

51. Paul Ferlazzo, "The Expatriate
in the Fiction of Glenway Wescott,"
Old Northwest 4, 1 (Mar. 1978): 33.

The Contributors

Ruth M. Alexander is assistant professor of history at Colorado State University. She is completing a book entitled *The "Girl Problem": Adolescent Sex Delinquents in New York, 1900–1930.*

Lester Alston teaches educational psychology at Baruch College. His clinical and research interests concern the ways in which social context has shaped the developmental experiences of black children at different periods of our history.

Liahna Babener is chair of the Department of English at Montana State University. Her special interests include regionalism and popular culture. She has written extensively about literary California and is now at work on a book, *Growing Up in the Heartland: Childhood Reminiscences by Midwesterners.*

Selma Berrol is professor of history at Baruch College of the City University of New York. A specialist in the history of immigration, she is the author of *Immigrants at School: New York City* (1978) and *Getting Down to Business: A History of Baruch College* (1989). She is working on a biography of Julia Richman.

Victoria Bissell Brown is professor of history at Grinnell College. She is currently writing a biography of Jane Addams and working on a film documentary of Addams's life as a social reformer.

Robert L. Griswold is associate professor of history at the University of Oklahoma. He is the author of *Family and Divorce in California, 1850–1890* (1983) and is currently finishing a book on the history of American fatherhood in the twentieth century.

N. Ray Hiner is Chancellors Club Teaching Professor of History and Education at the University of Kansas. He is the coeditor (with Joseph M. Hawes) of *Growing Up in America: Children in Historical Perspective* (1985); *American Childhood: A Research Guide and Historical Handbook* (1985); and *Children in Historical and Comparative Perspective: An International Handbook and Research Guide* (1991).

Miriam Formanek-Brunell is assistant professor at Wellesley College. She is the author of *Guise and Dolls: The Rise of the Doll Industry and the Material Culture of Girlhood, 1870–1930* (forthcoming).

Bernard Mergen is professor of American civilization at George Washington University, where he teaches courses in cultural history, material culture, and environmental history. He is the author of *Play and Playthings* (1982) and is at work on a history of snow in American life.

David Nasaw is professor of history at the College of Staten Island and the Graduate Center of the City University of New York and the author of *Children of the City: At Work and at Play* (1985) and *Going Out: The Rise and Fall of Public Amusements* (forthcoming).

Paula Petrik is associate dean of arts and humanities and professor of history at the University of Maine. The author of *No Step Backward: Women and Family on the Rocky Mountain Mining Frontier, Helena, Montana, 1865–1900* (1986), she is currently writing a history of toys in America.

Vicki L. Ruiz is the Mellon All-Claremont Humanities Professor at the Claremont Graduate School and Harvey Mudd College. A specialist in Chicano and women's history,

she is the author of *Cannery Women, Cannery Lives* (1987) and coeditor of *Women on the U.S.–Mexico Border* (1987, with Susan Tiano), *Western Women: Their Land, Their Lives* (1988, with Lillian Schlissel and Janice Monk), and *Unequal Sisters: A Multicultural Reader in U.S. Women's History* (1990, with Ellen DuBois).

William M. Tuttle, Jr., is professor of history at the University of Kansas. He is the author of *Race Riot: Chicago in the Red Summer of 1919* (1970), the coauthor of *A People and a Nation* (1982, with Mary Beth Norton and David Katzman), and the coeditor of *Plain Folk: The Life Stories of Undistinguished Americans* (1982, with David Katzman). He is at work on a book on America's homefront children during the Second World War.

Elliott West is professor of history at the University of Arkansas. A specialist in the history of the frontier and the American West, he is author of *Growing Up with the Country: Childhood on the Far-Western Frontier* (1989) and *The Saloon on the Rocky Mountain Mining Frontier* (1979).

Index